CW00765921

Hidden Landscapes in the Forest of Dean

Hidden Landscapes in the Forest of Dean

Jon Hoyle

 Historic England

Published by Historic England, The Engine House, Fire Fly Avenue, Swindon SN2 2EH
www.HistoricEngland.org.uk

Historic England is a Government service championing England's heritage and giving expert, constructive advice.

© Jon Hoyle 2019

Lidar images © Peter Crow. Forest Research; source, Cambridge University ULM (2004): Figs 1.8, 3.5, 3.7, 3.11, 3.12, 3.13, 3.14 , 3.15, 3.18, 3.19, 3.21, 3.22, 3.26, 3.31, 3.32, 3.33, 3.34, 3.35, 3.36, 3.37, 3.38, 3.39, 3.40, 3.41, 3.43, 3.48, 3.55, 3.58, 4.2, 4.9, 4.10, 4.11, 4.12, 4.13, 4.14, 4.15, 5.4, 5.5, 5.6, 5.7, 5.8, 5.16, 5.19, 5.24, 5.25, 5.26, 5.28, 5.36, 5.48, 5.51, 5.52, 5.53, 5.54, 5.55, 6.9, 6.11, 6.15, 6.22, 6.28

The views expressed in this book are those of the author and not necessarily those of Historic England.

First published 2019

ISBN 978-1-84802-258-4

British Library Cataloguing in Publication data
A CIP catalogue record for this book is available from the British Library.

The right of Jon Hoyle to be identified as author of this work has been asserted by him in accordance with the Copyright, Designs and Patents Act 1988.

All rights reserved
No part of this publication may be reproduced or transmitted in any form or by any means, electronic or mechanical, including photocopying, recording, or any information storage or retrieval system, without permission in writing from the publisher.

Application for the reproduction of images should be made to Historic England. Every effort has been made to trace the copyright holders and we apologise in advance for any unintentional omissions, which we would be pleased to correct in any subsequent edition of this book.

Brought to publication by Sarah Enticknap, Publishing, Historic England.

Typeset in Georgia Pro Light 9.5/11.75pt

Edited by Elizabeth Nichols
Indexed by Caroline Jones, Osprey Indexing
Page layout by Pauline Hull

Printed in the Czech Republic via Akcent Media Ltd.

Front cover: Ring cairn in the Forest of Dean after undergrowth clearance.

Back cover: Lidar imagery showing Welshbury hillfort with and without tree cover removed.

Contents

List of illustrations

Acknowledgements

The Forest of Dean Archaeological Survey was funded mainly by English Heritage (now Historic England) with contributions from the Forestry Commission, the Forest of Dean District Council, Gloucestershire County Council and the Countryside Agency (now Natural England).

The project was originally envisaged by Jan Wills, County Archaeologist for Gloucestershire County Council, who managed and supported the project through stages 1 to 3. The final stage of the project, which included the preparation of this book, was managed by her successor Toby Catchpole.

Laura Butler, Graham Tait, Danielle Wootton, Aisling Tuohy, Vanessa Macri, Jill Martin, Naomi Paine, Andy Walsh, Nick Witchell, Nathan Thomas, Briege Williams, Paul Nichols and Tony Roberts of Gloucestershire County Council Archaeology Service assisted with various stages of the project and Jo Vallender and Anna Morris assisted with the survey of Offa's Dyke undertaken in the mid-1990s. Tim Grubb and Anna Morris of the Gloucestershire County Council HER advised on the use of HER information and compatible recording systems and Kurt Adams, the Portable Antiquities Scheme Finds Liaison Officer, assisted with artefact identification.

The numerous specialists involved with the project have included Ross Dean (Substrata, geophysics), Tim Young (Geo-Arch, archaeometallurgy), Liz Pearson and Nick Daffern (Worcestershire Heritage and Archaeological Service, palaeoenvironmental analysis), Phil Toms (Gloucestershire University, OSL dating), Jane Timby (pottery analysis), Hilary Cool (metalwork analysis), Keith Wilkinson (ARCA, geoarchaeological assessment), Chris Salter (University of Oxford Department of Materials, bloomery iron working), Mark Campbell and Dave Owen (Gloucester Geology Trust, geological advice, particularly scowles), David Lowe (British Geological Survey, scowles formation), Colin Studholme and Sarah Rowlatt (Gloucestershire Wildlife Trust, the ecology of scowles).

The Forestry Commission were particularly supportive of the project and most of the fieldwork has taken place on their land. Special thanks must go to Tim Yarnell, Rob Guest, Jerry Gissop, Phil Morton, Ben Lennon, Pete Kelsall, Francis Raymond Barker, Dave Sykes and James Williams. Peter Crow of Forest Research (a branch of the Forestry Commission) advised on the applications of lidar and produced the lidar images used during the project.

Other specialists have discussed aspects of the Forest of Dean's history and archaeology with the author, commented on drafts or earlier reports or been helpful in other ways, and their ideas will have found their way into this book. These include Kate Biggs, Tim Copeland, Dave Cranstone, Bryn Gethyn, Carolyn Heighway, Neil Holbrook, Robin Jackson, Ian Standing and Elizabeth Walker. Nicola Wynne of the Dean Heritage Centre and David Rice of Gloucester Museums Service are also thanked for their help at various times.

Historic England staff who have provided advice and information throughout the project include Mark Bowden and Nicki Smith (topographical survey), Vanessa Straker (palaeoenvironmental and other scientific advice), Matt Canti (geoarchaeology), David Dungworth (archaeometallurgy), Alex Bayliss (radiocarbon dating and Bayesian analysis), Helen Winter and Simon Crutchley (National Mapping Programme). Nicola Hembry, Kathy Perrin, Buzz Busby and Helen Keeley acted as Historic England's Project Assurance Officers.

Many others have also been associated with various stages of the project and thanks go to Jasper Blake, Alf Webb, Doug Gentles and Phil Riches of Dean Archaeology Group; Brian Johns, Ian Pope, Averil Kear and Cecile Hunt of the Forest of Dean Local History Society; Penny Fernando, Tony Youles, Frank Colls and Ray Wilson of Gloucestershire Society for Industrial Archaeology; and also Keith Webb of Darkhill, Jonathan Wright of Clearwell Caves, Peter Bond for his work on the prehistoric period in Tidenham and also Joe, Grace and Isabel Powell who have identified a number of sites from Google Earth images which had not been found in other surveys.

Thanks also go to Marian Bullock, Madalene George, Ruth Hamblin and Pat Roberts who endured various stages of the work on the Forest of Dean. Pat Roberts also provided invaluable editorial advice on drafts of the text.

All errors, omissions and inconsistencies remain the responsibility of the author.

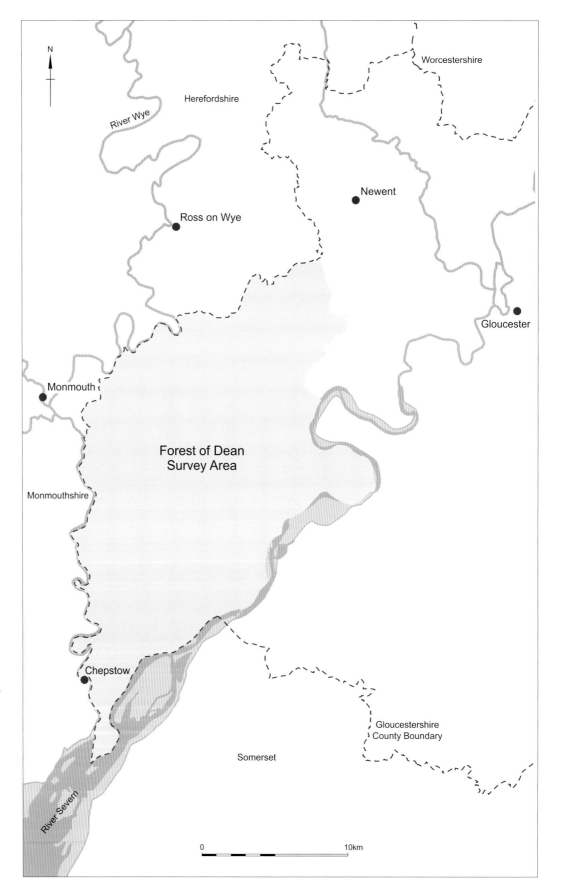

Fig 1.1
Location of the Forest of Dean survey area. The Forest of Dean Archaeological Survey covered different areas during different stages but was mostly focused on the area of approximately 337km² between the Rivers Severn and Wye. This area incorporated all of the Statutory Forest, the whole of the modern Hundred of St Briavels and all adjacent modern parishes. It also included nearly all the Forestry Commission woodland in the Forest of Dean in Gloucestershire and also much of the area within the legal and administrative boundary of the Forest of Dean at its most extensive on 1282.

The Forest of Dean

Fig 1.2
Woodland and the
Statutory Forest. The
Forest of Dean is the most
intensively wooded part
of Gloucestershire, with
around 118km² of wood-
land, much of which is
managed by the Forestry
Commission. 88km² of this
is in a largely continuous
block centred on the
Statutory Forest.

Although Forest of Dean District covers much of Gloucestershire west of the Severn, most people think of the Forest as the southern part of the district between the Severn and Wye and this area forms the basis of the discussion in this book. Historically the Forest was generally synonymous with the smaller Hundred of St Briavels, an area of high ground between Mitcheldean and Brockweir that has formed the basis of the Forest's administrative structure since the 12th century (Herbert 1996l, 85, fig 4; *see* Fig 1.2). This contains the relatively small area of approximately 9,308ha known as the Statutory Forest which is the core area of Forestry Commission woodland. The Statutory Forest's boundaries were not ratified until 1668, and it remained extraparochial until the 1840s (Herbert 1996a, 285), but it roughly corresponds to the area of uncultivated woodland and waste owned directly by the Crown during much of the medieval period.

Geology, topography and land use

Extensive tracts of woodland cover over a third of the area, dominating the higher ground and clinging precariously to its steep slopes. Outside the woodland the landscape is essentially rural in character with more or less equal proportions of arable and pasture. Small towns or villages are scattered throughout the area, although more haphazard settlement patterns, the legacy of post-medieval squatter communities, hug the fringes of the woodland in the central Forest encroaching into the former Crown estate.

The Forest has produced coal, iron ore and building stone while its woodland has been a source of timber and charcoal. Industries based on these resources have dominated the area for over 2,000 years, and although these have now vanished or been much reduced, their legacy of disfigured landscapes, crumbling structures or abandoned routes are still a significant characteristic of the Forest.

The Forest of Dean is geographically distinct from the rest of Gloucestershire and incorporates

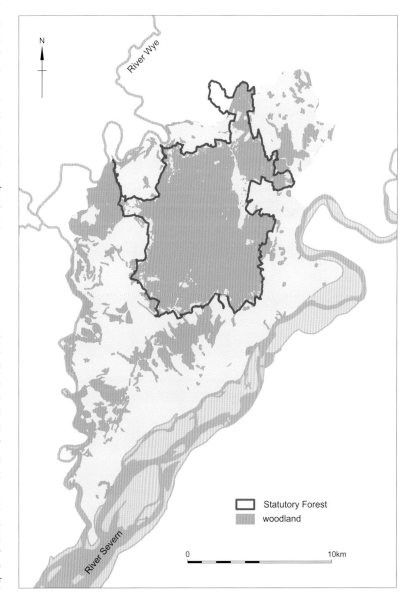

Statutory Forest
woodland

0   10km

a dramatic range of topographies, reflecting the underlying geology.

The central area of woodland (centred on the Statutory Forest) is mostly above 200m AOD (reaching a maximum height of 290m AOD) on a plateau incised by numerous streams and bisected by the wide north–south valley of the Cannop Brook. This Carboniferous Sandstone bedrock contains over 20 separate coal seams and overlies Carboniferous Limestone. These strata form a basin (the Dean syncline) and coal seams out-crop, or are close to the surface, throughout the area (Dreghorn 1968) and limestones, which contain iron ore, outcrop as a 'necklace' around the edge of the sandstone (BGS 1974).

Settlement consists of sprawling hamlets of haphazardly positioned cottages which ring the

Fig 1.3
Topography of the Forest of Dean.

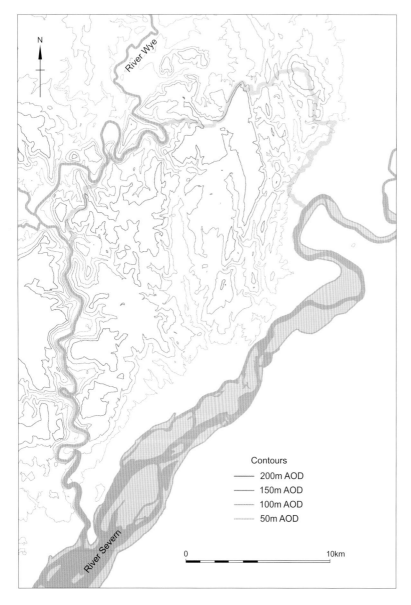

Contours

—— 200m AOD
—— 150m AOD
—— 100m AOD
—— 50m AOD

0   10km

Statutory Forest (Herbert 1996a, 293), largely the result of population expansion to meet the needs of expanding industries in the 18th and 19th centuries. In places these have developed a semi-urban character or even grown into small towns such as Cinderford.

To the north and west of this area much of the woodland is early 19th-century plantation and pasture, and arable fields are widespread in the vicinity of the settlements, such as Mitcheldean, Ruardean and Coleford, which are medieval in origin and close to the edge of former Royal Demesne.

To the south of the Statutory Forest an undu-lating plateau, tilted to the south, maintains heights of around 200m AOD. Enclosed farm-land (usually pasture, although arable and woodland is also found) is common here, and settlement tends to be in the river valleys which drain to the rivers Severn and Wye.

The western edge of the Forest is defined by the River Wye, which meanders through a nar-row gorge (generally less than 0.5km wide) cut through steep limestone cliffs, up to 100m high, that rise directly from the edge of the river at their base. There is considerable evidence of limestone quarrying in this area and woodland covers the steep slopes and abandoned workings. Further south the valley becomes less steep where the river cuts through brownstones and sandstones of the Old Red Sandstone Series (BGS 1974; BGS 1981). Settlement is mostly dispersed along the higher ground, although some small communi-ties extend from the Wye along the steep-sided valleys of the streams which flow into it.

The south-eastern part of the Forest is a broad alluvial plain along the northern shore of the Severn Estuary. Most of this is below 50m AOD, although there is some higher ground in the area of Sedbury at its southern edge. Settle-ment consists largely of small towns or villages either close to the river or linked to it by a navi-gable inlet.

The geology here is Lower Old Red Sandstone, Triassic Mudstones or Lower Lias clays, and significant deposits of sand, gravel and alluvium are found adjacent to the Severn.

History

The Forest of Dean is first recorded in the Domesday Survey of 1086, but simply as 'the Forest' and only with reference to settlements that were exempt from tax in exchange for 'guarding the forest', or that held land within it (Hart 1945, 167; Moore 1982, 167c).

Forests were introduced to England after the Norman Conquest in 1066 as distinct administrative areas set aside by the Crown and subject to separate Forest law and taxation.

They were a source of game, particularly deer, for the Royal table, although this would generally have been killed by professional huntsmen rather than for sport. Other resources, such as timber and minerals, were also important to the Forest's economy and they were not necessarily wooded but could include extensive open areas, heath and also settlements and agricultural land.

Although Forests, in the strict legislative sense, were introduced by the Normans, Royal hunting grounds had been designated in England since the reign of King Cnut in the late 10th century and Edward the Confessor, who ruled between 1042 and 1066, had maintained a number of 'Forest wardens' (Stenton 1998, 684). The Domesday entry for Dene (either Littledean and/or Mitcheldean) states that 'King Edward assigned these lands exempt from tax for guarding the Forest' (Moore 1982, 167c), and the Norman afforestation of Dean is likely to have been essentially a strengthening, and perhaps expanding, of regulations and restrictions in an existing Royal game reserve.

Forests also generated income for the Crown through revenues and fines for breaching Forest law and some medieval monarchs extended their boundaries to increase returns. The bounds of the Forest of Dean fluctuated considerably in the medieval period although it is not always clear exactly where the boundaries were at all times, or precisely which King ordered the extensions.

Antiquarian and earlier archaeological research

In 1977 a survey of the archaeological implications of forestry in the Forest of Dean stated that there is 'no great tradition of local antiquarian activity in the Forest of Dean and very little archaeological fieldwork has ever been carried out' there (Ellison 1977, 9). Antiquarian and archaeological research may have been limited, particularly when compared with other parts of Gloucestershire such as the Cotswolds, but it certainly occurred.

The earliest antiquarian reference to the Forest of Dean could be Leland's West Country Itinerary of 1542 which mentions that 'Flaxley Abbey, a Cistercian house stood in the Forest of Dean some five or six miles from Gloucester' (Chandler 1993, 177).

As the Abbey had only been dissolved for six years at this time, this reference could be regarded as current affairs rather than antiquarian research and Camden's *Britannia* of 1588 has a better claim as the earliest deliberate attempt to record the Forest's heritage. He records the 'more than half demolished' St Briavels castle and also evidence for early iron ore extraction (scowles) in Newland Parish, which he describes as 'vast mine-pits of sixty or seventy foot deep, and as large as a considerable Church'. He also recorded workmen at the numerous iron furnaces as 'very industrious in seeking out the

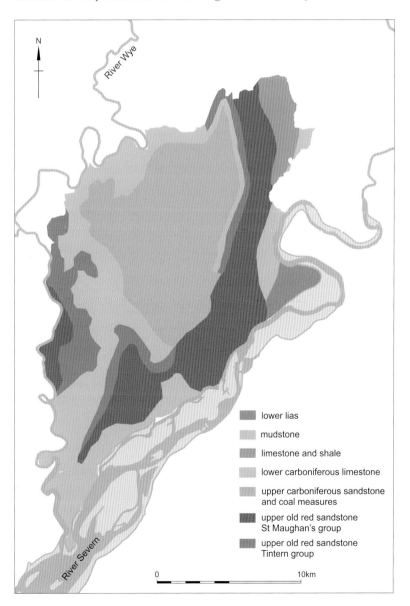

Fig 1.4
Simplified solid geology map of the Forest of Dean, after British Geological Survey.

lower lias

mudstone

limestone and shale

lower carboniferous limestone

upper carboniferous sandstone and coal measures

upper old red sandstone St Maughan's group

upper old red sandstone Tintern group

0   10km

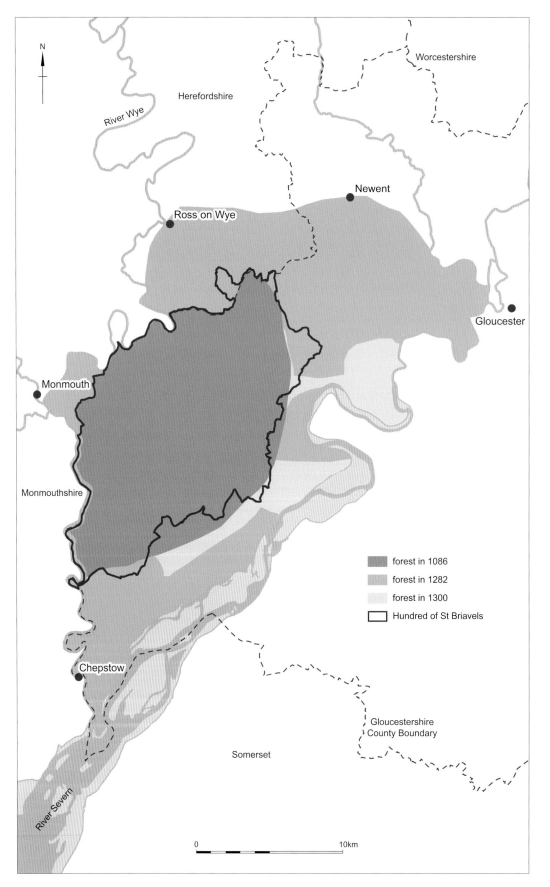

Fig 1.5
The modern Hundred of
St Briavels and the extent of
the medieval Forest (after
Hart 1945, maps I, II and
III). In 1086 the Forest
encompassed the area of
the modern Hundred of
St Briavels but was extended
between 1086 and 1282 to
include the area between
the Rivers Severn and Wye
from Gloucester, Newent
and Ross on Wye in the
north to the southern tip
of Beachley, south-east of
Chepstow, in the south. By
about 1300 the boundaries
had contracted, although
it extended to the River
Severn between Purton
and Awre and included
Walmore Common and
the Rodley area.

beds of old Cinders [the extensive mounds of waste from bloomery iron smelting]; which not being fully exhausted, are burnt again in the furnaces, and make the best Iron' (Camden 1588 reproduced in Atkyns 1712, 575). In the early post-medieval period these extensive spreads of bloomery iron furnace waste appear to have been one of the most notable visible features in the Forest of Dean, and in 1677 Andrew Yarrington wrote 'In the Forest of Dean and thereabouts, the iron is made at this day of cinders, being the rough and offal thrown by in the Romans' time; they then having only foot blasts to melt the iron stone' (Nicholls 1866, 49).

These observations are essentially notes of interesting features recorded within the context of descriptive accounts of the contemporary landscape, but in 1780 George Wyrall of Bicknor Court became a pioneer not only in recording the Forest's early history but also in the analysis of the meaning of archaeological evidence.

In a series of notes which were not published until 1878 (Wyrall 1878) he differentiated blast furnace from earlier bloomery smelting waste and drew conclusions on the industries they represented. Rather than relying on popular tradition, he suggested dates for past iron smelting based on artefacts found within waste dumps, and discussed past landscapes with reference to the resource needs of iron smelting (particularly woodland managed for charcoal production) and other sites which he thought contemporary.

In the latter part of the 18th century archaeological excavation was also undertaken at the Roman temple at Lydney Park by the antiquary Major Rooke who was 'frequently at Lydney and was allowed to dig wherever he was inclined' (Bathurst 1879, 3). Although his published results are limited, his approach was preferable to earlier investigators who were in 'the habit of searching for coins and other antiquities, and taking them away' or excavating 'into the old buildings without regard to the injury [to the surviving remains] thereby occasioned' (Bathurst 1879, 3). The Right Hon C Bathurst, who owned the site in 1805, undertook further excavation after tree planting exposed the remains of stone foundations. These excavations were exemplary for their time and involved the systematic exposure and recording of the temple's walls and mosaic floors and the cataloguing and illustration of a selection of the finds. After Bathurst's death the results were collated and published by his son, the Reverend William Hiley Bathurst (Bathurst 1879).

From the 19th century antiquarian research tended to focus on the identification and description of major earthworks either outside, or at the edge of, the central area of woodland.

The earliest of these was the Revd Thomas Fosbroke, the vicar of Walford in Herefordshire, who in 1831 recorded sections of Offa's Dyke overlooking the Wye to the south-west and north-west of St Briavels and a number of other 'camps' such as Symond's Yat Iron Age hillfort, the Norman ringwork at Newnham, a 'Roman camp' at Madget [sic] and a 'British settlement' at Coldharbour immediately west of St Briavels.

The southern section of Offa's Dyke was also investigated by George Ormerod, an antiquarian who had researched widely in the Chester area before moving to Sedbury Park, Tidenham in 1828. In 1841 Ormerod published his observations, which included a description of sections of Offa's Dyke to the south of Madgetts and continuing southwards beyond the area covered by Fosbroke (Ormerod 1841). Ormerod did not limit himself to Offa's Dyke, but had a broad interest in the antiquities of the Tidenham area, including observations of barrows, the course of the Roman roads, early passages across the River Severn and evidence for Roman occupation at Sedbury Park. This culminated in the private publication of over 30 years of research in a single volume ('*Strigulensia*') in 1861 (Ormerod 1861).

Later in the 19th century some antiquarian interest began to move away from the description and interpretation of specific earthworks or sites and the Revd H G Nicholls' *The Forest of Dean: an historical and descriptive account* published in 1858 (Nicholls 1858) was one of the first attempts at a more holistic, period-by-period, account of the history of the Forest from the earliest times. Although meticulously researched, it focused on industrial history (principally the iron industry) reflecting Nicholls' personal research interests, and he later went on to publish *Iron making in Olden Times* (Nicholls 1866), which may be the earliest 'comprehensive history of an iron industry to be published in monograph form' (Ian Standing in the introduction to Nicholls 1866, v). Throughout the 19th century antiquarian interest in the Forest continued with more descriptions of Offa's Dyke (Bellows 1877; MaClean 1893–4) and Symond's Yat promontory fort (MaClean 1879–80) although other earthworks were also included in early county-wide surveys (Playne 1877; Witts 1880). The wilful destruction of one of the Forest of Dean's ancient sites, the Long Stone near St Briavels, a Bronze Age standing stone destroyed by gunpowder, was also the occasion for an early call for 'legislative protection of our national antiquities' (Playne 1876, 106).

The earlier part of the 20th century saw some relatively high-profile investigations which were, in some ways, a continuation and consolidation of earlier work at key Forest sites. Sir Mortimer Wheeler undertook further excavation at Lydney Park between 1928 and 1929 (Wheeler and Wheeler 1932) and in 1931 Sir Cyril Fox concluded his survey of Offa's and Wat's dykes with the earthworks overlooking the River Wye in the western part of the Forest of Dean (Fox 1931; 1955). Local researchers were also active in the Forest of Dean, and between 1932 and 1935 A W Trotter surveyed the course of the Dean Road, a putative Roman road through the Forest (Trotter 1936).

In the mid-20th century Dr Charles Scott-Garrett, an Ulster-born chemist who settled in Aylburton, began a series of investigations into the archaeology of the area, often in collaboration with Frank Harris. These included groundbreaking excavations at The Chesters Roman Villa, Woolaston (Scott-Garrett and Harris 1938), Soldiers Tump Bronze Age round Barrow on Tidenham Chase (Scott-Garrett 1955), and the Norman fortification of Littledean Camp (Scott-Garrett 1958). There were also numerous smaller investigations (Scott-Garrett 1954; 1956; 1959; 1960; Scott-Garrett and Grinsell 1957) and he left a considerable body of unpublished notes and observations (Scott-Garrett 1918–58; Scott-Garrett and Harris 1932). Cyril Hart, who in the latter part of the 20th century dominated research into the history of the Forest of Dean's industry and forestry, drew heavily on Scott-Garrett's work (both published and unpublished) to form the basis of *Archaeology in Dean*, the first comprehensive synthesis of the history and archaeology of the area from the prehistoric to the Saxon periods (Hart 1967).

From the 1980s, investigation of all aspects of the Forest of Dean's history and prehistory

Fig 1.6
Excavations at Lydney Park in 1928/9. From Wheeler and Wheeler 1932. Society of Antiquaries of London.
[© Historic England Archive BB86/04361]

continued through active local groups, such as Dean Archaeology Group and the Forest of Dean Local History Society, along with some individuals. Brian Walters assessed the evidence for the Roman Iron Industry (Walters 1999) and also undertook extensive fieldwalking surveys that have added considerably to an understanding of the Forest's prehistory, particularly the Mesolithic period, which was virtually unknown prior to his work (*see* Saville 1984a, fig 4). In 1992 Walters' research culminated in the production of *The Archaeology and History of Ancient Dean and the Wye Valley* (Walters 1992a), an updating of Hart's earlier work (Hart wrote the foreword) drawing on research undertaken since the 1960s. A small number of subsequent investigations have also further explored some sites, such as The Chesters Roman Villa, Woolaston (Fulford and Allen 1992), Lydney Park Roman temple (Casey and Hoffman 1999; Young and Macdonald 1998) or Palaeolithic cave shelters in the Wye Valley close to Symond's Yat (Barton 1993; 1994; 1995; 1997).

Most of this research was directed towards sites outside of woodland, and although the rise of commercial archaeology, following changes in planning policies in the 1990s, increased the number of small-scale development-led archaeological investigations, very little (if any) work was undertaken within woodland.

Early mapped information

The Forest of Dean benefits from a number of 17th- and 18th-century maps (Standing 1997; Clissold 1982; PRO 1608a and b; PRO 1618; PRO 1782; Taylor 1777) along with mid-19th-century inclosure, tithe or industrial maps (Sopwith 1835; Gwatkin 1992a–1997d). Although these maps are of great value for historical and archaeological research, with a few exceptions maps of this date tend not to depict historical or archaeological sites unless these were significant landscape features at the time. Archaeological features were recorded by the Ordnance Survey whose mapping of the Forest of Dean area began between 1811 and 1816 and, after further revision between 1825 and 1829, was published in 1830–1 (Harley 1970a and b). Coverage of antiquities was far from comprehensive and although the original surveys were at a scale of 2" to the mile (Seymour 1980, 58) the maps were published at only 1" to 1 mile, which only allowed for the depiction

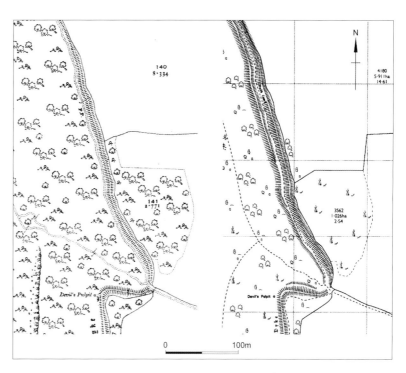

of earthworks as schematic lines, or simply denoted by a label stating 'Ancient Intrenchment' or 'Ancient Encampment'. More detail was shown on the County series maps, which were surveyed at a larger scale of 1:25,000 in the Forest of Dean. These were first published between 1880 and 1881 and subsequently revised at the turn of the 20th century and in the 1920s. The larger scale of these maps allowed for earthworks to be represented by hachures, and large earthworks such as Offa's Dyke or the Hillforts at Lydney Park, Welshbury Wood, Symonds Yat and Lancaut were depicted, often for the first time. Many smaller earthworks, however, particularly in woodland, were still overlooked and mapping of surveyed sites did not always include details of all associated earthworks (Hoyle and Vallender 1997, 44).

Why was the Forest of Dean Archaeological Survey needed?

By the end of the 20th century, despite nearly 200 years of archaeological and antiquarian research, the Forest of Dean's woodland (covering over one-third of the area) remained largely unexplored and with the exception of its rich and varied post-medieval industrial heritage and a handful of significant and highly visible earthworks from earlier periods, the archaeology of these areas was poorly understood. This was

Fig 1.7
Ordnance Survey maps dated 1921 (left) and 1974 (right), showing differences in the recording of earthworks associated with Offa's Dyke.
[© database right Landmark Information Group Ltd. All rights reserved 2018]

highlighted by the 1995 Monuments at Risk Survey (a survey of known archaeology in England), which indicated that the Forest of Dean contained less than half the average national density of recognised sites dating from the prehistoric, Roman or medieval periods (Darvill and Fulton 1998, figs 5.15, 5.16, 5.17).

There were suggestions that the woodland should contain more archaeology than was known. Sites such as Iron Age hillforts, which in other areas were components of an inhabited contemporary landscape, were known in the woods. Chance finds of Roman pottery or flint had also often been found where any form of archaeological investigation had taken place or where some knowledgeable or interested person had happened to be on hand during earthmoving operations.

Woodland is a difficult landscape for archaeologists. Nineteenth-century antiquarians recorded significant earthworks in some of the more peripheral areas or documented industrial features, but the large areas of Crown woodland in the central Forest were part of a working industrial landscape well into the 20th century and did not invite exploration. Conventional techniques for identifying archaeological remains (collecting finds from field surfaces, or identifying cropmarks from aerial photographs) are largely ineffectual in woodland where undergrowth can mask features, where limited sightlines can obscure relationships and where slight features can easily be overlooked or dismissed as insignificant. Even when earthworks are identified, bumps and hollows are so common in the woods that it can be very difficult to determine which are archaeologically significant.

In 2002 the Forest of Dean Archaeological Survey attempted to address this lack of knowledge by undertaking systematic research and, in particular, trying to find suitable ways of investigating evidence for archaeology hidden in the woodland.

The survey began with a desk-based stage that checked all existing Historic Environment records and systematically trawled through a range of published and unpublished text and map sources. This added over 4,000 new sites to the Gloucestershire HER (representing a 62 per cent increase), although most of these were post-medieval or modern industrial sites.

A daughter project, the Scowles and Associated Iron Industry Survey, mapped and collected information about scowles and pre-blast furnace iron smelting sites and the project also had close links with English Heritage's National Mapping Programme (NMP)) which ran concurrently with its early stages.

Following the desk-based work the decision was made to target future research on the large areas of woodland. A short programme of pilot fieldwork tested archaeological techniques such as excavation, geophysical survey, palaeoenvironmental sampling and rapid field reconnaissance at a number of wooded sites across the Forest. This coincided with a small lidar survey of the north-eastern part of the survey area undertaken by the Forestry Commission and the Cambridge Unit for Landscape Modelling. This tested an experimental technique to manipulate lidar data to reveal the ground surface below tree-cover and the project team were able to assess the accuracy and value of this application of lidar in a woodland environment.

Lidar proved to be such a valuable tool for the investigation of archaeology in woodland

Lidar imaging in the Forest of Dean

Lidar is a form of aerial survey in which short pulses of laser energy are fired from an aircraft towards the ground, and the time taken for these to be reflected back to the aircraft is measured. This measurement can be converted to distance by halving the return time and multiplying by the speed of light, and, so long as the height and position of the aircraft are known, this information can be used to create accurate maps of the topography of the ground surface. The Forest of Dean survey made use of an innovative technique developed by the Cambridge Unit for Landscape Modelling, which applied a 'vegetation removal algorithm' to the lidar data that separated out laser pulses that had not been blocked by the trees, and mapped the microtopography of the ground surface normally concealed by woodland cover. Further manipulation of this data was undertaken by the Forest Research branch of the Forestry Commission who produced a series of images of the ground surface illuminated from different directions to emphasise earthwork features. For more information about the archaeological applications of lidar see Crutchley and Crow 2010.

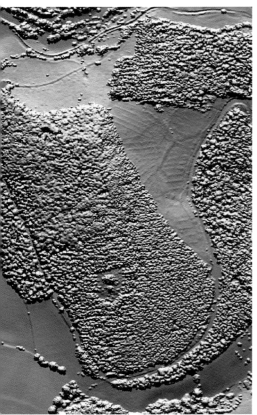 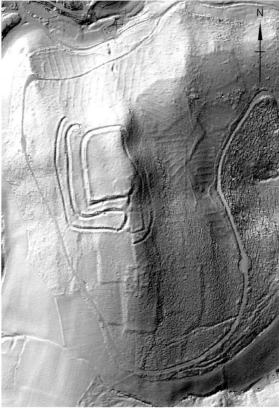

0   200m

Fig 1.8
Lidar imagery from the 2004 pilot survey showing Welshbury hillfort with and without tree cover removed. The Forest of Dean used an innovative technique developed by the Cambridge Unit for Landscape Modelling. This applied a 'vegetation removal algorithm' to the lidar data which separated out laser pulses which had not been blocked by the trees, and enabled the micro-topography of the ground surface, normally concealed by woodland cover, to be mapped.

Fig 1.9
Pilot fieldwork. Recording lidar-detected earthworks in Flaxley and Hope Woods. Lidar provided a landscape-scale overview of earthworks and their relationship with other features allowing 'borderline' features to be reassessed and interpreted with greater confidence. It also had the unexpected benefit of aiding navigation though woodland by showing tracks and other landscape features which were not recorded on maps. [© Gloucestershire County Council Archaeology Service]

that the third stage of the project was a lidar survey (in partnership with the Forestry Commission) of almost all of the Forest of Dean's woodland and the open areas in between, followed by a rapid preliminary analysis of the data, which identified hundreds of potential sites that had not been recorded previously.

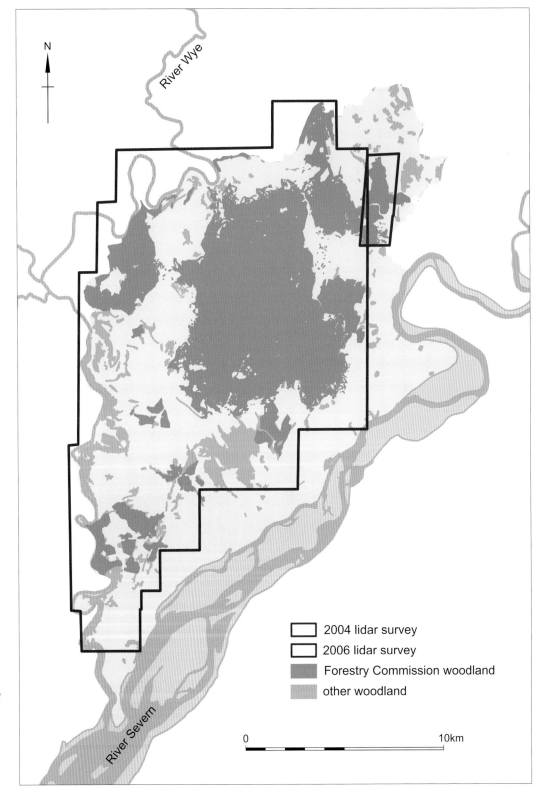

Fig 1.10
2004 and 2006 lidar surveys and woodland. Following a pilot stage to test lidar in a woodland environment an extensive lidar survey of approximately 278.3km² of the Forest of Dean was flown in March 2006. This covered almost all Forestry Commission woodland, and also extensive areas of private woodland. The results were processed to 'remove' the woodland cover and acted as a guide to further investigation.

2004 lidar survey
2006 lidar survey
Forestry Commission woodland
other woodland

0   10km

A small subset of these were then ground-truthed in Forestry Commission woodland and further, more intensive, fieldwork (small-scale exploratory excavation, geophysical survey and topographical survey) investigated four sites which represented examples of poorly under-stood features with the potential to be particularly valuable to an understanding of the archaeology

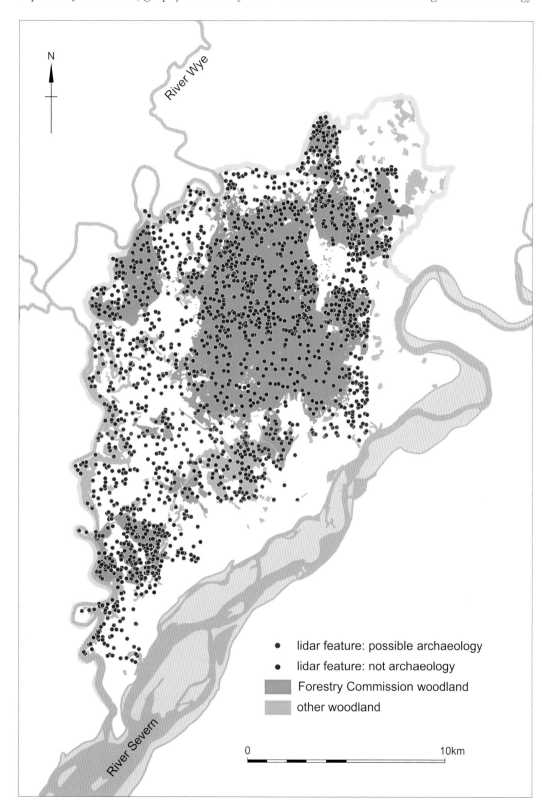

N

River Wye

River Severn

- lidar feature: possible archaeology
- lidar feature: not archaeology

Forestry Commission woodland

other woodland

0   10km

Fig 1.11
All features identified by lidar. Rapid preliminary analysis of the lidar images identified over 1,700 previously unrecorded areas of potential archaeological interest which would warrant further, more detailed analysis or fieldwork.

of the Forest of Dean and the survival of archae-ological features in its woodland. These proved to be late prehistoric to early Roman field sys-tems, an early Roman enclosure and a Bronze Age ritual monument demonstrating the range of potentially significant archaeological sites identified by lidar in the Forest, many of which remain to be fully investigated.

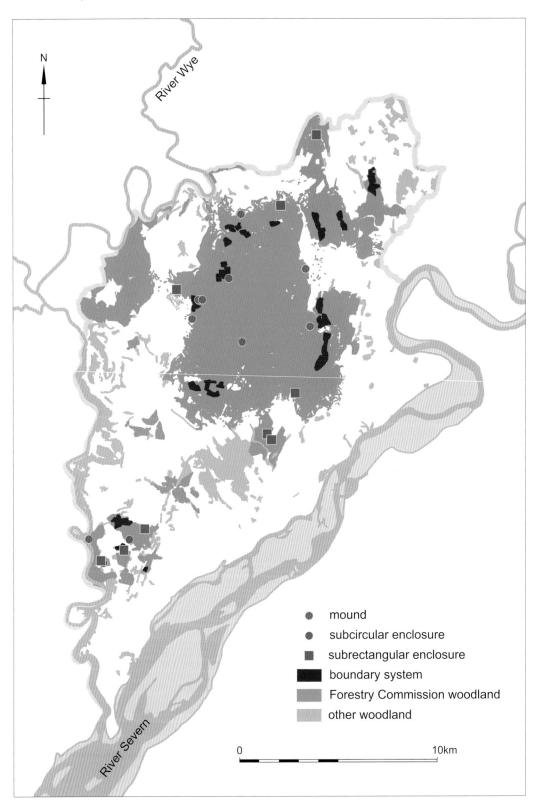

Fig 1.12
Rapid field evaluation ground-truthed 45 lidar-detected earthworks in Forestry Commission woodland. This prioritised undated mounds, boundary systems and enclosures which could not be confidently interpreted without further field survey.

2

The earlier prehistoric periods: Palaeolithic to Neolithic

The earliest inhabitants: the Palaeolithic period before the last Ice Age

The Palaeolithic period, which in Britain lasted for close to a million years between about 900,000 BC (Dinnis and Stringer 2014) and 10,000 BC, is the earliest period in which archaic humans (human-like predecessors of modern humans) or anatomically modern humans lived in Britain. The period saw many changes in climate and landscape, including four ice ages that would have rendered the area an uninhabitable arctic wasteland or freezing tundra fit only for seasonal hunting trips. Between these cold periods there were also long episodes in which the climate was temperate, or even warmer than today. The way people lived and exploited their landscape over this vast expanse of time adapted in response to changes in their environment, although throughout the period relatively small groups of people probably moved around the landscape, following resources as these changed with the season and supporting themselves by hunting, gathering or scavenging.

It is not clear when occupation of the Forest of Dean region began although isolated finds indicate there was an archaic-human presence during the Lower and Middle Palaeolithic periods before about 40,000 BC. These include Acheulean handaxes from Newent (Portable Antiquities Scheme database: GLO-3BE525) and Welsh Newton, Monmouthshire (Walters 1989, 9), a large quartzite tool from Upleadon (Glos HER 2015), a handaxe from Sedbury Cliffs, Tidenham and a Neanderthal Levallois blade from Sudbrook, Monmouthshire (Green 1989), but they tell us little about the nature or duration of any occupation.

From about 40,000 BC the earliest anatomically modern humans (*Homo sapiens*) began to settle in the British Isles, although as with earlier periods evidence for early human (Upper Palaeolithic) activity in the Forest is sparse. Surface finds of a flint core from Woolaston (James and Walters 1988, 39), a retouched blade from Morse Lane, Drybrook (Walters 1989, 9) and a large late notched blade from Taynton date to the Upper Palaeolithic, and a flint blade and scraper from excavations at Stock Farm, Clearwell may also be of that date (Atkinson 1986, 30). An early Upper Palaeolithic Solutrean shouldered point was reported as a chance surface find in the Wye Valley near Tidenham not far from the possible rock shelter at Pen Moel (*see* p 14). The significance of this find (which is now lost) is not clear as it was in very good condition and made of an unusual coarse brown flint, leading to suggestions that it may have been a recent facsimile, or an artefact from a private collection that did not originate in the area (Webb 2005, 23).

Fig 2.1
Possible Acheulean handaxe from Newent. Handaxes were ubiquitous and probably general purpose tools used by the predecessors of modern humans between about 1.5 million years BC and 40,000 BC.
[© Portable Antiquities Scheme]

0   5cm

After the Ice Age to the first farmers: the Late Upper Palaeolithic to the Neolithic

The Late Upper Palaeolithic

Fig 2.2
King Arthur's Cave Late Upper Palaeolithic rock shelter. The cave was used as a seasonal hunting camp on two separate occasions towards the end of the last Ice Age from about 12,000 BC. On the first occasion wild horse were hunted; then, after a break in use, another group of hunters used it as a base for hunting red deer (Jacobi and Higham 2011). It is no longer thought that the cave was used by Neanderthals (Homo Neanderthalensis) between about 60,000 and 40,000 BC (ApSimon and Jacobi 2004).
[© Paul Nichols]

Between about 25,000 BC and 12,000 BC, at the height of the last Ice Age, the area would have been too cold for most forms of vegetation and anything but the most sporadic human habitation, although people returned as conditions began to improve. King Arthur's Cave just outside the Forest of Dean on the Herefordshire side of the Wye Gorge was occupied, possibly as a seasonal hunting camp, on two separate occasions during this period (ApSimon *et al* 1992; Barton 1995; 1996; 1997; Jacobi and Higham 2011). Other rock shelters both sides of the River Wye may also have been used and Late Upper Palaeolithic flint tools (a penknife point and an abruptly backed bladelet) have been found in a rock shelter at Symonds Yat East (Barton 1994, 66). The bones of aurochs (*Bos primigenius*, an early species of wild cattle) and

Giant Beaver (*Castoroides leiseyorum*) have been found from Slaughter Stream cave, English Bicknor, and the tooth of a cave bear (*Ursus spelaeus*) from Pen Moel, Tidenham Chase, although it is not clear if these caves were used by humans.

Not all Palaeolithic occupation was in caves and evidence for two open-air settlements used at different times during the Late Upper Palaeolithic period has been found at Cophill Farm, to the west of Chepstow, Monmouthshire (Walker 2015). Artefacts from Llanishen near Cardiff and Thornhill Farm, Chepstow (Bevan 1996; Walker 2015) suggest other open-air settlements during this period.

The Mesolithic

By about 10,000 BC a warming climate had replaced arctic tundra with a landscape of woodland dominated by birch, alder, pine or hazel (Rackham 1995, 68). This process was sporadic, with warm spells interspersed with colder periods, and around 9,500 BC arctic conditions may

have changed to modern temperatures in as little as 50 years (Hosfield *et al* 2008, 30).

The hunter-gatherer lifestyle continued, and early Mesolithic (from about 10,000 BC to 6,000 BC) flint tools have been found at Soilwell Manor, Lydney and Tidenham, but are also known in the wider region with flints found at Taynton and Common Fields, Newent in Gloucestershire; Llanishen, Skenfrith, Hadnock and Dixton in Monmouthshire (Walters 1992a, 12–13); on the Black Mountains in Wales and at Usk and Shire-newton, Monmouthshire (Walker 2004).

Over the next few thousand years temperatures increased and the pine and birch woodland was gradually replaced by more familiar species such as lime, hazel, elm and oak (Mellars 1974). Thawing ice sheets caused sea levels to rise and by about 6,000 BC Britain was an island.

At about this time there was a change from relatively broad-bladed flint implements towards an increase in small microliths. The size and weight of smaller flints would have been attractive to mobile hunting groups and could be used to create composite tools such as arrow heads, although flint was also a valuable resource not readily available in the area, and may have been used sparingly (Darvill 2011, 51).

Although there are no known *in situ* Mesolithic features in the Forest of Dean, 50 sites have been identified where later Mesolithic (about 6,000–4,000 BC) flints have been found.

Some of these (such as a flint adze from the River Wye at Symonds Yat (Price 2001, 72)) were chance finds, although many were scatters of flint from the surface of ploughed fields, found during systematic fieldwalking by Brian Walters and members of the Dean Archaeology Group in the second half of the 1980s (Walters 1988, 36).

By the early 1990s Walters had identified concentrations of late Mesolithic flint scatters on Tidenham Chase, several sites around Bearse Common between St Briavels and Clearwell, Oldcroft near Lydney, Hangerberry between English Bicknor and Lydbrook, Blaisdon and Littledean, with similar sites just outside the area at Taynton and Newent in Gloucestershire and also Huntsman Hill near Symonds Yat and Great Howle in Herefordshire (Walters 1992a, fig 8). Further fieldwalking has increased the number of known sites and significant concentrations of Mesolithic flint have been found at Bream Cross, south-west of Bream (Walters 1996, 11), the Boughspring area to the south of Tidenham Chase, and the north-western part of Tidenham Chase to the south of Madgetts

Farm. King Arthur's Cave and other rock shelters in the upper Wye Gorge in Herefordshire were also occupied during this period (ApSimon *et al* 1992; Barton 1993, 337; Barton 1997).

Most Mesolithic flint concentrations overlie higher ground with well-drained soils over limestone geology and these may have been preferred by Mesolithic communities (Saville 1986, 229). The areas where concentrations of flint are most likely to have been found are most suitable for arable cultivation (Hoyle 2008a, 74–75) and other areas, such as woodland or pasture, where much less evidence for Mesolithic activity, has been recorded may also have been occupied.

At Goldcliff in Monmouthshire, to the south-west of the Forest of Dean, there is significant

Fig 2.3
Palaeolithic and Mesolithic finds. As recently as 1984 the Mesolithic in the Forest of Dean was almost completely unknown (Saville 1984a, fig 4). Fieldwalking by Brian Walters and Dean Archaeological Group in the 1980s revolutionised knowledge of the existence and spread of Mesolithic activity particularly in the area of Bearse Common to the east of St Briavels.

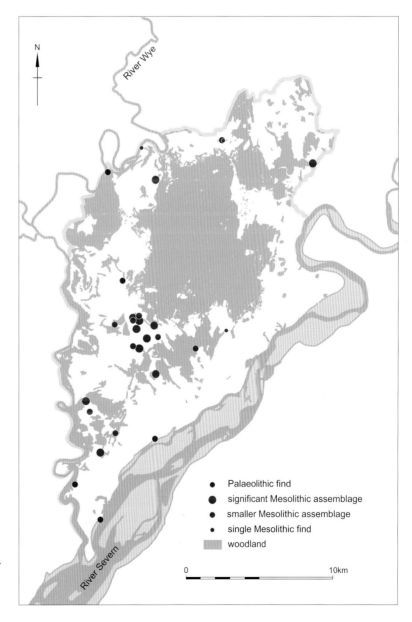

evidence for Mesolithic exploitation of coastal wetland sites in what are now sediment and peat deposits in the intertidal zone of the Severn Estuary (Bell 2007, 221). Much of the Severn Estuary would have been a broad, low-lying wooded landscape for much of the Mesolithic period (Allen 2001, 26, fig 4) before rising sea levels from about 6,000 BC produced a water-logged landscape of bogs and alder trees followed by reed swamp and then salt marsh by about 4,000 BC (Brown *et al* 2006, 77).

Evidence for Mesolithic exploitation of this emerging coastal environment in the Forest of Dean is limited, although charcoal from Woolaston (dating to the later Mesolithic period from about 4,700 to 4,220–3,890 cal BC) may be the result of seasonal burning of reed swamp to attract browsing animals to regenerative under-growth and making them easier to hunt (Brown 2007, 262).

The Neolithic

About 6,000 years ago new ways of living began to appear in Britain as people started to grow cereal crops, keep animals for food, make pottery and also stamp their identity on the landscape by constructing public monuments. Evidence for the transition from the late Mesolithic and early Neolithic is difficult to find (Darvill 2006, 18) and the change from mobile hunter-gatherer to sedentary farming community was probably gradual and piecemeal and occurred in different ways and at different speeds in different places. The earliest farmers may have lived in relatively mobile communities that combined hunting and gathering of wild foods with limited animal husbandry and cereal cultivation (Bell 2007, 16–17), and farming may have begun as a development of systems to manage food resources by controlling the movement of animals or encouraging preferred types of vegetation.

In the Forest of Dean, the evidence for the Neolithic consists almost exclusively of finds, mostly of worked flint. Some were chance finds or recovered during archaeological investigations (although these were exclusively residual finds in later features), but the vast majority were collected from ploughed fields during fieldwalking. Neolithic flints have been found at a number of sites on the Bearse between St Briavels and Clearwell, and also at Cottage Farm, Alvington; Chelfridge, Bream, Parsons's Allotment, Tidenham Chase, and also at Soldier's Tump round

barrow south-east of Chase Farm Tidenham, where possible early Neolithic pottery has been found (H N Savory in Scott-Garrett 1955, 30–31). Mesolithic flints have also been found at these sites, although this does not necessarily indicate continuous settlement and these sites may just have been periodically visited, perhaps for relatively short episodes, over a considerable period of time.

Other Neolithic finds from the Forest of Dean include five complete stone axe heads and a number of axe head fragments that were imported to the area from other parts of the country, showing that goods could be traded over considerable distances during this period. Two of the complete axes, from Newland and Mitcheldean, were made of polished flint. Two others (from Longhope and Clements End) were made of Greenstone from the Cornwall area, while the fifth (from Viney Hill, Awre) was from the Great Gable axe factory in Cumberland. Scott-Garrett also reported a story of a very old man who had found a 'celt' made of a 'slatey coloured material' on Tidenham Chase (Scott-Garrett 1918–58, entry for 19 November 1952) that was also presumably an imported stone axe.

Just outside the Forest of Dean, Cornish and Cumbrian stone axes have been found at Welsh and English Newton, Herefordshire. Others from Oxenhall near Newent and Walford, Herefordshire (Walters 1991a, 39) are from a currently unrecognised source, although one from Great Doward Hill in Herefordshire, on the opposite side of the River Wye, was from Scandinavia (Walters 1992a, 26).

Fig 2.4 (below right) Neolithic flint from Sallowvallets Wood north of Cannop. Apart from occasional nodules in gravel deposits the nearest source of flint is north Wiltshire. Mesolithic and Neolithic communities must have traded with other communities who were able to source this material. [© Gloucestershire County Council Archaeology Service]

Fig 2.5 (opposite) Neolithic Cornish Greenstone polished axe from Clements End, Coleford. Tools from diverse part of Britain and abroad clearly show that Neolithic people in Dean operated within a wide network of trade and communications. Precisely how goods were transported and by what routes, is not clear, but river transport along both the Wye and Severn must have played a major part in this distribution. [© Gloucester Museums Service. Photo Paul Nichols]

0   5cm

The majority of Neolithic finds are, like the Mesolithic assemblages (*see* p 15), from arable areas where fieldwalking is possible, with concentrations from the area between St Briavels and Bream, centred on Closeturf Farm, and also scatters centred around Nedge Cop near Bearse Farm, St Briavels. These concentrations contained many broken or burnt flints and may represent extensive temporary campsites established during hunting expeditions over an extended period (Walters 1988, 37).

Evidence for the Neolithic is found throughout the area, however, suggesting that activity was widespread, but there is no real evidence for long-term occupation.

The Neolithic is the period when ritual monuments begin to appear in the landscape and a range of these, particularly long barrows (large generally stone-built ritual structures used as communal burial sites), are known in the Cotswolds to the east and also in Wales to the west (Darvill 2004, 46–66, fig 34). These monuments suggest that communities lived nearby and were beginning to make their mark on the landscape, and their complete absence in the Forest of Dean is particularly striking.

The numerous field or place names that could indicate the sites of prehistoric burial mounds (Hoyle 2008a, 133) are not definitive evidence of Neolithic barrow sites. A possible long barrow identified by dowsing in Awre (Brian Johns pers comm) must remain speculative without further

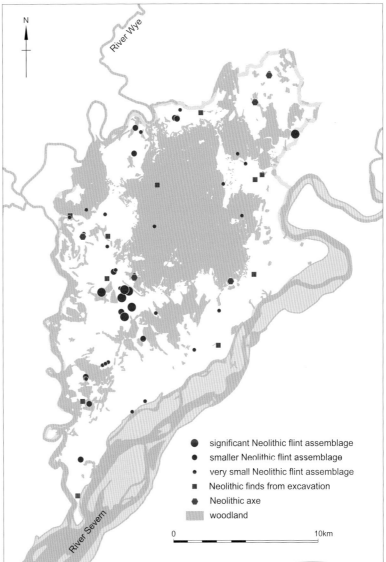

significant Neolithic flint assemblage
smaller Neolithic flint assemblage
very small Neolithic flint assemblage
Neolithic finds from excavation
Neolithic axe
woodland

0   10km

investigation, and a long barrow recorded by Scott-Garrett in Oakhill Wood near Tidenham Chase was subsequently discounted (Scott-Garrett 1918–58, entries for 19 September 1950 and 12 May 1951; Hoyle 2008a, 79). Sites may await discovery but neither the 2006 lidar survey nor the National Mapping Programme has identified earthworks or cropmarks that seem likely candidates for Neolithic field monuments (Hoyle 2008c; Small and Stoertz 2006) and it is possible that there were none in the Forest.

The implications of this are not clear but a lack of permanent field monuments could suggest that although people clearly visited and used the Forest of Dean during the Neolithic period this may have been primarily for seasonal hunting or foraging expeditions rather than for longer-term settlement and farming.

Fig 2.6
Neolithic finds. Although people were clearly active in the Forest of Dean during the Neolithic, there are no known Neolithic field monuments in the area.

3

The later prehistoric periods:
Bronze Age to Iron Age

There is more evidence for human activity during the later prehistoric periods and the Forest of Dean survey has had much greater impact on an understanding of how the area was inhabited and exploited from this time.

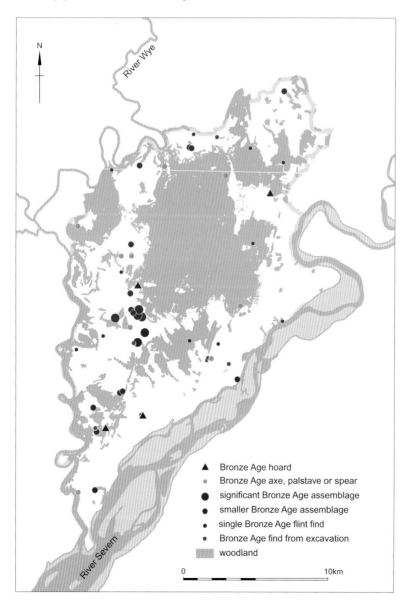

Fig 3.1
Bronze Age finds.

Later prehistoric settlement

There is very little excavated evidence for Bronze Age settlement in the Forest of Dean, but, unlike earlier periods, there are many more indicators in the form of ritual monuments and earthworks (*see* pp 39–49, Fig 3.60) that suggest that people were living in the area on a permanent basis.

Much of the evidence for the Bronze Age activity in the Forest of Dean consists of flint concentrations found by fieldwalking. This is known throughout the area, closely mirroring the spread of Neolithic finds, and significant concentrations are known around Bearse Common between St Briavels and Clearwell, with smaller scatters in the Tidenham Chase area. These areas of relatively well-drained soils on higher ground over limestone bedrock and outside of the areas of modern woodland (Hoyle 2008a, 98–100) may have been favoured during the Bronze Age, but fieldwalking has undoubtedly skewed the picture in favour of cultivated land. Neolithic and Mesolithic flints have also been found on Bearse Common (*see* pp 15, 17) suggesting that this area was occupied, perhaps as short-stay temporary campsites, over a considerable period of time.

Where fieldwalking has not taken place the evidence is more erratic and Bronze Age pottery is particularly rare.

Pottery and flints from the mound of Soldier's Tump round barrow on Tidenham Chase (*see* p 39) may be evidence for late Neolithic/early Bronze Age occupation disturbed during its construction (H N Savory in Scott-Garrett 1955, 30–1), and Bronze Age pottery from a group of small pits to the east of Lydney is also evidence for Bronze Age activity. The pits may have held upright timbers, but it is not clear whether these were a domestic structure (Barber 2009, 14, fig 7). Pottery from Rodmore Farm, St Briavels (Woodward 1995, 19), west of Drybrook Quarry (Chambers 1989, 6) and Lydney (Harris 1938,

Legend (within map):
- ▲ Bronze Age hoard
- • Bronze Age axe, palstave or spear
- ● significant Bronze Age assemblage
- ● smaller Bronze Age assemblage
- • single Bronze Age flint find
- • Bronze Age find from excavation
- woodland

0   10km

347) has been reported as Bronze Age, but this date is not certain.

Fourteen Bronze Age axe and palstave heads have also been found in the Forest of Dean. An early Bronze Age stone battle axe found at Roads Farm, St Briavels in 1978 is made from quartz dolerite from Whin Sill in the northern Pennines, although the rest are made from bronze. Most date from the early and middle Bronze Age (about 2,500–1,275 BC) and were isolated finds, generally discovered during quarrying, mining or other earthmoving operations.

Five late Bronze Age looped and socketed axe heads have been found on Clearwell Meend to the south of Coleford. One was found in 1956, two during excavations for house foundations in 1987 and two others, which may have been found sometime in the intervening period, have since come to light. These may have been part of a late Bronze Age founder's hoard where valuable scrap metal was buried for safekeeping by an itinerant metal worker, as the sockets of the axes found in 1987 contained scrap bronze and fragments of a bronze blade (Walters 1991a, 40). There are difficulties with this interpretation, however, as the axe heads were found over a period of more than 30 years, and it is not clear if they were all from precisely the same location. A middle Bronze Age spear tip has also been found in a garden at Boughspring, although no other artefacts were found with this (Walters 1991a, 39).

A possible Bronze Age settlement site has been suggested by earthworks to the south of Welshbury hillfort, Blaisdon (McOmish and Smith 1996, 57; see Fig 3.8) but this site has never been excavated.

There is much more earthwork evidence for settlement during the Iron Age (from about 800 BC), although some sites may have originated in the Bronze Age.

Hillforts

The Forest of Dean's four hillforts (Camp Hill, Lydney; Symonds Yat; Lancaut; and Welshbury Hill, Blaisdon) are the most tangible evidence of Iron Age settlement. A fifth site at Madgetts on the northern side of Tidenham Chase may also be a hillfort (see pp 26–7, Fig 3.13) and other hillforts are known just outside the Forest at Little Doward, Ganarew and Chase Wood, just south of Ross-on-Wye, Herefordshire.

Although hillforts are among Britain's best-known and easily recognisable prehistoric field monuments, it is not always clear how these sites were used. Hillforts vary enormously in layout and size (although most enclose an area of between 1.2 and 12 ha (Dyer 1992, 5) and however similar they may appear to us today, not all hillforts are necessarily contemporary or fulfilled the same function.

Excavations at a number of hillforts in Britain have shown them to have been defended settlements, perhaps the economic and political centres of a small region (Cunliffe 1984; Saville 1984b; Savory 1976), but it cannot be assumed that all hillforts were used in this way.

Defended hilltop settlements began to appear in Britain in the earlier part of the Iron Age (about 700 BC, Darvill 2011, 178) or possibly in the latter part of the Bronze Age from about 1000 BC (Savory 1976). Populations had been growing throughout the Bronze Age and a deteriorating climate may have caused a shortage of usable land which prompted the development of defended settlements. Many early hillforts were simple enclosures defended by a single (or occasionally a double) massive bank and ditch, although from about 400 BC some of these may have fallen out of use and more elaborate hillforts with multiple ramparts began to appear

Fig 3.2
Bronze Age barbed and tanged arrowhead from English Bicknor.
[© Portable Antiquities Scheme]

Fig 3.3
Bronze Age palstave from High Nash, Coleford. The sheer number of Bronze Age axes or other metalwork known from the British Isles has led some archaeologists to question whether they could all have been inadvertently lost or forgotten. Some may have been deliberately buried for safe keeping by itinerant metal workers and others may have been ritual deposits.
[© Gloucester Museums Service. Photo Paul Nichols]

0   5cm

(Darvill 2011, 188–9). Not all of these 'developed' hillforts were constructed from scratch and some early hillforts (for example, Danebury in Hampshire) were modified by adding further ramparts (Cunliffe 1984, 42–5). Some of the Forest hillforts may have been originally built during the earlier period and subsequently updated.

Camp Hill, Lydney

Camp Hill, Lydney was partly excavated by Sir Mortimer Wheeler between 1928 and 1929 (Wheeler and Wheeler 1932), and is the most extensively excavated hillfort in the Forest of Dean. The Wheelers were mainly investigating a Roman temple within the hillfort, but they sectioned the ramparts, cleared the area around the possible entrance on its eastern side and 'extensively trenched' the interior in the hope of finding 'traces of the hutments of the prehistoric inhabitants' (Wheeler and Wheeler 1932, 11). Pottery, animal bone and some stone tools (hone stones and a quern) along with a few brooches demonstrated that the site had been occupied in the Iron Age, but with the possible exception of some 'prehistoric' postholes and paving recorded below the temple (Wheeler and Wheeler 1932, 2–26; fig 2), no evidence of domestic structures was found.

The Wheelers' excavations suggested that the inner ramparts on the northern and eastern sides were originally built in the Iron Age, but were added to, and made higher, in the later Roman or post-Roman period. They found no dating evidence for the northern outer rampart, although there was no evidence for later additions, and they suggested that there had originally been only a single rampart, and that the outer northern rampart was added shortly after the end of the Roman period at which time the inner rampart was considerably enlarged (Wheeler and Wheeler 1932, 6).

More recent research has questioned the Wheelers' date for the heightening of the inner rampart (Casey and Hoffmann 1999, 101) and also the late or post-Roman date of the outer rampart, which the Wheelers based solely on an assumption that hillforts were entirely defensive, which meant that as the outer rampart was 'slightly higher' than the inner (Wheeler and Wheeler 1932, 5) it must 'on tactical grounds' be contemporary with the post-Roman rebuilding of the fortifications after which it was 'suitably dominated by the remodelled inner bank' (Wheeler and Wheeler 1932, 6).

The 1928–9 excavation records (Wheeler and Wheeler 1932, plate IV) do not show a marked disparity between the heights of the inner and outer ramparts (in fact the inner may be slightly higher) and hillfort defences are no longer assumed to be necessarily purely defensive and may have fulfilled less practical functions such as demonstrating the prestige of the inhabitants (Bowden and McOmish 1987, 77) or demarcating boundaries between areas of different social space (Hill 1996b, 108–10). There is no compelling reason to assume the outer rampart was late or post-Roman and, although the ramparts need not necessarily be contemporary, they should both be regarded as an integral part of the Iron Age hillfort (Casey and Hoffmann 1999, 113).

An alternative sequence for the hillfort development is suggested by lidar which provides

Fig 3.4
Hillforts in the Forest of Dean. All of these sites are around the periphery of the higher ground in prominent topographical locations, with a number of sides protected by either steep slopes or sheer cliffs. This combination of defensive advantage combined with visual prominence must have been a major factor in their siting and these may have been defended settlements.

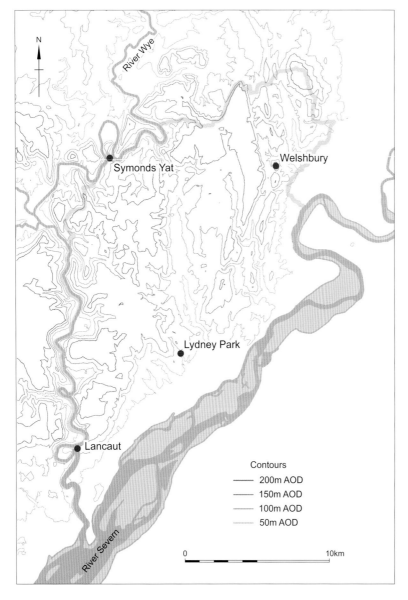

Fig 3.5 (left)
Section through the hillfort ramparts at Lydney Park 1928/9. From Wheeler and Wheeler 1932. Society of Antiquaries of London.
[© Historic England Archive BB86/04318]

Fig 3.6
Camp Hill, Lydney. The lidar shows a more extensive sequence of ramparts than that recorded by the Ordnance Survey or the Wheelers who surveyed the site in the late 1920s.

more information about the full extent of the ramparts than either the Ordnance Survey, which recorded the site as a univallate enclosure until the 1960s (OS 1880–1, 1902–3, 1921a, 1967), or the Wheelers' 1920s survey of the site (Wheeler and Wheeler 1932, plate LII).

The inner and outer northern ramparts (Ramparts 1 and 2) continue eastwards, beyond the junction with the inner eastern rampart (Rampart 3) before turning southwards along the eastern slope of the hill (Fig 3.7). These may have been the ramparts of the original hillfort protecting the shallower slopes on the hilltop's northern and eastern side. It is not clear if any ramparts ever existed above the much steeper western and southern slopes, where they could be deemed superfluous, although late 19th- and early 20th-century Ordnance survey maps (OS 1880–1, 1902–3, 1921a) show a short (about 30m) length of bank where the northern inner rampart turns to run along the top of the western edge of the plateau. This earthwork is not recorded on other maps (*see*, for example, Wheeler and Wheeler 1932, plate LII). Although the lidar shows a narrow bank in this area, it is not clear if this was ever part of the original ramparts here.

The inner rampart does not appear to have been part of the original scheme. It is relatively angular compared with the organic sweep of the eastern outer ramparts and was built from material quarried from its inner side rather than external ditches. When the Wheelers excavated the ramparts they recovered no finds from the outer rampart and only two animal bones and a

N

0   100m

single sherd of pottery were found in the Iron Age phase of the inner northern rampart. The earliest phase of the inner eastern rampart, on the other hand, produced numerous finds including 54 sherds of 'bead rimmed' pottery dating to the middle Iron Age, although no post-Iron Age material (Wheeler and Wheeler 1932, 4–7 and 94). They suggested that the inner eastern rampart was not constructed 'until the settlement had existed long enough to scatter the surface of the camp with debris' (Wheeler and Wheeler 1932, 10), but did not suggest it was built after the Iron Age.

Geophysical survey has suggested a further rampart may have originally run approximately 40m to the south of the existing banks on the northern side of the hillfort (Young and Macdonald 1998, 5), meeting the inner eastern rampart where there is a distinct kink in its alignment. To the north of this junction the northern section of the inner eastern rampart sits uncomfortably in the overall scheme and simply abuts the back of the inner northern rampart. This short section may have been a later addition and the inner rampart, when first built sometime in the Iron Age, may have defined an area within the hillfort enclosed by a single right-angled rampart roughly concentric with the earlier outer ramparts.

During the Roman period the southern part of the hillfort interior was used as a ritual centre with a temple and associated structures (*see* pp 69–70 and Wheeler and Wheeler 1932). The ramparts of the earlier hillfort are unlikely to have been maintained and any original ramparts on the southern and western part of the site, and perhaps also the original northern arm of the inner rampart, may have been levelled. During or shortly after the Roman period the hillfort defences were again strengthened, although this heightening of the banks was confined to the northern part of Rampart 2 and the eastern part of Rampart 3, which were linked by a new section and converted into a single right-angled enclosure.

The current entrance through the northern ramparts, which is merely labelled as 'gap' on Wheeler and Wheeler 1932, plate LII, is probably 'a comparatively modern opening' and the Wheelers suggested that the hillfort was originally entered from the south, through a wide cutting in the south-eastern corner of the hill. A terrace on the northern side of this opening was interpreted as 'the in-turned flanks of the original rock-cut entrance' (Wheeler and Wheeler 1932, 4), suggesting that more extensive earthworks originally existed in this area, perhaps destroyed to accommodate the Roman temple. The Wheelers also thought a small gap in the inner eastern rampart (Entrance B on Wheeler and Wheeler 1392, Plate LII), where there is a slight in-turn of the rampart, was an original entrance.

Welshbury

Welshbury hillfort, Blaisdon, in the eastern part of the Forest of Dean, appears to be the most complicated of the Forest's hillforts. A detailed topographical survey (McOmish and Smith 1996) has helped unravel the complex system of earthworks, and a geophysical survey has been undertaken in the interior (Hoyle 2008b, 92–4). There have also been two small excavations in

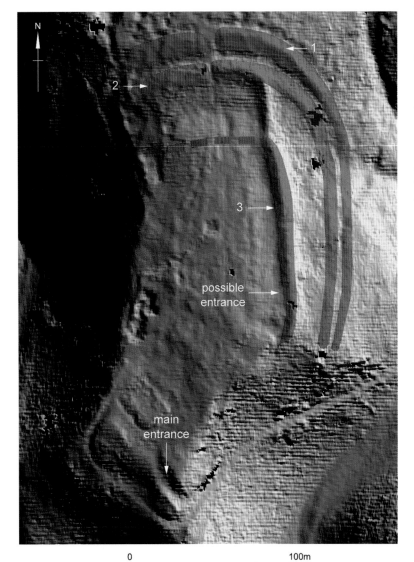

Fig 3.7
Camp Hill, Lydney, rampart sequence. During the Iron Age the outer two ramparts (ramparts 1 and 2) may have been constructed first and the inner (rampart 3) added at a later date possibly with a northern arm enclosing an area within the outer ramparts. During or shortly after the Roman period the site was remodelled.

ditches associated with the entrance earthworks and the middle rampart (Jarman 2015).

The earliest phase was the innermost ramparts that now form the north-eastern part of the hillfort complex, enclosing a roughly rectangular area of about 1.3ha, and may have formed a small early Iron Age hilltop enclosure. The northern, western and southern sides are defined by a large bank, ditch and counterscarp (partly derived from material scooped from the inner side of the bank). No rampart survives on the eastern side although the steep natural slope may have been modified to create a terraced scarp, and rubble on the slopes in this area may be the remains of a slighted rampart (McOmish and Smith 1996, 59).

The outer ramparts were constructed later, although how much later is unknown. The middle rampart appears to predate the outer, but this does not necessarily mean they were not part of a contemporary phase of refurbishment. In its final form the hillfort is consistent with a developed hillfort dating to the middle Iron Age period from about 400 BC and it is likely that either the whole hillfort or the outer ramparts were constructed at this time.

There may originally have been an entrance in the south-eastern corner of the inner enclosure approached via a linear scarp extending southwards from the hillfort and which enhances a natural geological ridge (Jarman 2015). An alternative approach would have been directly up the steep slopes to the east (McOmish and Smith 1996, 59) and it is possible that both routes were used.

There was evidence for extensive activity in the interior and much of the higher ground on its eastern side had been subdivided into a series of platforms or terraces defined by linear banks or ditches. There was some evidence of low-level burning, consistent with domestic hearths, although an area of more intense burning in the north-eastern corner may indicate some industrial process such as smithing or smelting. A number of small platforms in this area may have been the site of subrectangular structures and three later (but undated) charcoal platforms could have reused the site of earlier structures, such as roundhouses (McOmish and Smith 1996, 59; Substrata 2005a, 7–10).

The only excavated dating evidence from the site are nine sherds of Roman (probably 3rd to 4th century AD) pottery from the lower fills of the ditch of the middle rampart (Webster 2015; Jarman 2015) which suggest post-Iron Age

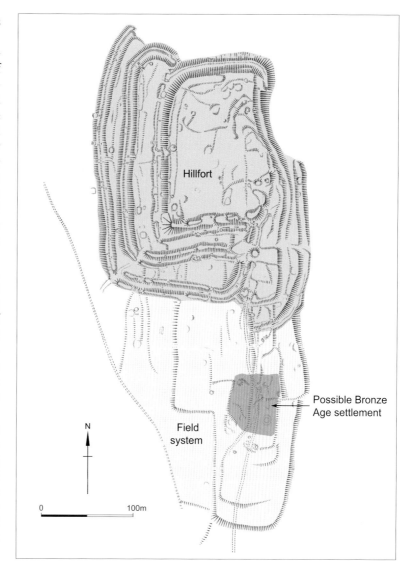

activity on the site, although precisely what this was is not known.

The 1995 survey also recorded evidence for a Bronze Age field system which probably remained in use after the hillfort was built (McOmish and Smith 1996, 57) and an extensive area of terraces and boundaries have been recorded to the south and east of the hillfort (Hoyle 2008c, 61, fig 25; Hoyle 2011a, 59–61). It is clear that the hillfort was not an isolated Iron Age feature but occupied a position within a contemporary landscape of small fields and paddocks.

Symonds Yat and Lancaut promontory forts

The remaining two hillforts at Symonds Yat and Lancaut are, unlike Welshbury and Lydney, promontory forts where a concentric arc of ramparts cuts off a roughly triangular area of level high

Fig 3.8
Welshbury hillfort. A detailed topographical survey deciphered the sequence of rampart construction and also recorded the remains of a field system to the south of the hillfort which may have originated in the Bronze Age. A cluster of platforms, within the field system were interpreted as the remains of 'an unenclosed settlement ... contemporary with the pre-hillfort phase of the field system' although the site has not been excavated. [© Royal Commission for the Historical Monuments of England]

Fig 3.9 (above)
Speculative reconstruction
of Symonds Yat
promontory fort. A series of
five banks and ditches cut
off one side of a triangular
area (approximately 2.5ha)
of high ground. The
remaining two sides
overlook the steep, high
cliffs of the Wye Gorge and
are undefended. Although
the reconstruction suggests
the hillfort was the site of a
small Iron Age settlement
no evidence for this has
been found.
[© Wye Valley AONB]

Fig 3.10 (right)
Iron Age ramparts at
Symonds Yat hillfort.
[© Gloucestershire County
Council Archaeology
Service]

ground, the remaining sides of which are defined by steep slopes with little surviving evidence of additional fortification.

Both hillforts occupy strikingly similar positions cutting off the narrow necks of high ground where the River Wye meanders through steep cliffs of the Wye Gorge. They command positions overlooking the river and also bar access to large areas of lower ground within the loop of the meander. Very little is known about either of these hillforts. A series of small-scale excavations and observations at Symonds Yat have recorded late Iron Age to early Roman activity on the site (Parry 1994; Walters 1992a), but not confirmed the date of the earthworks or shed light on how the hillfort was used or when it was constructed. In 2003 a section of Lancaut's outer ditch, to the east of the ramparts was exposed, but not excavated (Davis 2003, 7). Geophysical survey in the interior has identified a number of 'shallow cut features' that may indicate boundaries and curved gullies (possibly roundhouse foundations) associated with Iron Age activity on the site (Barker *et al* 2000, 8, fig 10), and also a number of possible ditches subdividing the interior and other possible small enclosures or pits (Roseveare 2018a, 3–5).

Very little is known about the status, date or longevity of the Iron Age hillforts in the Forest of Dean and it is not clear that they fulfilled similar functions, or were even contemporary features.

They are all in prominent positions and the limited archaeological evidence is consistent with an interpretation of defended settlements, perhaps controlling resources within a specific territory, although the boundaries of these territories can only be guessed at.

All of the hillforts are close to areas that are currently farmed (although evidence for an associated contemporary farmed landscape is known only at Welshbury) and all also have access to major watercourses (the Rivers Severn and Wye) that could provide both food resources and transportation links for trade.

Symonds Yat, Welshbury and Lydney are also close to the iron ore outcrops (scowles) and it is tempting to suggest that this resource was also controlled from these hillforts during the Iron Age.

Other prehistoric settlement

Most people during the later prehistoric period probably lived in small farmsteads rather than sites like hillforts. This type of settlement was not uncommon in the eastern part of Gloucestershire (Darvill 2011, 201–3) and numerous subcircular or subrectangular earthworks or cropmarks have been interpreted as small settlements or farmsteads to the west of the River Wye (Stoertz 2004, 27–9), in Wales (Wainwright 1971; Murphy 1983), the north of England (Cunliffe 1978, fig 12.24) and throughout central and southern England (Cunliffe 1978, fig 11.13, fig 11.6). Definitive evidence for Iron Age occupation outside hillforts is, however, limited in the Forest of Dean. A number of postholes recorded at Sedbury, Tidenham have been interpreted as Iron Age (Carew 2003, 84–5) and hearths and postholes found with Iron Age pottery at Coldwell Cave close to Symonds Yat also suggest a settlement site, although this is unlikely to have been typical.

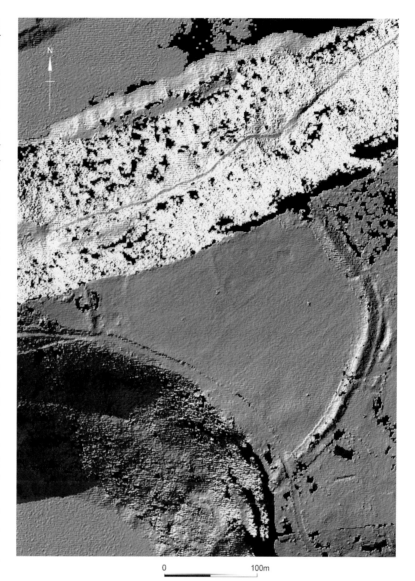

Fig 3.11

Lancaut promontory fort. A large bank and ditch with a smaller and discontinuous outer bank and ditch cuts off an area of 4.6ha defined by steep cliffs to north and south. The straight length of bank across the western edge of the plateau may be an original rampart. Earthworks visible in the interior may also be associated with the hillfort, although some correspond to boundaries recorded in 1974 (OS 1974). An additional outer bank in the central part of the eastern rampart may be part of an original entrance.

Fig 3.12
Soudley Camp encloses an area of only 0.16ha. To the west it is defended by a substantial bank (2m high) with an outer ditch (1–1.5m deep and 10m wide) with a central entrance. Steep slopes (possibly artificially enhanced) form the other two sides and there are intermittent remains of a bank along its northern side.

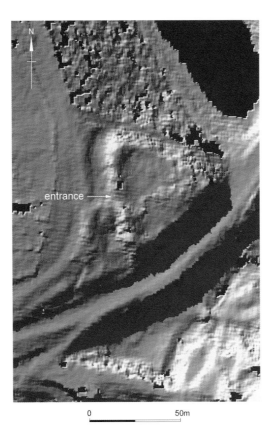

Fig 3.13
Possible enclosure predating Offa's Dyke at Madgetts. The curved line of Offa's Dyke here may have incorporated an earlier earthwork which is visible continuing to its east.

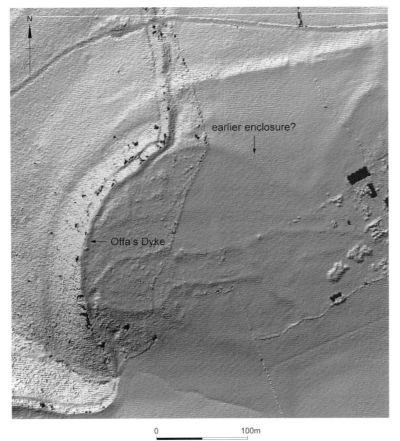

The Forest does, however, contain several small earthwork enclosures that have been tentatively interpreted as late prehistoric settlement sites.

The only one of these that has been dated in any way is Soudley Camp, Soudley, where a substantial bank with an outer ditch defends the western side of a small triangular area at the eastern end of a natural spur. This site has long been thought likely to be the remains of a small defended Iron Age settlement and has also been listed as a hillfort (Saville 1984b, 165, fig 1), although it had also been suggested as the remains of an early medieval 'castle' (Hart 1967, 53). A flint flake, iron ore, bloomery slag and five sherds of Roman pottery were found in molehills on the site (DAG 2000b, 25). A small excavation in 2017 showed the ditch to be surprisingly shallow (only 0.5 to 1.5m) and the defences may have been as much about display as defence. Little dating evidence was found, although a beehive quern recovered from a pit or posthole suggests that the site was occupied during the Iron Age and possibly into the early Roman period (Wheeler and Walsh 2019, 7–8).

Not all possible Iron Age settlements survive and two enclosures in Combesbury Wood, Tidenham were destroyed by quarrying in the 19th century while a third, identified as a crop-mark in Mitcheldean, is now under modern housing. Other earthworks at Ashbury and Yew-berry, Tidenham, and Oldbury and Dinnegar Camps in Stroat (Hart 1967, 14) cannot now be located with any certainty, although lidar has identified a short stretch of curved bank just north of Ashberry House, Tidenham (Hoyle 2008c, 48). Broad earthworks on the assumed site of Oldbury Camp correspond with banks recorded by Ormerod in 1841 (Hart 1967, fig 5). No earthworks have been found at the supposed site of Dinnegar Camp 'behind the orchard at Stroat farm' (Hart 1967, 14), although lidar shows a subrectangular earthwork on higher ground about 550m to it its east and next to a field recorded as 'Dinnegar' on the Tidenham tithe map of 1845 (Gwatkin 1995a).

Undated enclosures

Other subcircular enclosures that could repre-sent late prehistoric settlement have been identified in the Forest of Dean, although none have been excavated or produced finds which indicate their date or function.

There may have been a large subcircular enclosure to the west of Madgetts Farm on the northern side of Tidenham Chase where Offa's

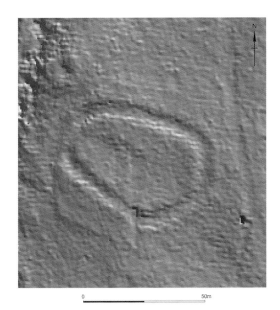

*Fig 3.14 (far left)
Sallowvallets enclosure.
A shallow ditch with a low
bank on both sides encloses
an ovoid area of about
54 × 38m. A metal detector
survey found 'pockets of
bloomery slag' in the
interior (Walters 1987a,
78), although these may
represent later iron
smelting on the site. The site
is undated and generally
considered prehistoric
(Standing 1986, 33)
although it could be a
medieval hunting lodge
(Newman 1988).*

*Fig 3.15 (left)
Enclosure in Flaxley
Woods. Its northern edge is
defined by a ditch 2m wide
and 0.5–1.5m deep with a
low bank on the inner and
outer sides. It has been
damaged by quarrying to
the south, although it could
be traced as a complete
circuit enclosing an area
of about 60 × 34m.*

Dyke follows a very regular arc at the western edge of the early medieval settlement at Madgetts. Some earlier authorities suggested that Madgetts was the site of an earlier earthwork that had been incorporated into the line of the Dyke (Fosbroke 1831, 1832; Playne 1877) and the site was recorded as 'Modesgate Roman Camp' in 1902 (OS 1902a). Cyril Fox, who surveyed Offa's Dyke in 1931, found no trace of this 'Camp' (Fox 1955, 203), and later surveyors suggested that the curve in Offa's Dyke simply followed the natural topography here (Hoyle and Vallender 1997, 68).

The lidar images of Madgetts, however, identified earthworks that gave the impression that Offa's Dyke may have incorporated the earthworks of an earlier hill-top enclosure.

There are small subcircular enclosures in Sallowvallets Wood north of Cannop and another in Flaxley Woods, both of which are undated but are similar to a small enclosure in Lord's Wood, just over the River Wye in Herefordshire, which is known to have been occupied in the Roman period (Hart 1967, 19).

These are similar in shape and size and both are sited on the edges of narrow elongated plateaux overlooking steep sloping ground, although neither would have commanded views in all directions. Both are also close to boundary systems identified by lidar [which in the case of Sallowvallets have been dated as late prehistoric and Roman (*see* pp 31–4)] and both have evidence for an internal and external bank on either side of a ditch.

A larger subcircular enclosure was visible in Dry Wood to the south-east of Soudley on an aerial photograph taken in 1946 when the area had been cleared of woodland. Like the enclosure at Sallowvallets and Flaxley this is sited on a narrow plateau overlooking steep slopes and possibly commanding views in all directions. No recognised boundary systems are in the near vicinity but some have been identified by lidar at Soudley about 1km to the west.

Cropmarks of a very large ovoid enclosure just to the south of Morse's Grove, Newnham

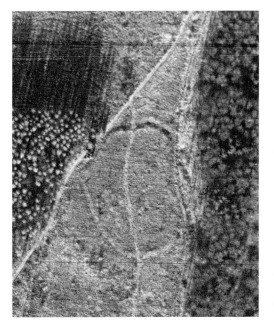

*Fig 3.16
1946 aerial photograph of
Drywood enclosure taken
after wartime clearfelling.
The site has been heavily
disturbed by post-war
forestry activity, but can
still be traced on the ground
as segments of a ditch
(particularly on its
northern side) with some
traces of an internal bank.
Photograph oriented with
north towards the top.
[© Historic England
Archive (RAF Photography)
RAF/CPE/UK/1913
frame 4029 (30-DEC-1946
LN 538)]*

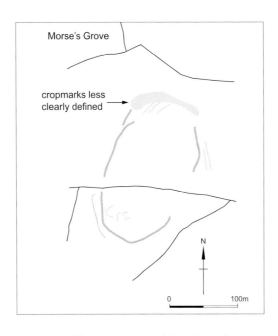

Fig 3.17 (right)
Cropmarks at Morse's Grove,
Newnham were thought to
be natural, although Google
Earth images show a clear
outline of a large ovoid
enclosure measuring
211m × 122m and hint at
internal activity and possibly
additional ramparts.
[Cropmarks from Google
Earth Imagery 2017]

Fig 3.18 (below right)
A 'rectangular
entrenchment' was recorded
at Highbury in the 19th
century (Maclean 1893–4,
26). It appears to enclose
at least three sides of the
southern end of the Highbury
plateau and is incorporated
into Offa's Dyke, which
follows its western boundary.
Its southern boundary
survives as a 3m-high
terrace and its south-western
corner appears to be abutted
by the section of Offa's Dyke
to its south.

Fig 3.19 (far right)
Fosbroke considered
Coldharbour to be a 'British
settlement' (Fosbroke 1832).
It predates the surrounding
fields, but is not in a
commanding position and
no ramparts have been
recorded. 'Coldharbour'
may indicate a place where
drovers could safely stay
overnight although nearby
fields called 'Walston' in the
19th century suggest an
association with a 'British'
site of some antiquity (Smith
1964a, 245; 1964b, 27).

also probably represent prehistoric settlement. These are on an east-facing slope overlooking the Severn, but with higher ground to the east, and were thought to be natural in origin (Hoyle 2008a, 118). More recent Google Earth images show the cropmarks more clearly, however, and suggest that this is a genuine archaeological feature with some evidence of internal activity (Amanda Adams pers comm).

A 'rectangular entrenchment' whose western side was formed by Offa's Dyke was recorded by Sir John Maclean in the late 19th century (Maclean 1893–4, 26) in Highbury Wood, a narrow ridge of high ground to the south of Redbrook. This site is associated with the place name Highbury and possibly also Coxbury (Coxbury Farm is only 200m to the south) and may be evidence for a late prehistoric enclosure on the southern end of the Highbury plateau, which later became incorporated into Offa's Dyke.

'Coxbury' may actually refer to an elliptical field that encloses a small hillock about 125m to the south of Highbury, although it is not clear if this site is archaeologically significant.

Another possible prehistoric enclosure is a large subcircular field at Coldharbour immediately to the west of St Briavels. This was considered to be a 'British settlement' by the antiquary Fosbroke in the early 19th century (Fosbroke 1832), but no surviving earthworks have been recorded and the site does not occupy a particularly commanding position, being overlooked from the north. It does, however, clearly predate the surrounding field pattern and there is place-name evidence that may suggest a site of some antiquity.

Less convincing is a circular enclosure on the summit of May Hill, Longhope which has been interpreted as prehistoric (Scott-Garrett 1918–58,

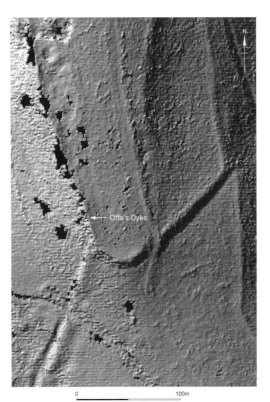

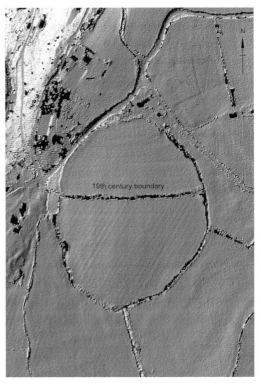

Fig 3.20 (left)
May Hill enclosure. This is a
low bank about 0.30m high
within a late 19th-century
common enclosure
boundary. Trees have been
recorded on the summit
since at least 1820 (Verey
1981, 23) and this may be
an enclosure to protect an
early 19th-century tree
plantation from browsing
animals (Hoyle 2004, 1).
[© Historic England
Archive NMR 23276/22.
07-NOV-2003]

entry for 12 May 1951; Small and Stoertz 2006, 25, fig 5), but may be a post-medieval enclosure to keep stock away from young trees.

There are two other undated earthwork enclosures to the east of Whitewalls Farm, Woolaston and Edge Farm; Woolaston may also be late pre-historic, but neither has been dated with any certainty and the Edge Farm site has been suggested as a small medieval ringwork (Townley 2004, 116).

From the 4th to 2nd centuries BC Iron Age farmsteads began to be enclosed by substantial

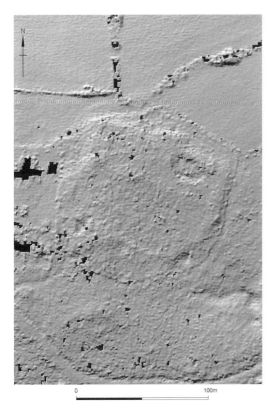

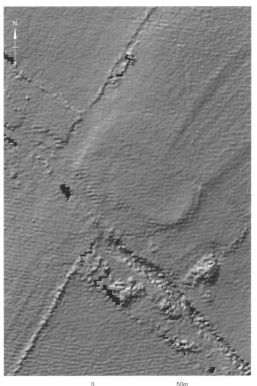

Fig 3.21 (far left)
Whitehills enclosure. Sited
on a spur of high ground
overlooking the Severn to
the east of Whitehills Farm,
this may be the Hwitan
heale 'the white nook of
land' recorded in the 9th
century (Grundy 1935–6,
242). It predates the
adjacent field pattern, but
no datable artefacts have
been found.

Fig 3.22 (left)
Edge Farm. Scott-Garrett
thought this was an Iron
Age settlement (Hart 1967,
21), although Townley
(2004, 116) has suggested
it was an early Norman
ringwork. There is 'hearsay
evidence' for Roman arte-
facts from the site (DAG
2000a, 27), but no clear
dating evidence.

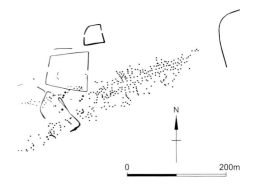

0 _____ 200m

*Fig 3.23 (far right)
Cropmarks of pits and
enclosures at Huntsham
north of Symonds Yat.
Three enclosures associated
with possible trackways
and numerous pits probably
represent an Iron Age
farmstead predating the
Roman villa (Taylor 1995).
In the Iron Age storage pits
were primarily used to
store grain and other food
products (Reynolds 1974).
[Cropmarks © Historic
England (NMP)]*

subrectangular earthworks (Darvill 2011, 195) and a number of undated subrectangular enclosures in the Forest may date to this period. In the Cotswolds to the east of the River Severn these seem to have a date range from the Iron Age to the Roman period (Moore 2006a, 14; 2006b, fig 5) and these sites are also discussed below.

Other evidence

Cropmark evidence for prehistoric activity is rare in the Forest of Dean, although cropmarks of an Iron Age farmstead predating the Roman villa have been identified at Huntsham, Herefordshire, just to the north of Symonds Yat (Small and Stoertz 2006, fig 6).

A number of other possible late prehistoric sites are worthy of note but their status, and often their precise location, are uncertain. A site at Wellhouse, south of Purton, may be associated with earthworks reported in nearby Warren's Grove although Hart (1967, 15) has linked it with Kear's Wood on uncertain placename evidence. There are also no known earthworks associated with Maidenham, south of Littledean, and the possible 'Iron Age camp' on Naas Cliff, Lydney, although there was an early post-medieval reference to a 'castle' on the site of the latter.

There is also some placename evidence to suggest possible sites, but without recognised associated earthworks these must be treated with caution.

At least 11 place names that contain the element 'bury' or 'berry' (which could indicate earthworks or burial mounds) are known that have no clear connections to known earthworks or cropmark sites, although none are linked with specific locations and any undiscovered sites could be within fairly wide areas. A large undated ditch has been excavated to the south of Berry Hill, Coleford (Mason and Egging Dinwiddy 2014, 4), although it is not clear if this is evidence for a prehistoric rampart.

The landscape in the Bronze Age, Iron Age and Roman periods

From the early Bronze Age Britain gradually became generally warmer and drier leading to a longer growing season and improved harvests. Communities flourished and marginal upland areas were farmed as more agricultural land was needed to feed a growing population (Darvill 2011, 133). In the south-west, cereal cultivation increased from the early Bronze Age (Wilkinson and Straker 2008, 73) and by the Iron Age much of lowland Britain was probably extensively farmed with fields and paddocks interspersed with occasional small farmsteads.

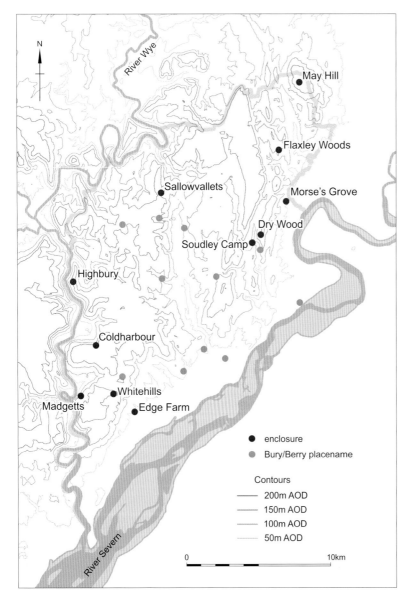

enclosure

Bury/Berry placename

Contours

——— 200m AOD
——— 150m AOD
——— 100m AOD
——— 50m AOD

0 _____ 10km

There is some evidence for Bronze Age farming in the Forest of Dean from the Soldier's Tump round barrow, Tidenham where carbonised white charlock, a plant which grows among cereal crops, was found with cremated bones buried below the cairn, suggesting that the cremation fire had been kindled with straw after the harvest (Scott-Garrett 1955, 27–8).

Terraces to the south of Welshbury hillfort (defining roughly rectangular areas of between 0.4ha and 0.8ha in area) have been interpreted as small fields that originated before the Iron Age hillfort was built (McOmish and Smith 1996, 57). In 1995 these were thought to be an unusual survival of a Bronze Age and Iron Age field system where the woodland had protected it from the destructive influence of several thousand years of farming.

The 2006 lidar survey identified numerous additional boundary systems that are beginning to transform our understanding of the Forest of Dean landscape during the later prehistoric period.

Some of these were similar to those found at Welshbury and appeared to form a coherent system of small (generally 0.5–1ha) conjoined subrectangular enclosures. Others were parallel linear terraces, generally 40–70m apart, and in some areas short straight terraces or banks, at right-angles to the main terraces, created a coaxial system of small rectangular enclosures. Some systems appeared to contain elements of both types.

A significant number of these were identified in areas of long-standing woodland, and with a few exceptions were not obviously the remains of medieval encroachment into the Royal Forest, or any recognised woodland management regime, but appear to represent a large-scale system of landscape organisation that predates the woodland. Similar boundary systems are found throughout central southern Britain (eg Woolbury, Hampshire [Cunliffe 1978, fig 11.16]; Danebury, Hampshire [Cunliffe and Poole 1991, fig 1.1]; Sidbury, Wiltshire and Segsbury, Berkshire [Fowler 1983, figs 40 and 57]), and have been interpreted as field systems which originated in the later prehistoric period (Fowler 1983, 119–28, figs 45–7) and survive in areas where they have not been obliterated by subsequent land use.

Late prehistoric fields: Sallowvallets Wood

Sallowvallets Wood to the north of Cannop contained two types of boundary system. A system of parallel linear terraces covered an area of only 10ha, although a more conjoined system to the east extended over an area 27ha, and similar systems on Worral Hill to the north suggest it may originally have covered an area of 70ha.

In 2011, the Forest of Dean Survey team excavated a small trench across one of the terraces in the southern part of the conjoined system in Sallowvallets Wood, demonstrating that it was a lynchet created by an accumulation of soil (colluvium) against the back of an earth bank, suggesting cultivation or stock management had destabilised the soil upslope.

The colluvium produced no pottery or other datable finds, although two fragments of hazel charcoal from its lower levels produced radiocarbon dates of 2330 ± 30 BP (SUERC-36801), corrected to 410 to 380 cal BC and 2268 ± 26 BP

Fig 3.24 (opposite, below) Subcircular enclosures and Bury/Berry placenames unconnected to known sites. These placenames (Cinderbury Croft, Wimberry Hill, Whimberry Slade, Boston/Bastonbury, Glastonbury Wood, Fox Berrys, Highbury, Hucklebury, Berry Hill and several Berry fields) generally apply to areas of relatively high ground overlooking a watercourse.

Fig 3.25 (below) Boundary systems identified by lidar in or close to woodland.

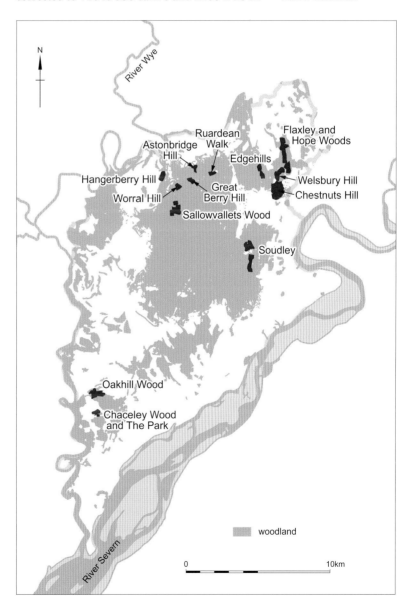

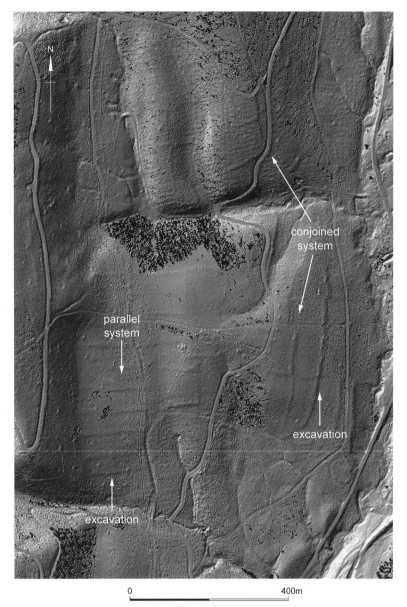

OSL

Optically stimulated luminescence dating (OSL) is a scientific dating technique based on the principle that some minerals, such as quartz, store a proportion of the radiation that naturally decays from the material in which they are buried. When these minerals are exposed to either temperatures above about 300 degrees Celsius or daylight, all the radiation they have absorbed is released. If the annual amount of radiation absorbed by these minerals is calculated, and the amount of radiation released when they are exposed to sunlight or heat is measured, this can be converted into years and the date when the minerals were last exposed to daylight or heat can be determined (Duller 2008, 4–5).

Statistical (Baysean) analysis of the OSL and radiocarbon dates suggested the system was laid out between 940 BC (in the later Bronze Age) and 260 BC (during the middle part of the Iron Age) and probably during the middle Iron Age around 500 BC. This area of woodland was a landscape of small cultivated or pasture fields in the later prehistoric period, although these may have fallen out of use by the early Roman period when there was iron smelting in the area. The economics of bloomery iron smelting favours sites close to a charcoal source and by the early Roman period the landscape of small fields and paddocks may have been replaced by woodland, possibly managed for charcoal production (Hoyle 2013a, section 3).

One of the terraces of the parallel system to the west was also excavated in 2011. This was also a lynchet formed by colluvium, although there was no surviving evidence for a boundary against which it had accumulated. The colluvium contained a few abraded sherds of Roman pottery (too fragmentary for more precise identification or dating), although two OSL samples produced dates of 304 BC–AD 56 and AD 1–AD 345 (Toms *et al* 2012, table 2b). Baysean analysis, comparing these dates with their stratigraphic relationship, suggested that this system had been laid out no earlier than the latter part of the first millennium BC (Toms *et al* 2012, 12) and the abraded Roman sherds suggest that these elongated terraced fields were cultivated during the Roman period but possibly originally laid out earlier.

Fig 3.26
Boundary systems in Sallowvallets Wood. The systems did not overlap and may have been used concurrently in the late prehistoric period, although the conjoined system may have fallen out of use in the early Roman period, after which the parallel system remained in use.

(OxA-25372), corrected to 400 to 210 cal BC (Toms *et al* 2012, table 1). Two samples were also taken for optically stimulated luminescence dating (OSL), one of which suggested the colluvium had formed sometime between 154 BC and AD 133 (Toms *et al* 2012, table 2b).

A layer of iron smelting debris, which overlay the colluvium, provided further dating evidence as this contained two sherds of early Roman pottery and charcoal fragments that produced radiocarbon dates of 1975 ± 30 BP (SUERC-36802), corrected to 50 cal BC to cal AD 90 and 1911 ± 26 (OxA-25373), corrected to cal AD 20 to cal AD 140 (Toms *et al* 2012, table 1) suggesting that the smelting occurred early in the Roman period.

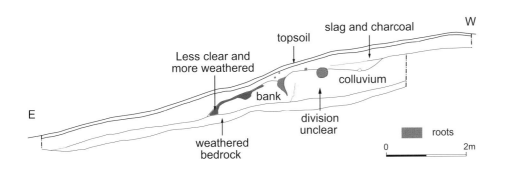

E ‖ W

slag and charcoal
topsoil
Less clear and
more weathered
bank
colluvium
division
unclear
weathered
bedrock
roots
0 ‖ 2m

Fig 3.27 (left)
Section of trench through a late prehistoric boundary in Sallowvallets Wood. This terrace, which was over 1.5m high, began with the construction of a field boundary made up of a rough earthen bank. The soil upslope of the bank was then destabilised, either through cultivation or livestock and gradually crept downhill as colluvium before accumulating against the bank's inner side to create a lynchet.

bank ‖ colluvium

Fig 3.28 (left)
Retaining boundary bank and colluvium in the section of a lidar-detected terrace in Sallowvallets Wood. Scale 1m (0.5m divisions). The outer side of the bank was much more compact than the colluvium, although this differentiation was less clear on its inner side where roots and earthworms had inter-mixed the two deposits, making the boundary more difficult to define.
[© Gloucestershire County Council Archaeology Service]

0 ‖ 5cm

Fig 3.29 (left
Roman Severn Valley ware pottery from Roman colluvium in a parallel boundary system in Sallowvallets Wood. Damage and wear to the pottery may have been caused by ploughing or other soil disturbance.
[© Gloucestershire County Council Archaeology Service. Photo Paul Nichols]

The two systems did not appear to overlap and may have co-existed side by side for a period. There was no evidence for contemporary settlement, although the areas between the two systems may warrant further investigation.

The boundary systems in Sallowvallets Wood are clear evidence for a late prehistoric landscape that included large areas of conjoining subrectangular fields or paddocks. By the early Roman period these may have fallen out of use and been replaced by woodland managed for charcoal production. An area of long, wide parallel terraces immediately to their west were fields that were worked well into the Roman period, although it is not clear if these superseded the earlier system or whether both operated side by side for some time in the latter part of the Iron Age. Why there are two distinct types of field system in Sallowvallets cannot be easily explained although differences in land use, agricultural technology, landownership or tenure could all have played a part.

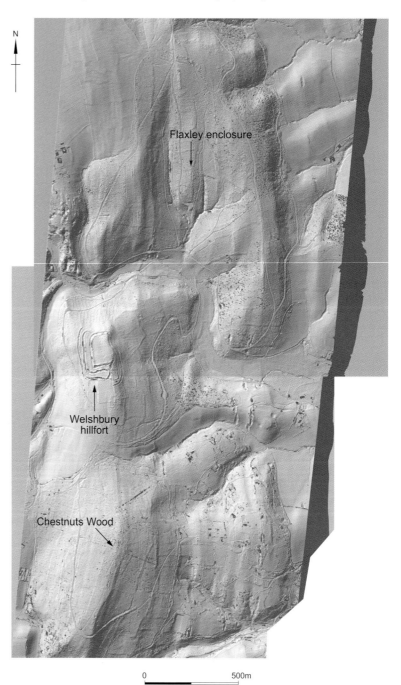

Fig 3.30
Boundary systems around Welshbury. The east–west terraces are clearly artificial, although most of the larger north–south banks or terraces are geological in origin and follow ridges of hard sandstone. These appear to have been modified and used with the artificial terraces to form a coherent coaxial field system.

Welshbury and the surrounding area

A Bronze Age field system has been identified immediately to the south of the Iron Age hillfort at Welshbury (*see* p 23) and field survey and lidar identified further boundary systems immediately to east of the hillfort, in Flaxley and Hope Woods to the north and Chestnuts Wood to the south. Some of the these systems extend outside the woodland into adjacent areas of open farmland and appear to combine modified outcrops of hard sandstone with artificial boundaries to create a coaxial field system covering a total area of approximately 300ha.

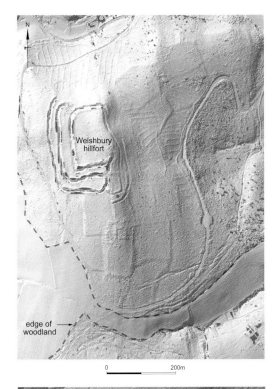

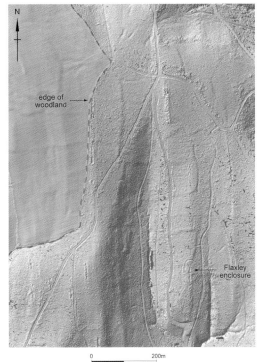

Fig 3.31 (far left) Boundary system in Welshbury Wood. Although the field system predated the hillfort (McOmish and Smith 1996, 57) it probably remained in use after the hillfort was built and formed part of a contemporary farmed landscape.

Fig 3.32 (left) Boundary system in the northern part of Flaxley and Hope Woods. These clearly extend out of the woodland and into the open farmland to the west.

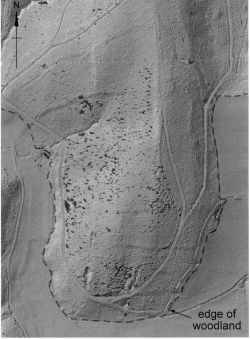

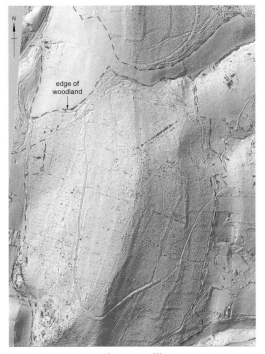

Fig 3.33 (far left) Boundary systems in the southern part of Flaxley and Hope Woods.

Fig 3.34 (left) Boundary system in Chestnuts Wood. This is dominated by parallel linear banks or terraces (running north–south), which follow outcrops of hard sandstone. Smaller terraces at right-angles to them create a coaxial field system enclosing areas between 0.69ha and 1.04ha. This system may have extended into open farmland to the north-west.

Other possible prehistoric field systems

Smaller undated boundary systems that may represent late prehistoric fields have been identified at Edgehills just over 1km to the west of Welshbury, to the north and south of Soudley in the eastern part of the Forest and also at Great Berry Hill and Ruardean Walk in the northern part of the Forest. There may also be a parallel boundary system within woodland on Astonbridge Hill to the south-west of Ruardean Woodside, although dense conifer in this area limited the area of ground surface that lidar was able to reveal. A hoard of 3rd-century AD Roman coins was also concealed within one of the boundaries of a parallel system at Hangerberry, English Bicknor (Portable Antiquities Scheme database: GLO-756722) suggesting that these boundaries were certainly in existence by the Roman period and may have originated at an earlier time.

Other undated boundaries have also been identified in the northern part of Tidenham Chase in Oakhill and Clayton Woods, the Park and the Madgetts area, while there are cropmarks of extensive relict field boundary systems outside woodland around Hewelsfield and St Briavels to the north-east. These systems are not contiguous and not all, particularly in Oakhill Wood, seem to form a coherent system and may represent boundaries of different dates. Some may be assarting recorded in this area in the 13th century (Herbert 1972a, 51), and others, particularly outside woodland, are close to known medieval settlement and may be medieval. Lynchets north of Madgetts Farm are clearly cut by Offa's Dyke (Small and Stoertz 2006, fig 22) and, although these may be following geological outcrops, probably represent land divisions that are prehistoric in origin even if they remained in use into the medieval period. Some of the boundaries in the northern part of Tidenham Chase could also be prehistoric, while others associated with medieval settlement may also have much earlier origins.

Not all of the boundary systems identified by lidar in woodland were necessarily the same date or were used in the same way and further investigation is needed. Lidar has, however, demonstrated that the Forest of Dean has undergone complex processes of landscape change since the prehistoric period and the woodland that covers much of the area today is just the latest phase in that process.

Fig 3.35 (right)
Boundary system at Edgehills. Two terraces and a rubble bank, each about 1.2m high, run east–west across the natural slope of the hill approximately 60–70m apart. Similar features to the south were much less clear on the ground.

Fig 3.36 (far right)
Boundary system at Great Berry Hill. East–west terraces at Ruardean Walk about 1km to the east and discontinuous boundaries at Smethers Tump about 300m to the north-west and Barnedge Hill 350m to the west may have been part of the same system.

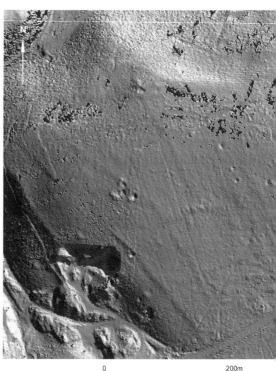

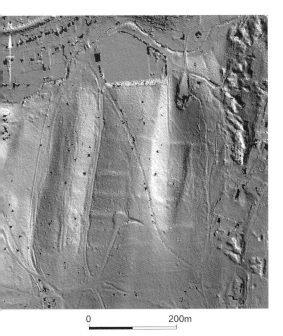

0 _____ 200m

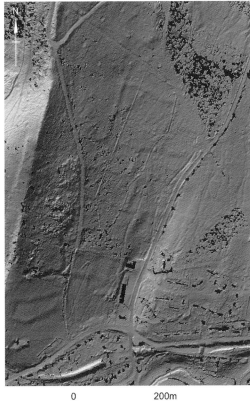

0 _____ 200m

*Fig 3.37 (far left)
Boundary system to the
south of Soudley. These
parallel east–west terraces,
each about 40–70m apart
covered an area of about
7.5ha.*

*Fig 3.38 (left)
Boundary system to the
north of Soudley. This
system covered about 16ha
and comprised parallel
linear terraces, segmented
by shorter boundaries to
form a coaxial pattern of
small rectangular fields.
On the ground the overall
layout was obscured by
small-scale quarrying and
later boundaries, which
may relate to medieval
coppicing.*

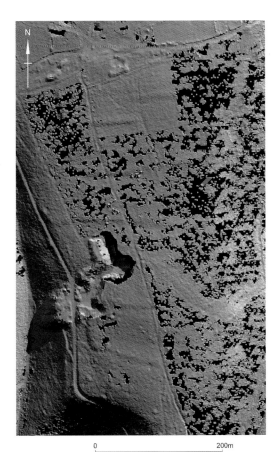

0 _____ 200m

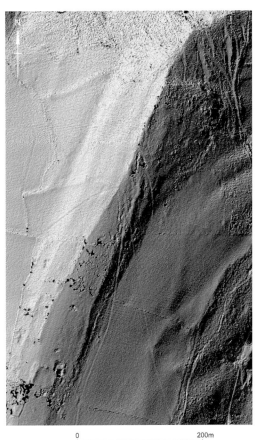

0 _____ 200m

*Fig 3.39 (far left)
Boundary system on
Astonbridge Hill south-west
of Ruardean Woodside.
These appear to represent
a series of parallel
boundaries running east–
west and about 40–70m
apart. Dense conifer, visible
as black pixilated areas,
has prevented much of the
lidar from penetrating to
ground level and has
obscured much of this
system.*

*Fig 3.40 (left)
Parallel boundary system
running approximately
north–south at
Hangerberry, English
Bicknor. A hoard of
3rd-century AD Roman
coins was buried in one of
these boundaries.*

Fig 3.41 (right)
Boundary system in Oakhill Wood, Tidenham. These do not form a coherent system and probably represent a number of boundaries of different dates and functions. Some of these, along with other boundaries in the area (both inside and outside woodland) may be relics of medieval farming, but none have been dated.

Fig 3.42 (far right)
Lynchets running approximately east–west to the north-west of Madgetts Farm Tidenham. Although these appear to be influenced by the underlying geology, and may represent medieval land divisions, they are clearly cut by Offa's Dyke and could be prehistoric in origin.

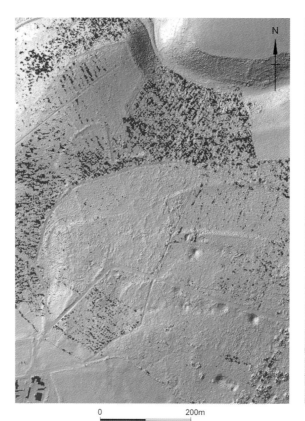

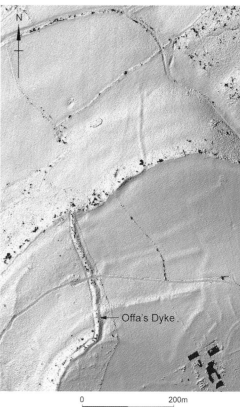

Fig 3.43
Lynchet to the west of Offa's Dyke at Madgetts Farm, Tidenham. Offa's Dyke is visible along the skyline with the lynchet, which is cut by the dyke, in the foreground.
[© Gloucestershire County Council Archaeology Service]

Late prehistoric religion and ritual

The Bronze Age

Late prehistoric ritual and religion in Gloucestershire is characterised by the numerous Bronze Age burial sites (round barrows or ring ditches), the majority of which are found in the Cotswold and Thames Valley (Drinkwater and Saville 1984, fig 1). Evidence from the Forest of Dean is much thinner; only one was recorded in Cyril Hart's *Archaeology in Dean* (Hart 1967, map II) and only three in 1987 (Darvill 1987, 95). All of these were in the Tidenham area in the southern part of the Forest of Dean and there is increasing evidence for Bronze Age ritual activity in this area.

Bronze Age ritual activity in the Tidenham area

The only excavated round barrow in the Forest is the Soldier's Tump Round Barrow, on the southern edge of Tidenham Chase, which was excavated by Scott-Garrett and the Forest of Dean Local History Society between 1951 and 1952.

A mound, originally about 16m in diameter, was defined by a circular stone wall or bank (Scott-Garrett 1955, fig 5) that retained a 'large amount of soft ochreous earth'. The site overlies Carboniferous Limestone but is less than 80m from the Carboniferous Sandstone (BGS 2012); the outer wall used both limestone and sandstone and the 'ochreous earth' was mainly derived from an area with sandstone bedrock.

In the centre of the mound the 'ochreous earth' sealed a stone cairn, nearly 2m high and over 5m wide, which had been laid directly on the ground surface. This was also built of limestone and sandstone (with the smaller limestones tending to be found in the centre of the cairn) and turves may have been piled around its base (Scott-Garrett 1955, 17–21, figs 1 and 5). There was no evidence that the mound had ever been surrounded by an external ditch (Scott-Garrett 1955, 23).

A small pit, about 0.5m wide and 0.6m deep, was below the approximate centre of the cairn. Its flat base was paved with three sandstone slabs and it had been closed by a sandstone capstone rebated into the lip of the pit so its surface was flush with the original ground surface, and its edges sealed with smaller stones and clay.

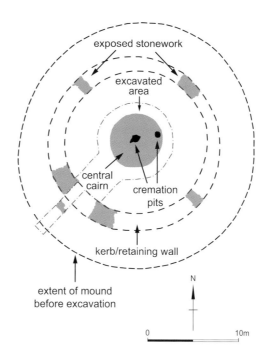

Fig 3.44
Excavated features at the Soldier's Tump round barrow. The mound was about 24m in diameter but had spread outwards and had originally been only about 16m in diameter. It was retained by a dry-stone wall which survived to a height of about 0.5m. [After Scott-Garrett 1955, fig 5]

Fig 3.45
Soldier's Tump round barrow under excavation. The stone cairn in the centre of the mound was nearly 2m high and over 5m wide. Smaller limestone slabs were more common in the centre of the cairn with larger sandstone blocks around the outside. [From Scott-Garrett 1955, Transactions of the Bristol and Gloucestershire Archaeological Society]

Two further sandstone capstones, whose edges were also sealed with smaller stones and clay, overlay this. A conical pile of cremated bone and charcoal laid on the paving slabs (perhaps originally in a bag) represented the remains of an adult female and a very young child (Scott-Garrett 1955, 28, fig 3). These had been buried with the blade of a short bronze dagger, a bronze pin, a flat shale pendant and three fossil beads (Scott-Garrett 1955, fig 3, plate IV).

There was a second, less regular, burial pit 2m to the north-east below the edge of the central cairn that contained the cremation of a single adult (whose sex could not be determined) and charcoal, but no grave goods. This measured about 0.5m × 0.4m and was about 0.30m deep with a rounded bottom. It had no paving, and its roughly triangular sandstone capstone was laid directly on the ground surface without a clay seal. Reddening of the ground surface between the burial pits along with burnt bone and charcoal suggested that the cremations took place on the site (Scott-Garrett 1955, 26, fig 6), probably sometime after 1,400 BC when cremations become more common than inhumation below round barrows (Darvill 2011, 141).

The grave goods are similar to those found in so called Wessex Culture barrow burials in Wiltshire and the Cotswolds to the east of the River Severn where a short dagger/knife often accompanies a burial or cremation, suggesting that the barrow builders had cultural links (or at least influences) from east of the River Severn (Darvill 2011, 141–4).

Another possible barrow is a roughly circular stone mound about 1km to the west of Soldier's Tump first recorded in the 19th century (Ormerod 1861, map opp p 8). This site is scheduled as a Bronze Age barrow, but there is no record of any excavation, although scattered stones suggest it has been disturbed in the past.

The third Bronze Age 'barrow' mapped in 1987 (*see* p 39) is a crouched inhumation of a young man that was discovered by workmen in Beachley in 1965. This was in a stone-lined cist, and has been interpreted as an early Bronze Age inhumation, although there were no grave goods or evidence of a former mound (Barnett and Savory 1961–4).

Other mounds interpreted as barrows were known in the Tidenham area before 1987. The antiquarian Ormerod recorded a mound in Sedbury Park, Tidenham, which he suggested was a barrow used as a beacon in the Roman period, and also mapped 'traces of an ancient mound' about 500m to the south (Ormerod 1861, 47, map opp p 8). Scott-Garrett and Harris also reported several mounds in the Sedbury Park area, and noted large slabs of conglomerate sandstone, from a source at least 2km to the north or west, on the surface (Scott-Garrett and Harris 1932). Other possible barrows included a slightly oval rubble mound in Caswell Wood south-west of Madgetts Farm on the northern side of Tidenham Chase (Rhodes 1965) and a small mound visible on the lidar to the west of Whitewalls Farm, Woolaston where Scott-Garrett recorded a 'small grassy tump' may also be a barrow (Scott-Garrett 1918–58, entry for 31 May 1953). Stone spreads north of Sycamore Cottage, Hewelsfield, to the west of Barrowell Lane, where Scott-Garrett reported 'a decided "tump" which may be all that remains of a barrow' in 1950 (Scott-Garrett 1918–58, entry for 11 October 1951), may be a ploughed out barrow (Hart 1967, 9). Two roughly circular features defined by dry-stone walls in East Vaga Wood may also be 'truncated round barrows' (Hart 1967, 22; Walters 1992a, 32), although Scott-Garrett interpreted them as probable prehistoric hut circles (Scott-Garrett 1918–58, entry for 24 May 1956).

Less likely are the one or more burial mounds reported to the east of Tump Farm, Sedbury

Fig 3.46
Grave goods from Soldier's Tump round barrow. Scale in centimetres.
[© Gloucester Museums Service. Photo Paul Nichols]

(Borthwick 1996, 11, 20) where no earthworks are known, and 19th-century records of levelling of mounds in Oldbury Field, Stroat (Ormerod 1861, 41), which probably refer to the earthworks of Oldbury Camp rather than barrows.

Other Bronze Age ritual monuments in the Tidenham area are the Broad Stone Stroat, one of the Forest of Dean's two surviving standing stones, and the Oudoceus Stone, one of the three former standing stones, which have now been lost (*see* pp 47–8).

A number of other possible Bronze Age ritual sites have been found in the Tidenham area, mostly by lidar or field survey, since the Forest of Dean Archaeological Survey began.

The most significant was identified as a sub-circular enclosure (with a possible central mound) by lidar in East Wood in the northern part of Tidenham about 2km to the south of Hewelsfield.

In 2011 the Forestry Commission cleared the site of undergrowth to enable a geophysical survey of the bank and interior and a detailed topographical survey. Finally topsoil and leaf litter was cleared in a small exploratory excavation (measuring 11.5m × 1.40m) where the bank had already been damaged by a forestry track.

The enclosure survived as a low spread bank about 7–8m wide and 0.50m high with an internal diameter of around 21m and enclosing an area of 288m². Over much of its surface, particu-

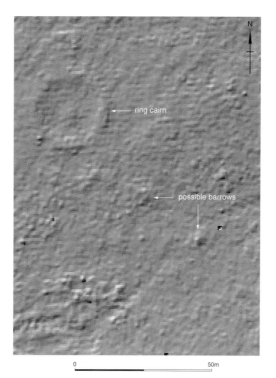

larly on its western and eastern sides, the bank was made up of mixed limestone and sandstone rubble. There was no sign of an entrance and a number of depressions in the bank were probably created by later tracks or vehicles crossing it. The mound visible on lidar could not be seen on the ground and this may have been the lidar

Fig 3.47
Ring cairn in East Wood, Tidenham and possible round barrows. The mound in the centre of the ring cairn was not visible on the ground and may have been caused by lidar picking up forestry detritus.

Fig 3.48
Ring cairn in East Wood, Tidenham before undergrowth clearance. When first identified the site was heavily overgrown and difficult to see from a distance.
[© Gloucestershire County Council Archaeology Service]

Fig 3.49
Fabric of the ring cairns's bank after removal of loose overburden. The bank made use of both limestone and sandstone and larger sandstone blocks tended to be on its outer side. Scale 1m (0.5m divisions). [© Gloucestershire County Council Archaeology Service]

picking up forestry detritus that had been in the centre of the enclosure when the survey was undertaken.

Where excavated, the bank was made up of limestone and sandstone blocks more or less randomly placed with no clear evidence of any structural elements. There was a slight tendency for larger sandstone blocks to be on the outer side of the bank (a general tendency observed across the monument as a whole, and particularly its south-western side) and for limestone fragments on the bank's inner face to appear placed upright and parallel to the bank, but these did not clearly represent walling or kerb stones on the bank's inner and outer faces.

Thirteen small vertically pitched slabs of white limestone (between 0.12m and 0.35m) were set into the top of the bank, generally on its internal face and with their long axes pointing inwards.

Nine of these were clearly small standing stones deliberately placed on the bank, although the status of others was less clear. Two on the western side of the enclosure were so close together that it was hard to interpret them both as deliberate standing stones, and one on the eastern side of the bank was interpreted as the stump of a broken stone, but this was unclear. Another was revealed in the excavation trench and did not protrude much above the height of the surrounding stonework, while a fourth, on the enclosure's north-western side, was, unlike other stones, on the bank's outer edge and although vertically pitched was loose, suggesting it was just part of its bank's rubble fabric.

The only finds were a single struck flint flake (identified as debitage with possible use wear), a

tiny fragment of burnt bone (too small to be identified) and a small piece of iron ore.

The East Wood enclosure can be interpreted as a ring cairn, a type of site known from the early or middle Bronze Age dating between about 2,500 BC and 1,000 BC (English Heritage 1989a, 4; Lynch 1979a, 2). Ring cairns come in a range of shapes and sizes and are found mainly in upland areas such as the Derbyshire Peak District, Cornwall and Devon and there are no other known examples in Gloucestershire or neighbouring English counties (English Heritage 1989a, fig 2). They are also fairly common in the uplands of Glamorgan and Gwent in south Wales (Evans and Lewis 2003, fig 4) and, with its relatively narrow bank and large central space, the East Wood ring cairn is similar to Welsh examples (Lynch 1979a, 9; Lynch 1979b, fig 1, English Heritage 1989a, fig 1). It is large with a diameter of about 25m, although ring cairns of similar size are known at Brenig, Denbighshire (Lynch 1979a, fig 1) and also at Morlais Hill, Pebyll and Cwm Cadlan in Glamorgan and Gwent, South Wales (Evans and Lewis 2003, 15), and the East Wood example could be seen as an eastern outlier of the South Wales group.

These probably fulfilled a similar ritual function to stone circles, contemporary Bronze Age monuments generally found in areas where there are no ring cairns and vice versa. Precisely what rituals took place is not always clear and, in

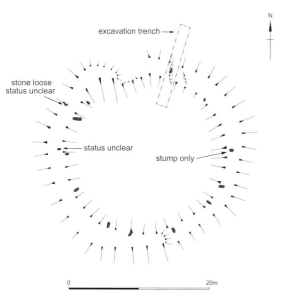

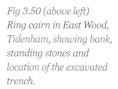

their current form, ring cairns and other ritual sites are the end product of a lengthy history during which they may have undergone a series of changes in both form and function (Bradley 1998, 134).

Geophysical survey at East Wood identified anomalies on the bank consistent with spreads of charcoal or other burnt material and also a probable area of burning, 3m in diameter, in the interior (Dean 2012). Rituals involving burning took place at ring cairns (English Heritage 1989a, 6) and spreads of ash and charcoal have been found at some sites (Lelong and Pollard 1998, 115; Lynch 1979a, 9). Two other anomalies at the bank's inner edge could have been pits, a common feature within ring cairns (English Heritage 1989a. 5). Burials or cremations have been found at some sites (English Heritage 1989a, 5; Lelong and Pollard 1998, 113), although these appear to be later additions and ring cairns do not seem to have been built as burial sites (Lynch 1979a, 10).

Two other geophysical anomalies were identified outside the enclosure. One, about 4–5m

Fig 3.50 (above left)
Ring cairn in East Wood, Tidenham, showing bank, standing stones and location of the excavated trench.

Fig 3.51 (above)
Standing stones in south-eastern quadrant of the ring cairn in East Wood, looking south. All the standing stones were made of white limestone, although none were higher than 0.35m. Scale 1m (0.5m divisions). [© Gloucestershire County Council Archaeology Service]

Fig 3.52
Ring cairn in East Wood after undergrowth clearance, looking east. [© Gloucestershire County Council Archaeology Service]

Fig 3.53
Speculative reconstruction
of East Wood ring cairn
nearing completion.
[© Anne Leaver]

Fig 3.54
Ring cairn and associated
features.

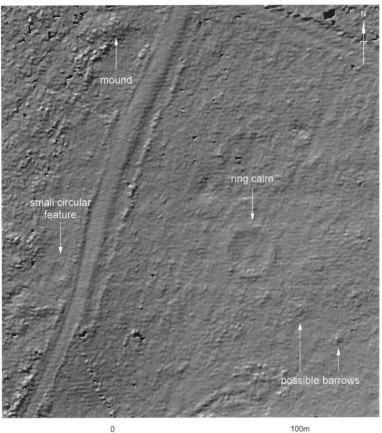

to the south-east, may have been a subcircular pit 6m in diameter, while the second suggested a linear boundary comprising an apparently segmented ditch and footings of a stone wall or similar structure (Dean 2012, 3–7).

The use of both limestone and sandstone, with some suggestion of deliberate differential use (all the standing stones for example were limestone), may be significant. Limestone pavement is visible on the surface immediately to its east and, although sandstone bedrock is recorded about 200m to the north (BGS 2012), sandstone boulders (upcast from later shallow quarries) litter the surface to the north and west of the ring cairn suggesting the site is close to the boundary between the two geologies.

Only 100m to the west of the East Wood ring cairn lidar identified a small subcircular earthwork. This was about 13m in diameter and up to 1m high with a shallow hollow (about 7m in diameter and 0.5m deep) at its centre. The interior was very charcoal-rich, but the feature was much more substantial than known charcoal platforms and could be a 'hengiform' monument, a loose category covering sites that include a range of later Neolithic and Bronze Age elliptical or circular ritual monuments (Harding and Lee 1987; Pollard and Healy 2008, 97).

Two possible barrows have also been found in East Wood to the south-east of the ring cairn. One, about 25m from the ring cairn, was an irregular subcircular mound, while the other, a further 23m to the south-east, appeared to use both limestone and sandstone in its construction (Hoyle 2013a, 69–70).

Other possible barrows recently found are a small subcircular mound in an area of open farmland on Tidenham Chase where flint flakes have been recovered, a circular mound in woodland to the east of Offa's Dyke, a roughly circular mound at the northern edge of The Park, Tidenham, and a smaller rubble mound (about 0.75m high and 4m in diameter) in Oakhill Wood, on the northern part of Tidenham Chase (Hoyle 2013a, 22). A large flat-topped mound (about 11m × 14m and 1.5–2m high) was also recorded about 130m to the north-west of the East Wood ring cairn, although as its western side was hard to define and its surface was extremely charcoal-rich; this may be forestry detritus rather than an archaeological feature.

There may have been a prehistoric cross-peninsula trackway, known as the Stone Row, across Tidenham Chase from the Severn at Stroat to a ford over the River Wye at Brockweir. This is marked by upright stones along part of its route (Hart 1967, 22, pl XI, b) and is mentioned as *Stanraewe* in a late Saxon charter (Grundy 1935–6, 241). The 'Hoar Stones on Garston Farm' south-west of Stroat, mentioned by Bigland in the 18th century (Herbert 1972a, 53) may have been part of this route and in 1952 Scott-Garrett reported that a Mr Barnard knew of 'three standing stones which stood in The Park on Tidenham Chase' which he thought were part of the Stone Row and had been 'uprooted and taken away' (Scott-Garrett 1918–58, entry for 19 November 1952). Whether this route has prehistoric origins or not is unknown and earlier records of stones could refer to other megalithic structures on Tidenham Chase that have now been destroyed.

Tidenham, and particularly the higher ground of Tidenham Chase in the northern part of the parish, is an area where there are a range of Bronze Age ritual monuments, and two Bronze Age hoards (*see* Fig 3.57) have also been recorded close to the area.

Tidenham Chase is a plateau of high ground and the watershed between the Rivers Severn to the east and Wye to the west. It overlooks lower ground on all sides but this is most dramatic to the west and east where there are steep slopes

leading down to both rivers and there is a clear sense of being a place where the two rivers are beginning to converge.

The area is geologically mixed with both limestone and sandstone forming the bedrock in different areas. Some areas of limestone pavement survive on the eastern edge of the plateau, and large sandstone boulders litter much of the surface in the sandstone areas.

Prehistoric ritual monuments were often associated with distinctive topographical or natural features (Jones 2006, 356) and this seems to apply on Tidenham Chase. The majority of known monuments are between 175m and 200m AOD and although not at the Chase's highest point are

Fig 3.55 (below)
Subcircular feature to west
of ring cairn in East Wood,
looking south-east. Scale 2m
(1m divisions).
[© Gloucestershire County
Council Archaeology Service]

Fig 3.56 (bottom)
Possible barrow to the
south-east of the ring cairn
in East Wood, looking north.
Note limestone and sand-
stone blocks. Scale 2m
(1m divisions).
[© Gloucestershire County
Council Archaeology Service]

in prominent positions, generally towards the edge of the plateau overlooking steeper slopes with views towards either the Rivers Severn or Wye. Most overlie limestone, but are close to the division between limestone and sandstone. These may have presented as visible geological exposures, such as the limestone pavement in the East Wood area, or in more subtle ways such as changes in soil colour, surface stone scatters, vegetation or drainage. These geological changes may also have influenced land use and monuments may have been placed deliberately at the edge of the lighter limestone soils, which may have been preferred for cultivation.

Where they have been sufficiently investigated the Tidenham Chase sites seem to celebrate the geological boundary in their construction, not only using both types of stone, but also using

them selectively or transporting them to sites where they were not readily available.

The other recognised barrow sites to the south, while not occupying such commanding positions are also close to geological divisions (generally the edges of gravel terraces) overlooking lower ground in at least one direction and generally with views towards one or both rivers.

The Tidenham area occupies a pivotal position at what would have been a hub of navigable prehistoric communications links and could easily have been a relatively prosperous area during the Bronze Age, able to support a flourishing and culturally rich population. It controls both the mouth of the Wye and the point at which the River Severn begins its transformation from a treacherous tidal estuary to a navigable sea route, giving it links inland to what is now Gloucestershire, Monmouthshire and Herefordshire and also seawards, via the Bristol Channel, to South Wales, southern England and beyond.

This is reflected in the (admittedly limited) evidence that the Bronze Age population of the Tidenham area were absorbing cultural influences from a number of sources. The ring cairn in East Wood was similar to Welsh examples while the Soldier's Tump round barrow, which is probably later, produced artefacts typical of the so-called 'Wessex Culture' in Wiltshire.

Other Bronze Age ritual sites

Not all possible Bronze Age ritual sites are found in the Tidenham area, although few sites in other parts of the Forest of Dean have been investigated.

Possible barrows include a circular stone mound (about 11m in diameter and 0.30m high) in the interior of Welshbury hillfort (McOmish and Smith 1996, 57) and another (16m in diameter) on Blakeney Hill, Blakeney where stone rubble in a 'stiff, yellow soil' was retained (in places) by upright kerb stones (Johns 1991, 5 and fig 2). Stone spreads near Eastbach Court, English Bicknor, found close to flint scatters, could also be ploughed-out barrows (Walters 1992a, 33), although a small mound (about 5m in diameter and 2.2m high) in Cadora Woods to the south of Redbrook may be a clearance cairn (Thomas 2000). Four subcircular flat-topped mounds (ranging from 15m to 25m in diameter and 1.5–2m high) are close to the Long Stone, Staunton (see Fig 3.60) and could be barrows, but iron ore outcrops in this area, and these could be the remains associated with later mining or iron smelting.

In addition the 2006 lidar survey identified almost 100 mounds of about the right shape or

Fig 3.57
Bronze Age ritual monuments on Tidenham Chase.

Fig 3.57
Bronze Age ritual monuments on Tidenham Chase.

River Wye

Madgetts Farm

ring cairn

East Wood

Soldier's Tump

East Vaga

● barrow/possible barrow
◉ other possible ritual feature

0   1km

size to be round barrows, although few have been ground-truthed, and most of these were waste from recent forestry or post-medieval coal mining. Possible barrows, however, include a mound (about 1m high and 8–10m in diameter) near the late prehistoric field system in Sallowvallets Wood (*see* pp 31–3) and two mounds associated with 19th-century field names 'Great Barrows' and 'Barrows' in Awre parish (Gwatkin 1995b).

Two cropmarks of ring ditches at Mitcheldean may have been round barrows, although these have now been destroyed by development (Small and Stoerz 2006, 23).

The Forest of Dean survey also identified almost 60 sites with names (Barrow, Berry or Tump) that could indicate the site of prehistoric burial, although none of these names can necessarily be taken at face value.

Other burial customs may have been practised during the period. Human remains have been found with late Neolithic/early Bronze Age flints and pottery at Hollybush pothole in Willscroft Wood, St Briavels, and with late Neolithic to Roman finds at King Arthur's Cave, Madawg rock shelter and Merlin's Cave near Symonds Yat in Herefordshire (Symonds 1871; Phillips 1931; Barton 1993–5, 1997). Prehistoric burial in caves, fissures, swallow holes or rock shelters is poorly understood, but at least 170 sites are known in England (Chamberlain and Williams 2001) and where suitable sites were available some individuals seem to have been buried in this way over very long periods.

Standing stones

Few standing stones have been dated with any certainty, although finds associated with standing stones from Wales have produced a date range from the late Neolithic to the late Bronze Age (Overy 1989, 2–3). There is evidence for seven standing stones in the Forest of Dean, although only three are known to survive.

The Broad Stone, Stroat is an irregularly shaped slab of limestone 2.7m high close to the Severn near Stroat in Tidenham while the Long Stone, Staunton, a sandstone monolith 2.5m high and 1m × 0.8m wide, stands in higher ground next to the A4316 south of Staunton.

The third surviving stone is the Queen Stone, Huntsham (in Herefordshire), which is a block of conglomerate sandstone close to the River Wye immediately north of Symonds Yat.

The Long Stone, St Briavels (which may also have been known as the Caradoc Stone [Wright 1980, 24]) was a sandstone monolith 3m high in a field called 'Long Stone' in 1842 (Gwatkin 1993a), probably about 15–20m from the field's northern boundary (Wright 1980, 24). In 1875 it was blown up, smashed with sledge hammers and carted away to an old quarry (Playne 1876, 105–6). Bones were found when the stone was destroyed, although it is not clear if these were associated with it (Hart 1967, 8).

Another lost standing stone was to the south of Coleford, close to an 18th- or 19th-century monument known as Gattles Cross on the northern part of Clearwell Meend. This is traditionally

Fig 3.58
Lidar-detected mound in Sallowvallets Wood.
[© Gloucestershire County Council Archaeology Service]

Fig 3.59
The Long Stone, Staunton. This sandstone monolith is about 2.5m high.
[© Gloucestershire County Council Archaeology Service]

thought to have replaced an earlier standing stone, known as the Cradock Stone, although the 1608 map marks a two-peaked monolith called Cradocks Stone approximately 450m to the south (Clissold 1982; PRO 1608a).

The Oudoceus Stone, Tidenham was next to the River Wye just north of Chepstow, and in the 1920s was reported as a slab of sandstone divided into two equal halves that had 'formerly' stood to a height of 3m (Crawford 1925, 201). By 1950, however, Scott-Garrett could only find 'a mass of detached outlier, in two pieces embedded in the silt' (Scott-Garrett 1918–58, entry for 6 August 1950) and the stone has not been reported since.

Another possible prehistoric standing stone was the Silverstone, which stood at the medieval boundary of Lea Bailey to the north of Drybrook and was referred to as 'the white stone' in 1282, perhaps suggesting it was made of limestone. It was recorded in the early 18th century but no longer survives (Hart with Clissold 2000, 25) and it is not clear if this was a prehistoric standing stone or a later boundary stone.

Standing stones may have been markers for small cemeteries (Darvill 1987, 109) or the ritual focus for a small community, although they may also (and perhaps simultaneously) have fulfilled more mundane roles such as territorial markers, meeting places or way markers (Overy 1989, 1).

All the recognised standing stones in the Forest are west of the Cannop Valley and seem to split into two distinct groups. The Long Stone, Staunton, Long Stone, St Briavels, and Cradock Stone, Clearwell are on higher ground (around 200m AOD) over a sandstone bedrock but close to the junction between sandstones and limestones and near (but not on) the top of gentle slopes, either at, or close to, the heads of the valleys of small streams.

The Broad Stone, Stroat, the Oudoceus Stone, Tidenham, and the Queen Stone, Huntsham are not close to significant geological divisions but are on lower, level ground next to navigable and tidal waterways (the rivers Severn and Wye). This group seem to be associated with river crossings and other routes. The Broad Stone marks the western end of a possible Severn crossing (Ormerod 1841, 9; Scott-Garrett 1918–58, entry for 18 October 1933), which may have been fordable at low tide, and the eastern end of the Stone Row, while the Oudoceus Stone was close to the Striguil Bridge, first recorded in the 12th century (Ormerod 1861, 8, footnote 1), which may have carried the Roman Road across the Wye, possibly following an earlier river

crossing (*see* p 77). The Queen Stone is close to the modern crossing of the Wye on the road running north from Symonds Yat, a gate place name that may have been associated with routes through the Mercian frontier in the 9th century AD (*see* below; Hoyle and Vallender 1997, 72).

It is of course impossible to be sure that these routes, which were first recorded in the medieval period or later, are actually contemporary with the stones, although even if they were, they may have been more than simple way markers. Religious structures, such as wayside crosses or chapels near bridges and river crossings, were associated with communications in the medieval period and reflected deep-seated anxieties about the dangers of travel, particularly across 'alien' environments like water. These standing stones may have fulfilled a comparable role, although it is no longer clear whether they were the focus for organised rituals giving thanks for safe passage, large-scale 'good luck' charms, something in between, or perhaps all three.

The stones on higher ground may also have been associated with communications as all are within 1km of the modern B4228, which is the natural north–south route following level high ground across the western part of the Forest. They are also close to areas where concentrations of prehistoric artefacts suggest contemporary settlement and at least one (the Long Stone, Staunton) may be associated with contemporary burial mounds (*see* p 46). They also share similar topographical locations and are close to geological boundaries that may have been discernible on the ground or signified changes in land use.

Bronze Age hoards

A number of Bronze Age hoards from the Forest of Dean may be Bronze Age ritual deposits, perhaps as a display of 'conspicuous consumption designed to increase the prestige of a powerful individual' (Parker Pearson 1993, 117).

Five late Bronze Age axe heads from Clearwell Meend found only about 250m from the original site of the Cradock Stone may be a ritual deposition, although these might have been a founder's hoard or not a hoard at all. Another Bronze Age hoard has been reported from the garden of a house on Tidenham Chase (Hart 1967, 58), although no details of this are known, while a miniature votive flat axe from Littledean may also be the remains of a hoard.

Six Middle Bronze Age bracelets and a copper alloy awl were found by metal detectorists in Woolaston in 2013, and further investigation

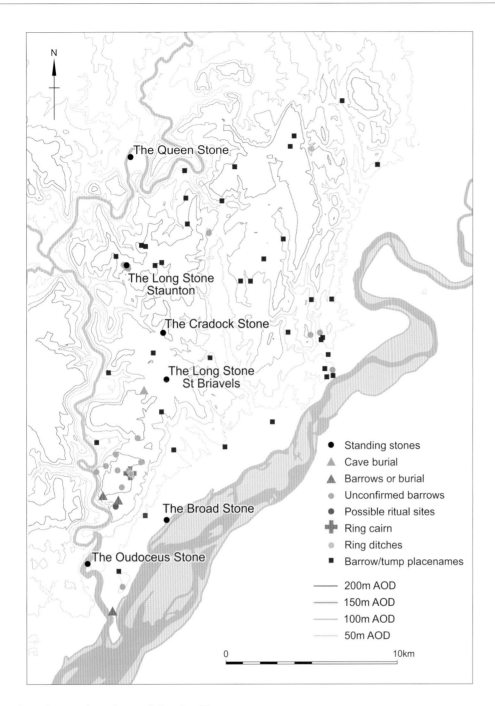

Fig 3.60
All recognised possible
Bronze Age ritual sites.

The Queen Stone

The Long Stone
Staunton

The Cradock Stone

The Long Stone
St Briavels

The Broad Stone

The Oudoceus Stone

● Standing stones
▲ Cave burial
▲ Barrows or burial
● Unconfirmed barrows
● Possible ritual sites
✚ Ring cairn
● Ring ditches
■ Barrow/tump placenames

——— 200m AOD
——— 150m AOD
——— 100m AOD
——— 50m AOD

0   10km

Fig 3.61
Small Bronze Age gold
bracelets found as part of
a hoard near Woolaston.
Eight gold bracelets were
wrapped around each
other in three groups of
four, two and two. Most
were in good condition
although the two on the
left may have been hit by
the plough.
[© Portable Antiquities
Scheme]

found another two bracelets and sherds of Bronze Age pottery from a single vessel (Raymond 2013, 14). These were probably part of a single hoard (Wilkin 2014, 7–8), although they were at the base of the topsoil and not in an easily recognisable archaeological feature (Hoyle 2013a, 5). Subsequent excavation of a larger area found only an undated posthole (perhaps for a post that originally marked the hoard site), although Bronze Age features downslope of the finds may have been sealed by a later accum-ulation of plough soil (Davis and Sharples 2014, 16).

0   5cm

Fig 3.62
Cupstone west of Madgetts
Farm, Tidenham. The stone
had been used during iron
smelting and the hollow
contained smelted iron.
Scale 1.10m.
[© Gloucestershire County
Council Archaeology
Service]

Fig 3.63
Late Iron Age enamelled
disc button from High
Nash, Coleford. This
formed part of a decorative
sword belt and was part of
a ritual deposit of military
equipment which may have
been a warrior burial. The
ring is about 37mm in
diameter and the 22mm
wide disc projects about
15mm from it.
[© Dean Heritage Centre,
SOYDH 2013.13, courtesy
of the Dean Heritage
Museum Trust]

Cup marked stones

Cup marked stones, another type of Bronze Age ritual site, are often mentioned when discussing the Forest of Dean and numerous examples have been found in the area.

Some consist of one (or sometimes two) large hollows (generally about 0.20m wide and 0.07m deep) or a larger number of smaller hollows (about 0.10m in diameter and 0.03m deep), sometimes apparently randomly positioned on their surface (Johns 1990, 19–22). Cup marked stones from Nottingham Hill and Cleeve Hill, Swell and Yanworth in the Gloucestershire Cotswolds have been interpreted as Bronze Age rock art (Darvill 2006, 28; 2011, 90–2), although in the Forest of Dean these stones may have been more functional. Stones from Blake-

ney Hill were found with rounded stones (Walker in Rawes 1991, 221), suggesting they were effectively mortars used in some crushing process. The Drummer Boy Stone south of Soudley (which has two holes) and a large cupstone near Offa's Dyke west of Madgetts Farm, Tidenham contained deposits of smelted iron suggesting they had been used in the smelting process (Standing and Tylecote 1977; Hoyle and Armstrong 2011), although some of these stones may originally have been prehistoric rock art reused for industrial purposes.

The Iron Age

An iron sword (which had been bent double), the remains of an iron shield boss, three bronze rings and fittings for a decorative sword belt were found at High Nash, Coleford in 1987 (Sindrey 1990, 25). Similar fittings were used by early Roman auxiliaries, but also in the late Iron Age (Webster 1989, 30–1; 1990, 294–5) and although no human bones were found in the acidic clay soil these were interpreted as a late Iron Age warrior burial (Walters 1999, 42). The only other late Iron Age finds in the area were a small pottery assemblage about 50m from the sword (Sindrey 1990, 29), although the site was within 100m of a Roman building which has been interpreted as a temple (*see* pp 72–3). The significance of these enigmatic finds and what they tell us about late Iron Age burial practices within the Forest of Dean is far from clear.

4

The Roman period

Late Iron Age – early Roman

The Forest of Dean during the late Iron Age (between about 100 BC and about AD 50) is not well understood. The distribution of Iron Age coins suggests that the area was within the western part of the territory of the Dobunni (Allen 1944, map 1), although whether the Dobunni were a distinct tribal group or their boundaries can be recognised through the distribution of artefacts has been questioned (Moore and Reece 2001, 25). In eastern Gloucestershire and much of southern Britain hillforts appear to have been abandoned as political influence refocused towards large defended lowland sites such as Salmonsbury, or partly defended territorial *oppida* such as Bagendon (Cunliffe 1995, 69). How much these political changes influenced the Forest of Dean is unclear, although political and cultural influence may have refocused towards Ariconium (the modern Weston under Penyard) only 4km to the north-west. This thriving civilian settlement was clearly an important economic centre as more Dobunnic coins have been found in the area than anywhere except Bagendon (Fulford 2003, fig 1; Jackson 2012, 180) and it may also have been a Dobunnic 'tribal centre', similar to Bagendon, perhaps controlling the production and distribution of Forest of Dean iron (Jackson 2012, 208).

By the mid to late 40s AD, a few years after the Claudian invasion of AD 43, the Roman army had established a military fort at Kingsholm close to a strategic crossing of the River Severn at the border of what is now the Forest of Dean (Copeland 2011, 37).

Most authorities think that at the time of the Roman invasion the area between the Severn and Wye was in the western part of the territory of a people known as the Dobunni who, according to the 2nd-century AD geographer Ptolemy, were based to the east of the Severn Estuary with their capital at Cirencester (Cunliffe 2003, 12).

Dobunnic coinage has been found west of the Severn and, in decreasing numbers, west of the Wye (Fulford 2003, fig 1), but this could just represent cultural or political spheres of influence rather than the boundaries of Dobunnic territory and does not establish whether borders were rigid or fluid, or to what extent the people who lived within them considered themselves to be a single coherent group (Darvill 2003, 5–6; Copeland 2011, 17). An alternative proposition that the area was in the eastern part of the territory of the Silures (Manning 1981) may be based on an over-literal interpretation of Tacitus's *Annals* (XII, 32). This mentions that the Silures needed to be suppressed by the construction of legionary camps (*castris legionem*), although the assumption that the Kingsholm fort was one of these, and that this would necessarily have been on the boundary of Silurian territory, cannot be proved. Tacitus's use of military terminology was not necessarily precise and '*castris legionem*' could be a stylistic way of referring to the need for military force rather than indicating established legionary forts (Hurst 1985, 121). A third suggestion that the Forest of Dean was occupied by an unnamed people who had no allegiance to neighbouring tribes (Walters 1992a, 60–1) appears to be based on 20th-century notions of the area's isolation and independence rather than any actual assessment of the available evidence.

Although the Dobunni appear to have been a relatively compliant group who largely submitted to Roman rule soon after the invasion (Copeland 2011, 31), the Silures, who occupied South Wales, were more resistant and were only suppressed after a 25-year military campaign between about AD 49 and AD 74 (Millett 1990, 51). The main route into Wales may have been the Roman road through the Leadon Valley to the north of the Forest of Dean (Margary 610, *see* Margary 1957, fig 2) and the early Roman fort at Kingsholm could have acted as a supply hub for this campaign (Millett 1990, 51), connecting the

Fig 4.1
Dobunnic sphere of
influence. This was centred
on the catchment areas of
the Rivers Severn, Wye,
Bristol Avon and the upper
Thames.
[After Darvill 2003]

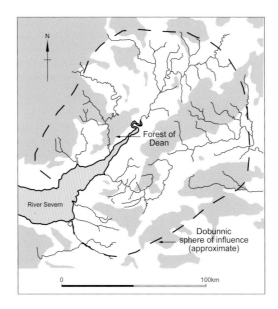

lives of the majority of the Forest's population, whose way of living may not have begun to alter in any significant way for a generation or more (Booth *et al* 2007, 42). Late Iron Age pottery continued to be used well into the Roman period, and it can be difficult to determine for sure whether sites with evidence for early Roman activity were founded after the conquest or were late Iron Age sites which continued largely unchanged into the Roman period.

The hillfort at Lydney Park was occupied into the mid-1st century AD although it may no longer have had political significance and was inhabited by a 'residue' of the former population who were 'declining in culture, initiative and wealth' (Wheeler and Wheeler 1932, 16–17). Two late Iron Age/early Roman brooches and a sherd of pottery from Chestnuts Wood, immediately south of Welshbury hillfort, do not mean the hillfort was occupied during this period and an undated 'Roman type' spearhead (Walters 1992a, 62) is certainly not evidence that the site was defended against the Romans. Late Iron Age/early Roman pottery has also been found at Symonds Yat hillfort (Parry 1994), but this does not mean the site was continuously occupied or maintained its original status.

Field systems in Sallowvallets Wood, Cannop originated in the late prehistoric period and some at least were cultivated into the Roman period, suggesting a late Iron Age/early Roman settlement should be nearby. The same may be true of other field systems (*see* pp 31–8), although no associated settlements have been identified.

At Huntsham, Herefordshire iron ore, slag and furnace lining which predated the 2nd-century AD villa may represent late Iron Age/early Roman iron smelting although no pottery earlier than the 2nd century AD has been found (Taylor 1995, 250–1). This could indicate continuous occupation from the Iron Age farmstead (*see* p 30, Fig 3.23) into the Roman period although other sites where Iron Age and Roman occupation has been found (for example, Birdlip in the Gloucestershire Cotswolds) may have been abandoned in the middle Iron Age and reoccupied in the early Roman period (Parry 1998, 55).

A polygonal enclosure at Reddings Lane, Staunton had late Iron Age/early Roman 'native' ware in the lower fills of its ditch, suggesting that although the settlement continued until the 3rd century AD it may have originated before the arrival of the Romans (Ellis 2013, 12, table 2). At Sedbury, Tidenham a number of small-scale archaeological evaluations to the south of

road with supplies transported either by the road network to the east or by water up the River Severn (Copeland 2011, 35–6). The Kingsholm fort may have been set back from the actual frontier with forward military positions to the west of the Severn in what may then have been regarded as 'friendly' territory, although evidence for these has been elusive. Some sites, such as Ariconium (Weston under Penyard), Dymock or Stretton Grandison, Herefordshire have been suggested; these have tended to be discounted due to lack of evidence.

Two sites interpreted as Roman military sites by 19th-century antiquarians were at Sedbury Park, Tidenham, and Castle Meadow, Staunton, although the status of both is not clear. At Sedbury Ormerod excavated right-angled ditches, which he interpreted as a military base associated with a 'fire beacon' to aid navigation on the Severn (Ormerod 1861, 46–8), although there is no particular reason to interpret the site as military and it may just be part of a wider complex of later Roman settlement in the area (*see* pp 63–4). Maclean described Castle Meadow, Staunton as 'within 100 yards of the south-west of the church', 'quadrilateral in form' and probably a 'Roman Speculum ... used for reconnoitring the country and signalling' (Maclean 1882–3, 227). No clearly visible remains of this site survive and excavations in the 19th century were inconclusive, although Staunton's medieval manor house was probably on the site (TBGAS 1881–2, 359) and late 18th-century references to the 'castle ditch' may refer to the remains of a moat (Herbert 1996d, 277).

The arrival of the Roman army may not have had an immediate impact on the day-to-day

Buttington Tump have identified at least one, and possibly two, enclosures with other ditches and pits, early Roman and late Iron Age style pottery and a quartz conglomerate quern, and this small early Roman farmstead may also have had late Iron Age origins. It appears to have fallen out of use by the mid-2nd century AD (Carew 2003, 40–1; Clarke 2007, 10; Riley 2010, 5), although the focus of settlement may have shifted to the slightly higher ground around Sedbury Park (under 1km to the north) where there is evidence for later Roman activity (*see* pp 63–4, Fig 4.23). 'Belgic' (late Iron Age) pottery and iron slag has also been found at Holm Farm, Lydney, where later Roman pottery (2nd to 3rd century AD), 3rd-century coins and a stone hammer have also been recovered (Harris 1936, 283–4; Harris 1937, 327), and this may also be a late Iron Age/ early Roman iron working settlement which continued into the 2nd or 3rd centuries AD. There may have been late Iron Age/early Roman iron smelting at a number of sites in the Ruardean area to the west of Drybrook Quarry where 'native ware' pottery, iron slag and 1st-century AD Roman pottery have been found (Chambers 1989, 6–7; Walters 1999, 4, 53–4). 'Malvernain'-type pottery, tiles and masonry remains have also been reported at the Grange Newnham (GADARG 1982b). These may also indicate an early Roman site which could have originated in the late Iron Age, although the site has never been investigated.

A small subcircular enclosure in Lord's Wood, Ganarew, Herefordshire, just west of Symonds Yat, was occupied in the Roman period (Hart 1967, 19), and some of the undated subcircular enclosures in the Forest, which probably represent prehistoric settlements (*see* pp 26–30), may have remained occupied after the Roman conquest.

Small subrectangular enclosures from the Cotswolds to the east of the River Severn have been interpreted as settlements dating from the

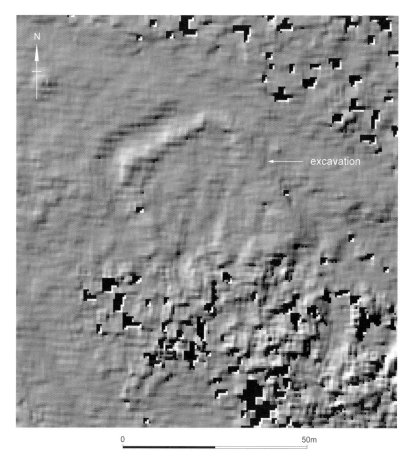

Iron Age to the Roman period (Moore 2006a, 14; Moore 2006b, fig 5) and a number of undated subrectangular earthworks in the Forest of Dean may fall into this category.

Ruardean Hill

One of these, which had been identified by lidar on the upper slopes of Ruardean Hill, was excavated in the winter of 2011.

A single excavation trench was cut through the bank and ditch. A small amount of early Roman Severn Valley ware and some sherds of

Fig 4.2 (above)
Subrectangular enclosure at Ruardean Hill. The enclosure is on the southern side of Ruardean Hill with higher ground to the north and overlooking lower ground to the south where it would have commanded views over a 180 degree arc from west to east.

Fig 4.3
Panoramic view of subrectangular enclosure at Ruardean Hill. This had an internal measurement of 27 × 36m and was defined by a low bank (0.35–0.7m high) with rounded corners and an external ditch. A dip in the bank on its northern side may have been an entrance.
[© Gloucestershire County Council Archaeology Service]

0   5cm

Fig 4.4
Late Iron Age and early
Roman pot from below the
bank of the subrectangular
enclosure at Ruardean Hill.
[© Gloucestershire County
Council Archaeology
Service. Photo Paul Nichols]

locally produced Malvernian limestone-tempered ware pottery in the late Iron Age tradition (Timby 2012) were found below the bank.

Although the bank was less than a metre high, the ditch was 1.8m deep, suggesting the bank had been considerably reduced. The lower ditch fill was weathering from the soft sandstone subsoil, which contained a few small fragments of iron slag, burnt clay, charcoal (probably oak) and a single small sherd of undated pottery. This was sealed by a thick layer of loose sandstone rubble and soil, similar to the bank material, containing a considerable amount of Malvernian pottery that spanned the late Iron Age/early Roman periods, but also some 1st-century AD Roman Severn Valley ware, 2nd-century AD Black Burnished ware and numerous fragments from what was probably a very large early Roman storage vessel (Timby 2012). There was also a cattle jaw bone and a small amount of bloomery slag and charcoal. Above this was a deposit of relatively stone-free sandy silt that produced no finds.

The rubbly layer was interpreted as the result of demolishing the bank and dumping it in the ditch, and the stone-free material also have

derived from the original bank although this was less clear.

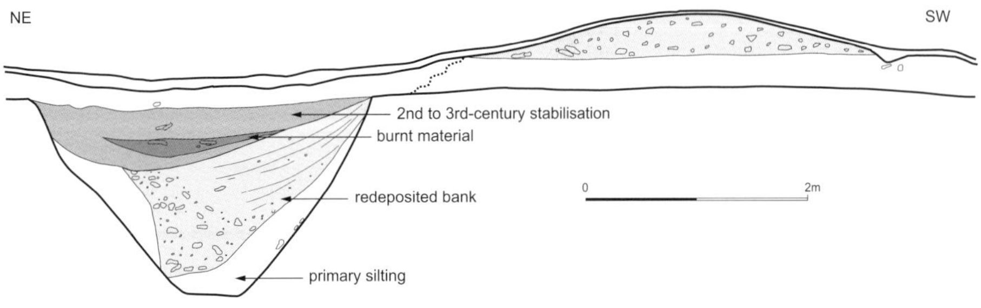

Sometime after this, the enclosure (which remained visible as low earthworks) was inhabited and the ditch's upper fills contained mostly late 2nd- and 3rd-century AD pottery, although also some abraded sherds of an imported central Gaulish colour-coated roughcast beaker probably dating to the late 1st/early 2nd centuries (Timby 2012). These later fills also contained charcoal, bloomery slag, three fragments of iron ore, part of a Roman bow saw blade and a small sandstone whetstone.

Precisely what this episode of occupation represented is not clear, although the bloomery slag, along with other burnt material and three fragments of iron ore and the bow saw blade, suggest that iron smelting and charcoal production were taking place here.

The quantity of transitional late Iron Age/Early Roman pottery from the site may support an interpretation that this site was a late Iron Age/early Roman farmstead, although the early Roman pottery found beneath the bank suggests it was built early in the Roman period and the sherds of late 1st-/early 2nd-century imported pottery from the site (albeit in a later context) are also puzzling finds for a late Iron Age settlement unless it was of particularly high status. It also appears that the bank was deliberately slighted shortly afterwards, sometime in the 2nd century AD.

The size and shape of the enclosure (particularly its rounded corners) are consistent with a small Roman military fortlet (Adkins and Adkins 1982) and similar to examples known at Barburgh Mill, Dumfriesshire, Martinhoe, Devon, and also in Germany (Breeze 1974, table IV). The ditch (1.60m deep and 3m wide at its lip) is also comparable with the ditches of early Roman military sites, although it lacks a cleaning slot at its base (Breeze 1974, fig 4; English Heritage 1988a, 4).

Known Roman fortlets are generally associated with the northern frontiers of Roman Britain, but examples are known in other parts of England and Wales although they are rare to the south of the Severn–Trent line (English Heritage 1988a, 4–5). They were built throughout the Roman occupation and garrisoned by a small detachment of troops (perhaps a single century of 80 men plus an officer) who fulfilled a specific task such as guarding river or road crossings or providing surveillance over particular areas (Breeze 1982, 101; 1994, 42–3) and could be occupied for a year or two or consider-

Fig 4.5
Excavated section through
the bank and ditch of the
subrectangular enclosure
on Ruardean Hill.

NE   bank   SW

2nd to 3rd-century stabilisation
burnt material
redeposited bank
0   2m
primary silting

ably longer depending on military requirements (English Heritage 1988a, 3).

If this is an early Roman military site it would have been built early in the Roman period as part of the consolidation of early Roman control west of the River Severn to support the advance westwards into Wales in the latter part of the 1st century AD. It may have been relatively short-lived, and abandoned once the Forest of Dean was no longer a frontier zone and the Roman army had moved on. Precisely what role this fulfilled is now unclear although it may have involved surveillance over communication routes, guarding approaches or garrisoning troops who patrolled particular areas. The site is also close to iron ore outcrops in the form of scowles (*see* pp 126–30) and although there is no clear evidence for direct military control of the Forest's iron industry as has been suggested (Sindrey 1990; Walters 1992a, 76), the area's iron ore resources and active iron industry must have been of some

0   2cm

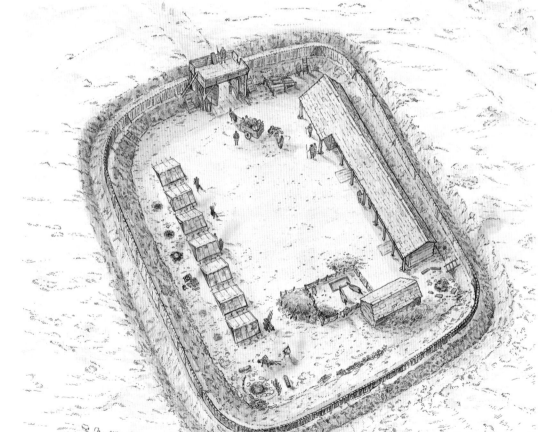

Fig 4.6 (above top)
Late 1st-/early
2nd-century AD Central
Gaulish colour coated
roughcast beaker from the
upper fill of the ditch of the
subrectangular enclosure
at Ruardean Hill.
[© Gloucestershire County
Council Archaeology
Service. Photo Paul
Nichols].

Fig 4.7 (above left)
Roman bow saw blade
from the upper fill of the
ditch of the subrectangular
enclosure at Ruardean Hill.
[© Gloucestershire County
Council Archaeology
Service]

Fig 4.8
Speculative reconstruction
of Ruardean Hill enclosure
as a Roman fortlet.
[© Anne Leaver]

interest to the Roman authorities in the early years of conquest. Any military sites may have had some role in securing control over a valuable mineral resource, particularly during the early years of conquest when this resource was at the frontier of Roman influence (Salway 1993, 94).

The interpretation of the Ruardean Hill site as an early Roman fortlet is not certain and there are reasonable arguments that this could be an early Roman settlement constructed soon after the Roman conquest in the late Iron Age tradition. This site may, however, represent the only excavated evidence of early Roman military presence in the Forest of Dean.

A number of other undated subrectangular enclosures have been identified, generally by lidar, in the Forest of Dean. Some could be early Roman military sites, late Iron Age/early Roman settlements or something else entirely and further work is needed to clarify what they are.

Small enclosures at Mile End near Coleford, Wigpool Common west of Mitcheldean, and possibly also Great Berry Hill near Brierley are comparable in shape, size and topographical position to the Ruardean Hill site, but a similar enclosure at Yorkley has recently been shown to date to the medieval period.

Other slightly larger enclosures in High Wood, Tidenham and Plump Hill near Mitcheldean may also be late Iron Age/early Roman enclosures or Roman military sites, but these are also similar to medieval keeper's lodges and, like the Yorkley example, are discussed more fully below.

Three other undated enclosures do look more like early Roman military sites.

One of these was a large earthwork on the top of a hill at Oldcroft, south-east of Blakeney. This overlooks the River Severn and Gatcombe Pill (a tributary of the Severn) with views in all

Fig 4.9 (right)
Subrectangular enclosure at Mile End Coleford. The site is on the southern side of a fairly level plateau with slightly rising ground to the east. An internal area of 27 × 34m is defined by a bank 1–1.5m high with evidence for an external ditch on all sides and a possible entrance on its eastern side.

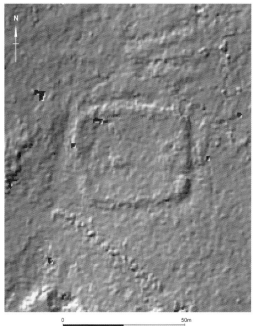

Fig 4.10 (below left)
Subrectangular enclosure at Wigpool Common. Although on the eastern side of a steep-sided plateau, the site does not command views and is overlooked by gently sloping ground to the east. Its interior measures 24 × 32m and is defined by a narrow bank between 0.2 and 0.7m high and only 2m wide. There is a small outer ditch, but no visible entrance.

Fig 4.11 (far right)
Possible subrectangular enclosure in Great Berry Hill. This may be a product of recent quarrying and trackways, although two sides are visible as a bank/terrace about 0.5m high, and there may be a connection with the placenames 'Great Berry' and 'Aconbury'.

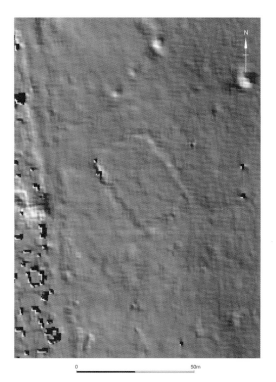

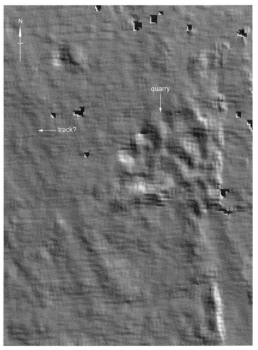

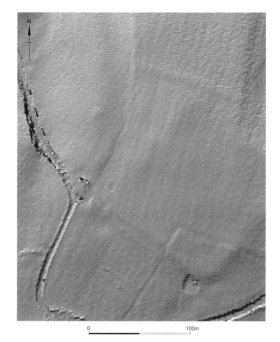

Fig 4.12 (left)
Possible subrectangular enclosure at Oldcroft, Blakeney, east of St Briavels. Only the southern and eastern boundaries survive as a broad shallow bank up to about 1m high on its outer side (but lower on its inner side). The western boundary is barely discernible as a low, wide and discontinuous rise (no more than 0.5m high) while the northern bank is not really visible as a surviving earthwork at all. This could have enclosed an area of (10,622m² and has a number of similarities to a Roman fort particularly the curved sweep of its south-eastern corner.

Fig 4.13 (top right)
Bivallate enclosure at Closeturf Farm, St Briavels. This enclosed an area of about 105 × 107m and cropmarks suggest external ditches and entrances on its southern and northern sides. The site is 200m west of Willsbury Farm, a placename suggesting an association with an 'ancient' earthwork.

directions, and is only about 500m to the south-east of the Roman road between Newnham and Caerwent. Only the southern and eastern ramparts (with a well-defined rounded south-eastern corner) are clearly visible where they appear to be cut by later field boundaries, and there is no evidence for an outer ditch. A Roman glass bead (Webb 1998, 7) and spread of bloomery slag (Johns 1995) have been found close to the site, but no other finds. The overall plan of the surviving earthwork, combined with its commanding position in the Roman landscape, suggests a Roman fort whose western and northern sides have been largely destroyed by ploughing.

There is also an almost square bivallate enclosure in open farmland between Closeturf Farm and Willsbury Farm, St Briavels, where a sherd of 1st-century AD Roman pottery has been found on the surface (Riches 2011–12, 35). The site is on a hillside and close to the edge of a steep valley and may be a small Roman fortlet or Iron Age settlement, although it also has some similarities with Roman temple sites such as the possible temple identified by cropmarks at Black-rock Farm, Lydney 4km to the east (*see* p 73).

A subrectangular enclosure at Hangerberry, English Bicknor is sited on the northern part of a steep-sided ridge overlooking lower ground to the west and east and commanding views over the Lydbrook Valley to the north-east. The enclosure has never been excavated, but Roman brooches dating from AD 70–150 and 3rd-

century AD Roman coins have been recovered by a metal detectorist from the site (Kurt Adams, Gloucestershire and Avon Finds Liaison Officer, pers comm). The site is also within an area of linear boundaries, one of which contained a hoard of 3rd-century AD coins (*see* above; Portable Antiquities Scheme database: GLO-756722).

Another site which may fall into this category is represented by what appears to be two sides of a square bivallate enclosure in Kidnalls Wood, north of Lydney. This is also on a hillside overlooking a steep valley, but there is no clear sign of its eastern or southern ramparts and the

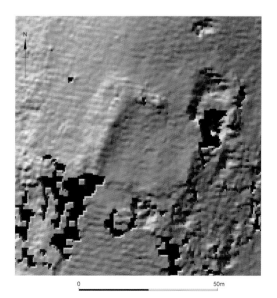

Fig 4.14 (left)
Subrectangular enclosure at Hangerberry, English Bicknor. This enclosure has an internal measurement of approximately 24 × 26m and its banks survive to a height of 0.5–0.8m. Early Roman brooches and 3rd-century AD coins have been found at the site and it is associated with the placename 'Hangerberry', which was recorded as 'Hangerbury' in the 17th century (Smith 1964a, 227).

Fig 4.15 (right)
Possible bivallate enclosure
in Kidnalls Wood, north of
Lydney. The earthworks
survive as two parallel low
banks about 0.6m high.

Fig 4.16 (below)
Evidence for late Iron Age
and/or early Roman
activity (1st to 2nd
centuries AD) and undated
subrectangular enclosures.
Some of these could be
early Roman fortlets but
others could be non-
military sites dating from
the late Iron Age to the
medieval periods.

visible earthworks seem to terminate just short of the valley edge to its south.

Although it is difficult to determine whether some 1st-century AD sites originated in the late Iron Age or early Roman periods, other sites clearly began after the Roman conquest.

Bloomery slag, roof tile and Roman pottery (none of which appeared to be later than the late 2nd or early 3rd centuries AD) have also been found over an area of about 20ha in Old Wood, Great Howle Farm, just over the county boundary in Herefordshire to the north of Ruardean, where a rectangular earthwork was recorded and destroyed in the 19th century (Walters 1986, 36). The site has not been investigated but is probably an iron working settlement active from the late 1st to the early 3rd centuries AD.

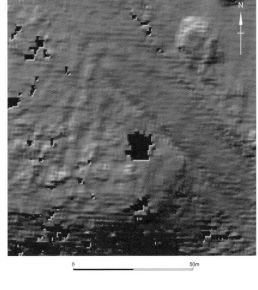

There is more evidence for early Roman activity in the Blakeney area where excavations at Legg House, between 1987 and 1992, recorded floor surfaces, building foundations and other features that suggested that a 1st-century AD timber structure had been superseded by a probably short-lived masonry structure sometime in the late 1st to early 2nd century AD. A 'large quantity of Flavian-period Samian' was found, suggesting the inhabitants had a certain degree of wealth or status, and *pilae* tiles (which were often associated with hypocausts) within deposits associated with the demolition of the 1st-century structures suggest that some rooms had under-floor heating (B Walters 1987a, 82; M Walters 1990a; 1992b).

Legg House is within the level base of the valley of Bideford Brook at its confluence with the Blackpool Brook. The Bideford Brook flows into the River Severn at Brims Pill about 2.5km to the east and may have been navigable during the Roman period, linking Blakeney to the Severn and beyond. The Roman road between Gloucester and Caerwent (Margary No 60a) also runs through this area and although its precise course across the valley is not clear, it probably ran either immediately south-east or north-west of Legg House (Margary 1957, 55–6). In the early Roman period this area would have been ideally placed as a transport hub with links to road and river communications, and although there is no reason to think the early Roman structure at Legg House had any military links, it may have had some sort of official function. The suggestion that it was the residence of the Roman government's administrator of the iron industry in the period

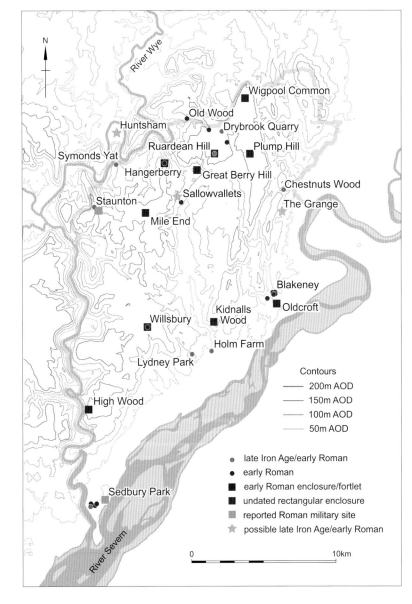

Contours
——— 200m AOD
——— 150m AOD
——— 100m AOD
——— 50m AOD

• late Iron Age/early Roman
● early Roman
■ early Roman enclosure/fortlet
■ undated rectangular enclosure
■ reported Roman military site
★ possible late Iron Age/early Roman

0   10km

immediately following the Roman conquest (Walters 1990a, 42), presupposes imperial control of the iron industry at that time (*see* Walters 1990b, 45–6), which has not been established, and a more reasonable explanation might be to see it as an early guest house or *mansio* associated with the nearby Roman road (Hoyle 2008a, 159; Copeland 2011, 133). These were built to provide accommodation for 'persons travelling with imperial permits' or associated with the imperial postage system (Salway 1993, 410) and although they varied considerably in layout and size, generally included a number of rooms and an associated bath house. From the 2nd century AD they tended to be built in stone, although some may have had earlier, timber, predecessors (English Heritage 1988b, 3).

Although the Legg House structures appear to have been short-lived and were probably demolished by the mid- to late 2nd century AD, late 1st- and early 2nd-century occupation in Blakeney may have been more extensive. Pottery from this period has been found at Brook House about 70m to the west (Walters 1987a, 82) and about 170m to the south (Johns 1995, 40) and the economic benefits of its favourable communication links may have attracted wider civilian settlement.

Later Roman settlement

Although almost 200 sites within the Forest of Dean have produced some evidence for Roman activity (generally as finds of Roman pottery), relatively few of these (only about 10 per cent) are known to represent evidence for settlement.

Villas

One category of settlement is villas, which are difficult to define but were well-appointed domestic buildings with some trappings of a comfortable Romanised lifestyle such as under-floor heating, wall plaster, mosaic floors and perhaps also a bath house. These generally begin to appear in the 2nd century AD (although some may originate in the late 1st century AD) and their earliest manifestation is often a relatively simple, and apparently less luxurious, building that was subsequently enlarged and improved, perhaps representing increased wealth or status of the inhabitants but also changes in fashion. Outbuildings, such as barns, suggest that villas were the centres of agricultural estates, although many also operated a

mixed economy (Branigan 1989, 42) and made enough profit for the owners to invest in at least some luxuries. Most villas in the Forest of Dean seem to have been associated with iron smelting to some degree, and this industry may have been a significant income stream for some of them, but how important this was for all of them is not clear.

Four Forest sites are classed as villas (not including the early Roman structure at Blakeney, which is also sometimes referred to as a villa) and another two are just outside the area at Huntsham, Herefordshire and Hadnock, Monmouthshire, both on the 'Forest' side of the River Wye. Other villas may remain undiscovered, particularly where stone structures associated with Roman industrial or agricultural activity have been found.

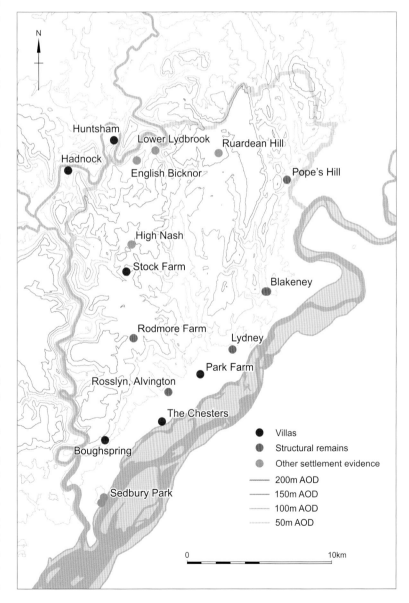

Fig 4.17
Roman villas, later Roman (3rd to 4th centuries AD) structural remains which may be associated with villas and other later Roman settlement evidence.

Riverside villas

Two villas (the Chesters, Woolaston and Park Farm, Aylburton) are close to the River Severn in the south-eastern part of the Forest of Dean.

The Chesters, Woolaston, on a ridge of land less than 200m from the Ley Pill, which flows into the Severn, was identified as a villa by Ormerod who noted reports of 'coins ... and remains of buildings', which he linked to the 'Chesters' placename (Ormerod 1861, 38), although it was not investigated until the 1930s when Scott-Garrett and Harris excavated a series of trenches to reveal the ground plan of the main villa building and associated structures to the north, south and west (Scott-Garrett and Harris 1938, 94–5; fig 2). From the 2nd to early 4th centuries AD the villa was a tripartite corridor type with a central block of four rooms flanked by smaller rooms or corridors. It had a courtyard to the west, rooms with under-floor heating, wall plaster and mosaic floors, and also a bath house at its southern corner. From the 4th to 5th centuries AD (or later) it was considerably remodelled with the demolition of part of the bathhouse and its northern and eastern rooms, and the construction of new sections extending the villa to the south-east (Scott-Garrett and Harris 1938, fig 2).

Other structures identified in the 1930s excavations included a boundary wall with a gateway, and a large rectangular building (approximately 23m × 9.5m) that had a corridor along its southern side and was interpreted as a barn with labourers' accommodation. A small square building in the south-eastern corner of the boundary wall and an area of flagstones to its north were interpreted as beacons which, when used in conjunction, could have guided shipping through a gap in Guscar Rocks at the mouth of Ley Pill (Scott-Garrett and Harris 1938, 108–10; fig 2). The remains of a hearth on one of the villa's broken flagged floors suggested temporary or squatter occupation after the villa had effectively been abandoned (Scott-Garrett and Harris 1938, 100).

Further investigation was undertaken to the south of the villa in 1987 and 1991. Geophysical survey indicated buildings in two areas where dark cropmarks and bloomery slag had been reported and subsequent excavations revealed padstones for a large timber-framed building, iron smelting furnaces, possible ore crushing areas and quantities of tap slag, charcoal, fired and unfired clay, and iron ore. Coins and pottery wcrc also found which suggested that iron smelting dated from the mid-3rd to the late 4th/early 5th centuries AD. Iron production had clearly contributed to the villa's economy during this period, perhaps with finished products exported by the River Severn via Ley Pill (Fulford and Allen 1992, 169–81), although it is not clear how central this was to the villa's economy.

The other riverside villa is Park Farm, Aylburton, which was also explored by Scott-Garrett between about 1955 and 1960, although his investigation was limited to exposing the sandstone wall footings of four structures (Fitchett 1986).

The main villa building was of tripartite corridor type with a central block of three rooms flanked by smaller rooms or corridors and with an additional long thin room or corridor at its western end. The width of wall footings suggested it may have had at least two storeys and a 'stairway base' was found at the end of one of the corridors. Three rooms had tessellated floors (although one was described as 'coarse') and the remaining floors were either stone flagged, mortared gravel, or *opus signinum*. No indications of under-floor heating or of painted wall plaster were recorded although the excavations were limited.

A smaller building to the south-west with a curved corner had stone flagged floors and included a narrow room with a 'much burnt' brick-lined furnace, a larger room with a 'much repaired' floor and a central sump connected to a drain and a tiny (2.5m × 3m) rectangular annex in its north-western corner. A third rectangular building to the east may also have had a heavy flagged floor. These structures were probably outbuildings rather than domestic structures, although it is not clear what they were used for.

Fig 4.18
The Chesters, Woolaston construction sequence. Scott-Garrett thought a '9-inch deposit' of soil between the phases suggested the villa had been abandoned or suffered some catastrophic event before it was refurbished, although he acknowledged that this could just have been deliberate levelling as part of the refurbishment process (Scott-Garrett and Harris 1938, 100, 124). [After Scott-Garrett and Harris 1938]

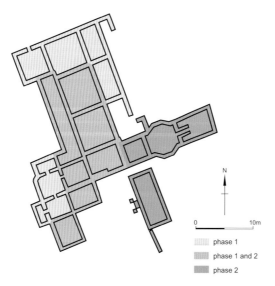

N

0   10m

phase 1
phase 1 and 2
phase 2

A record of 'glass chips' from the south-east corner of one of them (Fitchett 1986, 25), could have been a residue from some industrial process but may also have been broken window glass.

A fourth rectangular building to the south contained a 'brazier hearth' interpreted as the base of a beacon to guide shipping to a wharf, which survived as a wall running eastwards from it along the edge of the slightly higher ground on which the villa had been built (Fitchett 1986, 25 and site plan).

Although the site is now 1.75km from the River Severn it was probably closer during the Roman period. Some sections of the modern foreshore had been reclaimed from the river by the late 13th century or earlier (Herbert 1996e, 47–8; Townley 2004, 45, fig 21) and this may have removed navigable links between the villa and the Severn.

Details of finds are sketchy, although most of the pottery has been dated to the 2nd or 3rd centuries AD (Fitchett 1986, 25). An assemblage of early to mid-2nd-century Samian ware suggests the villa was built at that time (Walters 1992a, 85), but without detailed analysis of the finds it is not clear whether the villa continued in use beyond the 3rd century AD.

Iron slag was used in the floor make-up of one building (Fitchett 1986, 27) and later field survey has reported 'much furnace slag and hearth bases' on the site (Walters 1999, 10), which, although undated, suggests that iron smelting took place at the villa during the Roman period.

A third villa in the Severn Valley is at Boughspring about 4km to the south-west of the Chesters and this is often classed as a riverside villa as it is only about 1.5m from the Severn. Unlike the Chesters and Park Farm it is not on level ground with a navigable link to the river but on an artificial platform cut into the steep valley side nearly 100m above the Severn, and it seems to have been sited to take advantage of magnificent views rather than convenient trade links.

The site was discovered in 1969 when foundations and 3rd- and 4th-century AD pottery, *tesserae*, roof, floor and hypocaust tiles and a considerable quantity of bloomery slag were found (Bridgewater 1973, 7–8). Further excavation between 1979 and 1985 found evidence for a simple early 2nd-century AD rectangular stone building, which was enlarged in the later 2nd century with the addition of further rooms. Although still a simple structure, this building was decorated with painted wall plaster and a geometric mosaic floor was laid in at least one room (Neal and Walker 1988, 196). In the later 3rd century a corridor with a porch/entrance hall was added but the final phase of villa construction took place in the 4th century AD when major renovation almost doubled its size. All existing rooms were refurbished and two new wings with under-floor heating, painted wall plaster and *opus signinum* floors (although no evidence for mosaics) were added. A new room or corridor was also added to its north-western side.

In 1989 an extensive area of wall foundations was recorded to the south-east. These have not been investigated in detail but seem to represent a rectangular building with massive foundations (1–1.2m wide), perhaps suggesting more than one storey. Wings or corridors extend south-westwards possibly enclosing a courtyard, although traces of wall foundations in the central area hint at a more complex ground plan. There was also evidence for a boundary wall and an additional small stone structure to the north-west. Sometime after the villa had fallen out of use, probably in the late 4th or 5th centuries AD, two human burials were placed in the abandoned structure (Pullinger 1990, 13–16, 18–19).

Iron slag has been found on the site, but it is not clear how significant these deposits were or whether they were Roman and iron smelting need not have been a significant part of the villa's economy.

The two villas just outside the Forest of Dean (Huntsham, Herefordshire and Hadnock, Monmouthshire) are also close to a river, although in this case both are close to the River Wye.

At Huntsham the villa complex included the main villa building (which replaced a mid- to late 2nd-century house), an aisled barn and a smaller house. The villa was occupied from the late 2nd

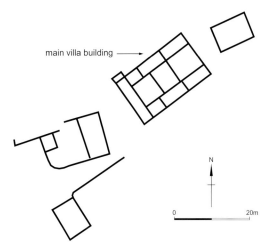

main villa building →

N

0   20m

Fig 4.19
Park Farm villa. Excavation in the 1950s hinted at further buildings and/or courtyards extending northwards. A section of stone wall, which continued westwards for at least 37m and contained at least one entrance, may have been a boundary to the villa compound. [After Fitchett 1986]

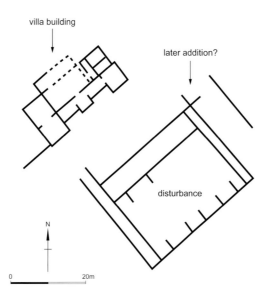

villa building

later addition?

disturbance

N

0   20m

Fig 4.20 (right) Boughspring villa. The villa had magnificent views over the River Severn and although the south-eastern building may have been outbuildings, it is tempting to see it as a completely new complex of domestic accommodation built in the 4th century at which time the original building (plus the new extensions) may have been converted into a bath house (Pullinger 1990, 18). [After Neal and Walker 1988; Pullinger 1990]

Fig 4.21 (below) Stock Farm villa and associated cropmarks. It has been suggested that the villa housed an official associated with the administration of iron ore extraction (Walters 1999, 17), although cropmarks suggest that it was not an isolated country house but a typical rural villa at the heart of a complex of boundaries and ancillary buildings. [Cropmarks © Historic England (NMP)]

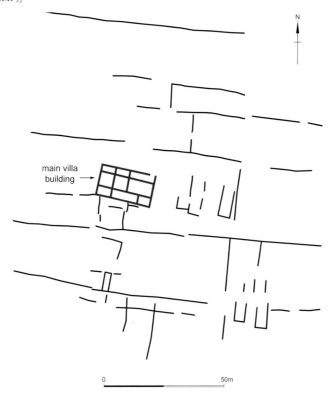

N

main villa building →

0   50m

to late 4th centuries AD, and although at least one room appeared to have had under-floor heating it was never particularly luxurious (Taylor 1995, 224, fig 3). The barn suggests its economy had an agricultural basis, although its short period of use, and evidence for short-lived diversification projects, suggest this was not particularly sustainable or profitable. Evidence for iron smelting has been found but this predated the construction of the villa in the 2nd century (Taylor 1995, 224) and there is no evidence that the villa's economy was reliant on iron smelting.

Hadnock villa comprised two stone buildings, at least one of which had under-floor heating. It appears to have been occupied from the 2nd to 3rd centuries AD and may have been part of a larger complex of buildings or close to further settlement immediately to its east (RCAHMW 2015). The site has produced bloomery slag which may date to the 3rd century (Walters 1992a, 95), although it is not clear whether iron smelting was a major part of the villa's economy.

Other villas

Not all the Forest's villas were close to major rivers and the villa at Stock Farm, Clearwell is several kilometres from the Severn and Wye. Air photographs taken in 1976 revealed the outline of a rectangular structure divided into three large rooms flanked by a series of narrower rooms or corridors representing a tripartite corridor villa remarkably similar to the main villa building at Park Farm, Aylburton (*see* Fig 4.19 and Blake 2004, fig 3). Small-scale excavation in 1985 found sandstone walls and 3rd- to 4th- (or possibly 5th-) century AD pottery, along with some animal bone (pig, sheep and horse) and a few fragments of iron slag (Atkinson 1986, 29, 30–5). Although the site is close to iron ore outcrops (ie scowles; *see* pp 126–30), a relatively small amount of slag has been found at the site (Blake 2004, 15; Catchpole 1996, 5; Cook 1995, 2) suggesting that if smelting did take place it may not have been a significant part of the villa's economy.

Other later Roman settlement

High status 'villas' would not have been isolated within an otherwise unpopulated landscape, and a range of lower status sites, from isolated farmsteads to small settlements, would be expected in the contemporary landscape. Few have been investigated and little is known about their layout, status, date and economic basis. Although many (but not all) were probably associated with iron smelting, this is likely to have been part of a mixed economy undertaken when the labour force was not engaged in other activities such as agriculture.

Pope's Hill and Rodmore Farm

Evidence for Roman iron smelting (and possibly also charcoal production) was found by Scott-Garrett at two sites about 500m apart at Pope's Hill and Chestnuts Hill in the eastern part of the Forest. A rough semicircular platform paved with large flagstones and possibly with associated postholes was recorded between Chestnuts Hill and Welshbury Hill immediately to the north. The flagstones sealed charcoal deposits and pottery (including some Samian), which suggested a date range of between about the 2nd and 4th centuries AD. A 5m-deep well within the platform may have been Roman in origin but contained fragments of medieval and post-medieval pottery (Scott-Garrett 1956, 199). The second site on Pope's Hill found evidence for a wooden structure with a rammed earth floor, a stone-lined hearth and a pitched stone threshold with Roman pottery, including 2nd-century AD Samian, burnt daub and an abundance of iron slag. About 5.5m to the west a dished rectangular area of stone slabs was interpreted as the base of a bloomery furnace, although it did not appear to have been burnt and may have been an ore crushing unit similar to those at the Chesters villa, Woolaston. More iron slag and fragments of 'partially baked furnace walls' were also found in this area (Scott-Garrett 1956, 200–2).

Another iron working site was excavated at Rodmore Farm, about 1.5km to the west of St Briavels, where Roman pottery and bloomery slag had previously been found close to fields recorded as 'Chess Redding' in the 19th century (Gwatkin 1993a). Excavation and geophysical survey between 1993 and 2003 identified stone footings of a rectangular building divided into three separate rooms (Blake 2004, fig 3) with cobbled stone floors that contained a carved sandstone mortarium (Blake 2001, 7) and a heavily reinforced stone basework that may have supported some apparatus connected with smelting (Blake 2003, 11) or other industrial processes. Iron slag and pottery dating from the 2nd to the 3th centuries AD were also found (Blake 2002, 15). Geophysical survey found a roughly rectangular enclosure about 60m to the south of the building (Blake 2002, 16, figs 1 and 2). This was defined by a V-shaped ditch and contained a circular patch of burning and three small slag-filled pits, interpreted as the base of a bloomery furnace and slag tapping pits, along with quantities of iron slag and charcoal (Blake 2003, 8–11). Geophysical survey appeared to show other structures and boundaries to the south and east of the excavated features (Blake 2002, figs 1 and 2), although the significance of these is not clear (Blake 2003, 13). Iron smelting and possibly other industrial processes were clearly taking place at Rodmore Farm in the 2nd to 3rd century AD.

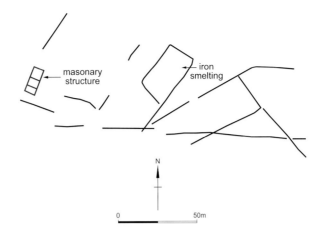

Although no evidence of domestic settlement was found at these sites it seems likely that these were part of larger complexes rather than isolated smelting sites, although it is unclear whether these were associated with villas or small rural settlements.

Sedbury Park

There is a concentration of Roman activity centred on Sedbury Park, Tidenham, although, unusually, there is no evidence that this site was associated with iron smelting. Roman remains were first recorded here by the antiquarian George Ormerod, who lived at Sedbury Park between 1828 and 1873. A 'few years' before 1860 he discovered the remains of a Roman pottery kiln and associated clay pits about 350m to the north-east of Sedbury Park (Ormerod 1861, 46, fig opp p 48) and in 1860 unearthed Roman pottery and 'deeper ancient lines' during the excavation of drainage ditches. These proved to be large backfilled ditches with the outer face considerably steeper than the inner, and similar to 'punic' ditches recorded at some Roman military defences (Jones 1975, 106; fig 20). These formed two contiguous subrectangular enclosures, although there was also a suggestion of a right-angled feature on a slightly different alignment. Roman pottery (including *amphorae*, *mortaria* and also some Samian) was found in the ditch fills along with animal bones (cattle and sheep, some of which had been butchered and cooked) and also coal, 'cinders of coal' (clearly not iron slag), lead, glass and some corroded iron (Ormerod 1861, 46–8 and fig opp p 48). The precise date of these remains is not clear as Ormerod simply records them as 'Roman' and there has been no detailed modern analysis of the pottery. The assemblage included fine table wares such as Samian and 'a vessel encaustically coloured, and raised in bas-relief [which]

Fig 4.22
Rodmore Farm. Masonry building and associated geophysical anomalies. The site was probably part of a larger complex, although there is no evidence for a nearby villa or other settlement. 'Chess' placenames have been recorded less than 150m to the west, although no Roman finds have been recorded at that location. [After Blake 2002]

Fig 4.23 (right)
Cropmarks and
archaeological sites around
Sedbury Park. Although none
of the cropmarks have been
dated with any certainty and
the precise date of the Roman
remains is not clear, the
Sedbury Park area does
appear to have been a focus
of occupation during the
Roman period. After
Ormerod 1861.
[Cropmarks © Historic
England (NMP)]

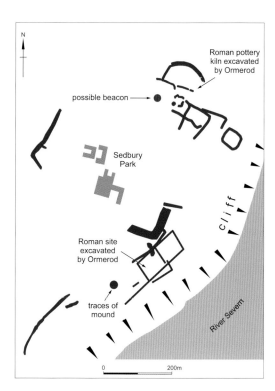

Fig 4.24 (below)
Roman sites in the Blakeney
area.

represented the chase of a hind by a dog' and was probably a colour-coated hunt cup, popular during the 2nd and 3rd centuries AD (Swan 1988, 25–6, plate 16). Ormerod also found ceramic tiles (although no evidence of masonry structures), which suggests reasonably established buildings with at least some degree of comfort.

He interpreted this site as a military base, but apart from the shape of the ditches there is no reason to think this was the case and more recent research suggests these may be part of a larger complex of occupation centred on Sedbury Park. Aerial photographs taken in 1947 recorded a number of roughly rectangular cropmark enclosures reminiscent of 'Celtic' field patterns close to the site of Ormerod's pottery kiln, and geophysical survey in the area has found anomalies that could represent ditches

and pits (Stratsocan 2013, 5, fig 03). There are cropmarks of a large D-shaped enclosure immediately north-west of Ormerod's pottery kiln and roughly square platforms and ditched enclosures to its south. Other cropmarks have been recorded to the west and east of Sedbury Park. Early Roman (and possibly late Iron Age) settlement is known to the south of Buttington Tump about 750m to the south-west and the Sedbury Park sites may represent evidence for a sequence of occupation throughout the Roman period that gradually migrated around the area of high ground.

Blakeney

Later Roman activity dating to the 3rd and 4th centuries AD has also been found at Millend, Blakeney, about 200m to the west of the early Roman building at Legg House (*see* pp 58–9), although unlike Legg House, Millend was clearly an industrial site associated with iron smelting. The earliest phase consisted of narrow enclosures defined by ditches filled with slag and charcoal and also a slab-lined oven-base with a cobbled surface, postholes and charcoal-filled cuts and pits. Subsequently further ditches, one of which incorporated a stone-lined culvert, were dug and cobbling was laid over earlier charcoal accumulations. Other features included waste pits containing charcoal, a hearth, slab-lined channels and a pit which contained two iron

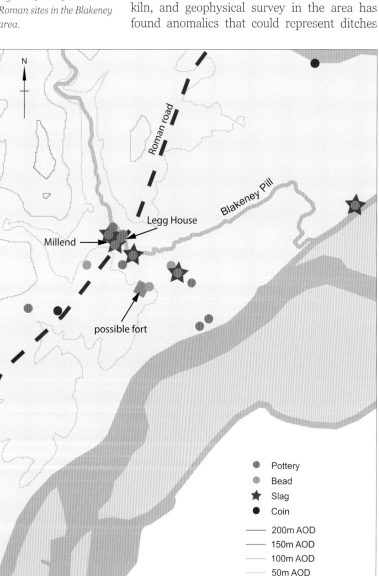

bucket rings and nine 4th-century AD Roman coins (Barber and Holbrook 2000, 35–9).

Despite their proximity the Legg House building and Millend site are not connected, but may be part of a wider Roman settlement in the Blakeney area. In 1786 Bigland reported structural remains (including 'four semi-circular walls ... with two square rooms') in a field called Church Croft, about 100m to the south-east (Rudge 1803, 118). These have been interpreted as the remains of a Roman bath house (Walters 1992b, 10) and Roman pottery (not closely dated) has also been recorded from Brook Cottage less than 100m to the north-east (Fitchett 1987). Other finds of Roman pottery (some dated to the 3rd and 4th century AD) associated with bloomery slag have been found to the south of Blakeney (Johns 1995, 40–8) and between the village and the River Severn to the south-east, and other Roman finds are known from this area (Johns 2005b).

It is not clear if Roman occupation at Blakeney represented a single settlement or if it was continuous throughout the Roman period. It is possible that the combination of road and river access, which had made the site desirable in the early Roman period (*see* pp 58–9), encouraged later settlement on a site that had been abandoned for a generation or more.

English Bicknor

A number of sites in the vicinity of English Bicknor have produced evidence for later Roman settlement in conjunction with iron slag or other evidence for Roman iron smelting.

Roman brick and tile (including a box flue tile usually associated with Roman under-floor heating systems) and some possible *tesserae* have been found in molehills in the churchyard of English Bicknor Church, where a concentration of bloomery slag was also noted.

Just over 1km to the east, fieldwalking at Barnfield, Eastbach Court in 1986 identified areas of bloomery iron slag, charcoal and burnt clay along with Roman pottery (at least one sherd of which was 4th century in date) and a coin of Constantus II minted in AD 353. Excavation the following year revealed the base of a Romano-British iron smelting shaft furnace and associated slag tapping pit along with two slag furnace bases, more Roman pottery and a Roman glass bead (Rawes 1987, 246; Walters 1987b, 50; Walters and Walters 1987, 50). Cropmarks of right-angled boundaries may also be associated with this site.

Pottery of 3rd to 4th century AD date has been found with a concentration of bloomery

slag and a partly smithed iron billet in the northern part of one of the fields of Cow Meadow Farm less than 500m to the south of the church (Walters 1999, 6), and a small excavation in the garden of Whitehouse Farm house, just over 1km to the south of the church, found Pennant Sandstone roof tiles over a Roman pit that contained more tile fragments, a large amount of unabraded Roman pot (suggesting settlement in the very near vicinity), a bronze spoon, five honing stones and bloomery slag (Milford 2000, 1).

It is not known whether the Roman occupation around English Bicknor is evidence for a single dispersed settlement or a number of smaller broadly contemporary sites, although iron smelting clearly formed part of the economy of people living in the area during the later Roman period.

Fig 4.25
Roman sites in the English Bicknor area.

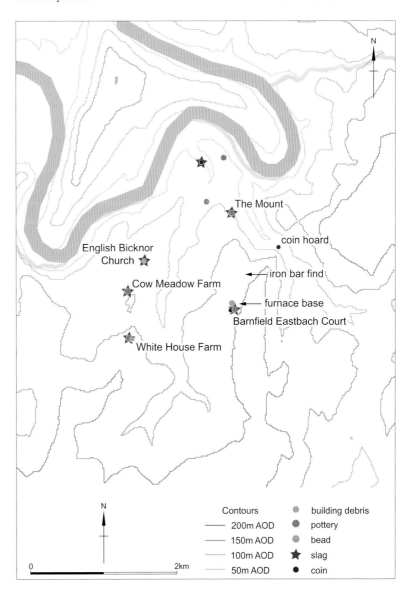

The Lydney area

The Lydney area is known to have been occupied during the later Roman period with the Roman temple at Lydney Park and the villa at Park Farm, Aylburton less than 1km to the west of the modern town. Numerous chance finds of Roman pottery and coins have been recorded in the area and many small excavations are beginning to piece together the story of Lydney's Roman past.

On the eastern side of the modern town, immediately to the east of Rodley Manor, two Roman ditches and spreads of Roman ceramic building material in a discrete area (about 100m²) were interpreted as the remains of one or more timber buildings, at least one of which

was substantial enough to have a tiled roof. These were probably agricultural rather than domestic, but may have been outbuildings associated with a large farm or villa. A number of small and abraded sherds of Roman pottery, generally coarse wares but also some sherds of fine table ware (Samian), were also found, suggesting the buildings had been used in the 3rd and 4th centuries AD (Wessex Archaeology 2003a, 24, 30–1, fig 4).

Roman ditches, pits and postholes containing pottery dating to the 3rd and 4th centuries AD have also been found overlying a gravel terrace just over 1km to the south. Significant amounts of charcoal and bloomery slag, and a small amount of hammerscale were also found, suggesting that iron smelting (and also smithing) had taken place on the site (Brett 2004, 13–14).

A similar range of features was also found about 400m to the north-east of this, also on a gravel terrace. Pits and gullies containing pottery dating to the 3rd and 4th centuries AD, iron slag and hammerscale were interpreted as evidence for later Roman occupation and iron smelting (Barber 2009, 14–15). About 250m to the north-east of this a possible Roman gully contained iron slag and fired clay (presumably the remains of a bloomery), although the dating of this feature is reliant on a single small abraded sherd of Roman pottery that may be residual (Wessex Archaeology 2003b, i).

Further west there is evidence of more Roman settlement along the line of the modern A48, which corresponds approximately to the line of the Roman road between Newnham and Caerwent (*see* p 77). In 1936 Frank Harris reported Roman pottery and iron slag in fields north-west of the town and also reported 'banks in the field', which suggested 'a native settlement' (Harris 1936, 283), although these earthworks have now been destroyed by housing development.

Just under 2km to the south-west, near Tump Farm, Aylburton, Scott-Garrett reported Roman pottery in an area he interpreted as 'a small occupation site' (Hart 1967, 41). The view that a curved field boundary was the remains of an enclosure earthwork is thought doubtful (Ordnance Survey, Antiquity Record Card for Gloucestershire, SO60SW, 15), although the placename 'Chesnals' is recorded only 500m to the north-west (Gwatkin 1994b).

Further evidence for Roman occupation has been uncovered at Rosslyn, Alvington, about 3.5km to the south of Lydney (just to the south of the probable line of the Roman road) where a

Fig 4.26
Roman sites in the Lydney area.

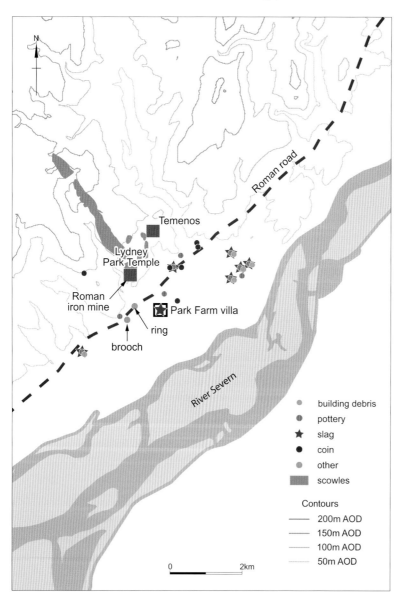

2nd-century AD terrace and stone cobbled surface was replaced by further surfaces, a stone structure and a slag-filled refuse pit in the 3rd to 4th centuries AD. The site had clearly been used for smelting iron in the later Roman period. There was no direct evidence for domestic occupation, although the pottery assemblage included a relatively high proportion of fine table ware (Samian), suggesting that a reasonably high-status building, perhaps a villa, was located nearby (Hood 2013, 16–19).

Lower Lydbrook

Another Roman occupation site has been found at a D-shaped enclosure on the western side of a promontory overlooking the River Wye at The Mount, Lower Lydbrook. A small excavation between 1985 and 1986 found evidence for Romano-British settlement comprising rectangular and circular buildings along with 2nd- to 4th-century AD pottery (including some Samian) and both iron and bronze slag (Walters 1985a, 24). Like many other Roman settlement sites in the Forest of Dean, iron was smelted at The Mount, although this settlement also appears to have been involved in bronze working, the only other evidence for which is from Dymock, about 18km to the north, where bronze brooches were made in the early Roman period (Dungworth 2007, 186).

High Nash, Coleford

Bloomery iron slag and iron ore have also been found with 3rd- and 4th-century AD pottery at High Nash, Coleford where rescue excavation found robbed-out foundations of what may have been a rectangular structure with an apsidal addition on its western side (Walters 1987b, 50). The structure was interpreted by the excavator as a temple (*see* pp 72–3) but this is far

Fig 4.27
The Mount, Lydbrook looking east. This enclosed an area of 27 × 34m and had an internal division. After a break of about 4m a boundary runs from its western side northwards for 46m.
[© Historic England Archive NMR 23327/10. 07-NOV-2003]

from certain; the evidence may represent buildings associated with later Roman iron smelting and/or occupation on the site.

Ruardean Hill

The possible early Roman fort at Ruardean Hill was also occupied in the 3rd century, after its defences had been reduced in the 2nd century (*see* p 54). Finds of iron slag suggest that the occupants were involved with iron smelting, and a saw fragment and hone stone hint at woodland management and/or charcoal production. It is not clear how long the site was used, or whether this represented permanent or seasonal occupation.

Wider settlement evidence

Chance finds or scatters of Roman material are found throughout the Forest of Dean. The precise meaning of these is difficult to determine without detailed analysis of the finds, although where these are found in the vicinity of known Roman remains they may indicate the extent of settlement.

Clusters of finds (mostly pottery), and some 'chester' place names (a name derived from the Latin *castra* and generally interpreted as indicating masonry remains that are probably Roman [Smith 1964b, 110]) are known around Blakeney and Lydney, along the line of the A48, the Roman road that linked Newnham and Caerwent (*see* p 77), and also in the area of Chestnuts Wood, north of Littledean, around Stock Farm Roman villa, Clearwell and in the vicinity of English Bicknor and Lower Lydbrook in the northern part of the Forest. Scatters of Roman finds from other areas (for example to the north of Ruardean and to the south-west of Coleford) are not focused enough for likely sites to be identified.

Concentrations to the north and west of Close Turf Farm, St Briavels may be skewed by the amount of fieldwalking that has taken place here, but other evidence for Roman activity such as the enclosure near Willsbury Farm and structural remains at Rodmore Farm (*see* pp 63–4) and the 'chester' place names (Castors and Chess Reading) suggest that Roman occupation was widespread in this area.

Three other 'chester' place names (Chess Grove, west of Chess Grove Farm, south-west of Longhope (Gwatkin 1992a), Chestnut Ground, south-east of Bigsweir House, St Briavels (Gwatkin 1993a) and 'Chestley Furlong' near Bullo,

Newnham (Gwatkin 1992b)) are not close to known evidence for Roman activity and may indicate sites that have yet to be discovered.

Roman ritual and religion

Religion and ritual in the Roman period was extremely diverse and would be confusing to the modern mind in its ability to accommodate apparently contradictory or at least inconsistent views on the nature of the spiritual world. On the one hand private devotion often focused on local (and often pre-Roman) deities who were tied to particular locations or had specifically domestic responsibilities, while on the other hand public observance to a pantheon of gods and goddesses was inextricably bound up with social cohesion and the individual's public duty as a participant in the Roman state. Roman religion assimilated pre-Roman deities into its own pantheon, often conflating them with existing Roman gods, and was extremely tolerant of a variety of religious practices so long as these did not involve secret or closed societies (which could be seen as conspiring against the state) or human sacrifice. In addition to these there were also religious cults imported into Britain from other parts of the empire, often by auxiliaries serving in the Roman army. This latter group included the mystery religions, which generally originated in the Middle East and often involved initiation rites and a belief in salvation and eternal life (Salway 1993, 469–73). This tolerant (and pragmatic) approach to alien belief systems facilitated the integration of conquered peoples into the Roman state, but makes it difficult to unravel the actual beliefs or rituals of the inhabitants of Roman Britain, particularly where the only evidence is the ground plan of religious buildings or items of statuary whose design imitates those of a classical culture that may have been dedicated to a different deity (Salway 1993, 469).

There is limited evidence for Roman religious practices and belief in the Forest of Dean, and what there is may only represent a small sector of the totality of religious belief in the area at that time. Some religious sites, particularly those associated with pre-Roman deities, may just have been semi-natural features such as groves or springs that would have left no evidence unless they were subsequently enhanced in some way, and other sites are doubtless awaiting discovery.

Temples

Lydney Park

The best-known Roman religious site in the Forest of Dean is undoubtedly the temple in the southern part of the Iron Age hillfort at Lydney Park on the edge of a promontory with steep slopes on three sides and commanding views across the Severn Vale (*see* Bathurst 1879, pl II).

The site has been known since at least the late 18th century when the antiquary Major Rooke was 'allowed to dig wherever he was inclined' (Bathurst 1879, 3). Rooke published his results (Rooke 1777), but was not the first person to dig on the site, which had previously been damaged by stone robbing and treasure hunting expeditions (Bathhurst 1879, 3). In 1805 foundations exposed during tree planting prompted further excavation by the owner, the Right Hon C Bathurst, whose systematic record of walls, mosaic floors and finds were collated and posthumously published by his son (Bathurst 1879). Bathurst's record of the temple and associated buildings was particularly impressive. The earliest was a large building with multiple rooms surrounding a courtyard. Immediately to the west of this (and on a different alignment due to the constraints of the topography) was an extensive bathhouse with under-floor heating and connected to a cistern about 45m to the north-east. A long suite of rooms linked by a corridor or portico ran southwards from the bath house along the edge of the plateau, and next to this was a rectangular temple. Finds from the temple included two bronze and lead tablets (one of which had been offered by Silvanus cursing the family of Senicianus whom he accused of stealing his ring) dedicated to a god whose name was variously spelt Nodon (or Nodons), Nuden and Nodens and to whom the temple was dedicated. All of the buildings had some mosaic floors and the whole complex was within a walled precinct (*temenos*), the limits of which were constrained by the natural slopes of the promontory. There was an entrance into the precinct on its northern side, between the bath house and the courtyard building, although the main approach, which led directly to the eastern entrance to the temple, was through a rock-cut gully in its south-eastern corner (Bathurst 1879, 5–12, pl IV). In addition to the tablets (*see* above), Bathurst's excavation also recovered a wide range of finds including Samian pottery, iron tools, jewellery, spoons, bone pins, nail cleaners, combs, a number of impressed bronze letters and decorative strips

and hundreds of coins. There were also a number of clearly symbolic or ritual finds including bronze models of human limbs, an axe, effigies of Victory, Jupiter, Ceres, a cockerel and nine dogs, including an unusually well-made model of a wolf hound. He also found a stamp used by an oculist (Julius Jucundus) to authenticate his medicines (Bathurst 1879, 33–124).

Bathurst interpreted the site as the official residence of 'the principal military commander for the area' and his retinue (Bathurst 1879, 4–5) and thought the temple was an integral part of the official residence, which would have had a civilising effect on the native population by exposing them to Roman culture and religion. He also suggested that the god Nodens may have been associated with Aesculapius, the classical god of healing (Bathurst 1879, 13–16).

Fig 4.28
Location of Lydney Park temple complex within the earlier hillfort.
[After Wheeler and Wheeler 1932]

The site was excavated again by Sir Mortimer and Tessa Wheeler between 1928 and 1929, who added little to the recorded ground plan of the buildings (compare Bathurst 1879, pl IV with Wheeler and Wheeler 1932, plate LII) but did offer fairly precise dates for the buildings and identified their construction sequence and modifications. The Wheelers determined that the temple was not built before AD 364 on the basis of coins buried in or under its floors (Wheeler and Wheeler 1932, 47) and also pointed out its unusual 'basilical' design with a central nave or *cella* with three shrines at its north-eastern end. An outer aisle surrounding the *cella* had a continuous stone bench and incorporated seven small rectangular bays. Soon after its construction parts of the temple collapsed into earlier iron mines (*see* p 131); it was rebuilt and three of the bays were converted into small rooms or chapels by adding enclosing walls which projected into the aisle.

The Wheelers thought the temple was designed as a 'consecrated meeting place' for a mystery cult, and compared it to continental examples at Bakchtheon, Athens or Pesch near Cologne, Germany (Wheeler and Wheeler 1932, 35–9).

Rituals involving offerings to the god Nodens probably took place in the *cella* where over 350 of the coins had been found, and where a small funnel in the floor may have been used for liquid libations (Bathurst 1879, pl VIII; Copeland 2011,

150). Nodens was probably linked with healing as the numerous votive items from the site included effigies of dogs (associated with healing in classical mythology), human limbs and a large number of pins (associated with childbirth). The Wheelers also suggested that the chapel-like structures may have been places where the sick slept to receive help from the gods in their dreams – another aspect of classical healing shrines (Wheeler and Wheeler 1932, 40–3). The oculist's stamp may also indicate that professional healers were present at the site. The Wheelers also reinterpreted the letters *D.M. Nodonti* on a votive tablet and suggested that Nodens was a local pre-Roman healing deity who was conflated with Mars in the official Roman pantheon (Wheeler and Wheeler 1932, 100–1).

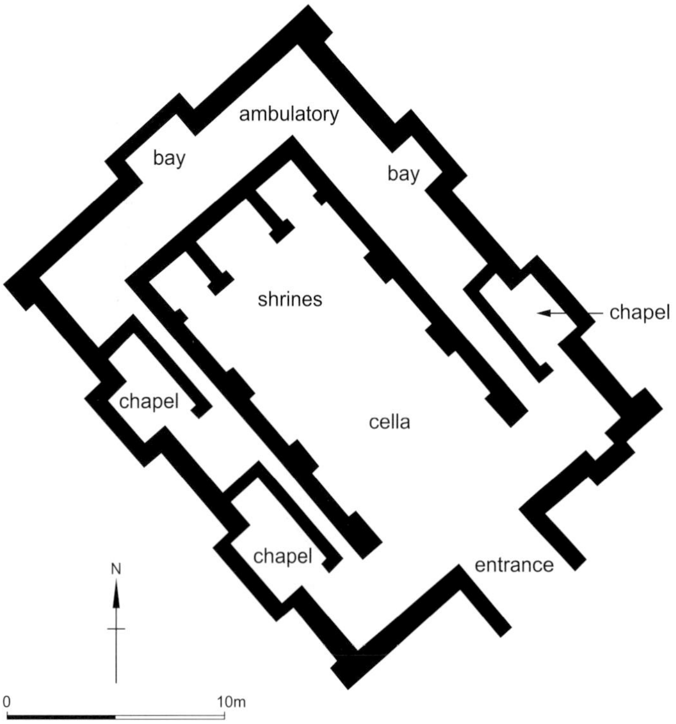

The Wheelers interpreted the courtyard building as a guest house and the long building to the west of the temple as either additional accommodation or an *abaton*, where visitors prepared for sacred sleep. They also considered the baths 'both by design and in scale' were intended for public rather than private use (Wheeler and Wheeler 1932, 47, 51–2, 57). The temple was clearly designed for large numbers of visitors or pilgrims, perhaps in search of a miracle cure for some ailment, and the Wheelers considered the cult of Nodens had 'flourished exceedingly' from the later 4th century well into the post-Roman period in the 5th century (Wheeler and Wheeler 1932, 61–3).

Since the Wheelers' excavation the temple layout has been reassessed and its 'unusual' basilical design reinterpreted as a more common Romano-Celtic style where an inner area is surrounded by an ambulatory passageway containing open or closed side chapels, and with a similar example known at Caerwent, Monmouthshire only about 23km to the south-west (Muckelroy 1976, 187). Their post-AD 376 date for the complex has also been questioned and the temple and associated buildings were probably constructed in the second half of the 3rd century AD (Casey and Hoffmann 1999, 114), although there was considerable 'embellishing of the structures' probably after about AD 364. The temple may not have remained in use well into the 5th-century period as the only indication of this is a 5th-century brooch (*see* Wheeler and Wheeler 1932, fig 15), but material evidence for immediate post-Roman activity is often elusive and precisely when the temple ceased functioning is unknown (Casey and Hoffmann 1999, 115).

Fig 4.29
Lydney Park Roman temple.
[After Wheeler and Wheeler 1932]

This re-assessment does not diminish the significance of the Lydney temple and really just suggests that it was founded a century or so earlier and had a more complex history of development than the Wheelers suggested. The temple of Nodens at Lydney flourished in the latter part of the 4th century AD as a popular (and lucrative) pilgrimage centre probably attracting large numbers of the sick and other pilgrims from a wide area.

Other possible temples

The temple at Lydney Park was, for many years, thought to be the only Roman temple in the Forest of Dean. Two other possible sites were discovered in the 1980s, but the interpretation of both of these as temples is not straight-forward.

The foundations of a substantial stone building, which had been damaged by later stone robbing, and evidence for iron smelting were uncovered close to Littledean Hall, Littledean. Some Roman pottery, tile and *tesserae* were found and the site was interpreted a Roman springhead temple (probably dating to the 2nd or 3rd century AD) that had been built over an infilled (and possibly sacred) pool (Jones and Maude 1987, 40–1). The structural sequence is not absolutely clear, but there may have been an earlier timber structure on the site that was replaced by a square building with stone footings and an eastern entrance. This was superseded by a new building on a slightly different alignment that had a rectangular *cella* with aisles on its northern and southern sides, an apsidal shrine to its west and a porch to its

east. After an unspecified period of time, the *cella* and apsidal shrine were demolished and replaced by a court with an ambulatory on three sides. The western wall of this structure contained a number of small niches and a small rectangular porch with a narrow opening. A stone drain ran from the central court towards its northern wall (Macer-Wright and Fitchett 1984, 3, fig p 9).

In 1986 a hoard of 85 Roman coins was reported from the site (Jones and Maude 1987, 41) and two further hoards (of 32 and 115 coins) were found in the vicinity by metal detectorists in 1986 and 1987.

The interpretation of this site as a temple has, however, been questioned. Its plan, especially in

Fig 4.30 (above)
Speculative reconstruction of Lydney Park temple complex.
[From Wheeler and Wheeler 1932, Society of Antiquaries of London (NMR CC86/00098)]

Steps into
temple entrance

Fig 4.31
Lydney Park temple looking west into the entrance.
[© Gloucestershire County Council Archaeology Service]

■	masonry
▨	robber trench
⫽	presumed
•	post hole

Fig 4.32
Littledean, possible Roman temple. A series of postholes were interpreted as a polygonal timber structure similar to other possible late Iron Age ritual sites (Jones and Maude 1987, 41), although when originally discovered these were not thought to be early features (Fitchett 1985, 10–11) and their interpretation remains problematic.
[After Macer-Wright and Fitchett 1984]

its final phase, has no direct parallels in Roman Britain and the small wall niches in particular are unique. Apart from the coins very little Roman material has been found (Macer-Wright and Fitchett 1984, 2) and there is a lack of the sort of 'votive' items often associated with temples. This is particularly puzzling as it would have been the second largest Roman temple in Britain after the temple at Colchester dedicated to the Emperor Claudius, and almost 40 per cent larger than Lydney Park temple (Macer-Wright and Fitchett 1984, 4).

The remains have also been interpreted as a late medieval or post-medieval farmhouse with a central dairy (Smith 1985), although this would have been a particularly large example (Jones and Maude 1987, 40) and this interpretation also has its difficulties.

Another possible Roman temple has been found at High Nash, Coleford. In 1985 'sparse' amounts of 3rd- and 4th-century AD pottery had been found on the site (Walters 1985a, 34) and a four-day rescue excavation in 1987 recorded the robbed-out foundation trenches of a rectangular building with a semicircular apse on its western side. A small rectangle of flat stones in the centre of the apse was interpreted as the base for an altar, and pottery from the 3rd and 4th centuries AD was found in the foundation trenches. Other finds included a 4th-century coin, iron nails, pennant sandstone (interpreted as flagstone remains), some 'crude sandstone *tesserae*', bloomery iron slag and fragments of iron ore, but no votive offerings or other items (such as statuary fragments), which would be expected from a temple. Immediately to its west the possible remains of sandstone floors with 2nd- to 4th-century pottery and nails suggested a second building and both seem to have been enclosed within a boundary ditch (Sindrey 1990, 26–7).

The interpretation as a temple complex is based mainly on the ground plan of the apsidal structure, although the layout visible on the only published record (Sindry 1990, fig xi) appears less coherent. The apse stands out but the linear

Fig 4.33
Possible Roman temple at Littledean under excavation, looking north. Scale 2m (0.5m divisions).
[© Gloucestershire County Council Archaeology Service]

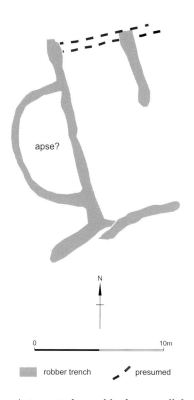

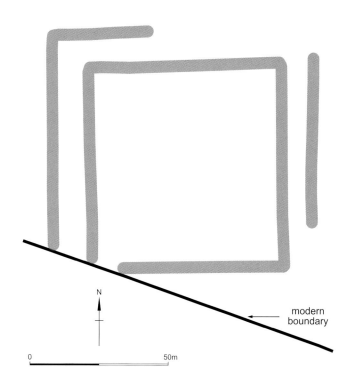

robber trench   presumed

ditches, interpreted as robbed-out wall footings, do not obviously form a rectangular building and may be several unrelated linear trenches. The southern wall is particularly problematic and seems to be two separate trenches, one of which continues beyond the supposed south-western corner of the building. Roman pottery has been found on the site, and late Iron Age military equipment (possibly from a burial) and a 'small' assemblage of late Iron Age pottery was recorded less than 100m to the north-west. Clearly there was Roman and possibly also late Iron Age occupation on this site, and possibly evidence for 3rd to 4th-century AD buildings, but it is far from clear that these were the remains of a temple and they may be evidence for later Roman iron smelting and associated occupation.

A fourth possible temple was identified at Blackrock Farm, Lydney from Google Earth images in 2015. Cropmarks clearly show two concentric square enclosures similar to the 'double-box' plan of a Romano-Celtic temple or *temenos* enclosure common in the north-western provinces of the empire (Salway 1993, 474–7), with similar examples known in Gloucestershire at Sapperton, Nettleton and Uley to the east of the River Severn (Moore 2012, 6).

Other undated enclosures (particularly the concentric subrectangular earthworks at Willsbury, east of St Briavels [*see* p 57] and perhaps also the rectangular enclosures at Plump Hill,

Mitcheldean and Morse Lane, Ruardean [*see* pp 116–17]) may also represent Roman temple sites but are currently thought most likely to be other types of site.

Other evidence for Roman religion

Altars

Small altars were used in Roman sacrificial rituals (Henig 1984, 128–31) and two Roman altars have been found in the Forest of Dean.

One of these, like most small Roman altars, has a squared shaft with a protruding pedestal and a more decorative capital (Scarth 1880–1, 67; *see* for example Clifford 1938, figs 1–30) but no inscription (Clifford 1938, 299) and was reportedly found 'within a tumulus' on Tidenham Chase in 1825 close to where a Roman coin had been found (Ormerod 1861, 39). Ormerod presented the altar to the Archaeological Institute (later the British Museum) which listed it as from a tumulus in Sedbury Park, Tidenham (Franks 1852, 13), while the Ordnance Survey recorded it from a mound on Parsons Allotment on the eastern side of Tidenham Chase (OS 1881), which was subsequently shown to be the site of an 18th-century gazebo or folly (Scott-Garrett 1954, 237–41). Ormerod himself, however, when describing the possible Roman 'camp' at Madgetts describes 'tumuli, proved to be Roman by the

Fig 4.34 (above left)
High Nash, possible Roman temple.
[After Sindrey 1990]

Fig 4.35 (above)
Cropmarks of Roman probable temenos *at Blackrock Farm, Lydney. The site was discovered from Google Earth images and did not show up on earlier aerial photographs or lidar. It is also close to a spring and associated with the placename 'Stonebury' (Stonebury Wood and Stonebury Coppice are immediately to the east and south respectively) suggesting a site of some antiquity.*
[Cropmarks from Google Earth Imagery 2015]

discovery therein of a sepulchral altar in my possession' (Ormerod 1841, 14), which was the same altar he 'presented ... to the Archaeological Institute' (Ormerod 1861, 4, fn 2). By 1861, however, Ormerod seemed less clear about precisely where this tumulus was, as although it was clearly on Tidenham Chase in the Madgetts area, he mentions other tumuli between it and Madgetts Camp, suggesting it may not have been within the camp itself (Ormerod 1861, 39). It is still not clear precisely where this was, but likely candidates are a mound immediately east of Offa's Dyke within the rampart of the speculated Madgetts Camp, or a small elliptical mound at the edge of the headland to the west of Offa's Dyke in Caswell Wood, although other mounds are known in the vicinity. Why a Roman altar was in a Bronze Age barrow remains a mystery, though earlier ritual sites may have retained some ritual/folkloric significance into the Roman period.

The second altar was found in 1982, about 500m to the north of Closeturf Farm on St Briavels Common in an area of swampy ground. This has a tapered base rather than the more usual pedestal and would not have been free standing (Johns 2005a, 38), but the altar appears to have had a secondary use as a post-Roman grave marker (*see* p 107, Fig 5.38) and the pedestal may have been removed at that time.

The stone font at Staunton Church may also have been carved from a Roman altar, although this has been questioned since the late 19th century and is doubtful (Scarth, 1880–1, 67–8).

Other stone objects that have been interpreted as evidence for Roman ritual are four crudely carved sandstone heads (in fact two heads, a bust and a stele) found in a garden at Ruspidge in 1970 (Fowler 1971, 22; GADARG 1982a; David Rice, Gloucester City Museum, pers comm) and another reportedly found in a neighbouring garden (Marlene Wilkinson pers comm). These may have been associated with a Romano-Celtic shrine, but some authorities consider the heads to be modern (McGrath and Cannon 1976, 94–8).

Another stone head found at Dean Hall, Little dean in 1991 has been associated with the pre-Roman springhead temple at Littledean Hall (*see* pp 71–2; Walters 1992a, 54), although the provenance of this artefact and its association with the putative temple site has not been established.

Burial

The Romans tended to bury their dead in cemeteries close to settlements and although no large Roman settlements are known in the Forest, burials could still have taken place in cemeteries serving small settlements or even villas or farmsteads. Evidence for Roman burial and cremation has been found at Dymock (Cole 2007, 192), and possibly also Newent (Catchpole 1993b), but there is little evidence from the Forest of Dean.

Two skull fragments (from different individuals) have been found at the later Iron Age to Roman iron working settlement at Reddings Lane, Staunton. One fragment may have been from a decapitated head (Ellis 2013, 13), but postmortem decapitation was rarely seen before the 4th century AD (Philpott 1991, 226) and these are more likely to be disturbed bones from pre-Roman (Iron Age or earlier) burials. A cremation and pottery found at Lindors Farm, St Briavels in about 1883 may also be Roman, but these are undated and their current whereabouts are unknown (Allen 1883–84, 356). Two burials in the 'ruined remains' of the Boughspring Roman villa are probably post-Roman (Pullinger 1990, 19).

The only other possible evidence for Roman burial is a rectangular stone basin from Whitecliff, Coleford, which had been used as a water trough and has been tentatively interpreted as a Roman sarcophagus (Beachus 2000, 10, fig 8).

4.36
Roman altar from a possible Bronze Age barrow to the west of Madgetts Farm, Tidenham Chase. The altar is made from coarse brown sandstone and is about 0.48m high.
[From Clifford 1938, plate IV, fig 8, Transactions of the Bristol and Gloucestershire Archaeological Society*]*

This would be an unusual find for the Forest as only 30 Roman sarcophagi are known in Gloucestershire, all east of the Severn, and only four outside Cirencester (Russell 2010, 15, table 2), although this may be a relic of a Roman cemetery in the vicinity.

Coin hoards

Although there have been numerous finds of Roman coins in the Forest, only 21 of these have been classed as hoards, which can be defined as a group of coins deliberately deposited together (FISH 2018), and the status of a number of these is not clear. All but seven were found in the 19th century and details of their discovery, the numbers or dates of the coins or even their precise location is not always clear.

Four hoards contained no coins later than the 2nd century AD, including 'several' coins from Chepstow Bridge, Tidenham (Watkin 1878, 42), 100 coins from Lydney (Bagnall-Oakeley 1881–2, 108), 155 coins from near an area of scowles at Bream (Hart 1967, 42) and a large hoard of more than 1,000 coins from Kidnalls Wood (*The Gloucester Journal*, 3 May 1879). Five of the hoards contained no coins later than the 3rd century AD. These included about 500 coins from Crabtree Hill, Cinderford, a large hoard of about 3,000 coins from scowles in Perrygrove Wood near Coleford, about 100 coins probably from near the Dean Road in the Soudley area and over 1,000 coins from Parkend (Bagnall-Oakeley 1881–2, 108–10). A hoard of about 1,300 coins from Hangerberry, English Bicknor may also only comprise 3rd-century coins, although at the time of writing this hoard awaits full analysis (Portable Antiquities Scheme database: GLO-756722). The remaining hoards contained mainly coins from the 4th century AD. These included 'several thousand' coins from Tufthorn, Coleford (Bagnall-Oakeley 1881–2, 110), two hoards of about 3,150 and 548 coins from Old-croft, Lydney (Rhodes 1974, 15; Rhodes and Wild 1974, 65–70), two hoards of 126 and 1,646 coins from Lydney Park Temple (Wheeler and Wheeler 1932, 112–29), and another hoard of 'several hundred' coins from Woolaston (Bag-nall-Oakeley 1890, 262) which may represent two separate hoards. Over 200 3rd- to 4th-century AD coins from Littledean Hall, Littledean may represent one or more hoards (Glos HER 2015), a 'great number' of coins from Lydbrook may also represent a 4th-century AD hoard (Bagnall-Oakeley 1881–2, 108) and a hoard of nearly 500 4th-century AD coins has also been

found at Yorkley (Portable Antiquities Scheme database: GLO-24A5E0).

Twenty-four 4th-century AD coins from the Chesters villa, Woolaston (Scott-Garrett and Harris 1938, 113–14) and 12 from Yorkley Slade (Portable Antiquities Scheme database: GLO-BEC0A0) may also be small hoards although this is not clear, while three from Tidenham (Grinsell 1968, 64) may be all that remains of a larger hoard found in 1862.

Six of the hoards (from Chepstow Bridge, Kid-nalls Wood, Crabtree Hill, Perrygrove, Tufthorn and Parkend) were found in one or more pottery jars, while the hoard probably from the Soudley area was in a brass vessel and three of the hoards (both the Oldcroft hoards and the hoard from Yorkley) were probably contained in bags. One

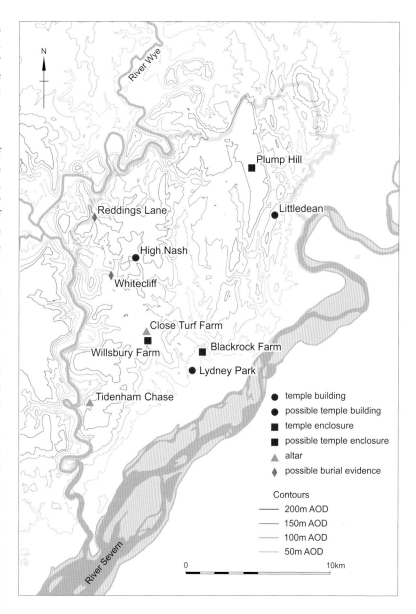

Fig 4.37
Roman ritual sites.

of the Oldcroft hoards was concealed within a wall, while the Hangerberry hoard appears to have been inserted into a field boundary, although there was no evidence that these coins had originally been placed in a container or bag.

Roman coin hoards defy generalisation as a diverse range of complex processes can have contributed to the deposition, location and lack of recovery of individual hoards (Reece 1987, 46–9). Some may be the result of people burying valuables during times of political and economic instability (Salway 1993, 174) and there may have been an increase in coin hoards during the 3rd and 4th centuries, but hoards are not restricted to this period and many are of little monetary value (Casey 1999, 60).

The two hoards from Lydney Park Temple and possibly the hoard from Littledean may

have been ritual offerings and other hoards, even where not obviously associated with religious sites, may also fall into this category. Other hoards, particularly where deliberately hidden or buried in pottery containers, could just have been cash stored in a safe place (Casey 1999, 53) and funds could have been deposited or withdrawn as required, much as a 21st-century person would use a bank account.

Late Roman Christianity

Christianity was officially recognised by the Roman Empire in AD 313 (Ling 1968, 180), although how widely it was practised, particularly at the western limits of the Empire, is unclear. A few items from east of the Severn, such as a Chi-Ro symbol at Chedworth Roman villa and lead baptismal tanks and a ring depicting the Good Shepherd from Bourton-on-the-Water, have been interpreted as evidence for late Roman Christianity, which may have been more common in the higher classes who lived in towns or villas. Evidence for Christianity among the rural or poorer population is elusive (Heighway 1987, 93) and no evidence for late Roman Christianity has been found in the Forest of Dean. It has been suggested, on architectural grounds, that the late Roman temple at Lydney Park may have been used for late Roman or early post-Roman Christian rituals (Townley 2004, 237), but no specifically Christian artefacts have been recovered from the site.

Roman communications

Roads

Military roads

Throughout the prehistoric period the Forest of Dean would have been criss-crossed by a network of routes linking settlements to each other and with the resources they needed. Over time some would have gained or lost prominence, new ones would have been created and others abandoned, reflecting changes in the significance the inhabitants placed on certain places within the landscape in which they lived.

When the Roman army arrived in the middle of the 1st century AD, the established route system would not have been completely superseded but a number of new roads were built by the Roman army that were unlike any previously seen in the area. Roman roads did not follow dead straight lines regardless of practical or

Fig 4.38
Roman coin hoards and possible hoards by period.

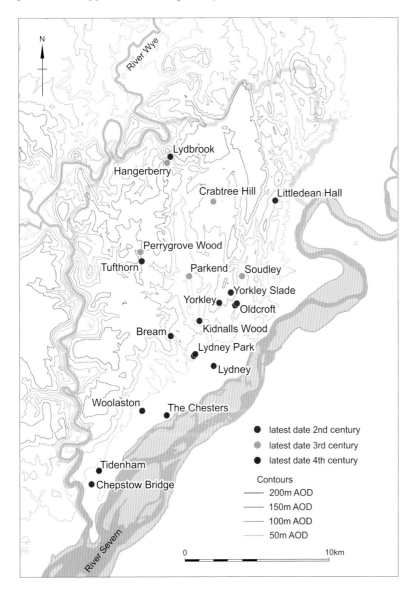

topographical considerations, but were designed to be as straight as possible and were constructed in straight sections (generally along sight lines between high points), only deviating where topography or other landscape features made this logistically necessary and ignoring existing boundaries. These roads were important to the authorities for a number of reasons. They provided a rapid, direct and all-weather surface for the Roman army to move men and supplies between military installations and enabled the speedy and efficient movement of messages (relayed by the *cursus publicus* or Imperial postal service) and officials for the effective administration of the province (Salway 1993, 385). Less apparent, but equally significant, would have been their cultural impact on the native population. These new roads were significant features, with a cambered stone surface on a raised linear bank (*agger*) and drainage ditches to either side. They drove new routes across the landscape, cutting across existing cultural boundaries, and would have been a very tangible symbol of the power the Roman state held over their conquered territories (Copeland 2011, 45).

Two of the Forest's Roman roads, the road between Gloucester and Mitcheldean and a branch from this road at Huntley that connects it with Ariconium, the modern Weston under Penyard in Herefordshire (Margary 61 and 611; Margary 1957, 59–62), run through the northern part of the Forest of Dean. These were probably built early in the Roman period to facilitate the campaign against the Silures of South Wales between about AD 49 and AD 74 (Copeland 2011, 35–6), and also to link the regional power base at Kingsholm/Gloucester with the late Iron Age iron production sites at Ariconium and with the iron ore resources they exploited at Wigpool Common, north-west of Mitcheldean. These are thought to have followed the approximate lines of the modern A4136 and A40 respectively, and although traces of Roman road have been recorded at Linton Farm, Highnam, none have been identified from the Mitcheldean and Longhope area.

This road may have continued westwards from Mitcheldean towards Drybrook, and also further west to the Wye at Lower Lydbrook, through English Bicknor to link with another Roman Road at Staunton. Although Roman settlements in the northern Forest would have been linked, the projected course of this road is based largely on references to 'Traces of Roman paving' on early Ordnance Survey maps (for example at Ruardean; OS 1878–1891) (Hart 1967, 36) and no Roman road along this course has been verified by modern excavation.

The other road probably built by the Roman army in the early years of the conquest runs southwards from Newnham to Caerwent northwest of Caldicot, South Wales (Margary 60a; 1957, 55–6). This road may have commenced at Newnham where a ford across the Severn at low tide (passable until 1802) connected it to the Roman road at Arlingham and then to the road between *Abonae* at Sea Mills, Bristol and Gloucester (Margary 1957, 55). To the south of Newnham it more or less follows the course of the modern A48 until Bledisloe about 2.5km to the south, where it follows a straight line to the east of the modern road, crossing Stretfield Hill, a 'street' place name, probably referring to the Roman road. Its course through Blakeney is not clear, although it probably followed a direct route over Old Hill, Nibley to rejoin the modern road at Old Street House (another 'street' place name) just over a kilometre to the south. Southwest of Lydney it runs slightly to the north-west of the modern road where lidar has identified a slight holloway and linear ridge, before rejoining the modern road at Wyvern Farm. It then continues through Stroat (also a 'street' place name) until just beyond Tidenham from where it veers westwards across fields to cross the Wye at the site of Striguil Bridge north of Chepstow Castle. Ormerod recorded 'a rude pavement in sinking foundations' in this area (Ormerod 1861, 8) and its route can be traced by cropmarks and lidar.

Whether this road continued northwards from Newnham, perhaps following the line of the modern A48 (Catchpole *et al* 2007, fig 1) is unknown. 'Traces of Roman paving' are marked on (OS 1884) in places along this route, but this does not necessarily mean that the road is actually Roman.

Another road often considered to be Roman is the Dean Road that runs north–south from Lydney to Mitcheldean and links the two Roman roads that skirt the northern and southern borders of the Forest, although its status and date remain controversial.

Where exposed (Walters 1985b; Hoyle 2017a, 2) this road is generally about 2.5m wide with a visible surface of roughly laid sandstone blocks between near vertical sandstone kerb stones. An excavation in 1985 identified a small ditch running parallel to one side (a corresponding ditch on the other may have been destroyed)

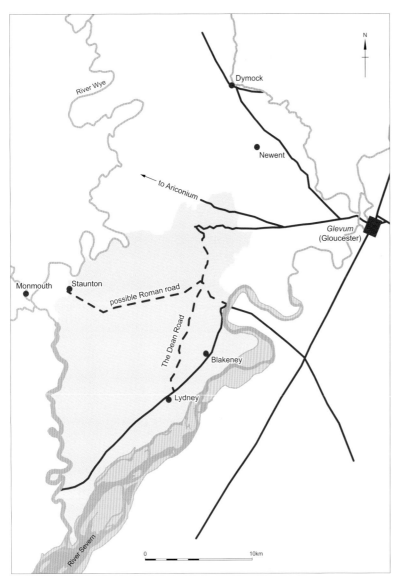

the Roman period (Trotter 1936, 5, plan 1), although he found no evidence that it was Roman (Hart 1967, 38). This interpretation was accepted by Margary (1955, 64) (although his preferred course diverged slightly from Trotter's, and he pointed out that, at about 2.5m wide, it was narrow by Roman standards) and also in more recent histories (McWhirr 1981, 131; Sindrey 1990; Walters 1992a; 1992b).

No excavations of Roman roads close to Ariconium have, however, found examples with a paved and kerbed construction like the Dean Road's (Bridgewater 1959), and Bridgewater (1968, 3) argued that the road had none of the characteristics of a Roman road but was typical of a metalled pre-turnpike road.

Roads are extremely difficult to date from their construction alone, but the Dean Road is not typical of a Roman road, particularly one built by the Roman army. Known Roman roads were generally between 4m and 24m wide, and at 2.55m the Dean Road is relatively narrow. Its paved surface is unusual (but not unknown) for Britain (although its actual surface may be missing) and it lacks the heavy camber of a 'typical' Roman road. It may also lack side ditches (although again this is not absolutely clear) and also shows no sign of the successive phases of resurfacing that are a typical feature of Roman roads, which were used for several hundred years (English Heritage 1989b, 2–4).

None of this is definitive proof that the Dean Road is not Roman but a radiocarbon date from a sample of a charcoal layer 'completely sealed' below the road surface to the south of Soudley (Walters 1985b, 5) produced a date that was not earlier than 1660, suggesting that, in this area at least, the metalled road surface is post-medieval at the earliest (Standing 1988, 37–41).

Standing (1988, 38–9) has pointed out that the road respects post-Roman features such as churches and, unlike many Roman roads, was not used as an early parish or bailiwick boundary. It was not mapped as a single continuous entity on the earliest large-scale map of the Forest (Taylor 1777) and it cannot definitely be linked to medieval references to the *Via Regia* (literally the 'king's highway'). There is documentary evidence for the cost of 'stoning' and 'filling' roads in a document dating between 1680 and 1720 and the Dean Road (or at least sections of it) may have been built, perhaps by the government, to serve increased post-medieval timber and coal traffic and anticipated naval timber production following the Dean Forest

Fig 4.39
Roman roads in the Forest of Dean and vicinity

(Walters 1985b, 5, 8), but ditches have not been recorded in other areas (Hoyle 2017a; Trotter 1936). The road surface at Soudley was a single layer of stones about 20cm thick (Walters 1985b, 5), while another to the south of Oldcroft was similar but may have overlain a layer of smaller stones below a clay sub-base (Hoyle 2017a, 2).

The earliest published account refers to it only as 'ancient' (Nicholls 1858, 198), but it has been known locally as 'the Roman road' since at least the 19th century (Standing 1988, 35), and this date was largely accepted by historians at that time (Codrington 1905, 360; PCNFC 1914; Witts 1880). Its course between Lydney and Mitcheldean was established by Trotter in 1936, who also suggested it had been built to transport iron ore between Lydney and Ariconium during

4.40
The Dean Road at Blackpool Bridge to the south of Soudley, looking south.
[© Gloucestershire County Council. Photo Steve Dorey]

Reafforestation Act of 1668 (Standing 1988, 39–43).

More recently Walters has cast doubt on the reliability of the radiocarbon date, suggesting that the sample was not securely sealed and cites a 4th-century AD coin hoard possibly in a boundary wall that ran parallel to and 'only 12m to the east' of the road alignment near Oldcroft as 'conclusive evidence' of its Roman date (M Walters 1991b, 9; B Walters 1992a, 68), and it is possible that there was a Roman road along this route. The balance of probability, however, combined with what little evidence does exist, suggests that the road in its current form at least may be considerably later.

Minor Roman roads

There are numerous examples of 'traces of Roman paving' on 1st Series 25" scale Ordnance Survey maps (*see* for example OS 1878–91; 1884), although most of these were interpreted as Roman by John Bellows, a 19th-century antiquarian and cartographer, who advised the Ordnance Survey. These should be treated with considerable caution as Bellows boasted that he had identified 'every carriage road but two in the Forest of Dean' as Roman on the same basis (Standing 1988, 35) and these probably represent the remains of extensive road repairs carried out in the 19th century (Codrington 1905, 286).

There may have been a Roman road between Newnham and Monmouth, passing through Littledean, Cinderford Bridge, Broadwell and Staunton, but much of the evidence for this is 'traces of Roman pavement' (Hart 1967, 38–40), and a reported terrace at Staunton. Short stretches of putative Roman road have been identified at Lydney Park Temple (Witts 1880, 34), between Tidenham and Stroat, and at Boughspring Roman villa (Bridgewater 1973, 8), and also along the edge of the Severn from Warrens Wood to Naas House east of Lydney (Scott-Garrett and Harris 1932, 7), but the actual evidence for these is also largely circumstantial. Stone paving and kerbing have been recorded at Silver Street, Mitcheldean (Hart 1967, 33–4), although as with the Dean Road (*see* p 78) this does not necessarily mean the road is Roman. Test pits over the course of the Dean Road to the south of Oldcroft in late 2016 identified two adjacent metalled surfaces (one kerbed, the other not) in some areas, although the relationship between these was not established and no dating evidence was found (Hoyle 2017a; Phil Riches pers comm).

During the Roman period the Forest of Dean would have had a network of roads and tracks as variable as that which exists today, and some of these roads or references to metalling may be Roman in origin. As with the major roads above, however, conclusive dating evidence is extremely elusive and much more work would be needed to clarify the Roman road system in the Forest.

River traffic

The Rivers Severn and Wye are also likely to have been important communication routes during the Roman period, although the evidence for this is limited.

A river crossing between Newnham and Arlingham, on the Severn's eastern bank, is implicit in Margary's route for the Roman road from Newnham to Caerwent (*see* p 77). In the Roman period a ford probably followed a shelf of rock that was connected to the shore by a firm bed of sand and was passable at low tide. This was used by pedestrians and vehicles until 1802 when the sand bed was washed away (Elrington 1972a, 29; O'Neil 1946–7–8, 420). Newnham and Arlingham also had a ferry link by the 14th century AD (Elrington 1972a, 29) and the Romans may have had a similar arrangement.

Medieval ferries crossed the Severn between Beachley and Aust, Sedbury and Sheperdine near Oldbury on Severn (Herbert 1972a, 54, 57), Rodley and Framilode (Elrington 1972b, 157) and also at Purton (Herbert 1996e, 51). The earliest dates for these are difficult to establish but these routes (or similar ones) may have been used during the Roman period. The River Wye was probably crossed by a bridge just north of the later site of Chepstow Castle, where a medieval bridge (Striguil Bridge) was recorded and where timbers are still visible at low tide. Ferries may have operated in other places, although apart from the crossing at Waterscross north of Lydbrook (Jurica 1996a, 232) few known ferries are thought to be early.

Rivers would also have been used as routes and the villas at the Chesters, Woolaston and Park Farm, Aylburton (where a possible wharf was recorded) almost certainly used the Severn to transport goods out of the Forest, and other settlements (for example Blakeney and Lydney) may also have had links to the river. There may have been navigation beacons at the Chesters, Woolaston (Scott-Garrett and Harris 1938), Park Farm, Aylburton (Fitchett 1986) and possibly also at Sedbury Park (Ormerod 1861), although this has not been proved.

5

The medieval period

Early post-Roman: 5th and 6th centuries AD

Very little is known about the Forest of Dean during the period immediately following the withdrawal of the Roman army in AD 410 and before the establishment of Anglo-Saxon rule sometime between the 6th and 8th centuries AD, and any picture of this period draws on (the generally limited) evidence from other areas augmented by clues from the Forest itself.

Britain is generally thought to have left the Roman empire in AD 410 when the Emperor Honorius issued a letter informing British cities that they could no longer rely on the Roman Army to defend them against Anglo-Saxon incursions (Frere 1978, 410), although if this letter ever existed it may have been addressed to the province of Brettania in southern Italy rather than Britain (Copeland 2011, 175). It is not certain what actually happened in AD 410, but Britain had severed links with Rome on two previous occasions in the preceding 30 years (Heighway 1987, 2) and the events of 410 may have just been an incident in the gradual loosening of political links between Britain and the Roman empire rather than a catastrophic turning point in British civilisation. By 410 'almost all effective forces had long ago gone to Italy or Gaul' to defend core parts of the empire against barbarian incursions, and the circulation of new coinage had been declining since the late 4th century (Frere 1978, 409, 414). No new coins were issued after about 402, and the resultant cash flow problem may have caused the collapse of some key pottery industries (Copeland 2011, 17). Some villas in the Gloucestershire Cotswolds seem to have been declining since the latter part of the 4th century (Copeland 2011, 176–8) although for others this may have been a period of relative prosperity (Heighway 1987, 1–2) and the decline of towns appears to have begun before this time. By AD 410 the forum in Gloucester may have been largely dismantled and a number of buildings were being used for industrial rather than domestic purposes (Copeland 2011, 176). Parts of late 4th-century Cirencester appear to have had a rural rather than urban character with demolished buildings replaced by 'dark earth' (Holbrook 1994, 75–6) suggesting cultivation or at least a lack of urban hard surfaces.

The lack of datable coins or pottery makes this a particularly difficult period for archaeologists to unravel, especially when it is remembered that both could have been used for decades. Evidence for 'decline' can also have other interpretations. Reuse of derelict sections of villas, demolition of public buildings or industry and cultivation in urban areas may be changes in function or fashion rather than indicators of an impoverished society, and the British may have continued living in a Roman manner and thought of themselves as part of the Roman world, for a generation or more after 410. By the end of the 5th century, however, things certainly seem to have changed and many villas had fallen out of use or reverted to 'peasant' farmsteads (Heighway 1987, 5). The major towns still held some position as both Gloucester and Cirencester were recorded in 557, and both seem to have been occupied in some way at this time (Copeland 2011, 176). Precisely what form this took is open to question and it is not known if they still functioned as administrative centres, or towns as we would understand them.

Some hillforts in western Britain seem to have been reoccupied and refortified during the early post-Roman period with examples known at Cadbury Congresbury, South Cadbury and Ham Hill in Somerset, Castle Ditches, Whitsbury in Hampshire and Cleeve Hill in Gloucestershire. Post-Roman finds are also known from Maiden Castle and Hod Hill in Dorset and Old Sarum, Wiltshire and post-Roman reoccupation may be far more widespread than the excavated evidence currently suggests (Corney and

Payne 2007, 142–3). Precisely what this reoccupation meant is not fully understood, and not every case is necessarily an example of the same thing. Some (for example South Cadbury, Somerset [Alcock 1972]) may have been strongholds of sub-Roman British warlords, although others may have just been settled as relatively safe havens during troubled times.

The barbarian incursions threatening post-Roman Britain were seaborne, with raiders from Ireland to the west and north Germany, Denmark and northern Holland to the east. The Severn Estuary would have been an ideal route for these groups to gain access to the heart of the west of Britain and both Lydney Park and Welshbury hillforts would have been in strong strategic positions to identify and respond to any threats from that direction. The hillforts at Lancaut and Symonds Yat overlooking the River Wye would also have been in a commanding position to guard against incursions from that route.

There is no known evidence for post-Roman refortification at Lancaut or Symonds Yat but at Welshbury 'haphazardly placed' rubble recorded on top of some of the ramparts might be evidence for this (McOmish and Smith 1996, 61) although without further excavation this can only be surmised.

At Lydney Park the Wheelers suggested that the hillfort was refortified sometime in the 5th century as their excavations had indicated that the inner rampart had been enlarged with material containing residual detritus from demolished buildings (including a number of *tesserae*) along with pottery and coins dating to the later 4th century AD (Wheeler and Wheeler 1932, 6–9). They assumed this must have taken place after the temple complex had fallen out of use, partly because 'the roughly piled earthen rampart' could 'have no place' in the ordered Roman temple complex and must belong to a 'period of recrudescent barbarism after the beginning of the 5th century' (Wheeler and Wheeler 1932, 64). A trench excavated through the eastern rampart in the early 1980s found a similar sequence but the pottery could only be broadly dated to between the mid-3rd and later 4th centuries AD, and the excavators suggested that the rampart may have been rebuilt during mid-4th-century refurbishment of the temple rather than after it had fallen out of use (Casey and Hoffman 1999, 100, 114). In fact the only post-Roman find from the site is an unusual 'Gothic' brooch, with Romanised decoration and workmanship, which the Wheelers considered to date to the 'latter part of the 5th cen-

tury' (Wheeler and Wheeler 1932, 79–81, fig 15) although their report does not make it clear where this brooch was found or even if it was found during their excavations in the 1920s. The material culture of the immediate post-Roman period is, however, notoriously difficult to identify (Casey and Hoffman 1999, 115) and even a single find could be significant. There may have been post-Roman activity at Lydney but what form this took is unknown, and there is no particular reason to think the hillfort defences were strengthened as a temporary base for a post-Roman cavalry force (Walters 1992a, 118) or to protect the temple from raiders as the rule of law began to break down (Hart 1967, 43).

Other evidence for settlement in the Dean during this early post-Roman period is equally tantalising.

Excavations at the Chesters villa, Woolaston found a hearth in the broken floor of one of the villa's former domestic rooms which, although undated, was interpreted as post-Roman squatters in the former villa building (Scott-Garrett and Harris 1938, 99). A similar hearth was found at Huntsham villa, Herefordshire, although again this was undated (Taylor 1995, 236). Two undated burials found in the 'ruined remains' of Boughspring Roman villa probably date to sometime after the 5th century AD, after the villa had fallen out of use (Pullinger 1990, 19). These have parallels with post-Roman burials at some villa sites to the east of the Severn (eg Frocester and Barnsley Park), interpreted as evidence that official burial sites had ceased to function and people were now being buried close to their farms (Heighway 1987, 3). It is not clear if this is the case at Boughspring, but people seem to have been making use of the decaying villa in some way.

It is tempting to think of these as evidence of impoverished post-Roman peasant farmers living in the ruins of the old villas and eking out what Mortimer Wheeler called 'a sort of second-hand existence' among the ruins of former grandeur (Wheeler and Wheeler 1932, 65). We should, however, be cautious of assuming that the reuse of apparently ruinous structures necessarily indicates a society in decline or the collapse of any form of social order.

The only other find which may date to this period is a Roman altar from Closeturf Farm, St Briavels Common which appears to have been reused as a grave marker sometime in the 5th to 9th centuries, although this is not associated with any known settlement evidence (p 107).

Fig 5.1
Fifth-century 'Gothic' brooch from Lydney Park. [From Wheeler and Wheeler 1932, 80, fig 15, Society of Antiquaries]

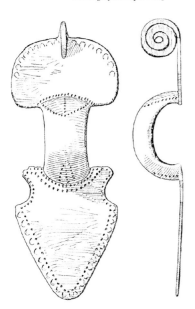

The arrival of the Anglo-Saxons

Precisely when Germanic people known as the Anglo-Saxons first arrived in the Forest of Dean area is unknown but the Anglo-Saxon Chronicle records that three British kings (Conmail, Condidan and Farinmail) were defeated and killed at the battle of Dyrham in AD 577 by the West Saxons who also captured three of their cities: Bath, Cirencester and Gloucester. The Anglo-Saxon Chronicle is not necessarily reliable history for these early periods but this record does suggest that the West Saxons had begun to take control of the Severn Valley by the later 6th century (Heighway 1987, 18–19). It is not clear if groups of ethnic Angles, Saxons or some other Germanic group moved into the area or if this was an elite extending their political influence and assimilating the local population into their dominant culture, although reality may be somewhere between these two positions.

In the Severn Valley, the Cotswolds and the Upper Thames Valley to the east of the Forest there is an increasing amount of evidence for the early Anglo-Saxons consisting of pre-Christian cemeteries or evidence for distinctive buildings such as timber halls or sunken featured buildings. Early Anglo-Saxon settlement has been found at Bishops Cleeve, Cheltenham and Uckington on the eastern side of the Severn Valley (Lovell *et al* 2007, 104; Sheldon *et al* 2010, 4; Williams 2011, 9), although none has been found in the Forest of Dean, or west of the Severn in Gloucestershire.

There are, however, signs of Saxon cultural influence and early settlement is a distinct possibility. Early Saxon finds include an early 7th-century coin from Newent to the north of the Forest, and spearheads of pagan Saxon style from Tutshill, Tidenham (Hart 1967, 49) and at Mork to the west of St Briavels (Webb 1997a, 15; 1997b, 291). Evidence for 7th- to 9th-century iron smelting has also been found at Clearwell Quarry, Newland (Pine *et al* 2009), although there was no evidence for a contemporary settlement.

There are also a number of placenames which suggest early Saxon or contemporary settlement (Hooke 2009, 31–50).

Placenames suffixed 'ton', derived from the Saxon *tun*, may not have gained common usage until after about 730, although the name is thought to indicate a small Saxon farming community occupied by an extended family (Hooke 2009, 45). Seven *tun* placenames (Alvington, Alverston near Lydney, Purton in Awre, Staunton, Woolaston, Whippington near Staunton and Poulton) were first recorded in the Domesday Survey of 1086 (although Allaston, a manor in Bledisloe hundred, was recorded, but not named) (Moore 1982, 37.5; 1987, 121–2). Another three, Bishton (now Bishton Farm), Kingston (now Sedbury) and Middleton (Beachley) all in Tidenham parish, were recorded in a late Saxon charter (Grundy 1935–6, 244–5), although Buttington (also in Tidenham) is probably not the Buttington where a battle between the Mercians and the Danes was fought in 893 (Heighway 1987, 43; Fox 1955, 90) and was not recorded until the 14th century (Smith 1964a, 264).

Most of the recognised *tun* placenames are in the south-western part of the Forest close to the

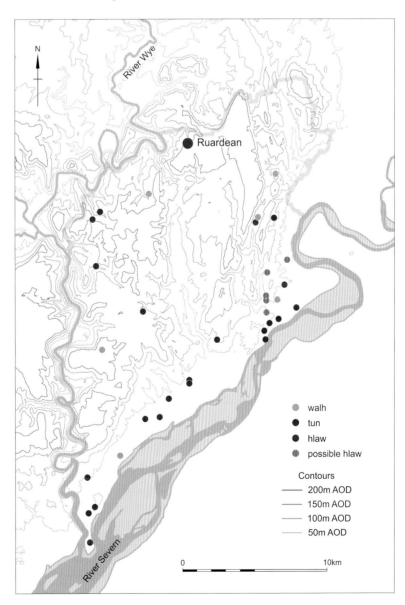

Fig 5.2
Tun, hlaw and walh placenames suggesting settlement in the early Saxon period. There may also have been an early Saxon settlement near Ruardean as the name (first recorded as Rwirdin in 1086) is probably derived from the Welsh rhiw, meaning hill and a Mercian Saxon word worthign meaning an enclosure (Smith 1964a, 241).

northern shore of the Severn Estuary. To the north of the Forest *tun* placenames are also found in the Leadon Valley, either close to the River Leadon or a tributary of it (Hooke 2009, fig 11) suggesting that the Saxons settled near the rivers they used during their early incursions into the area. Many settlements with a *tun* placename are also close to former Roman roads which probably still survived as important thoroughfares at this time.

Staunton and Welinton in the western part of the Forest look towards the river Wye which may also have been a route for early Saxon settlers, although neither name was recorded before the 12th or 13th centuries (Smith 1964a, 237, 247). Welinton, the original name for Newland (Herbert 1996g, 195) is over 1.5km from the river but is close to the Valley Brook which joins the Wye at Lower Redbrook. Staunton is over 2km from the river and on much higher ground, but is close to the Roman road which leads through the Forest towards Monmouth.

Only one *tun* placename, Noxon, first recorded as Noxton in 1317 (Smith 1964a, 237), is close to the central Forest between Clearwell and Bream, although this is not far from the River Lyd which joins the Severn at Lydney.

An intriguing group of placenames contain the element *loe* or some derivative of it, and are derived from the Old English *hlaw* meaning a mound or tumulus (Smith 1964b, 139). In the north of England this frequently indicates natural hills, although in the south it tends to denote artificial mounds (Gelling 1997, 134–7), often associated with the meeting places of hundreds, early Saxon burial mounds or earlier mounds reused at this time (Heighway 1987, 25), or Roman roads (Hooke 2009, 41).

Smith (1964a and b) lists a number of *hlaw* placenames in the Forest or its vicinity. Botloe Hundred, which includes the towns of Newent and Dymock, is about 7km to the north of the Forest and Baglaw (the modern Bagley Farm, also a *hlaw* name) about 5km to the east at Westbury on Severn. A cluster of these names is also found in, or close to, Awre, a low-lying headland within a bend in the River Severn and nearly all within 1km of the Roman road through the parish. Hagloe, Bledisloe (or Blidesloe) and Etloe are all farms or settlements; Dodloe is recorded in the Awre tithe map (Gwatkin 1995b), and Mutloes on the Newnham tithe map about 3km to the north of the parish boundary (Gwatkin 1992b). A number of other placenames in Awre (Broadlow Field, Pillows

Field, Lowfield Orchard and Lullo Pit) and also Bullo just north of the parish boundary in Newnham and Bollow in Westbury on Severn may also be *hlaw* placenames, but this is less clear and these names could have other derivations. Hart (1967, 49) also records Barrow How close to Etloe which may also have been a *hlaw* placename, although it is not clear precisely where this was.

This placename has been used to suggest an early Saxon presence in the Severn Valley in Worcestershire and Herefordshire (Hooke 2009, 43) and this unusual concentration around Awre is suggestive of early Saxon burials and possibly settlement on the Awre headland. Apart from these names, however, there are no other indications of early Saxon settlement at Awre. A number of 'barrow' or 'tump' placenames (Great Barrows, Little Barrows, Barrows, Great Berry Field and Tump Orchard) are close to *hlaw* placenames and two are associated with small mounds, but none have been excavated. Bledisloe Tump, immediately south of Bledisloe Farm, was partially excavated in the 1960s but was probably built in the late 12th century (Dornier 1966, 61–3).

In Awre there is an early 17th-century reference to a Walles Hill (Smith 1964b, 255), which may have been near fields called Upper and Lower Wallis Mead to the east of Blakeney (Gwatkin 1995b). The name probably derives from the Old English *walh* (Smith 1964a, 18) meaning a serf or Welshman (Smith 1964b, 183) and may have denoted people who spoke a Celtic rather than Germanic language (Gelling 1997, 93). These would have been regarded as British, as opposed to Anglo-Saxon (Heighway 1987, 35) and they may have been settlements of ethnically British people at a time when the two different cultural groups were living side by side. Other *walh* placenames (identified in Smith 1964a and b) include Welshbury hillfort, Blaisdon (Walesbury in about 1275) which may support the possibility of early post-Roman reoccupation of the hillfort site (*see* p 82), while Walson or Walston (le Walestone meaning Welshman's/Serf's/Briton's Farmstead in about 1275) near the possible enclosure at Coldharbour, St Briavels (*see* p 28, Fig 3.19) may indicate a similar situation. Other Walstons are at Newnham (Walleston in 1419), English Bicknor (le Walestone in about 1275) and Tidenham (Waleston), although the precise location of these is no longer clear and they may be later medieval references to Welshmen (Smith 1964b, 27). Walmore Common in Westbury, immediately north of the Forest of Dean (Walemor in 1221) is also a *walh* placename. These may have originated in the 7th or 8th centuries (Hooke 2009, 39), although none are recorded before the later Middle Ages and these should not be uncritically accepted as evidence for British settlements. Most are, however, close to the Rivers Severn or Wye, the main routes Saxon settlers may have used to approach the Forest, and it is tempting to see these as a reflection of settlement patterns during early contact between Saxon colonists and the native population.

By the early 7th century AD, much of what is now Gloucestershire was part of the Anglo-Saxon world (Heighway 1987, 20) and within the kingdom of the Hwicce, a sub kingdom of Mercia which covered much of the English Midlands (Heighway 1987, 35). The Forest of Dean was not ruled by the Hwicce (Hooke 2009, 13) and its northern part appears to have been within the kingdom of the Magonsaetan (also a subkingdom of Mercia) whose territory included much of Herefordshire and South Shropshire.

In the 7th and early 8th centuries, parts of the southern part of the Forest may have been under Welsh control, although the evidence for this is a single grant of land in about 703 when a Welsh king Morgan ap Athrwys granted the church of *Istrat Hafren* to the Welsh Bishopric of Llandaff along with an *uncia* of land between *Podum Ceuid* and the sea (Herbert 1972a, 73). *Istrat Hafren* is probably Beachley, Tidenham (Clammer and Underwood 2014, 8) and *Podum Ceuid* has been identified with the Lancaut peninsula, also in Tidenham (Smith 1964a, 26), although it is not clear if this grant included all of the land between Lancaut and the Severn Estuary or a much smaller area.

Between 757 and 796 Mercia, the largest and most powerful of the Anglo-Saxon kingdoms was ruled by Offa, who extended Mercian control over neighbouring kingdoms. Although Mercia's precise western boundaries are still unclear, most of the Forest seems to have been under Mercian control by this time.

Later Saxon settlement

Nearly all the evidence for pre-Norman settlement in the Forest is found in the Domesday Survey of 1086, which was commissioned by William the Conqueror to make a record of the value of his newly acquired kingdom 20 years after the conquest.

A handful of places in the Forest were recorded by name before the Norman Conquest of 1066 and although Domesday records names which are now towns, villages or hamlets, it was primarily a record of taxable property (generally manors) rather than a comprehensive list of settlement, and smaller properties could be subsumed within larger holdings and not recorded by name (Hey 1996, 136). Domesday records the value of manors in 1066 (at the time of the Norman Conquest) and 1086, but does not tell if people were living in recognisable villages, hamlets or dispersed farmsteads or small groups of cottages scattered throughout the manor.

In what is now the Forest of Dean the Domesday Survey records 29 places although a number of these, such as Staunton, Ruardean, Whippington

Fig 5.3
Places recorded by 1086.
Pre-Domesday records are
Wyegate (Uuiggangeat) in
972, Tidenham
(Dyddanhame) in 956,
Lancaut (Lann Ceuid)
around 700, and Lydney
(Lideneg) in about 853
(Smith 1964a). Bishton
(Bispetun now Bishton
Farm), Kingston (Cingestun
now Sedbury) and
Middleton (Middletun now
Beachley) were recorded in
a late Saxon charter
(Grundy 1935–6, 244–5).

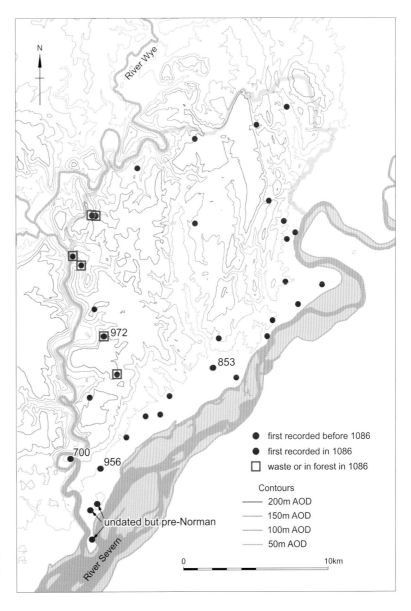

and Alvington, were in Herefordshire at that time (Moore 1987, 121–2). One placename (Dene) has been interpreted as both Littledean (Smith 1964a, 225) and Mitcheldean (Moore 1982, 167c) and may represent two settlements which had tenurial links at that time (Jurica 1996b, 173). Many are along the northern shore of the Severn, reflecting the distribution of early Saxon placenames (*see* pp 83–4, Fig 5.2) although many more Domesday manors are found on the higher ground at the edge of the Wye Valley.

Later medieval settlement

The establishment of the Norman Forest between 1066 and 1086 does not seem to have had a major impact on the Forest's settlement pattern. The area outside the Royal Demesne remained inhabited and farmed, although the inhabitants would have been subject to separate courts and taxation systems under Forest Law (Herbert 1996k, 295).

Only the Royal Demesne within the wider Forest (an area roughly correlating with the modern Statutory Forest [Herbert 1996a, 285]) was set aside for game and this area was probably a late Saxon royal hunting ground and already devoid of permanent habitation before the Norman Conquest. The Domesday Survey records that Whippington, Lower Redbrook (*Brocote*) and Staunton with Upper Redbrook (which are part of the same manor) 'were waste and are still in the King's Wood' or 'they are waste and were waste' (Moore 1982, E3, E4, E6; Moore 1987, 121–2), suggesting that they were already waste and had presumably been depopulated before 1066 (Herbert 1996d, 272; Jurica 1996c, 101). Hewelsfield and Wyegate to the north of St Briavels were, however, recorded as depopulated and placed in the Forest 'by order of the King' between 1066 and 1086 (Moore 1982), suggesting the Royal Demesne was extended following the Norman Conquest (Herbert 1996j, 354) although this process may already have been underway by the time the Normans took over.

Most places recorded in 1089 are now recognised settlements of some sort, although they have probably changed beyond recognition since 1086. Some have become small towns such as Lydney, Mitcheldean and St Briavels, while others such as Madgetts on the northern part of Tidenham Chase, Bledisloe in Awre parish and Stears near Newnham are now isolated

farms. Only two, Newarne and Whippington (*see* p 87), are no longer linked with any sort of settlement.

Many other settlements were first recorded later in the medieval period, although most had probably existed in some form before they are first mentioned. Some medieval settlements were founded after the Norman Conquest.

Staunton and Hewelsfield, which had no recorded population in 1086, were resettled by the mid-12th century when churches were built at both sites (Herbert 1996c, 150; 1996d, 272) and a Norman motte constructed at Hewelsfield. Wyegate, which also had no population and was 'in the forest' in 1086, was returned to cultivation by 1338 (Herbert 1996g, 209), although it was not necessarily established as a settlement. Newland was created by asserting into the western side of the Royal Demesne and had its own church in the early 13th century. Newland (*Nova Terra*) was recorded as Welinton in 1220 and as 'the new land of Welinton in 1232 and 1247 (Herbert 1996g, 195). Welinton is a *tun* placename, generally associated with Saxon settlement (Smith 1964a, 237; Hooke 2009, 45) and this may represent the recolonisation of an earlier settlement (Welinton) which like Staunton had been abandoned before the Norman Conquest.

Fig 5.4
Boundaries south of Bishton Farm, Tidenham visible as lidar images and cropmarks (shown red). Very little is known about the medieval settlement, although there were nine tenants in 1584 and an open field in the late 16th/ early 17th century (Herbert 1972a, 39).

There is little evidence for medieval settlements which are now completely deserted, although a number are now much reduced and only represented by a few houses or an isolated farmhouse.

Two completely deserted settlements are Newarne and Whippington both of which were mentioned in the Domesday Survey of 1086.

Newarne (recorded as *Niwar* in 1086) is the only place Domesday records within the Royal Demesne. The name means 'New House' (Smith 1964a, 218) and the manor contained 2.5 hides (300 acres) before 1086, although its site is currently unknown. There is a suggestion based on the 1282 perambulation of Forest bounds that it was to the south or south-west of Cinderford (Smith 1964a, 218–19) although it has also been placed near the Speech House in the central Forest between Cinderford and Coleford (Moore 1982, map of North-west Gloucestershire Ha: 4, E2). More recently a site about 1km to the north of Speech House in the triangle formed by the Cannop Brook (parts of which were called Newarne Brook in the 17th century) and one of its tributaries has been suggested (Hart with Clissold 2000, 17–18).

Whippington is the only other place mentioned in Domesday with no modern equivalent. It was already waste by 1066 and the site of the manor or any associated settlement has never been discovered, although the name survives as a road junction (Whippington Corner) to the south of Staunton and as the stream (Whippington Brook) which separates the parishes of Staunton and English Bicknor (Hart with Clissold 2000, 27).

Bishton, Tidenham was also a pre-Norman settlement recorded as *Bispetun* in a late Saxon Charter (Grundy 1935–6, 244–5), but was not mentioned in Domesday, presumably as it was within the manor to Tidenham. Sherds of 12th-to 14th-century pottery have been found at the site (Ellis 1984, 204) and it survived as a settlement into the early 18th century with 16 families recorded in 1710 (Herbert 1972a, 59), but all that remains now is a small group of houses on Bishton Lane in an area recorded as Old Bishton in 1845 (Gwatkin 1995a), Bishton Farm and a number of relict boundaries to the south of Bishton Farm.

Placenames which include the suffix 'gate' may have been access points through Offa's Dyke (Gelling 1983; Wood 1900–1 to April 1902) and places with these names may have been settlements which originated when the Dyke was in use from the late 8th century.

Madgetts (recorded as *Modiete* in 1086) may have been a settlement immediately west of Madgetts Farm, Tidenham. Evidence for iron working (bloomery slag and a large cupstone containing iron) has been found although the only datable medieval find is a silver penny of King Edmund who ruled from 939 to 946 (Portable Antiquities Scheme database: GLO-D7E0AE). By 1086 Madgetts included fisheries on the Wye but only one villager and a plough were recorded (Moore 1982, 164b, 167d) suggesting that any settlement was in decline at that time.

Another possible settlement site with a gate placename is Wyegate (*Wigheiete* in 1086 and *Uuiggangeat* in 972 (Ekwall 1960; Smith 1964a, 244), presumed to be around Wyegate Green

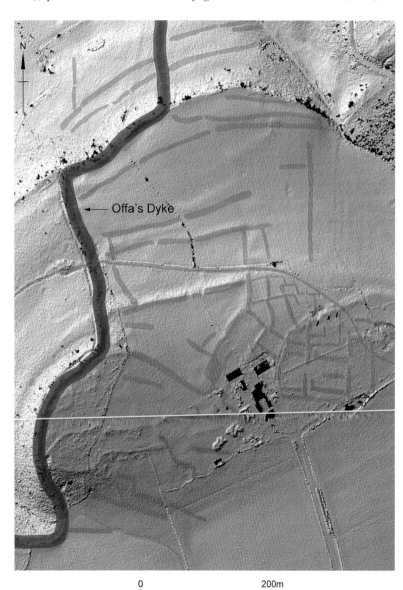

Fig 5.5
Earthworks and cropmarks (shown red) of linear boundaries and small enclosures at Madgetts, Tidenham. Madgetts may have been a pre-Norman settlement sheltering behind Offa's Dyke although some boundaries predate the Dyke and the settlement may be within a prehistoric enclosure (Hoyle and Vallender 1997, 68; Hoyle 2008, 47; Small and Stoertz 2006, 34–6).

N

← Offa's Dyke

0   200m

Fig 5.6 (below)
Linear and right-angled boundaries visible as cropmarks (shown red) and lidar in the Wyegate Green area may be remains of fields, or enclosures associated with the pre-Norman manor, although these could relate to cultivation recorded in the 14th century.

Fig 5.7 (below riight)
Settlement remains at Lancaut identified by lidar, cropmarks (shown red) and field survey. Outside the settlement there are earthworks, cropmarks and evidence for ridge and furrow where an open field was recorded in 1549 (Herbert 1972a, 69).

just under 2km to the north-west of St Briavels. In 1066 the manor was worth 60 shillings, but in 1086 is referred to in the past tense, had no recorded villagers or plough teams and had been included in the forest 'by the kings order' leaving only a fishery worth 10 shillings (Moore 1982, 166d).

Staunton was recorded as *Stantonesgate* around 1300 (Gelling 1983, 12) but only as Stanton in 1086 at which time it was 'waste and in the Kings Wood' (Moore 1982, E4), although the suffix *tun* suggests early Saxon settlement. No surviving sections of Offa's Dyke are known near Staunton but it is close to the modern county boundary, which may roughly correspond to the border of Offa's Mercia (Stenton 1998, 201) and straddles the probable Roman road to Monmouth. Staunton may have been an access point through the Mercian frontier although it is not clear if the '*gate*' suffix, which

was not recorded before about 1300, refers to this or not.

Lancaut, which was recorded as *Podum Ceuid* about 703 (Smith 1964a, 263), may have been founded as an early Welsh monastic settlement (*poda*) dedicated to the 6th-century Celtic saint St Cewydd (Parry 1990, 55). Lancaut is not mentioned in the Domesday Survey (Moore 1982) and, although it may have been included in the manor of Tidenham at that time, there need not have been continuous settlement on the peninsula from the 8th century, or a secular settlement in 1086 (Parry 1990, 55). The present church was largely rebuilt in the late 12th or early 13th centuries (Parry 1990, 90–2), but there is no evidence for a church before the early 12th century (Parry 1990, 55) and the secular settlement may have originated around then. Lancaut had 10 tenants in 1306 and 19 communicants in 1551 but by 1750 the settlement had

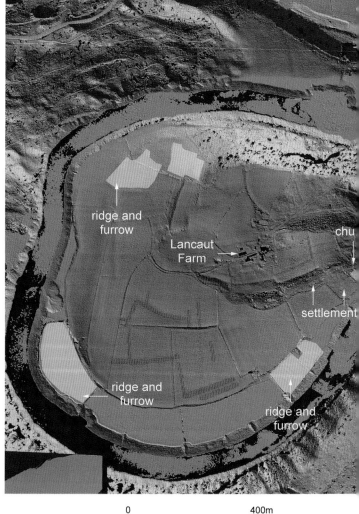

site of former
mansion house

Highmeadow
Farm

0   200m

Medieval military and defence

Early medieval: Offa's Dyke

Offa's Dyke, the longest linear earthwork in Great Britain, runs through the English and Welsh borders from Treuddyn, near Mold in North Wales, to Sedbury on the Severn Estuary in Gloucestershire. It is not a continuous earthwork but is made up of a number of lengths separated by gaps of up to about 23km, the longest of which separates the northernmost section in the Forest at Lydbrook with the section which runs northwards from Bridge Sollers, west of Hereford.

Within the Forest the Dyke is a linear earthwork generally on high ground overlooking the Wye Valley between Lydbrook and Sedbury. Although this is a distance of over 30km, only about 15.2km of earthwork survives in five discrete sections, each of which contains a number of smaller gaps. Sections of the Dyke were recorded in the 19th century (Fosbroke 1831, 1832; Ormerod 1841; Maclean 1893–4) and in 1931 Sir Cyril Fox concluded his major survey of Offa's Dyke with the Forest section (Fox 1955). The Forest section was included in research undertaken by Frank Noble (Gelling 1983) and in 1995 and 1996 Gloucestershire County Archaeology Service's survey recorded management issues and also attempted to identify and characterise the visible monument (Hoyle and Vallender 1997).

There has, however, been very little field investigation of the Dyke. In 1931 a small excavation at Tallard's Marsh, Sedbury, where a small earthwork at the western end of the Dyke overlooks the River Wye, found evidence for a ditch and an undated iron lance head (Fox 1955, 204). There have also been a handful of small-scale watching briefs or excavations (Catchpole 1993a; Ellis 1979; Hill 1996a), and some sections through the bank and ditch have been recorded (Hoyle 1996b; Lewis 1963; Rhodes 1965; Wills 1986).

Was it built by Offa?

Offa ruled Mercia from 757 to 769 and during his reign extended Mercia's borders to extend from Bath to London in the south, London to the Wash in the East, the Humber to the Mersey in the north and along more or less the modern boundary between England and Wales as far as the Severn Estuary in the West (Stenton 1998, 201). The Dyke is generally thought to have

Fig 5.8
Settlement remains at Highmeadow, identified by lidar and as cropmarks (shown red). The village may have been cleared when the owners built a mansion in about 1680.

declined and only two houses were inhabited (Herbert 1972a, 60). The earliest settlement was probably about 40m to the west of the church, where geophysical survey suggests stony banks and burnt debris (Bartlett 1994) and where the earthwork remains of house plots and yards, and the remains of stone walls have been recorded (Iles 2017, 1). Geophysical survey may also have found evidence for landscaping or features in the area between the former settlement and the church although the interpretation of these is not clear (Roseveare 2018b, 3). Lidar and aerial photographs have also identified earthworks and cropmarks of linear boundaries on the higher ground around Lancaut Farm about 170m to the north-west.

The hamlet of Highmeadow between Coleford and Newland is now also largely deserted, but existed by the early 13th century and at least 14 families lived there by the mid-16th century. A number of houses were demolished when the Hall family built a mansion in about 1680 and the remainder, if not deliberately cleared at that time, fell into decline (Herbert 1996d, 275). The mansion itself was demolished early in the 19th century and only a single farmhouse is now occupied. The remains of boundaries and enclosures still survive as earthworks and cropmarks on the site, although some of these may date to the Civil War when Highmeadow Farm was a Royalist garrison (Gaunt 1987, 58).

been built late in his reign, around 784 (Macinnes 1986), to consolidate Mercia's western frontier, but its association with Offa stems from an almost throw-away reference to him as 'he who had the great rampart made from sea to sea between Britain and Mercia' in Bishop Asser's *Life of King Alfred* written about 893.

Parts of the monument were considered to be Offa's Dyke from an early date. There is a 14th-century reference to the earthwork at Lindors Farm as '*Offedich*' (Herbert 1996f, 249), and sections in Tidenham and Newland were referred to as Offa's Dyke by 1712 (Atkyns 1712, 722, 573). This does not necessarily mean it was

built by Offa in the 8th century and the Offan date for the Forest section has frequently been questioned. In 1841 Ormerod discussed whether the Forest sections were Offa's Dyke, and although he concluded they were, he suggested that some sections might have followed or reused earlier earthworks. He also refuted a view held by Sir Richard Colt Hoare (among others) that the Sedbury section was a Civil War defence by quoting the deeds to his own house which described this earthwork as the 'fforce ditch' in 1638 (Ormerod 1841, 17). In 1877 Sir John Bellows was probably referring to the Iron Age ramparts at Symond's Yat and Lancaut hillforts when he suggested that parts of the Dyke at least were 'on the tract of far more ancient encampments' (Bellows 1877), while Playne (1876) suggested that the southern section across the Sedbury Peninsular had not been built by Offa. M'Kenny Hughes (1892) argued that some sections were Roman and also suggested that earthworks of different date may have been linked together to form a single boundary, a possibility suggested in more recent studies (Hoyle 1996a). More recently Hill and Worthington (2003) have argued that none of the Forest earthworks are part of Offa's frontier earthwork.

Ray and Bapty have examined the form and structure of Offa's Dyke and its position in the landscape along its entire length between North Wales and Sedbury. They highlight parallels between the Forest of Dean sections and other parts of the Dyke to the north and make a compelling argument that when viewed as a whole Offa's Dyke can be interpreted as a single monument built in accordance with a coherent concept of design and purpose and that the Forest of Dean sections, even though physically detached from the Dyke to the north are an integral part of this scheme (Ray and Bapty 2016, 336, 371).

The limited available evidence combined with the historical records of Offa's power, aspirations and relations with his Welsh neighbours is consistent with the Dyke being constructed by Offa sometime in the later 8th century AD (Ray and Bapty 2016, 22). The earthwork, however, remains undated, although some limited dating evidence has been found in excavations to the north of the Forest.

A radiocarbon date from a hearth below Wat's Dyke near Oswestry, Shropshire (generally considered to be broadly contemporary with Offa's Dyke) produced a date around the mid-5th century AD (Hannaford 1999) showing it was post-Roman. Optically Stimulated Lumi-

Fig 5.9
Offa's Dyke in the Forest of Dean. Inset showing Offa's Dyke nationally.
[After Hoyle and Vallender 1997]

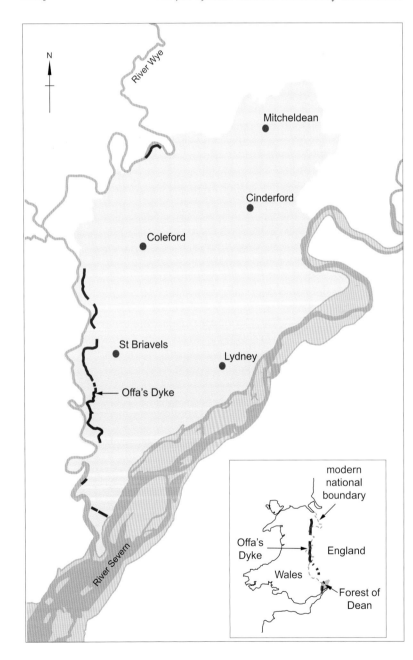

nescence dates from another section north of Oswestry suggested that Wat's Dyke was constructed around the mid-9th century AD (Hayes and Mallim 2008 cited in Ray and Bapty 2016, 20).

Offa's Dyke at Ffrith Village, Flintshire has also been shown to postdate the Roman period as it overlies a Roman settlement, although the date of the Dyke's construction was not established (Fox 1955, 40–1; Turner-Flynn *et al* 1995 cited in Ray and Bapty 2016, 19). Excavations of a section of Offa's Dyke at Chirk, Wrexham, however, produced four radiocarbon dates from samples of apparently undisturbed turf near the base of the bank (*Current Archaeology* 2014). These ranged from AD 430–643 to AD 887–1019 and the earlier dates are probably from earlier material which became incorporated in its construction and simply indicate that the earthwork was built after the Roman period. The later date (about 100 years or more after Offa's death) is more problematic and may suggest that the bank, at least in the Chirk area was built after Offa's reign, although further analysis of the significance of these dates is required before any definitive statements about the date of Offa's Dyke can be made (CPAT 2014).

Why was the Dyke built?

There has also been considerable debate about why Offa's Dyke was built and how it might have operated. Fox thought it had been built for 'visual control over enemy territory' and argued that the Forest sections did not demarcate the Mercian frontier, which was the River Wye (Fox 1955, 196). The Domesday Survey account of Chepstow mentions tolls from river traffic, a Saxon survey of Tidenham mentions 'Welsh shipmen' at Beachley (Gelling 1983, 3) and the Dyke terminates at the maximum tidal reach of the River Wye at Redbrook (Fox 1955, fig 94). Fox thought a frontier agreement allowed Welsh river boatmen access both to the river itself and to the Mercian bank, and the Dyke's position along the edge of the Wye Valley marked the limit of the free access zone within Mercian territory. Burn (1959) suggested that, in the Wye Valley at least, the Dyke was a last line of defence to the east of the actual border to which Mercian frontiersmen could retreat in times of trouble. Frank Noble, however, has argued that it was a patrolable line with a defensive function, which allowed visual control of the actual boundary (the River Wye) and channelled access across the frontier through specific access points. He also thought the massive construction and commanding position of some of the Forest sections represented a tangible 'show of strength against the kingdoms of Gwent and Glamorgan' (Gelling 1983).

A more recent survey has highlighted the sophistication of the Dyke which was faced in stone or turf, incorporated look-out posts and fortified watchtowers and was built in a way and sited in a position to create maximum visual impact when viewed from the west (Ray and Bapty 2016, 188, 247–50). Clearly it was more than a simple boundary marker and in the Forest dominated the actual boundary between Mercia and the Welsh Kingdoms (probably the River Wye). Its commanding position along the sky line overlooking the Wye Valley would have been an impressive demonstration of the power of Offa's Mercia and his ability to control the western borders of his territory, clearly visible from the Welsh kingdoms to the west.

The Dyke was probably not built for a single purpose and could have simultaneously fulfilled a number of roles (Ray and Bapty 2016, 363). In the Forest of Dean it would have affirmed Offa's claim to relatively newly acquired territory (Gelling 1983, 1; Keynes 2005 cited in Ray and Bapty 2016, 363) and would also have been a practical way of controlling access across the frontier, which could be channelled through designated entrances and monitored. It may also have been built in response to direct threats to Offa's borders or as part of a long-term strategy for Mercian domination of the Welsh Kingdoms to the west. Practical considerations need not have been the only reason, and an aging Offa may have wanted to impress neighbouring rulers and build a lasting memorial to his own power, perhaps by emulating 'great works' of antiquity such as Hadrian's Wall (Ray and Bapty 2016, 363; Wood 1981, 96).

Although Offa's Dyke is mentioned in numerous annals from the 12th century or later, it is not referred to by name in earlier charters. The significance of this is not clear, but could imply that despite the enormous resources and organisation expended in its construction, its political and strategic significance may have been relatively short-lived (Ray and Bapty 2016, 23).

Offa's Dyke in the Forest of Dean

There appears to be considerable variation in the present form and size of the Dyke in the Forest of Dean. In places it survives only as a terrace, but it more commonly consists of a bank with a

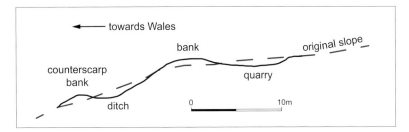

ditch, terrace or counterscarp bank on its outer side and often with shallow quarry scoops on its inner side. The height of the terrace or bank ranges from a few centimetres to more than three metres and the depth (or presence) of ditches or quarries is also extremely variable.

To the north and south of St Briavels Common, and in the detached northern section between Lydbrook and English Bicknor, it is 'sensitive to the relief of the countryside' (Fox 1955, 119) and takes a meandering route generally closely following the break in slope at the edge of the Wye Valley overlooking steep slopes to its west, but overlooked by more gently sloping higher ground to its east. In this area the bank often has a relatively low inner face (often 1.5m or less) with a much higher outer face (3m or more) where the builders have used the natural topography and artificially steepened the slope of the valley side (Hoyle and Vallender 1997, 21–4). At its outer face there is generally a ditch, either with or without a counterscarp, or sometimes just a step. The remains of quarries follow its inner side as a series of shallow interconnected hollows, or sometimes just a continuous hollow.

Fig 5.10 (top)
Typical profile of Offa's Dyke overlooking the Wye Valley showing principal components.
[After Hoyle and Vallender 1997]

Fig 5.11 (above)
Outer face of Offa's Dyke overlooking the Wye Valley.
[© Gloucestershire County Council Archaeology Service]

Fig 5.12 (right)
Inner side of Offa's Dyke overlooking the Wye Valley.
[© Gloucestershire County Council Archaeology Service]

Where the Dyke crosses St Briavels Common the topography is much less dramatic. From north to south the Dyke takes a more or less straight course up the slope from the lower ground around Lindors Farm, west of St Briavels before taking a sharp turn to the west to follow the edge of the Wye Valley with steeper ground on its outer side and overlooked by gentler slopes on its inner side. It then turns to the south to cross the common following a much less dramatic break in the slope with slightly higher ground to its east. Where the common begins to slope down towards the Brockweir Brook the Dyke follows a slightly sinuous route down the relatively gentle slope towards the bottom of the valley at Brockweir before taking a more or less straight route up the much steeper valley opposite to resume its position on higher ground just north of Madgetts Farm, Tidenham. Throughout this stretch the topography is considerably less dramatic and there is much less disparity between its inner and outer faces, although where it overlooks steeper ground its outer face is consistently higher than its inner. The visible remains of associated features such as quarries or an outer ditch are less common in this area, although these can be discerned in places suggesting that they were originally present (Hoyle and Vallender 1997, 223–43; Hoyle 1996a, 30).

Where it crosses the Sedbury Peninsula in the southern part of the Forest, the Dyke takes a direct route across generally fairly level ground

between the slight eminence of Tallard's Marsh overlooking the Wye with the high ground of Sedbury Cliffs overlooking the Severn. To the east of Buttington Tump it survives as a bank which is higher on its southern (outer) face where it overlooks slightly lower ground. There is a clear ditch on its outer side, and the remains of quarries are discernible on its inner side. West of Buttington Tump, where it runs through modern housing development, it survives only as a terrace as landscaping associated with house construction or earlier cultivation has cause soil to accumulate against the bank's inner face. This has also obscured visible signs of quarry pits, and evidence for a ditch or other earthworks on its outer side has been removed by recent road construction (Hoyle and Vallender 1997, 223–43; Hoyle 1996b).

Numerous suggestions have been made to explain differences in the Dyke's appearance in different areas. Fox argued that this was influenced by geology and land use and the Dyke took different forms if it was built in open farmland or woodland (Fox 1955, 218–19). Other suggestions are that these reflect the work of different gangs of builders (Hill 1985), the Dyke fulfilled different functions in different places (Gelling 1983) or discrete earthworks of different dates may have been incorporated into a single frontier system (Hoyle 1996a). More recently Ray and Bapty (2016, 174) have pointed out that these apparent differences need not indicate different gangs or construction

towards Wales

bank

quarry?

Fig 5.13
Offa's Dyke crossing
St Briavels Common.
[© Gloucestershire County
Council Archaeology
Service]

dates, but are actually the product of a consistent approach to Dyke construction in differing topographies and geologies which the builders encountered.

The Dyke in the Forest of Dean is actually a remarkably consistent earthwork. Its basic components (bank, inner quarry, outer ditch) are either present or are likely to have been destroyed, and it is consistent in the way it responds to the landscape. Where it is built on a slope it always uses the natural topography and is higher on its outer face. Where it follows more level ground, goes up or down a slope or crosses a valley, the height of its inner and outer faces generally evens out, even when it does this for only a short section such as where it crosses narrow valleys (Hoyle and Vallender 1997, 24–5).

How the Dyke was constructed and what it originally looked like is not always clear. A section through the bank at Lippets Grove, west of Madgetts Farm, Tidenham, suggested it was constructed as a simple dump of clay and rubble (Gelling 1983; Rhodes 1965), typical of the type of construction recorded in other areas (Ray and Bapty 2016, 188). No evidence for external revetting or internal walling was recorded in this section, although the remains of what appears to be laid stonework have been recorded on the bank's outer face in some areas between Madgetts Farm and Lancaut and also on St Briavels Common and in the Lydbrook area (Hoyle and Vallender 1997, 48–9).

This has also been recorded on sections of the Dyke north of the Forest (Ray and Bapty 2016, fig 5.16) suggesting that in these places it was faced with stone to present a vertical or near vertical wall-like appearance. Where the Dyke follows the steep slopes of the Wye Valley this effect may have been enhanced by exposing bedrock below the bank's face and evidence for this has been recorded north of Devil's Pulpit and also to the south of Redbrook (Hoyle and Vallender 1997, 49). Where suitable stone was not readily available the Dyke may also have been faced. A section through Buttington Tump, where the Dyke crosses the Sedbury peninsula, recorded steep tip lines angled away from its outer face as if originally dumped against a revetment which has since been lost (Lewis 1963, fig 1). Turf was used as both revetting and for internal stabilisation of the Dyke's bank at Chirk in Clywd and Forden in Powys (Hill 1977, 221). The bank at Buttington Tump may also have been faced with turf (Hoyle and Vallender 1997, 49) and turf may have been used in other areas (Ray and Bapty 2016, 188).

Where the Dyke has been investigated to the north of the Forest larger stones may have been deliberately placed against the rear of the bank to contain its dumped construction (Ray and Bapty 2016, 188). Evidence for this has been noted where the Dyke overlooks the Wye to the south of Devil's Pulpit and also possibly where it crosses the Sedbury Peninsula (Hoyle and Vallender 1997, 49–50).

Ray and Bapty have identified what they refer to as 'adjusted segments' in some sections of Offa's Dyke which are slight variations in the orientation of short segments of bank which create an optical illusion enhancing the perceived scale of the earthworks when viewed from particular directions (Ray and Bapty 2016, 202–8). In the

Fig 5.14
Selected profiles across Offa's Dyke.
[After Hoyle and Vallender 1997]

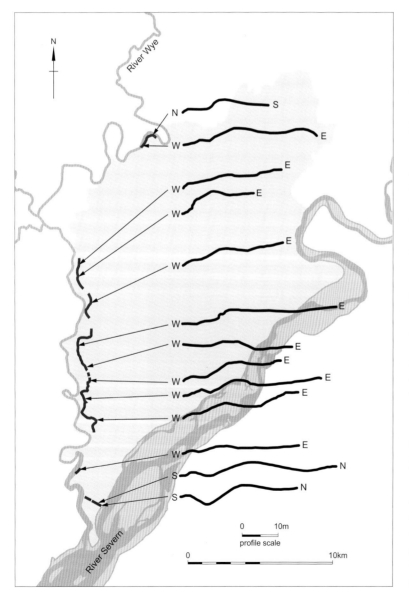

Fig 5.15
Exposed stone facing on
Offa's Dyke at Highbury to
the south of Redbrook.
[© Gloucestershire County
Council Archaeology
Service]

Forest this type of construction has been identified to the north and south of Devil's Pulpit where it overlooks the Wye (Ray and Bapty 2016, 206–8).

Features associated with Offa's Dyke

Apart from the bank and ditch there are also a number of features in the Forest of Dean which may have been an integral part of the frontier works.

A small elliptical enclosure (measuring about 40m × 75m) occupies a natural knoll at Tallard's Marsh. This overlooks the Wye at the western end of the section across the Sedbury Peninsula (Fox 1955, fig 90), and Ormerod interpreted it as a fortlet protecting a landing place from the Wye (Ormerod 1841). Its southern boundary was recorded as a natural cliff overlooking a drainage ditch, its eastern side appeared to be a natural rise, while its western side was bounded by the Wye. Fox excavated a ditch on its northern side and although he interpreted a layer of disturbed clay as the truncated remains of an internal bank, he thought the ditch was a natural hollow that had been cleaned out to act as a ditch, suggesting the site was essentially a natural eminence that had been modified to create a 'fortified spur' which he considered to be 'the only fort on the line of the Dyke which has any claims to be considered as a Mercian work and an integral part of the Offan frontier'. Apart from

a 19th-century coin in later deposits, the only find was an iron lance head from the ditch which could not be securely dated (Fox 1955, 204, figs 89 and 90). The bank and ditch on the northern side have now been destroyed by modern housing development (Hoyle and Vallender 1997, 77).

Buttington Tump is a discrete mound along the line of the Dyke where it crosses the Sedbury Peninsula. This has been recorded as a separate, and unusually high, section of the Dyke since at least 1824 (O'Neil and Grinsell 1960, 135), although its western part is now made up of redeposited material removed from the eastern side during road widening in 1960 (Lewis 1963). The *Butt* element in the name may signify an 'end' or a 'thicker end' (Ekwall 1960, 79), perhaps suggesting that the present mound is a remnant of an originally more pronounced portion of the Dyke. The road immediately to its east may have been an original entrance through the Dyke leading down to the early river crossing at Beachley and the mound could be a relic of an original entrance feature, perhaps the base of a watchtower guarding the entrance and overlooking the relatively gentle slope down to the Beachley Peninsula to the south (Hoyle and Vallender 1997, 37).

Other fortified watchtowers or lookout posts have been identified along Offa's Dyke to the north of the Forest (Ray and Bapty 2016, 249–50), and

Fig 5.16
Possible bastion/look out
post overlooking the Wye
Valley and the valley of the
Brockweir Brook where
Offa's Dyke changes course
to the north-west of
Madgetts Farm, Tidenham.

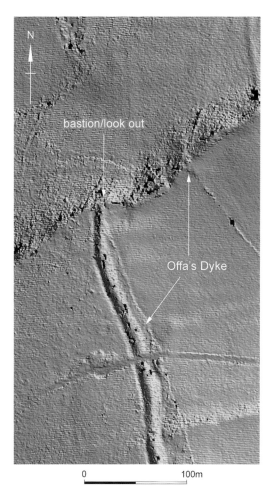

Fig 5.16
Possible bastion/look out
post overlooking the Wye
Valley and the valley of the
Brockweir Brook where
Offa's Dyke changes course
to the north-west of
Madgetts Farm, Tidenham.

a distinct 'bastion' projecting from the Dyke where it overlooks the Wye at Madgetts Farm may have served a similar purpose (Ray and Bapty 2016, 251, fig 6.16).

Fox thought Llanymynech Iron Age hillfort, Shropshire had been used as part of Offa's Dyke (Fox 1955, 202) and Hill has suggested that Old Oswestry hillfort in Shropshire and other hillforts may have been used as access points (Hill 1977).

In the Forest the earthworks of Lancaut Hillfort across the neck of the Lancaut Peninsula are marked as 'Offa's Dyke' on Ordnance Survey maps dating from 1881 to 1921 (OS 1881–6, 1902b, 1921b). The hillfort defences are not connected to surviving sections of the Dyke (although these may have been destroyed by quarrying [Hoyle and Vallender 1997, 56–7]) and face in the 'wrong' direction with no apparent signs of modification. These could, however, have been incorporated into the Dyke (Gelling 1983; Fox 1955; Hoyle and Vallender 1997, 57), perhaps acting as a defended access point leading towards the Wye through the hillfort's

original entrance (Hill 1977). Other earthworks at Madgetts Farm, Tidenham and at Highbury to the north of Coxbury Farm, Newnham (*see* pp 27–8, Figs 3.13, 3.19) may also have been incorporated into the Dyke, although the status of these earthworks is less clear.

Access points through Offa's Dyke

Buttington Tump and Lancaut Hillfort may have acted as access points through the Dyke, although Madgetts and Wyegate (*see* pp 87–8, Fig 5.17), both of which are names containing the element 'gate', may also have been associated with routes through the Dyke (Hoyle and Vallender 1997, 71–6). Wyegate Hill overlooks the road which crosses Offa's Dyke at Mork and leads to the River Wye at Bigsweir, while Madgetts is close to an early route which leads to the Wye at Brockweir, both of which may have been early river crossings. Other gate placenames may also have been on early access routes through the Mercian frontier in areas where there are no known sections of Offa's Dyke. The Iron Age hillfort at Symonds Yat (Hoyle and Vallender 1997, 71) may be on an early route which crossed the Wye to the north and Staunton (recorded as *Stantonsgate* around 1300; Gelling 1983, 12) is on the line of the Roman road which would have crossed the Wye leading to Monmouth. The Roman road which crossed the Wye north of Chepstow would also have been an early access point through the Dyke, although there is no place name associated with this (Hoyle and Vallender 1997, fig 11a).

Gaps in Offa's Dyke

Offa's Dyke in the Forest of Dean is not recognised as a continuous earthwork. A short section, just over 2km long, runs from Lydbrook to the north of English Bicknor, after which there is a gap of about 8.5km before it starts again just south of Redbrook. From here it runs more or less continuously until about 0.5km north of the Lancaut peninsula where it peters out in an area of disused quarries. Another short stretch about 350m long runs from just south of Lancaut to the Roman road which crossed the Wye just north of Chepstow Castle. After another gap of about 2km, where steep cliffs overlook the Wye opposite Chepstow, the final section crosses the Sedbury Peninsula between Tallard's Marsh (overlooking the Wye) and Sedbury Cliffs (overlooking the Severn).

There is evidence to suggest that the Dyke was originally continuous between Redbrook and the area just north of Chepstow and that gaps in this stretch are the result of more recent destruction either through cultivation at Lindors Farm (Hoyle and Vallender 1997, 58) or quarrying to the north and south of Lancaut and to the south of Coxbury Farm, Newland (Hoyle and Vallender 1997, fig 12 A–C).

Quarrying or landslip may also have destroyed some sections of the Dyke between English Bicknor and Symonds Yat, and possibly also to the west of Symonds Yat, although this is less certain (Hoyle and Vallender 1997, 61–2).

The absence of a visible earthwork between the area just north of Chepstow and Tallard's Marsh is less easy to explain. A substantial terrace (the Elm Villa lynchet) between the recognised Dyke and the 19th-century bridge across the Wye east of Chepstow Castle may be a remnant of the monument (Gelling 1983, 2) and cliffs above the Wye to the east of this may have rendered further defences unnecessary (Fox 1955, 196). An alternative explanation is to suggest a Mercian bridgehead on the site of Chepstow controlling the lower Wye at its lowest bridgeable point (Gelling 1983, 2).

The large gap between Redbrook and English Bicknor is perhaps the most intriguing. It is possible that surviving remains of the Dyke have yet to be discovered in this area, although other possibilities have been suggested. The present national boundary between England and Wales approximately corresponds to the boundary between Mercia and the Kingdom of *Ergyng*, the modern Archenfield (Gelling 1983, map 4), although the precise status of this area in the late 8th century is unclear. The area was originally controlled by the kings of Gwent, but grants from them ceased in the early part of Offa's reign at which time it may have fallen out of Welsh hands (Gelling 1983, 10–11). If it was under Mercian control, perhaps as a subordinate 'buffer state', a frontier earthwork along its boundary may not have been needed.

The frontier may, however, have been marked by a timber fence or cleared ride (Gelling 1983, 12), although natural features may have been used as boundary markers. The Buck Stone and Suck Stone are two large natural blocks of Quartz Conglomerate Sandstone to the west and north of Staunton, and both very close to the modern national boundary. There is a considerable folkloric tradition attached to these stones (Wright 1980, 13–23, 32) suggesting they have been significant landscape features for some time.

Another prominent natural feature in this area is a ridge of upper Old Red Sandstone/Quartz Conglomerate, up to 4m high, which runs parallel to the modern national boundary (about 300m to the east of it) for a distance of just under 1km through Bunjups Wood about 1.5km to the south-west of Staunton. A similar ridge is also found close to the national boundary in Highmeadow Wood, just to the north of Staunton. Although there is no particular reason to suggest that these natural ridges were converted into frontier earthworks, they may have been significant enough to demarcate and influence the location of the Mercian boundary at this point (Hoyle and Vallender 1997, 60–1).

The Dyke may terminate immediately west of Lydbrook at the edge of the steep valley where

Fig 5.17
Offa's Dyke in Gloucestershire showing principal sites mentioned in the text.

the River Lyd meets the Wye. In the 19th century, however, Maclean found a section of earthwork he described as 'sufficiently distinct for identification' as part of Offa's Dyke in woodland overlooking the Wye to the west of Ruardean (TBGAS 1881–2; Maclean 1893–4). Fox dismissed these as weathering out of an unusually hard band of limestone (Fox 1955) and when this area was visited in 1995 these could have been a combination of linear dumps of quarry spoil and natural outcrops of limestone. They could be interpreted as a surviving portion of Offa's Dyke which had been seriously damaged by later quarrying, although further investigation would be needed to verify this. They appeared to terminate at the edge of a steep valley which forms the modern county boundary between Gloucestershire and Herefordshire (Hoyle and Vallender 1997, 64–5).

Norman fortifications

The Norman Conquest of 1066 saw a wholesale change in landownership as the Saxon landowning class was replaced by new Norman lords. There are a number of fortifications (ringworks and mottes) in the Forest of Dean which are thought to have been built in the first 100 years or so after 1066, although few have been dated with any certainty.

Some may have been built soon after the conquest as a practical way of controlling a newly conquered territory and as a tangible symbol of the power and presence of the new regime, although others may date to the civil war between the Empress Matilda and her cousin Stephen from 1135 to 1154, known as the Anarchy, when numerous 'adulterine' castles were constructed without royal consent (Leach 1988a, 5). Many of these 'adulterine' castles were demolished during the reign of Henry II between 1154 and 1189.

Ringworks

The Forest of Dean contains at least three ringworks (although some other earthworks may be ringworks) that are thought to be early Norman although only one has been dated by excavation and some late Saxon examples are known (Leach 1988a, 5).

The undated ringwork at Stowe, just under 2km north of St Briavels, is at the head of a small valley leading down towards the River Wye approximately 2.6km to the west. The ground to its south rises slightly and it is clearly sited to command views down the valley towards the river. Scott-Garrett excavated some trial holes at the site in 1947, although all he found was a layer of 'coal' and some undated bones (Scott-Garrett 1918–58, entries for 7 and 8 July 1947). A late 8th-/early 9th-century coin (recorded as of Boemeric or Britric, but possibly of Beorhtric, king of the West Saxons who died in 802) has been found at Stowe (Hart 1967, 49), although not from the ringwork itself. A spearhead, thought to be Saxon (Hart 1967, 49) but possibly later (Kurt Adams, Gloucestershire and Avon Finds Liaison Officer pers comm), and an axe head dating to the 12th to 14th centuries have been found at Brook Farm (Webb 1997a, 15; Webb 1997b, 291) about 800m to the west, although it is not known if these were associated with the ringwork in any way.

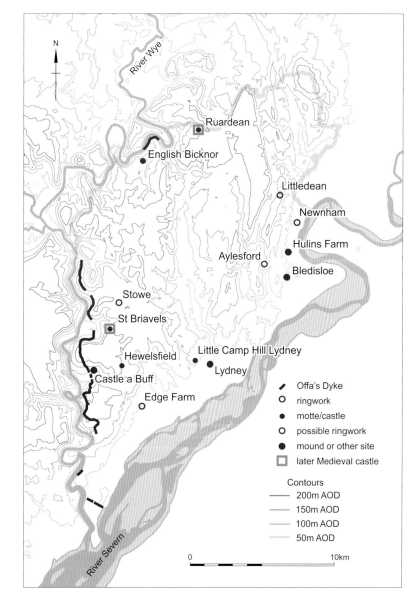

Fig 5.18
Medieval fortifications in the Forest of Dean.

The ringwork at Newnham is at the southern end of a ridge which forms the south-western boundary of the town and overlooks steep slopes to its south-west. Although not at the cliff edge this site commands views up and down the Severn in both directions and overlooks the river crossing between Arlingham and Newnham, and the Roman road south from Newnham. It is thought to have been partly excavated in the 19th century, although the results were never published and are now presumed lost.

Townley (2004, 114) has suggested that Stowe may be pre-Norman and possibly associated with an access point through Offa's Dyke, guarding the head of the valley to the south of Wyegate Hill (a 'gate' placename; see pp 87–8) which leads down through the Dyke to the river crossing at Bigsweir. The late 8th-/early 9th-century coin and possible Saxon spearhead from Stowe (but not from the ringwork itself) and Brook Farm, Mork (see p 98) may support this but no other Saxon finds are known from the area.

The Newnham ringwork may also be pre-Norman as it appears to have no particular relationship with the layout of the town (Townley 2004, 114–16) and was already known as the 'old castle' by the mid-12th century (Elrington 1972a, 30). This certainly suggests it was no longer acting as a fortification by then, but does not necessarily mean that it was built before the Norman Conquest (see Littledean Camp below).

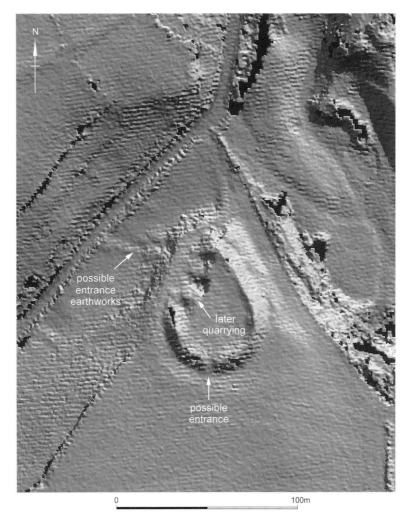

possible entrance earthworks

later quarrying

possible entrance

0   100m

Fig 5.19 (above) The ringwork at Stowe survives as irregular subcircular/oval bank (3.5m high in places) enclosing an area of about 35 × 50m. A gap in the southern side of the defences may have been an entrance, although parallel banks to its north may be part of an original entrance which has now been destroyed by quarrying (Townley 2004, 106, fig 36). No external ditch is visible, but there is a distinct step on its northern and eastern sides.

Fig 5.20 (left) Stowe ringwork, looking east. [© Gloucestershire County Council Archaeology Service]

Fig 5.21
Newnham ringwork looking east towards the River Severn.
[© Gloucestershire County Council Archaeology Service]

Fig 5.22
Ringwork at Newnham is roughly oval and encloses an area of about 36 × 25m. Its bank is less than 2m high on its inner face, although higher on its outer side. The linear bank running northwards along the edge of a natural ridge is thought to have been added during the English Civil War (Elrington 1972a, 30) when Newnham was a Royalist garrison (Atkin and Laughlin 1992, 25). [Hachures from Landmark digital copy of the 1973 1:2500 scale Ordnance Survey map. © database right Landmark Information Group Ltd. All rights reserved 2018]

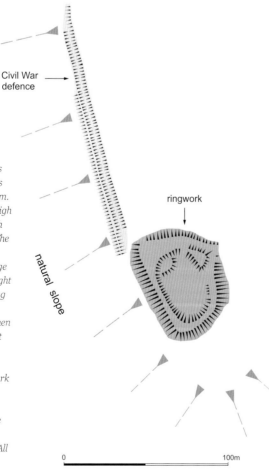

Civil War defence

natural slope

ringwork

0   100m

Unlike Stowe and Newnham, which are fairly large open subcircular areas enclosed by a bank, the ringwork at Littledean Camp is an almost perfect circle and its massive banks enclose a relatively small area. It is at the northern end of a long ridge with views in almost all directions and overlooks the road leading into the central Forest through Littledean and also the Severn Valley with views towards Gloucester and the Cotswolds.

In the 1950s Scott-Garrett excavated the site. In the interior he found a rough, pitched sandstone 'floor' and evidence for later charcoal burning, along with some nails and pottery dating to the first part of the 12th century. The bank was made of dumped rubble, and Scott-Garrett suggested that a levelled platform and an adjacent high point overlooking the entrance was the site of a watchtower (Scott-Garrett 1958).

Littledean has been identified as 'the Old Castle of Dean' mentioned in charters of Henry II (r 1154–89) and it was probably already 'old' and abandoned by the latter part of the 12th century. It was occupied during the early 12th century and served a role during the Anarchy of 1135 to 1154, but may have been constructed earlier.

There is another small ringwork on Cern Hill, Aylesford, west of Awre. This is in an extremely good defensive position on the summit of the hill in a bend of Soudley Brook at the end of a ridge on the eastern side of the Soudley Valley, but only has views along the valley as there is higher ground between the motte and the River Severn and the Roman road to its east. The slight remains of a small roughly circular earth bank are on a level area on the top of the hill. A slight rectangular terrace (encompassing about 25 × 17m) on the eastern side of the hill immediately below the ringwork may also have been part of its defences. It was surveyed in 1984 (RCHME 1984) but no excavation has ever been undertaken and its date or function is unknown, although it may have been a watchtower or similar monitoring the eastern approaches to the Forest along the Soudley Valley.

Motte and bailey castles

The other type of Norman fortification in the Forest is motte and bailey castles, where an earth mound within a defended enclosure would have been topped by a tower and a palisade wall, probably originally of timber, and sometimes replaced with stone (Leach 1988b, 6). Unlike ringworks, motte and bailey castles, with very few exceptions, were not introduced until after the Norman Conquest (Leach 1988b, 1).

The motte and bailey at English Bicknor is at the northern end of a shallow ridge commanding views to the south and over the Wye Valley to the north. It may have replaced an earlier castle at Castle Hill near Eastbach Court about 1km to the south-east (Walters 1992a, 143), although it is only about 500m to the south of Offa's Dyke, and Townley (2004, 118–19) has suggested that the Norman castle may have superseded a Saxon fortification on the same site. Maclean thought it was an adulterine castle built during the Anarchy and destroyed during the reign of Henry II, although the 'bailiwick and castle of Bicknoure' are mentioned in deeds in 1223 (Maclean 1879–80, 310–11) and there is a 14th-century reference to a residential property (a *capital messuage*) which may have been the 'Castle Hall' recorded near the church in the early 17th century (Jurica 1996c, 107). Neither of these, however, indicate that the castle was in any way operational after Henry II's reign, and it may just have been inhabited as a high-status residence.

If the original castle was built of timber it was certainly superseded by a masonry structure as a 'small room' constructed of 'Norman masonry' was recorded on the motte's north-western side in the late 19th century (Maclean 1879–80, 304). This structure was uncovered again in a recent watching brief (Craddock-Bennett 2015,

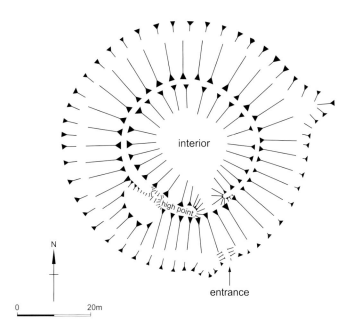

6–7, illus 4) and its position at the edge of the motte, along with its size (at least 6.6 × 4.6m with walls over 3m thick enclosing an area of only 2 × 1.8m), suggests it was the foundations of a gatehouse or tower. This may have been attached to a stone shell keep, a type of Norman castle where the top of the motte was enclosed by a circular or polygonal curtain wall which included towers and a gatehouse (Leach 1988c, 4–6, fig 1). The lidar, however, suggests a rectangular structure with further towers on its

Fig 5.23
Littledean Camp is almost perfectly circular and has a very large bank, over 3.5m high and 10.5m wide at its base. Its footprint encompasses an area of about 60 × 60m, but encloses an area of only about 20 × 16.5m. It has an external ditch between 1.5 and 2.5m deep and a narrow entrance on its southern side.
[After Scott-Garrett 1958, Transactions of the Bristol and Gloucestershire Archaeological Society]

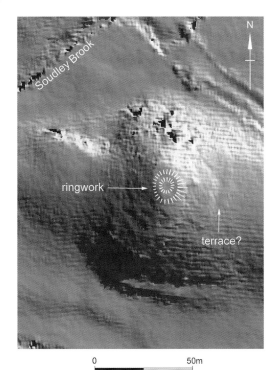

Fig 5.24
Ringwork at Aylesford. The earthwork covers 17.6 × 15.5m, although the bank is 6.5m wide and only encloses an area 4m in diameter. The bank is between 0.2m and 0.7m high and a slight lowering on its north-eastern side may be an entrance, although this is not clear (RCHME 1984).

Fig 5.25
English Bicknor Castle. The motte is up to 4m high and within a subrectangular inner bailey (59 × 59m) defined by a ditch with low traces of an inner bank. An outer bailey, which contains the 12th-century church, is defined by a bank with a ditch linked to a leat which may have supplied it with water.

Fig 5.26 (below)
Little Camp Hill, Lydney, looking south.
[© Gloucestershire County Council Archaeology Service]

Fig 5.27 (right)
Little Camp Hill, Lydney. Structural remains after Casey 1931.

eastern side and this may have been a type of castle known as a tower keep (Leach 1989) consisting of a substantial stone keep with additional towers projecting from its corners.

Another stone Norman castle was on the summit of Little Camp Hill, Lydney, to the south-west of the Iron Age hillfort and temple at Lydney Park, which commanded views overlooking the River Severn and also the former Roman road between Newnham and Chepstow.

This was excavated in the late 1920s exposing the remains of a large stone keep (measuring about 15 × 17m) in the north-eastern corner of a roughly diamond-shaped stone castle whose walls incorporated a gatehouse on its eastern side and another tower at its south-western corner. Immediately east of this a large ditch separated the castle from a D-shaped outer bailey, the northern part of which was defended by a bank and outer ditch, although these were absent on its southern side where the natural slope of the hill was steepest. Finds included a number of metal objects (keys, a pick, a lead plumb bob), part of a bird-bone whistle and 12th-century pottery, which led the excavator to suggest it had been built between 1100 and 1189, and probably during the Anarchy. An enormous amount of rubble over these remains did not seem to be the result of casual stone robbing, and the castle was probably deliberately demolished during the reign of Henry II (Casey 1931, 248–50).

There is another motte and bailey castle at Hewelsfield, near the 12th-century church and occupying a dominant position on high ground between the Severn and Wye, but there is no record of when it was built and no excavations have been undertaken. Although Hewelsfield was depopulated between 1066 and 1086 (*see* p 86; Moore 1982) it was reconstituted as a manor

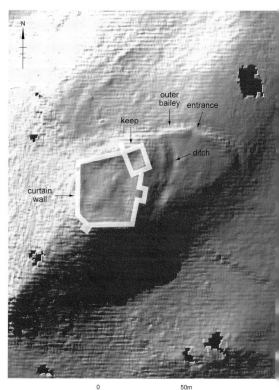

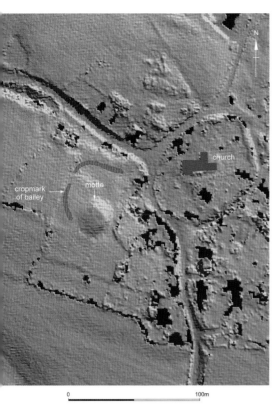

by the mid-12th century, at which time a church was recorded (Herbert 1996c, 150). The castle may have been constructed at that time, but could also have been an adulterine castle built during the Anarchy of 1135–54.

The small stone fortified manor at Ruardean may have been built on the site of an earlier 'earthen' castle (Hart 1967, 53), and St Briavels Castle also superseded an early motte and bailey castle (Herbert 1996f, 251, 257–8).

The castle at Ruardean was immediately north of the 12th-century church on a spur of land overlooking steep slopes to the north. St Briavels, which was also close to the 12th-century church and recorded as a royal castle in 1130 (Herbert 1996f, 255), commands views over the Wye Valley and towards the central Forest. There may originally have been a wooden tower at Bailey Tump west of the castle although this had been replaced by a stone keep (about 30m high) on a mound in the southern part of the later castle by the end of the 12th century (Salter 1998, 2–3). There are no definite remains of a bailey although this was probably the same area occupied by the curtain wall and moat of the 13th-century castle.

Fig 5.28 (left)
The motte at Hewelsfield is 24–27m wide at its base and about 3–3.5m high and was within a subcircular bailey (51m across) visible as a cropmark (shown red). Scattered possibly worked stones have been recorded on the motte and earthworks to its south may be structures or compounds associated with the castle.

Fig 5.29 (above)
Hewelsfield motte looking south.
[© Gloucestershire County Council Archaeology Service]

Fig 5.30
Ruardean Castle looking south-east. The later castle was on what may be an artificial mound, or enhancement of the natural bluff.
[© Gloucestershire County Council Archaeology Service]

Fig 5.31 (right)
Bledisloe Tump. The
mound, which was about
2m high and 18m in
diameter at its top, may
have been constructed as
early as the late 12th
century. Although it
replaced an earlier
watchtower it is not clear if
this was built as a motte
(Dornier 1966, 61–3).
[After Dornier 1966.
Transactions of the Bristol
and Gloucestershire
Archaeological Society]

Fig 5.32 (far right)
Possible motte at Hulins
Farm, Bullo. This mound is
very similar in size to the
Bledisloe mound and there
may be an artificially
raised area on its north-
eastern side (Townley
2004, 117, fig 39).
[After Townley 2004]

Fig 5.33 (below)
Undated mound north of
Lydney Tin plate works.
The mound is about 13 ×
20m, and about 1.75m high.
The tree growing on it is
130–50 years old (Standing
and Wills 1988, 62).
[© Gloucestershire County
Council Archaeology
Service]

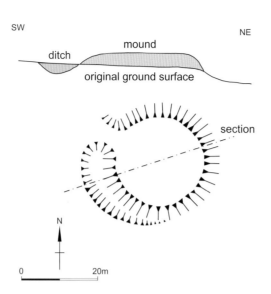

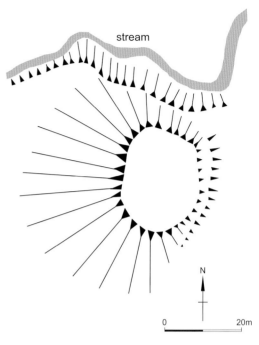

There may also have been a small Norman motte at Bledisloe Tump, Awre, where a mound on the edge of rising ground with views overlooking the Severn Valley to the north, east and south was partially excavated before it was levelled in the 1960s. Postholes below the mound were interpreted as the foundations of a timber watchtower which was burnt and demolished in the 12th century and may have been an adulterine castle destroyed by Henry II following the Anarchy. The mound was built soon afterwards, but as it was only partly surrounded by a ditch and there was no evidence for a tower it may never have been completed, or may have been built as the meeting place of the Bledisloe Hundred rather than as a motte (Dornier 1966, 61–3, plan 1). Evidence for a

14th-century building on top of the earlier mound was interpreted as a domestic dwelling belonging to Bledisloe Manor (Dornier 1966, 68–9).

Other possible mottes which could be watchtowers rather than castles include a small mound at Hulins Farm, Bullo overlooking a stream leading to Bullo Pill (Townley 2004, 117, fig 39), and a mound at Lydney which overlooks the River Severn and the former Roman road between Newnham and Chepstow. The status of neither site is known, although local legend has the Lydney mound as a burial mound following Civil War fighting around Whitecross Manor and it may also be a windmill mound (Standing and Wills 1988, 62).

There may also have been an early Norman fortification on Mill Hill, Brockweir, a rounded knoll overlooking the steep valley which leads up from the River Wye (Hart 1967). A farm at the foot of the hill was called 'Castle a Buff' and fields about 500m east of this were recorded as 'Baileys Hill Meadows' in 1841 (Gwatkin 1993a), but no conclusive evidence for a castle is known. The site is close to Offa's Dyke and the name (the origin of which is unknown) could relate to a Saxon fortification associated with the Mercian frontier.

With the exception of the castles at St Briavels and Ruardean (and possibly also English Bicknor), all the early Norman fortifications in the Forest appear to have fallen out of use by the end of Henry II's suppression of adulterine castles following the Anarchy of 1135 to 1154. What is not clear, however, is whether these were all adulterine castles established during the Anarchy or whether some of them were built earlier in the Norman period and had already been abandoned, or were perhaps refortified during that period.

The ringworks at Stowe and Newnham, which Townley (2004) has suggested may be pre-Norman, are also of interest, particularly as they are very different from the ringwork at Littledean, which has been shown to date to the Anarchy period, although further investigation of these sites is needed before clear conclusions can be drawn.

Later medieval castles

The only surviving later medieval castle in the Forest of Dean is St Briavels Castle which was the administrative centre of the Forest by the 13th century (Herbert 1996j, 355) and was a pivotal site in the manufacture and distribution of quarrels (cross bow bolt heads) from about 1241 (Webb 1992, 19–21). The Castle began to take its current form during the 13th century, enclosing the 12th-century keep and earlier motte within a curtain wall which included a large gatehouse and range of domestic buildings. Subsequent alterations, such as extending the castle to the south and raising the height of the gatehouse, were undertaken in the 14th century and at its height the triangular area of Bailey Tump to its west and possibly also a triangular area to its east (subsequently used for housing) may have been part of the castle grounds.

The manor house on the site of the Norman castle at Ruardean was also fortified during the later medieval period. In 1311 Alexander of Bicknor was granted a licence to crenellate his house (Herbert 1996i, 236) and the castle included a stone tower and domestic buildings surrounded by a stone wall (Hart 1967, 53). It was recorded as a square enclosed area with one (or possibly two) towers on a map of 1608, by which time it may already have been ruinous (Vallender 2002, 8, fig 3). Some sections probably remained standing in 1611, but the castle was demolished and extensively robbed by the early 19th century (Herbert 1996i, 236). Earth mounds on the site conceal collapsed masonry and probably intact footings, although only the ruined remains of part of the tower and a section of adjoining wall survive above ground.

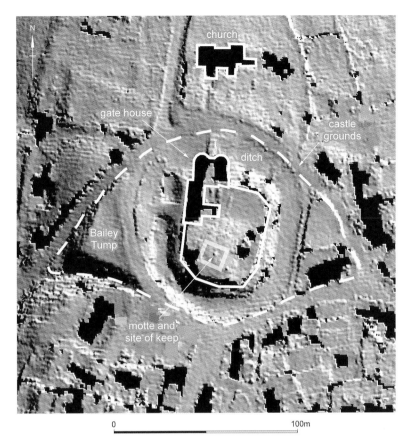

0   100m

Scott-Garrett undertook some excavation (unpublished) at the site and found evidence for part of a round tower and possibly two outer wards (Townley 2004, 119) and there are reports that the remains of a small chamber were uncovered by local treasure hunters in the 1930s (Herbert 1996i, 236).

Fig 5.34 (above)
St Briavels Castle.

Fig 5.35 (below)
St Briavels Castle. Late 13th-century gatehouse.
[© Gloucestershire County Council Archaeology Service]

*Fig 5.36
Ruardean Castle. The
remains of a tower, the
probable curtain wall and
rectangular outer ward are
clearly visible.*

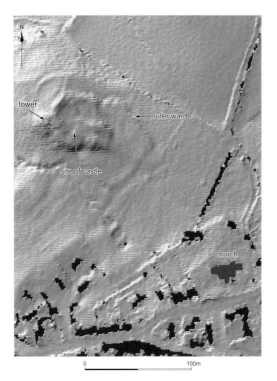

There may have been other later medieval fortifications in the Forest of Dean, but the evidence for these is much less clear.

Moseley Castle (*Moseleyscastel*) and Saintlow Castle (*Seynteleyscastel*), are mentioned in 1282 (Hart 1967, 56) and were probably in the Royal Demesne at Moseley Green to the east of Parkend and Saintlow Enclosure about 1.5km to the north. These may have been medieval fortifications set up to establish control of the Royal Demesne, although Hart (1967, 56) has suggested that the names Saintlow and Moseley are likely to indicate

areas of cleared woodland and these could have been watchtowers or other structures which guarded valuable Royal pasturelands.

Other possible fortifications include Naas Castle, mentioned in 1558, which may have been a small fortification at Naas Point. This would have overlooked Lydney Pill, east of Lydney, and the approach to the town from the River Severn (Herbert 1996e, 63) but no trace of a fortification has been found at this point (DAG 2000–2001, 2). Masonry remains of a square room or tower recorded at Woolaston before 1953 (Scott-Garrett and Harris 1932, 10–11) have not been precisely located, and may have been remains of a domestic building (Hart 1967, 56), while building foundations reported at Churchcroft, Blakeney in the 18th century (Rudge 1803, 118) may be the remains of a medieval chapel (DAG 2000–2001, 4).

Early medieval ritual and religion

The early Anglo-Saxons were not Christian and would have introduced new beliefs and practices to the area. The most tangible evidence for this is generally barrows or cemeteries, although none have been found in the Forest of Dean and there is no clear evidence for early medieval pagan ritual or religion. A concentration of *hlaw* placenames around Awre has been suggested as evidence for early Saxon burial mounds (*see* p 84, Fig 5.2), but no suitable mounds have been found.

Anglo-Saxon pagan beliefs seem to have had little impact on the populations in the areas which came under their control (Heighway 1987, 93) and pre-Saxon beliefs, one of which may have been Christianity, are likely to have survived well into the early Saxon period, particularly in areas in the western part of what is now England where substantial British populations survived (Hare and Heighway 2012, 6). The extent to which the British population were Christianised in the later Roman period is not clear, although the late Roman temple at Lydney Park suggests that non-Christian beliefs certainly survived in the Forest of Dean in the later Roman period.

There are suggestions for early post-Roman Christianity to the east of the Severn. There are legends of a 5th-century bishop (Aldate) at Gloucester, and possible (but not certain) 5th- to 6th-century Christian structures or burials

*Fig 5.37
Surviving stonework from
a tower at Ruardean
Castle.
[© Gloucestershire County
Council Archaeology
Service]*

below later churches at Gloucester and Frocester (Heighway 1987, 94). At this time Christianity would have been part of a western British Christian tradition (sometimes referred to as the 'Celtic Church') that was descended from late Roman British Christianity and had developed independently from the church in Rome, with its own liturgy and traditions (Hey 1996, 71; Salway 1993, 322). Evidence for this in the Forest is limited to a modified Roman altar from Closeturf Farm, St Briavels which has crudely carved irregular letters on each side. Some of these could represent NO NO leading to the suggestion that it was removed from the temple of Nodens at Lydney, about 4km to the east (Sindrey 1990, 22). Others could be deciphered as *fecit* and the altar was probably reused as a crude copy of a type of early Christian memorial stones known in south-east Wales from the 5th to the 9th centuries AD which have Latin inscriptions (Bryant 2012, 241–3). This find might suggest an early Christian burial site and possibly also a settlement close to where it was found (Townley 2004, 235), although there is no other evidence for this, and it is not clear if it was found anywhere near its original position.

Christianity was certainly present in the Tidenham area by the early 8th century when a Welsh king, Morgan ap Athrwys of Glywyssing, granted the church of *Istrat Hafren* (Beachley) and land at *Podum Ceuid* (Lancaut, where there was probably an early monastic settlement) to the Welsh Bishopric of Llandaff (Clammer and Underwood 2014, 8; Herbert 1972a, 73; Parry 1990, 55).

The small chapel or hermitage dedicated to St Twrog (St Tecychius, a 7th-century Welsh hermit) on a tidal island at Beachley Point, Tidenham may also have been established in the early medieval period. This was first recorded in 1290 (Herbert 1972a, 75), although masonry remains which appear to predate the 13th-century structure have been recorded at the site (Townley 2004, 242). Another hermitage dedicated to either St Margaret or St Briavels (another Celtic saint) may also have been established at Stowe, north of St Briavels, in the 7th century (Walters 1928, 136), although this was not recorded until 1220 (Herbert 1996f, 259) and its date of origin can no longer be established.

There may also have been early Christian churches at Woolaston and Hewelsfield where there are subcircular churchyards. In Cornwall and south-eastern Wales these are often taken as an indication of an early Christian foundation

(Owen 1897, 229–30; DoE 1988, 13, 118; Edwards and Lane 1992), possibly within a pre-Christian ritual monument (Child 2007, 28). The existing churches at both these sites, however, were built after the Norman Conquest and neither has produced any other evidence for an early Christian foundation or a pre-Norman church.

Fig 5.38 (left)
Roman altar from Closeturf Farm probably reused as an early medieval grave marker. The former base of this is now conical and its original capital appears to have been repurposed as its base (Johns 2005a, 39), the crude carvings on each side are mostly illegible, but seem to be approximate copies of letters produced by someone who was either illiterate or semi-literate. [© Carolyn Heighway and Mick Sharp]

Fig 5.39 (below)
Churchyards at Woolaston and Hewelsfield. The ovoid churchyard at Woolaston was originally a smaller irregular circle with the church in its centre. This influenced the boundaries of the gardens of almshouses formerly on its north-eastern edge. Churches at neither of these sites were recorded in the Domesday survey of 1086 (Moore 1982). [Mapped information from landmark digital copies of 1:2500 scale 1902–3 and 1973 Ordnance Survey maps. © database right Landmark Information Group Ltd. (All rights reserved 2018)]

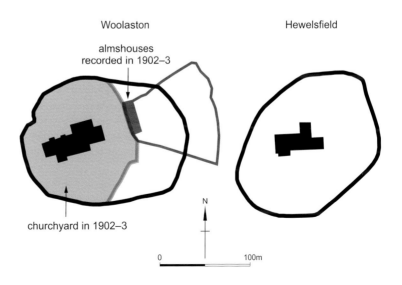

In the later Saxon period there was no established parish system, although churches began to be built by local landowners to serve the needs of their estates from around the 9th century (Hey 1996, 339–40). It is difficult to date the origin of what later became parish churches (fewer than 0.5 per cent of medieval churches have a known foundation date [Morris 1990, 4]) and some Saxon churches must have existed in the Forest of Dean.

Direct archaeological evidence for churches which predate 1066 is, however, very rare, especially when compared with the surviving evidence for pre-Norman churches east of the Severn.

A fragment of cross slab reused in the construction of the George Inn, St Briavels may be a late Saxon grave marker although it could be from the nearby early Norman church and stylistically it is not definitely pre-Norman. There was a church at Awre in 1086 (Moore 1982), although no evidence for this has been found in the fabric of the present 13th-century church (Verey 1970, 93). A chapel at Newnham, recorded in the early 11th century, may have been close to the river crossing between Newnham and Arlingham (Leech 1981, 62), although this reference could be to a Newnham in Northamptonshire or Warwickshire (Douthwaite and Devine 1998, 103).

Another form of religious house established by powerful Saxon landowners was the minster, in which a community of priests administered to the spiritual needs of the territories under their control (Hey 1996, 314–15). From the end of the 7th century minsters were founded in the Christian kingdom of the Hwicce, including Gloucestershire to the east of the River Severn, often centred on hundreds (Heighway 1987, 97–8), a land division established in the late Saxon period (Hey 1996, 226).

Minsters were often headed by members of the ruling elite (Blair 1988, 38) and Townley (2004, 234) has suggested that the Mercians used them as a tool for consolidating political hegemony and that they could have established minsters west of the Severn when the area came under their control. There might have been a minster at Westbury on Severn, just outside the Forest of Dean (Heighway 1987, 97, 168), although the evidence for this is largely circumstantial. Westbury is an unusually large parish which in 1066 was owned by a particularly powerful landowner, the king (Moore 1982, 1.11). It was also the centre of a large hundred which, in 1066, included the manors of Westbury, Churcham, Longhope, Bulley, Blaisdon and Minsterworth and also Stears, Hyde and Ruddle in Newnham (Smith 1972a, 1) and in the later medieval period the churches of Newnham and Minsterworth were chapels of Westbury (Herbert 1972b, 98), suggesting it originally had ecclesiastical jurisdiction over the hundred. There may also have been a minster at Lydney, although again there is no direct evidence for this. Lydney was, however, a large parish which originally included Aylburton (Herbert 1996e, 46) and before 1066 the hundred of Lydney extended from the Severn to the Wye and included Hewelsfield and St Briavels. Its church also had ecclesiastical jurisdiction over a wide area and later in the medieval period the churches of Aylburton, St Briavels and Hewelsfield were chapels of Lydney (Townley 2004, 234).

Later medieval ritual and religion

Churches and chapels

Whatever the date of origin of churches in the Forest, the arrival of the Normans provided an incentive for church building as new landlords stamped their identity on the landscape and new churches were built and existing ones replaced or improved beyond recognition. Churches were built at Lancaut, Alvington, Bulley, English Bicknor, Pauntley, Preston, Ruardean, St Briavels, Staunton, Woolaston, Newnham and Aylburton in the 11th and 12th centuries (Verey and Brooks 2002) and probably also at Tidenham, Awre, Lydney and Littledean (Herbert 1972a; 1996e; 1996h; Jurica 1996b) although this is less clear.

At four of these sites (English Bicknor, Hewelsfield, Ruardean and St Briavels), where the Norman church was built close to a Norman fortification, these were probably built by the same feudal lord, demonstrating the unity of church and state and the power they both held over the lives of the population.

Many of these were modified or added to over the centuries and new churches, possibly replacing earlier churches, were built later in the medieval period (mainly during the 13th and 14th centuries) at Lydney, Tidenham, Mitcheldean and Abenhall, while churches at Newland and possibly also Coleford and Bream may have been new foundations. The original 12th-century church at Newnham was also abandoned and replaced by the present church in the 14th century.

At least 21 medieval chapels are known in the Forest although three of these, at Newnham, on St Twrogs Island off Beachley Point and at Stowe near St Briavels, may have been pre-Norman (*see* p 107).

These were built for a variety of purposes and St Mary's Chapel, St Briavels, St David's Chapel, Rodmore and a small chapel at Purton were chantry chapels where masses were said for the soul of the chapel's patron or their family. Others such as Stowe Grange, St Briavels, and St Whites near Littledean were hermitages (Herbert 1996f, 259; Jurica 1996g, 148) occupied by a hermit or anchorite who often also acted as a guide or operated ferries (Hey 1996, 217).

Others were built to benefit travellers seeking divine protection, and, as crossing water was seen as particularly perilous, many chapels were sited near river crossings. St Peter's chapel, Newnham housed an anchoress who operated the ferry, and the chantry at Purton generated income from the river crossing (Townley 2004, 254). St Ewan's Chapel, Beachley and the chapel at Woolaston Grange were also close to ferries across the Severn, although less difficult cross-

ings also warranted divine assistance, and St David's Chapel, Tutshill was built for travellers crossing the Striguil Bridge over the Wye between Tutshill and Chepstow. Chapels were also sited by roads and Margaret's Chapel, Lindors, north-west of St Briavels, was a roadside chapel, while

Fig 5.40
Norman church at Hewelsfield.
[© Gloucestershire County Council Archaeology Service]

Fig 5.41
St Twrog's Chapel, Beachley Point. This small chapel or hermitage is dedicated to St Twrog (St Tecychius). It was first recorded in 1290 but may have been an early medieval foundation.
[© Gloucestershire County Council Archaeology Service]

the chapel at Dryslade Farm south of English Bicknor was near 'an ancient road junction'.

Both St Whites and Stowe were attached to monastic granges (an outlying farming estate owned by a monastery and run by lay brothers), and there was also a chapel attached to the grange of Tintern Abbey at Woolaston, and possibly also to the grange at Madgetts (*see* p 111).

Most medieval chapels are not known to survive and their precise location is often not clear. Most are only recorded in documentary sources, although three (Aylburton, St Margaret's Chapel, Lindors, west of St Briavels, and St David's Chapel, Tutshill) are recorded on early maps but not depicted as actual buildings (Hoyle 2008a, 192).

One chapel (St Mary's Chantry, St Briavels) has been converted into a dwelling and another

three (St Twrog's Chapel, Tidenham, Woolaston Grange, Woolaston and St Margaret's Chapel, Stowe) survive as ruins. Another, the chapel at Mork, was reported to be incorporated into the fabric of a garage in 1951 (Scott-Garrett 1918–58, entry for 18 October 1951), but has not been recorded since.

Monastic sites

The only monastery known in the Forest of Dean is Flaxley Abbey, a Cistercian monastery founded by Roger, Earl of Hereford at Flaxley between 1151 and 1154 close to the site where his father had been killed in a hunting accident 10 years previously (Graham 1907, 93). The Cistercian ideal of a remote site far from civilisation where the monks led a simple, contemplative life could rarely be achieved in Southern England and, like many other Cistercian abbeys, Flaxley was founded on relatively poor-quality land close to areas of woodland and/or a Royal Forest. The site (which was just within the bound of the Royal Forest in the 12th century) was not wild untamed countryside in the 12th century and it was not uncommon for peasants to be evicted to allow Cistercian orders to maintain a suitable quality of remoteness (Aston 1993, 77–8). There is no evidence for this at Flaxley, but the abbey appears to have had some impact on the landscape as pollen from a palaeoenvironmental sample about 600m to the west of the abbey suggested that an open, cleared landscape of dry grassland became an increasingly wet landscape with alder and hazel woodland sometime in the late Saxon/early Norman period (Hoyle 2008b, 89–90).

Although the monks themselves may have led a life of prayer and contemplation, Cistercian monasteries relied on lay brothers who worked the granges (monastic farms) which provided the monastery with an income (Aston 1993, 74). There was a grange attached to the monastery at Flaxley and fishponds were created by damming the Westbury Brook. There were also detached granges at St Whites, south of Cinderford (which included a hermitage and fish ponds), and also outside the Forest at Dymock, where there was a mill and barn, and Walmore to the east of Westbury on Severn where the monastic fishponds can still be seen (Townley 2004, 255). The abbey was also granted the right to pasture cattle, sheep and pigs and a tithe of all chestnuts in the Forest. It had a forge at *Edland* (presumably *Ardlonde* which has been identified as St Whites Farm,

Fig 5.42
Medieval religious sites.

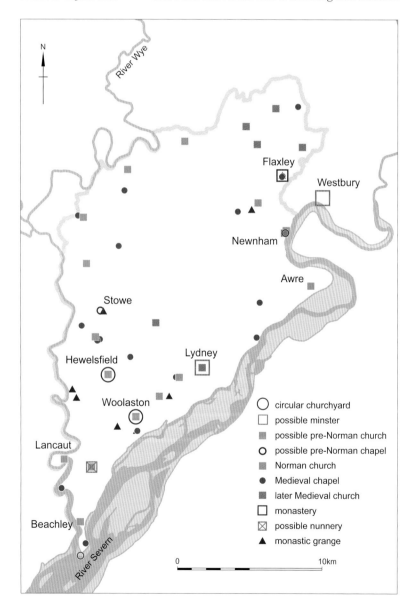

circular churchyard
possible minster
possible pre-Norman church
possible pre-Norman chapel
Norman church
Medieval chapel
later Medieval church
monastery
possible nunnery
monastic grange

0   10km

Fig 5.43
Flaxley Abbey from
Welshbury Hill. The abbey
was built on land taken
from the Royal Forest
where the gentle Severn
Vale meets the more
rugged high ground of
the Royal demesne.
[© Peter Crow, Forest
Research]

Cinderford [Jurica 1996g, 140]) and the right to two oaks per week to provide fuel (subsequently rescinded in exchange for Abbots Wood, Soudley). It was also granted a fishery at Rodley near Newnham, woodland in Dymock and other meadows and assarts (Graham 1907, 94) and sheep folds at Newnham, suggesting they exported wool by river (Townley 2004, 257). Despite these wide business interests the abbey was never a particularly wealthy house. In 1279 it was one of the poorer Cistercian houses, heavily in debt, and there was disease in its sheep flock. Things did not improve and by the time the abbey was dissolved in 1537 there were only seven monks and one lay brother, the church had burnt down, other buildings were in a ruinous state and the bells had been melted down to fund repairs (Graham 1905, 95; Robinson 1998, 108).

After the dissolution much of the abbey was demolished, with the exception of the range of buildings on the western side of the cloister. This included a section of the wall of the abbey church, part of its cloistral range and the 12th-century refectory, which were incorporated into the 17th- and 18th-century country house that now stands on the site (Middleton 1881–2, 280–3; Jurica 1996g, 142), although the foundations of the chapter house were revealed in the late 18th century (Crawley-Bovey 1921, 57–8).

Flaxley Abbey was not the only medieval monastic house with interests in the Forest and wide tracts of land outside the Royal Demesne were held by a number of religious orders (Townley 2004, fig 68). Blanton Priory, Gloucester had a grange at Alvington Court, although no medieval structures are known to survive. There was also a grange at Stowe, north of St Briavels, held by Grace Dieu, Monmouth where the remains of a chapel (St Margaret's Chapel) survive in a ruinous condition incorporated into later structures (see p 109) and unpublished small-scale excavation suggests the potential for other buried remains (Townley 2004, 261).

Tintern Abbey also had extensive holdings in the Forest of Dean with at least two granges in Woolaston (Woolaston Grange and Ashwell Grange), one at Madgetts, Tidenham and also one at Brockweir (Smith 1972b, 106–9).

Fig 5.44
Blocked monastic door at
Flaxley Abbey recorded
during restoration work.
The door may originally
have led from the church to
the cloister.
[© Gloucestershire County
Council Archaeology
Service]

Woolaston Grange had a chapel, a barn and a mill, although only the chapel survives as a ruin, but medieval masonry appears to have been used in later farm buildings (Townley 2004, 250). There was also a series of fish ponds created by damming the Black Brook which flowed towards the River Severn at Grange Pill and where there was a timber and stone quay from the middle of the 12th century (Fulford *et al* 1992).

There may also have been a chapel attached to Madgetts Grange, as a 19th-century fieldname 'Chapel Meadow' is immediately to the east of Madgetts Farm (Gwatkin 1995a), although it is not known that this is the site of a former chapel and other interpretations of this placename are possible (Hoyle 2008a, 192).

Brockweir Grange was probably centred around the area of Brockweir Farm where the Brockweir Brook meets the River Wye (Smith 1972b, 104). This area and a narrow strip of land in the valley of the Brockweir Brook was a detached portion of Woolaston Parish until 1935 (Smith 1972b, 102) and probably echoes holdings owned by Tintern Abbey at Woolaston and Brockweir.

Very little is known about Brockweir Grange. The Malthouse just to the north of Brockweir Farm may be the only surviving monastic structure (Verey and Brooks 2002, 204), although recent research has suggested it is an early post-medieval building on the footprint of an earlier monastic building which reused medieval masonry and architectural fittings (Hickling 2007, 15). The Old Post Office just to the north of the Malthouse, on the opposite side of the road, is another early post-medieval building which has earlier (15th-century) windows (Verey and Brooks 2002, 204), and a number of the buildings in this part of Brockweir may contain masonry reused from demolished monastic structures. The grange also had a watermill on the Brockweir Brook, although its precise site is not known. A section of Offa's Dyke, just below Mill Hill and about 700m east of the Wye, was repurposed as a dam for a mill pond. The mill must have been downstream of this dam, although whether it was close to other grange buildings (perhaps on the site later occupied by post-medieval watermills less than 100m from Brockweir Farm) or higher up the valley is not known.

A nunnery has also been reported on the site of Tidenham House, Tidenham (Scott-Garrett

Fig 5.45
Section of Offa's Dyke converted into a monastic dam at Brockweir.
[© Gloucestershire County Council Archaeology Service]

1918–58, entry for 18 October 1933), although no remains of this are known and the validity of this claim is not clear.

The medieval landscape

Unenclosed open fields

The Domesday Survey (Moore 1982; 1987) records the number of plough teams in each manor, providing a general indicator of the spread of cultivated land in 1086. Tidenham, with 38 ploughs, was probably the most extensively cultivated area, although arable farming was clearly important along the northern shore of the Severn between Newnham and Stroat where 89 plough teams are recorded. Ruardean, Mitcheldean (*Dene*) and Longhope on the northern side of the Forest had 30.5 ploughs between them (although some may have been in Littledean which may also have been part of *Dene* in Domesday [Smith 1964a, 225]). There was much less arable land in the western part of the Forest with only four ploughs recorded at St Briavels and only one at Madgetts on the northern side of Tidenham Chase, while English Bicknor only had half a plough. No ploughs were recorded on the higher ground above the Wye Valley between English Bicknor and St Briavels as much of this area seems to have been largely woodland and waste within the Royal Demesne at that time.

Evidence for former open fields (Hoyle 2006) and cropmarks of ridge and furrow indicate that the relatively level fertile low-lying ground on the northern shore of the Severn continued to be cultivated throughout the medieval period, although there were also later medieval open fields around Hewelsfield, between St Briavels and Newland and English Bicknor, where new or growing settlements had converted former woodland or waste to agriculture. Open fields were also recorded to the south of Staunton (Herbert 1996d) and possibly also in Longhope (Jurica 1996e, 182; Jurica 2010, 236), although little ridge and furrow has been recorded in these parishes and few former open field boundaries were fossilised in later enclosure patterns (Hoyle 2006). There is also no documentary evidence that Mitcheldean, Abenhall, Littledean or Ruardean ever had any open fields (Herbert 1996i, 238–9; Jurica 1996e, 182; 1996b, 167), although small pockets of ridge and furrow have been identified from aerial photographs in these parishes.

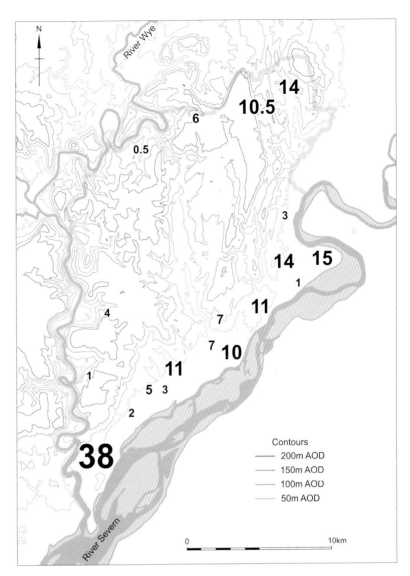

Fig 5.46 (above) Ploughs recorded in the Domesday Survey of 1086.

Fig 5.47 (left) Aerial photograph, taken in 1946, of ridge and furrow surviving as earthworks to the south-east of Alvington between the village and the River Severn to the right of the picture. These earthworks have now been much reduced or levelled by cultivation. [© Historic England Archive (RAF Photography) RAF/106G/UK/1295 frame 3008. 26-MAR-1946]

Enclosed fields

Open fields were not the only sort of farming in the medieval period and in some parts of the Forest of Dean, particularly areas of high or steep ground, there was a long-standing tradition of a more enclosed landscape often referred to as wood pasture. This is often found in wooded areas where livestock could be grazed at certain times of year (Hey 1996, 505) and although there may have been areas of unenclosed open fields, small enclosed fields or closes for livestock were equally important.

Even where open fields are recorded, cropmarks and lidar have also found evidence for small enclosures. These are most common on higher ground away from the Severn Valley and have been found close to the medieval settlements of St Briavels, Hewelsfield, Brockweir, English

Bicknor and between Newland and Redbrook and also around the former medieval settlements at Lancaut, north of Tidenham, Harthill west of Hewelsfield, High Meadow Farm, Newland and Madgetts Farm, Tidenham (Small and Stoertz 2006; Hoyle 2008c, fig 25). Some of these may be survivors of earlier (possibly prehistoric) enclosure patterns which continued into the medieval period (Small and Stoertz 2006, 48–9) although others, for example around Hewelsfield or on the Lancaut peninsula, appear to fossilise former open field boundaries and probably represent late or post-medieval enclosure.

Pasture and meadows

Livestock was pastured in open fields during fallow periods, although there may also have been more permanent areas of grazing particularly on the higher ground of Tidenham Chase and Bearse Common and on the slopes of the Severn Valley at Woolaston and Aylburton Commons, north of Lydney and on May Hill (Hoyle 2006). In wood pasture areas pigs, cattle and sheep could be commoned in areas of woodland and waste and in the late 12th century the Crown collected revenues for grazing cattle or feeding pigs on beech mast in the Royal Demesne (Herbert 1996j, 360).

The only meadows recorded in the Domesday Survey were at St Briavels and Alverston, although there were extensive areas of grazing and meadow close to the Severn at Awre, Aylburton and Alvington later in the medieval period. Some areas of arable may have been used as meadow as part of open field rotation and some former open fields also reverted to meadow following population decline after the Black Death of 1348–52 (Townley 2004, 83). Smaller areas of meadow were recorded at Whitecliff, west of Coleford, Hewelsfield and along the Westbury Brook west of Flaxley and the Valley Brook (a tributary of the Wye) between Lower Redbrook and Clearwell, and also in narrow strips of land close to the Wye (Hoyle 2006).

Woodland and assarts

The Roman period may have seen an increase in areas of woodland managed for charcoal production (*see* p 143), although charcoals from 8th- and 9th-century smelting at Clearwell Quarry, St Briavels produced no direct evidence for coppicing. The charcoal from Clearwell was dominated by mature oak with a secondary use of

Fig 5.48
Medieval landscape of small enclosures and open fields around Hewelsfield identified by lidar and as cropmarks (shown red).

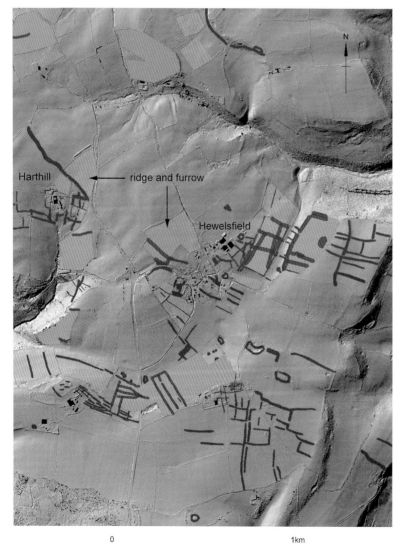

hazel, birch, wild cherry or ash, the types of trees which would be expected in the wood pasture landscape (Pine *et al* 2009, 36) envisaged for this area later in the medieval period.

Some of the Forest's woodland was certainly being managed as coppice by the late medieval period as eight areas of coppice are recorded on the 'fringes' of the Royal Demesne in the mid-16th century, most notably at Chestnuts Wood, Littledean, Bradley Hill, west of the Soudley Brook, and the Kidnalls, north of Lydney (Herbert 1996j, 362), and by the mid-17th century coppicing was widespread with over 16 coppices named in legal documents dating between 1634 and 1656 (Hart 1995, 68, 108–11).

The Royal Demesne appears to have been largely depopulated and used as a royal game reserve by the late Saxon period and much of this area would have been taken up with woodland and also extensive areas of more open waste which were probably used for grazing. In the 12th to 13th centuries new or refounded settlements (such as Newland, Staunton and Hewelsfield) and their associated farmland were set up in this area. In the late 12th century the Royal Demesne was not just a royal game reserve and revenues were collected for grazing cattle (*herbage*) or allowing pigs to forage for beech mast (*pannage*), and by 1223 local inhabitants could collect brush wood (*estover*) in the Forest (Herbert 1996j, 360). Charcoal production also took place in the Forest's woodland, and the Crown grappled continually with illegal (or semi-legal) charcoal burning throughout the medieval period (Jurica 1996d, 346).

Woodland was more widespread than the Royal Demesne and in 1086 woodland was recorded at Lydney, Newnham, Alverston (probably south-west of Lydney), St Briavels and Tidenham (Moore 1982), although details of these woods are not always clear.

The extent of this woodland was not constant in the medieval period and there are numerous records of illegal and semi-legal encroachment and assarting (cultivation of former woodland or waste) into the Royal Demesne.

Sections of the woodland in the Demesne were sold in the 14th century (Herbert 1996k, 298–99; 1996j, 362) and there are historic records of assarting relating to 13th-century grants of land to Flaxley Abbey, Flaxley and Abbots Wood, Soudley and also mid-14th-century assarting at Elwood and Bream (Herbert 1996k, 298–9). To the south of the Royal Demesne, 267 acres of assarts were reported in the area of Tidenham Chase in 1282 (Herbert 1972a, 51).

Forest administration

The system of post-medieval forest lodges to manage Crown woodland is well documented (Herbert 1996j; Waygood 2003; 2004), although less is known about medieval administration.

The Royal Demesne was administered from St Briavels Castle, under the Constable, who was also Warden of the Forest of Dean. For practical purposes the Forest was divided into a system of bailiwicks administered by a woodward who maintained under-foresters or 'serjeants in fee' who patrolled the forest to monitor illegal activities. Six bailiwicks (Ruardean, Lea, Mitcheldean, Blakeney, Staunton and Bicknor) were recorded in 1119, but by 1282, when the boundaries of the bailiwicks were recorded, there were also

Fig 5.49
Generalised map of principal components of the medieval landscape derived from cropmark evidence. [© Historic England (NMP) and historic landscape characterisation data (Hoyle 2006)]

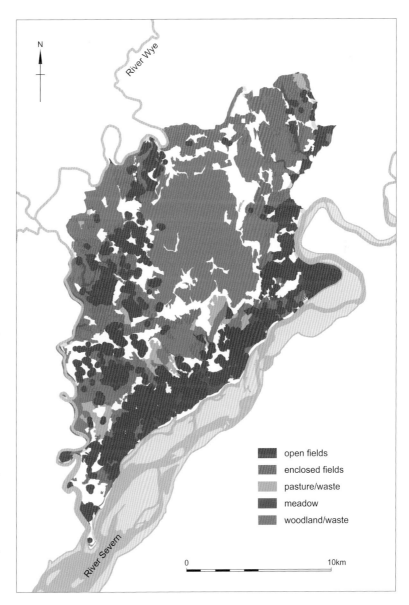

open fields
enclosed fields
pasture/waste
meadow
woodland/waste

0   10km

bailiwicks centred at Abenhall, Blaize, Bearse and Littledean (Grundy 1936, 110–55; Herbert 1996j, 355–8).

Although, unusually for a medieval forest, the boundaries of Dean's bailiwicks are well documented (Grundy 1936, 110), there is little known physical evidence for structures relating to medieval forest management.

Two sites recorded in 1282, Moseley Castle (*Moseleyscastel*) and Saintlow Castle (*Seynteleyscastel*), may have been structures built to guard royal pasture lands in the Forest (Hart 1967, 56), although apart from the fact that they were probably at Moseley Green to the east of Parkend and Saintlow Enclosure about 1.5km to the north, these sites are not known.

Several subrectangular earthworks in the New Forest, Hampshire have been interpreted as medieval hunting or keeper's lodges, although this is reinforced by historical references to the construction of lodges and details of roofing material, the remains of which have been found at these sites (Smith 1999, 23–6, fig 14).

The only historical reference to medieval keeper's lodges in the Forest of Dean dates to 1611 when two lodges (one of which was already 'old') were recorded at Noxon Park, which was outside the Royal Demesne (Herbert 1996g, 212). A number of subrectangular enclosures consistent with the general size and shape of the New Forest's lodges are within or close to the edge of the Royal Demesne (Hoyle 2008c, 40).

Only two of these have been dated, and one (on Ruardean Hill) has been shown to be early Roman (*see* pp 53–4). Another, at Yorkley, however, dates to the 12th to 14th century, and although there was evidence for iron smelting in its interior, this may not have been its primary function (Jackson *et al* 2016, 48; Wheeler and Walsh 2019, 7). This enclosure was on a southeast facing slope (although not at the highest point) and may represent the remains of a hunting or keeper's lodge, perhaps associated with the bailiwick of Blakeney (Grundy 1936).

None of the remaining enclosures have been dated, and all could have other interpretations.

A possible candidate for the medieval Forest lodge within the Royal Demesne is a square earthwork enclosure at Plump Hill, Mitcheldean on the western side of a linear ridge with westerly views. This is reported to have been excavated in 1958 but no records of this are known. A geophysical survey, undertaken in 2005, confirmed an outer ditch and possible counterscarp bank beyond this, although evidence from its interior was confused by a recent iron water pipe and disturbance from later tree planting and charcoal burning. A linear anomaly parallel to the southern bank may, however, have been internal division of some kind (Substrata 2005b, 6, fig 1).

Two other enclosures are close to the edge of the Statutory Forest, and presumably were close to the edge of, or just within, the Royal Demesne.

One of these is a polygonal enclosure in Kidnalls Wood, north of Lydney which would have had views towards the south-west over the valley of the River Lyd.

The other is a square enclosure at Morse Lane, Ruardean, only 250m to the north of the Statutory Forest boundary, which would only have commanded views over the head of the Drybrook Valley to its east. It is similar in shape and size to medieval keeper's lodges from the New Forest,

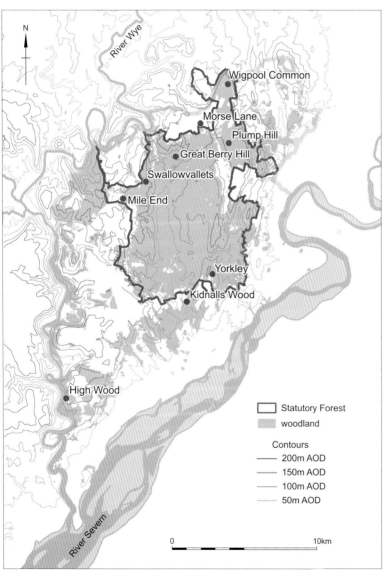

Fig 5.50
Possible medieval keepers' lodges. Only the small subrectangular enclosure at Yorkley is known to be medieval and all the remaining features shown have produced no dating evidence and could date to other periods.

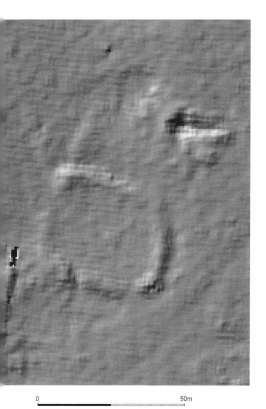

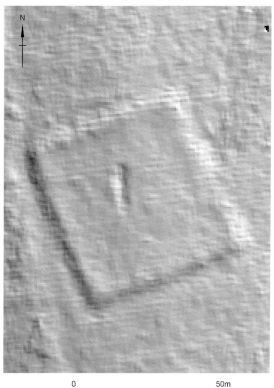

0   50m

0   50m

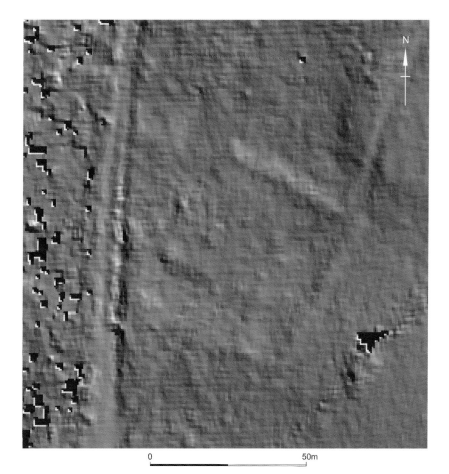

0   50m

Fig 5.51 (far left)
Subrectangular medieval enclosure at Yorkley Slade. The Yorkley enclosure has an internal measurement of 27 × 34m and was defined by a bank (1–1.5m high). There was no clear evidence for an entrance but the bank was breached in three places where modern footpaths crossed the site and one of these may have made use of an original entrance. There was some evidence for an external ditch, particularly on its eastern side.

Fig 5.52 (left)
Undated enclosure at Plump Hill. This square enclosure has an internal measurement of about 45 × 45m and is enclosed by a bank in places 1.30m high on its outer face, although only 0.4m high on its inner side. There is evidence for an outer ditch and possibly also a counterscarp bank and a gap in the eastern bank may have been an original entrance.

Fig 5.53
Undated enclosure in Kidnalls Wood. This consists of a rectangular area enclosing about 40 × 31m with a small rectangular extension or annex (about 13 × 16m) on to its south-eastern side. The enclosure is defined by low earth banks or terraces between 0.4m and 0.6m high and 4–4.5m wide, but there is no evidence for an external ditch.

Fig 5.54 (right)
Undated enclosure at
Morse Lane, Ruardean.
This is almost square
(about 60 × 59m) and
defined by a ditch. The lidar
hints at an internal bank
(enclosing an area of about
50 × 43m), but this is not
clear and only the eastern
and north-eastern sections
of the earthwork appear to
have survived in good
condition.

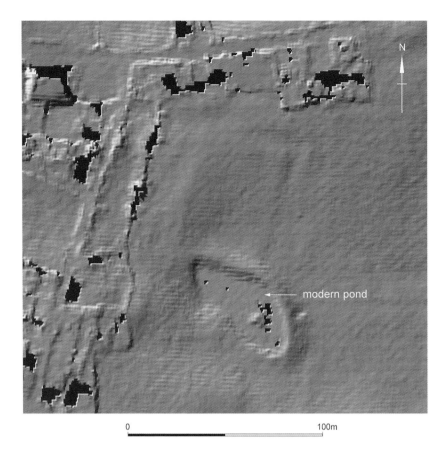

Fig 5.55 (far right)
Undated enclosure in
High Wood, Tidenham.
This encloses an area of
56 × 46m and its outer
rubble bank is up to 0.75m
high and 3.5m wide. Its
interior was divided by two
more rubble banks. There is
no clear evidence for an
external ditch, but a gap in
its south-eastern bank may
be an entrance.

but could also be a medieval moated site with no association with Forest administration.

Another undated enclosure in High Wood, Tidenham close to the edge of the Wye Valley (and also just inside Offa's Dyke) is some distance from the Statutory Forest and if it is a medieval lodge may relate to Tidenham Chase rather than the Royal Demesne. This was close to the top of a rise with views over the Wye Valley and the southern part of Tidenham Chase.

A number of other undated enclosures in the Royal Demesne may also be the remains of medieval keeper's lodges, although they have been given other interpretations. The subcircular enclosure in Sallowvallets Wood is thought likely to be prehistoric, although Newman (1988) has suggested it may be a medieval lodge. Subrectangular enclosures at Mile End, Wigpool Common and the possible enclosure on Great Berry Hill may also be medieval keeper's lodges, although they have been suggested as possible early Roman military sites or late prehistoric enclosures (see above).

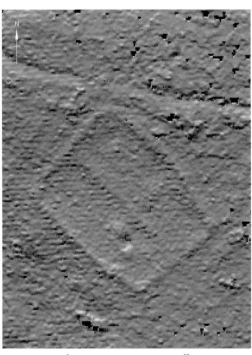

6

Industry and trade from the prehistoric to the early post-medieval periods

The post-medieval industrial history of the Forest of Dean is one of the area's defining characteristics and has been the subject of considerable and widely published research (Hart 1971; Cross 1982; Bick 1980; Jurica 1996d). The Forest's earlier industrial history, however, is less well known.

Extractive industries

The Forest of Dean is a geologically complex area with limestone, sandstone, coal and iron, often in close proximity. The Statutory Forest is centred on an area of Pennant Sandstone which contains Coal Measures and some iron ore. The Sandstones overlie Carboniferous Limestones which contain most of the iron ore, and which in turn overlie earlier Sandstones of the Old Red Sandstone Series (BGS 2014). Coal either outcrops or is very close to the surface in many areas in the central Forest and the iron ore is easily won from the limestones at the edges of the Pennant Sandstone.

These resources have been mined or quarried in the Forest of Dean 'since earliest times' (Cross 1982, 26) and there is widespread evidence of this exploitation.

Stone

Stone has been quarried in the Forest since at least the Bronze Age when limestone and sandstone were selectively used in the construction of the Bronze Age ring cairn in East Wood, Tidenham (Hoyle 2013a) and also of the Soldiers Tump round barrow to the south of Chase Farm, Tidenham (Scott-Garrett 1955). In the Iron Age, stone was used to construct the banks of Iron Age hillforts where it was excavated from the rampart ditches or from quarries on their inner sides (McOmish and Smith 1996; Wheeler and Wheeler 1932).

The Romans also used sandstone and limestone to construct buildings, particularly from the 3rd century AD. Sandstone was used most often for wall construction, although limestone was also used in some of the footings at Boughspring Villa (Pullinger 1990, 21) and at the Chesters, Woolaston (Scott-Garrett and Harris 1938, 113).

Forest of Dean sandstones can be split along horizontal bedding planes to create flat slabs of varying thicknesses and sandstone paving slabs were used at a number of Roman buildings including the Guest House at Lydney Park Temple (Wheeler and Wheeler 1932, 46), the Chesters villa, Woolaston (Scott-Garrett and Harris 1938, 113) and also at High Nash, Coleford (Sindrey 1990, 27).

Sandstone was also used to make roof tiles. The guest house at Lydney Park Temple, at least in its latest phase, was roofed with hexagonal sandstone tiles (Wheeler and Wheeler 1932, 46), and flat Pennant Sandstone fragments from a Roman pit at Whitehouse Farm, English Bicknor may also have been broken roof tiles from a Roman building (Milford 2000). Stone roof tiles were also used at the Chesters, Woolaston, although the excavators did not specify whether these were limestone or sandstone (Scott-Garrett and Harris 1938, 113).

Sandstone roof tiles were also used to roof the barn at Huntsham Roman villa, Herefordshire (Taylor 1995, 242) and are known at a number of sites to the east of the Severn. Hexagonal Old Red Sandstone roof tiles were used on a Roman building at Ladybellgate Street, Gloucester (Roe nd, 2) and Old Red Sandstone roof tiles were found at Hucclecote Roman villa to the east of Roman Gloucester (Clifford 1933, 328–9; 1961, 45–6; Shaffrey 2012; Roe 2003, 51). Old Red Sandstone roof tiles have been found at other Roman sites around Gloucester (for example at Brockworth [Rawes 1981, 73], The Portway [Rawes 1984] and Frocester Court villa [Price

2000a, 131]) and Cirencester (for example at Beeches Road [McWhirr 1986, 44]), and tiles may have been exported to these centres for wider distribution (Shaffrey 2012, 50).

Sandstone from the central Forest was also used for honing or rubbing stones during the Roman period and Old Red Sandstone rubber stones were found at Millend, Blakeney (Roe 2000, 49) and Dymock (Crooks 2014, 76). Whetstones were exported outside the Forest and have been found at Frocester Court (Price 2000b, 187), Kingscote to the south of Stroud (Gutierrez and Roe 1998, 178) and Haymes to the north of Cheltenham (Rawes 1986, 90). Some of these may have been reused roof tiles rather than purpose-made tools, as honing marks on sandstone roof tiles are not uncommon (Shaffrey 2012, 50). Whetstones were also found at the Chesters villa, Woolaston, although it is not clear if these were sandstone (Scott-Garrett and Harris 1938, 121).

Stone continued to be quarried during the medieval period, and quarries are associated with Offa's Dyke, which may have been built in the later 8th century (Hoyle and Vallender 1997, 43). Limestone was used mainly for lime production, and lime produced in Dean was shipped to Gloucester in the mid-13th century. Sandstone, on the other hand, was mainly used as building stone or for millstones (Jurica 1996d). There are historical references to medieval quarries at Bixhead, Abenhall, Blakeney, Mitcheldean and Hanewye (Hanway) in Ruardean (Jurica 1996d, 337) and St Briavels Castle was built of local sandstone (Hart 1971, 297). Churches or other buildings throughout the medieval period were almost certainly built of stone quarried locally where suitable sources were available.

Some of the Forest's inhabitants acquired and exercised the right to quarry stone (subject to certain qualifications) within Crown land during the medieval period, although whether the Free Miners' customary privileges to mine in the Royal Forest included stone working was debatable (Hart 1971, 298–301; 2002, 5).

Aerial photographs and lidar have identified many small-scale and undated quarries throughout the Forest which are not obviously modern, although quarries are difficult to date, even with detailed documentary research or careful excavation, and evidence for earlier workings may have been obscured or removed by later activity at the same sites.

Querns and millstones

Sandstone was also used to produce querns and millstones for grinding corn or other items. These were generally made from Upper Old Red Sandstone which has a conglomerate form containing quartz pebbles which is found in the Wye Valley both in the Forest of Dean and to its west (Roe 1993, 199), although similar stone can also be found around Thornbury, north of Bristol (Price 2000b, 195). Stone from these outcrops is quite variable and ranges from a rough mixture of coarse quartz pebbles in a sandstone matrix to fairly coarse sandstone without pebbles (Roe 1993, 199). The grittier quartz conglomerates may have been preferred for millstones, although the smoother pebble-free type was also used and, on occasion, millstones were made from other suitable stone such as the Drybrook Sandstone from the edge of the central Forest (Mullin 1988, 53). Upper Carboniferous Pennant Sandstone was also used, but the provenance is not always clear as this is found both in the central part of the Forest and also to the east of Bristol (Green 1992, fig 10).

There were two types of milling process. Rotary querns made of two relatively small circular stones (an upper and lower stone) were domestic implements and the upper stone was usually turned by hand. Millstones were larger (up to about 1m in diameter) and were driven

Fig 6.1
Old Red Sandstone roof tiles from Hucclecote Roman villa.
[© Gloucestershire County Council Archaeology Service. Photo Paul Nichols]

0   20cm

by water power to mill cereals on a more industrial scale.

Fragments of sandstone rotary querns are known at a number of Roman sites in the Forest of Dean, such as the Warren, Lydney (Buckman 1856), Millend, Blakeney (Barber and Holbrook 2000), and Buttington Tump, Tidenham (Clarke 2007), and also to the east of the Severn. Outside the Forest Upper Old Red Sandstone querns have been found at Kingscote, a small Roman town south of Stroud (Gutierrez and Roe 1998, 176), Uley, about 4km to the west of Kingscote (Roe 1993, 199), Wortley Roman villa, Wortley (Taylor and Bagnall 1990), Ashchurch near Tewkesbury (Roe 2008, 53), Haymes, north of Cheltenham (Rawes 186, 90) and Brockworth near Gloucester (Shaffrey 2012, 51). Pennant Sandstone and Conglomerate Sandstone querns have also been found at Frocester Court Roman villa, Frocester, although petrological analysis suggests that these were probably made of stone from the Bristol region (Price 2000b, 193–8).

Millstones, which would have been used at permanent mill sites with a water source and some level of hydraulic engineering to ensure a reliable supply, are rarer. Two Old Red Sandstone millstones were found at the Chesters villa, Woolaston (Scott-Garrett and Harris 1938, 109), and a broken millstone was reused as part of the floor of Park Farm villa, Aylburton (Fitchett 1986, 26). Outside the Forest Pennant Sandstone millstones have been found at Frocester Court villa, although these were probably made in the Bristol area (Price 2000b, 195).

Rotary querns were used after the Roman period, although by the 11th century they had been largely replaced by water-driven mechanical mills. In the 15th century quarries at Mitcheldean and Hanway south of Ruardean probably produced millstones, and quarries in the Wye Valley were producing millstones for export to Bridgwater in Somerset throughout the 16th century (Jurica 1996d, 337). There were also early post-medieval millstone quarries at Redbrook (and possibly also Clearwell which had probably operated in the medieval period (Herbert 1996g, 220–1).

Most quern and millstone quarries were on the western side of the Forest close to the Wye Valley,

Fig 6.2
Roman Sandstone Conglomerate quern stone from Bourton-on-the-Water, Gloucestershire. This is the lower stone and is 0.35m in diameter.
[© Gloucestershire County Council Archaeology Service. Photo Paul Nichols]

Fig 6.3
Roman millstones at the Chesters, Woolaston reused as paving. These two runner (top) stones were placed with the grinding face downwards. The bow-like central hole would have fitted flanges attached to a vertical shaft which rotated the stone. The holes drilled into their backs may have improved balance.
[© Gloucester Museums Service]

although sites are also known where there were suitable outcrops to the east (Mullin 1988; 1990; Glos HER 2015). Many of these were probably last used during the post-medieval period and no definite prehistoric, Roman or medieval millstone quarries have been found, although some sites may have been used for a considerable period and evidence of earlier quern or millstone manufacture will now be either destroyed or masked by later workings.

Grindstones (which were used to sharpen edged tools) were also produced in the Forest of Dean during the medieval period, although these could be manufactured from the softer Carboniferous Sandstones from the central Forest. Grindstones may have been produced before the

mid-13th century (see Lewis and Vellacott 1907, 217) although they were certainly made at Bixhead, to the east of Coleford, by the mid-1430s, and a 'grindstone hewer' was recorded at Clearwell in 1608 although he may have been making millstones (Mullin 1988, 53). No medieval or earlier grindstone quarries are known for certain although there are numerous undated quarry workings in suitable areas.

Coal

With the possible exception of iron ore, coal is the mineral resource most often associated with the Forest of Dean.

Coal is found in the central part of the Forest district where the Upper Carboniferous Sandstones contain over 20 coal seams. These were laid down as horizontal layers, but are now upturned around their edges and outcrop as surface or near-surface deposits (Dreghorn 1968). On the western side of the Forest these dip down at an average angle of 10–15 degrees (Trotter 1942, 37), although in places this can be as steep as 20 degrees (Youles *et al* 2008, 47). On the eastern side of the Forest the dip is much steeper, generally between about 50 and 70 degrees but becoming almost vertical in places (GSGB 1957–9).

Coal has been exploited in Britain since at least the Roman period when it was probably used for domestic heating or industrial processes which did not require high temperatures (Travis 2008) and has been found at Roman sites in the Forest and neighbouring areas. No Roman coal mines have been found, however, and little is known about how coal was mined during this period, although the near surface outcrops were almost certainly exploited first, probably using pits or shallow shafts.

Coal from the Chesters villa, Woolaston, is assumed to be from the Forest of Dean (Fulford and Allen 1992), although coal from other sites has been analysed and its source determined. Coal used at Glendower Street, Monmouth in the 1st and 2nd centuries was probably from the area to the north-west of Coleford at the north-western edge of the Coal Measures (Williams 1988), while coal used at Frocester Court villa in the 3rd and 4th centuries, and at Chedworth, was also probably mined somewhere between Coleford and English Bicknor at the western edge of the Coal Measures (Dearne 2000, 259).

This would suggest that the Forest's Roman coal industry was concentrated in the north-

Fig 6.4
Identified millstone quarries in the Forest of Dean, based on information from Mullin 1988 and 1990, and Gloucestershire HER.

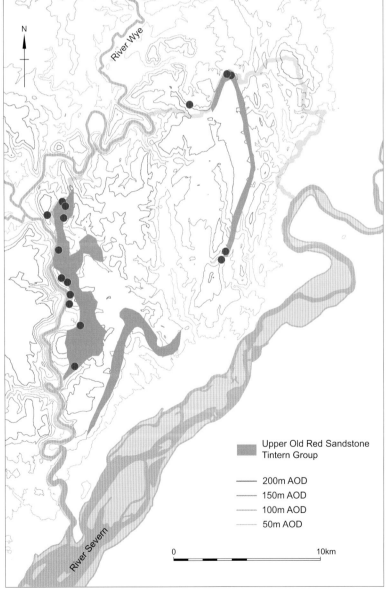

Upper Old Red Sandstone
Tintern Group

—— 200m AOD
—— 150m AOD
—— 100m AOD
—— 50m AOD

0   10km

Fig 6.5
Millstone rough out from
Oaken Grove, Newland.
Tape 600mm. Many
former millstone quarries
still contain roughouts
which broke, were defective
or were never completed
(Mullin 1988, 53).
[© Gloucestershire County
Council Archaeology
Service]

western outcrops in the Coleford area, close to where iron ore outcrops are also found, although coal can be relatively easily won in many other parts of the central Forest and further research may identify other sources. Coal from outside the Forest of Dean was also exploited during the Roman period as some coal used at Frocester Court villa in the mid- to late 4th century probably came from the coalfields in the Bristol area (Dearne 2000, 259).

During the medieval period coal was thought to be inferior to charcoal although it was used for domestic purposes or industrial processes such as smithing or lime burning (Hart 1971, 254; Townley 2004, 182). Coal was certainly

less important than iron during the medieval period and in the Forest of Dean no coal mining was recorded before the 13th century when mines are documented in the bailiwicks of Blakeney, Staunton and Abenhall (near Mitcheldean) and also at Bearse, Littledean, Mitcheldean, Ruardean, English Bicknor and Lydney (Jurica 1996d, 326; Oldham 2002, 2).

At this time extraction appears mainly to have been in the hands of small-scale private individuals licensed by the crown and the rights of free miners, most of whom mined iron rather than coal, were ratified (Hart 1971, 254; Hart 2002, 513). There are, however, no useful records of the scale of coal mining or the processes

Fig 6.6
Geological cross section
of the Forest of Dean. The
Carboniferous Sandstone
contains over 20 separate
coal seams and overlies
Carboniferous Limestone.
The strata form a basin
(the Dean syncline) and
coal seams outcrop
throughout the area. Iron
ore, within the Carboni-
ferous Limestone, outcrops
around the edge of the
sandstone.
[© Gloucestershire Wildlife
Trust]

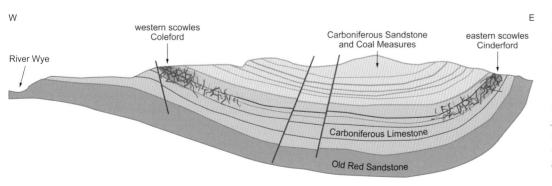

123

Fig 6.7 (right)
19th-century handbill
advertising coal for sale
at Futtrell near Coleford.
Futtrell is probably Fetter
Hill to south-east of Coleford
and the name is derived
from footrill meaning a
drift mine. This name was
first recorded as Fitteralls
in 1608.
[© Jon Hoyle]

Fig 6.8 (below)
Location of surface mining
remains and undated drift
mines identified on the
Gloucestershire Historic
Environment Record.

involved during much of this period, although it was probably limited to exploiting relatively shallow outcrops or superficial seams through surface pits, shallow workings, or short adits (also known as levels or drift mines) which were tunnels driven into hillsides or slopes towards coal seams (Jurica 1996d, 326).

Although at least 45 drift mines are known in the Forest, it is not clear how extensive this type of mining was in the medieval period and most known mines have been identified from 19th-century maps or 18th-century records (Hart 1971, 265). This type of mining was certainly practised by the early post-medieval period as an area to the south of Coleford is recorded as *Fitteralls* on the 1608 map of the eastern part of the Forest (Clissold 1982; PRO 1608a) which can

COAL! COAL! COAL!

HOPEWELL ENGINE COLLIERY,

FUTTRELL, near COLEFORD,

GLOUCESTERSHIRE.

GEORGE OLDLAND

Has now for Sale at the above Colliery, as under:-

GOOD HOUSE COAL 8s. PER TON.

SMITH'S COAL 4d. PER CWT.

LIME COAL 4s. 6d. PER TON.

P.S.—Allowance made in the Lime Coal if a quantity is taken.

COME AND TRY IT.

Bird, Printer, Coleford and Cinderford.

be interpreted as a variant of the word *footrill*, one of the many alternative terms for a drift mine (Gill and Newman 2015, 20).

The most common evidence for early coal mining in the Forest is undoubtedly the extensive areas of small subcircular pits and mounds, over half of which have been identified by lidar, which are widespread in the central Forest where coal outcrops (Hoyle 2008c, 72–5).

Most of these have not been investigated or dated but they have a very wide potential date range from the Roman period to the 20th century when some surface coal extraction was reported (Brian Johns, pers comm). The majority, however, will predate the later post-medieval periods after which steam-powered pumps allowed deeper seams to be exploited (Hart 1971), and some can be linked to recorded early post-medieval coal mines. A group of pits are known at Haywood Plantation, north-east of Cinderford where John Wade had coal workings in about 1656 (Hart 1995, 146–7), and also in Hawkwell Enclosure, north of Cinderford where 'colepits' were recorded in about 1710 (Hart 1995, map VIII, 206–7). Another area of pits at the Delves, north-west of Coleford, was probably worked between about 1550 and 1600 (Youles 2004, 5–6).

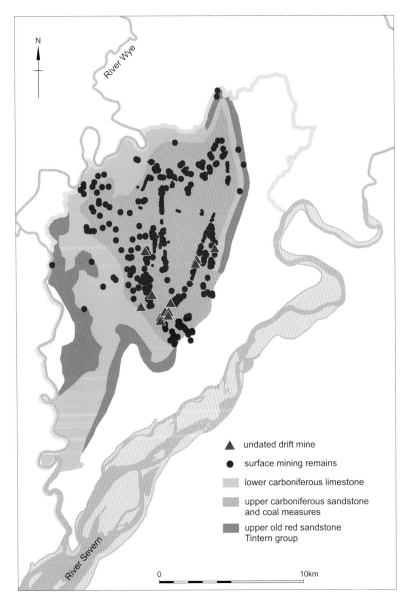

N

River Wye

River Severn

▲ undated drift mine
● surface mining remains
lower carboniferous limestone
upper carboniferous sandstone and coal measures
upper old red sandstone Tintern group

0   10km

These complex palimpsests of superficially similar hollows and mounds probably represent the visible remains of a range of mining techniques and workings of different dates which now survive in close proximity, while some depressions in these systems may be subsidence into collapsed shallow workings rather than former shafts or pits (Gill and Newman 2015, 18; Youles *et al* 2008, 47–50).

The earliest mines may have just been pits over surface deposits although shallow shafts leading to horizontal workings which followed a coal seam may also have been used from an early date. These may have been similar to bell pits (shallow shafts which 'bell out' at their base as coal is removed from the seam) known in other areas, but in the Forest of Dean any horizontal workings from their bases would have been shallow due to the thinness of the coal seams. These would also have almost always have needed shoring due to the instability of the overburden (Youles *et al* 2008, 47), although this was probably a fairly primitive 'stick and lid' affair consisting of a plank supported by a short prop (Ian Standing, pers comm in Youles *et al* 2008, 47). The miners' ability to follow seams as they dipped further below the surface would have been limited by the danger of roof collapse, flooding and poor ventilation, and once the limits of safe working were reached the shaft would have been abandoned and another sunk nearby (Gill and Newman 2015, 17).

As surface deposits were exhausted, deeper seams would have been exploited and new techniques were probably introduced from the later

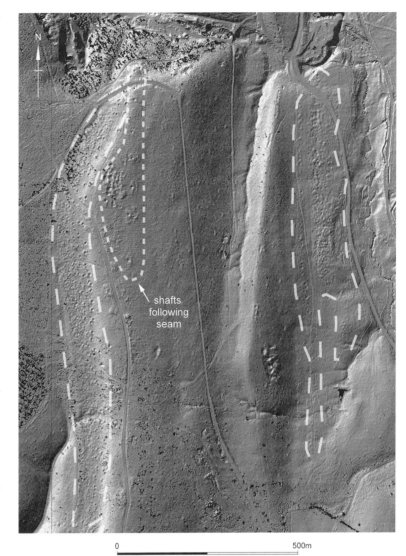

shafts following seam

0   500m

Fig 6.9 (above)
Palimpsest of surface coal mining remains in Nagshead Plantation and Fetter Hill south-east of Coleford. More regular shafts follow the coal seams between the two main groups of pits.

Fig 6.10 (left)
Surface coal mining remains to the west of Cinderford.
[© Gloucestershire County Council Archaeology Service]

medieval and early post-medieval periods. Coal mining increasingly took place in subterranean galleries linked by a system of shafts, generally no more than 20–30m apart and often lined with timber and brick (Gill and Newman 2015, 18; Hart 1971, 266), although in the Forest of Dean these mines would rarely have been more than about 25m deep due to water level difficulties (Hart 1971, 266).

To the south of Ruardean widely spaced mounds are the remains of early post-medieval coal shafts (Riches 2009, 21). Below ground these may be linked by galleries following the coal seam, although they could be single shafts which were abandoned due to flooding or other problems. A line of four smaller mounds in Bourts Enclosure, south of Lydbrook are proba-

bly also shallow shafts linking underground working following the coal seams.

Access and the removal of coal and waste were particularly problematic where mining involved vertical shafts. Ladders or human-powered winches may have sufficed for shallower workings, but became increasingly impractical as shafts deepened and horse whims (horse-powered windlasses) were recorded by the late 18th century, although they were probably used from an earlier date.

Flooding and drainage difficulties may have limited coal extraction to the summer months (Hart 1971, 258) and water levels restricted mining depth. Drift mines tended to slope upwards to facilitate drainage (Gill and Newman 2015, 20) and additional adits or soughs were excavated to drain mines. A surfe (drainage adit) drained John Wade's coal workings in Haywood Plantation around 1656 and allowed year-round working, although another pit in the area was abandoned the same year as it was 'sunk as deep as it could possibly be worked for water' (Hart 1995, 147). Some pits were emptied by bucket and human- or horse-powered pumps, although water-powered pumps were used in some mines by the mid-18th century (Hart 1971, 257).

Ventilation was also an issue. Some shallow shafts or short levels were probably abandoned due to flooding or risk of collapse before poor ventilation became a problem, although if necessary these could be ventilated by lowering a fire bucket into the shaft to draw up foul air and carbon dioxide. Drift-mines could also use air shafts to draw fresh air in through the mine entrance and discharge foul air through the shaft (Gill and Newman 2015, 24). For deeper mines, or more complex workings, air-flow was maintained by permanent fires at the base of shafts, ideally at the lowest point in the air-flow circuit (Court and Standing 1979, 10–13).

Iron

Historically the Forest of Dean has been closely associated with the iron industry and iron ore extraction and processing to produce iron have taken place in the area.

Scowles

The features most commonly associated with early iron ore extraction are the scowles which consist of irregular pits and hollows following the

Fig 6.11
The remains of coal shafts following the coal seam to the south of Ruardean. These probably date to the 18th century (Riches 2009, 21).

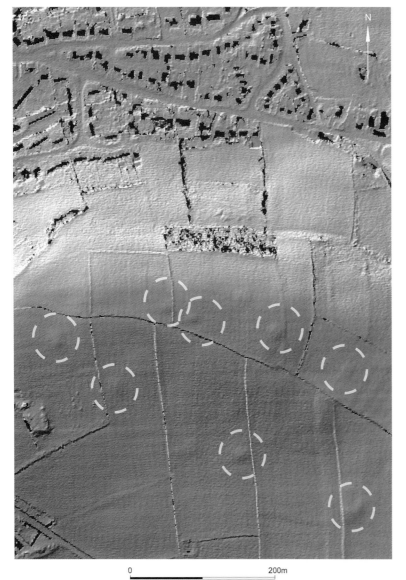

0   200m

Scowles

The origin of the word scowle is not entirely clear and there are a number of suggested derivations including from the verb 'to scowl' which describes their gloomy or threatening appearance (Geode Consulting 1998), and from *scowle* an early modern English word for rubbish or debris, which refers to the debris found in some scowles (Smith 1964a, 214). The most likely origin, however, is probably from the British word *crowll* meaning a cave or hollow or the Welsh word *ysgil* meaning a recess (Oldham 2002, 1). The word, however, is colloquial and has no scientific

definition and in the Forest of Dean it is used to describe a hollow of varying size or depth, from which iron ore has been extracted, and there is not always a clear distinction between surface features and the subterranean cavities which often lead directly from them (Hoyle *et al* 2007a, 74). The earliest documentary use of the word is in the name of Scowles village west of Coleford which was recorded as *Scwelle* in 1287, and is probably a back-formation from what was already the accepted name of these features (Smith 1964a, 214).

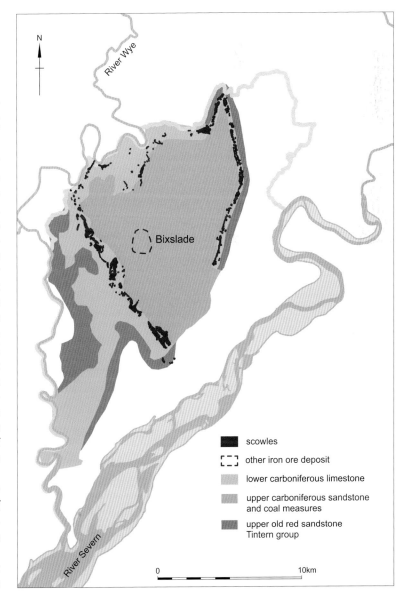

Fig 6.12
Scowles and other known iron ore sources in the Forest of Dean.

scowles
other iron ore deposit
lower carboniferous limestone
upper carboniferous sandstone and coal measures
upper old red sandstone Tintern group

Bixslade

River Wye

River Severn

N

0   10km

outcrops of Carboniferous Limestones at the edge of the Upper Carboniferous Coal Measures in the central area of the Forest (BGS 1974). Scowles are the result of complex geological and geomorphological processes, and human intervention, and are in two main bands between Staunton and Lydney in the west and between Drybrook and just south of Soudley in the east (Hoyle *et al* 2007a, fig 1; Wildgoose 1993, fig 2.1).

Although scowles are very variable and defy easy classification, they fall broadly into two main types. The first is a labyrinth of interconnected cavities, often several metres deep, which form a strange landscape of cavernous hollows or irregular trenches with exposed rocky outcrops or pillars and cave entrances leading deep underground. Vegetation and trees (often yew trees) cling precariously to their exposed rock faces and they are filled with varying amounts of scree or other debris. These can be discrete features although they generally consist of a more-or-less uninterrupted group, sometimes several kilometres long, although rarely more than about 0.5km wide and often narrower, particularly on the eastern side of the outcrop where the geological strata are pitched more steeply. Although these are thought of as typical, this type of scowle actually only makes up about half of the area of recognised surface iron mining remains (Hoyle *et al* 2007a, table 5, 30–1).

The second broad type are generally fairly shallow subcircular hollows or depressions of varying sizes, and although most have some visible rock exposures about a third do not (Hoyle *et al* 2007a, table 5, 30–1).

These have been interpreted as evidence for infilled scowles which may be true in some cases

Fig 6.13
Scowles as a cavernous
rocky landscape at Puzzle
Wood, Clearwell.
[© Gloucestershire County
Council Archaeology
Service]

Fig 6.14
Scowles as amorphous
hollows at Dockham to the
east of Cinderford.
[© Gloucestershire County
Council Archaeology
Service]

as there is evidence that some scowles have been filled in to create usable farmland (Hoyle *et al* 2007a, 54–9). Over half of these, however, are in woodland where it is hard to find an incentive for backfilling scowles, and this type probably also includes the remains of pits or trenches excavated in search of iron ore and also natural swallow holes or collapse from underground mine workings or caves (Hoyle *et al* 2007a, 61).

Scowles began to form over 300 million years ago when water running off the impermeable Carboniferous Sandstones and Coal Measures of the central Forest began to percolate into fissures in the Carboniferous Limestones exposed around its edge. This run-off was slightly acidic due to sulphur from the Coal Measures and reacted with the limestone which dissolved to create cavities. The Crease Limestone was most susceptible to this, but adjacent formations were also affected, and, over time an extensive cave system developed (Hoyle *et al* 2007b, 45–6).

The water run-off also contained iron which produced the Forest's iron ore deposits, although the precise mechanism of this deposition remains controversial. One theory is that the iron ore was deposited around 250 million years ago, after the caves had already formed (Lowe 1993). This may have occurred in two complementary phases producing two types of ore. The first was alteration of the cave walls to replace calcium and magnesium carbonate with hematite (metasomatic replacement), effectively transforming the cave wall into a thin layer of hard iron ore. The second was the precipitation of ore from iron-rich water filling the cavities to produce Goethite or 'brush ore', a relatively pure and friable ore containing few impurities (Solari and Lowe 1974, 69, 76). This was not necessarily a uniform process and there were probably some caves where iron ore has never accumulated (Lowe 1993) or which were 'incompletely filled with ore' (Wildgoose 1993, 202).

Another view is that ore was deposited when the cavities were created and the parent limestone was replaced by iron solutions (metasomatic replacement) transported into joints in the limestone by water runoff (Dreghorn 1968, 148–9). Both mechanisms may have played a part in the process with existing cavities modified and enlarged by metasomatic replacement during later deposition of ore deposits (Owen in Hoyle *et al* 2007b, 49).

Over millions of years further geological processes and erosion exposed the ore-rich cavities around the edges of the Carboniferous Sandstone and further erosion sculpted them into the scowles visible today.

Scowles are a complicated landscape, and although the essential grain of these features is the result of a long process of natural geomorphological action, human activity to remove iron ore deposits has undoubtedly made a major contribution to their present appearance. The extent to which their present form is the result of natural processes or human intervention is not always clear (Hoyle *et al* 2007a, 75–9), and they were probably a distinct landscape feature before

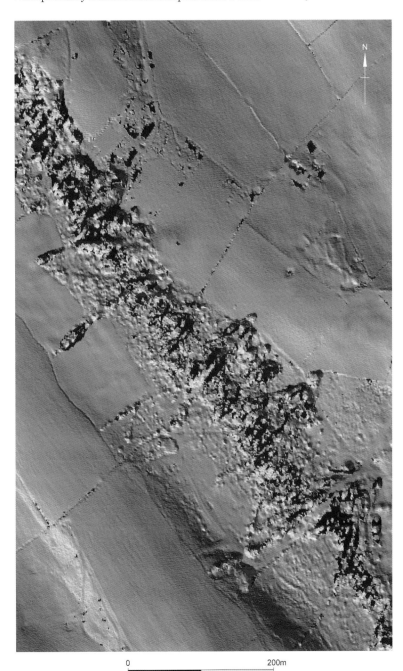

Fig 6.15
Scowles at Devil's Chapel, Lydney. The large irregular and cavernous scowles are flanked by an irregular landscape of pits and hollows. Some lines of mine pits radiate from the southwestern side of the main band of scowles.

0   200m

Fig 6.16
Formation of scowles and
iron ore deposits. There are
two main types of iron ore
in the Forest of Dean.
According to Mushet the
'brush ore' could be 'dug
easily, somewhat like
gravel', while the harder
haematite on 'the sides of
the chambers ... requires
gunpowder to detach from
the rock' (Mushet in
Nicholls 1858).
[© Gloucestershire Wildlife
Trust]

any human intervention. Precisely what they would have looked like is now unknown, but they may have been visible hollows, possibly with some rocky outcrops and variably infilled with eroded iron ore and rock.

Scowles are not the only source of iron ore in the Forest and small quantities have also been found in the Bixslade area of the central Forest where there is an underlying geology of Pennant Mudstones and Sandstone (BGS 1974), and where the precipitation of iron-rich water has left a residue of brush ore (goethite) in natural fissures in the sandstone.

Bog ores, which form below wet acidic soils, are also an important source of iron ore (Tylecote 1986, 125) and can yield very pure iron (Whitten and Brooks 1972, 56) which may have been easier to smelt than the 'stubborn haematites and

limonites of Dean' (Bick 1990, 39). Bog ores are known close to the Forest in Herefordshire (Bick 1990, 39), Trellech, Monmouthshire (Walters 1999, 21) and around High Nash, Coleford (Ian Standing, pers comm), but there is no evidence that they were smelted in the Forest of Dean.

Iron ore extraction

Ochre, derived from iron oxide, has been used as a pigment from the earliest periods of prehistory (Bray and Trump 1982). It is found in some parts of the iron ore deposits in the Forest (Hart 1971, 244) and may have been exploited at an earlier date than iron ore. Worn pebbles, and possible stone hammer fragments from near scowles at Drybrook and worn pebbles from disused iron mines have been tentatively interpreted as evidence for early ochre mining (Bowen 2003; Strassburger nd; Timberlake 2001). This interpretation is not certain, however, particularly as none of the tools appeared to display signs of ochre impregnation (Chris Salter, pers comm; Hoyle *et al* 2007a, 86).

Iron ores were certainly exploited in Dean during the Iron Age (McWhirr 1981), although the evidence for this is not always clear. Iron ore from the Iron Age hillfort of Midsummer Hill, Herefordshire was tentatively linked to the Forest of Dean (Walters 1999, 41) and the only datable Iron Age artefact from a scowle is a coin of about 50 BC from Bream (Allen 1961, 136) which is not necessarily evidence of mining (Hoyle *et al* 2007a, 85).

The main evidence for Iron Age exploitation of Forest ore does not come from the scowles themselves but from analysis of datable iron artefacts, ores or processing waste. Iron Age currency bars from Beckford in Worcestershire (dated to between 400 BC and 100 BC) have a low phosphorous content consistent with ores from the Forest of Dean or the Bristol Mendip region and were probably produced in the Forest (Hedges and Salter 1979; Paynter 2006). Late Iron Age iron slag from Frocester Court villa east of the River Severn had a low uranium content, consistent with outcrops on the eastern side of the Forest of Dean (Thomas 2000), indicating that Forest ore was also exported to other areas before it was smelted.

There is no direct evidence for Iron Age mining although it is generally assumed that surface deposits would have been exploited during this period (Hart 1971). Subterranean mining is, however, a feature of early mineral extraction in

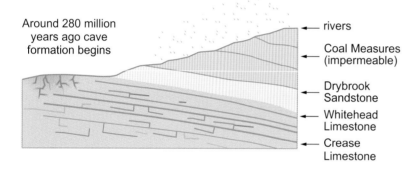

Around 280 million years ago cave formation begins

rivers

Coal Measures (impermeable)

Drybrook Sandstone

Whitehead Limestone

Crease Limestone

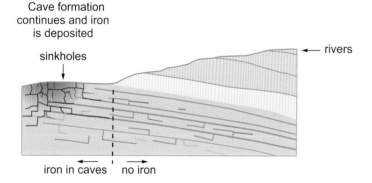

Cave formation continues and iron is deposited

sinkholes

rivers

iron in caves   no iron

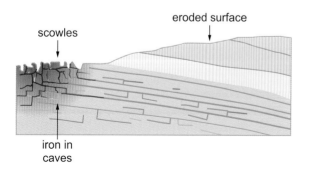

scowles

eroded surface

iron in caves

Britain, and Bronze Age copper mines have been investigated in North Wales (Crew and Crew 1990). Although there is no firm evidence for prehistoric subsurface mining in the Forest, this may have been masked by later mining activity (cf Timberlake 1990, 20–1) and may come to light in the future.

There can be little doubt that the Forest of Dean was a major producer of iron ore throughout the Roman period, and perhaps one of the two major iron-producing areas during the 3rd and 4th centuries AD (Cleere and Crossley 1985; LUAU 1998, 9; Sim and Ridge 2002). Attempts have been made to assess the scale of the Roman iron industry based on estimates of the quantity of slag produced by smelting process (Walters 1999, 127) or the size of scowles (Wildgoose 1993), but hard evidence for the extent of iron ore extraction or how the industry was organised during this period is elusive.

A small mine at Lydney Park predated a Roman hut and has been interpreted as a Roman iron mine (Wheeler and Wheeler 1932, 18–22). A second mine from Lydney Park may also have been Roman (Scott-Garrett 1959), but could have been later (Hoyle et al 2007a, 87).

Iron ore from 3rd- to 4th-century AD deposits at the Chesters Roman villa, Woolaston, and Frocester Court Roman villa, east of the Severn, are consistent with Forest of Dean ore, but could be from other sources in the Carboniferous Limestones of the Bristol/Mendip region (Fulford and Allen 1992, 204; Standing 2000, 92) and may not have been mined in the Forest of Dean.

Scientific analysis of dated iron artefacts, ores or smelting residues is likely to be the most reliable way of identifying sites where iron ore was extracted during the Roman period.

Slags from the 2nd- and 3rd-century AD layers at Ariconium (the modern Weston under

Penyard, Herefordshire) have a low uranium content consistent with iron ore from the eastern outcrops of the Forest of Dean (Young 2012, 164), the closest of which are scowles at Wigpool Common north of Mitcheldean, only about 3km to the south-east.

Slag from late 1st-/early 2nd-century smelting in Sallowvallets Wood, north of Cannop has also been analysed, and although it was not possible to identify the ore source with any precision, it was probably from an unknown source in the western outcrops. These were similar to slags reused in the construction of the 2nd-century forum-basilica at Caerwent, and also with Roman slag from Usk, perhaps suggesting that Forest of Dean ores from the western outcrops were exported westwards early in the Roman period (Young 2013, 241).

This analysis of smelting residues and ores is not yet refined enough to identify specific Roman mining sites, and it is not yet possible to apply this to speculation on the scale or organisation of ore extraction during the Roman period.

Fig 6.17
Iron Age currency bars from Beckford, Worcestershire. Iron currency bars have a variety of forms, although most are long thin flat bars with raised flanges at one end. It is thought these were produced close to smelting sites as a way of trading iron and showing off its forgeable properties (Crew 1995). These currency bars were between 880 and 760mm long and were probably made from Forest of Dean iron.
[© Bill Britnell with permission]

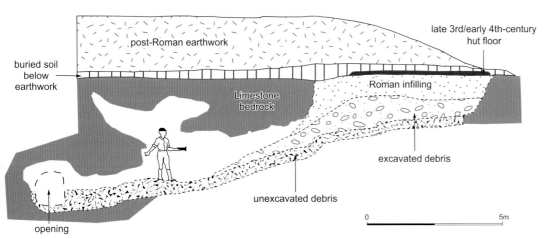

Fig 6.18
Roman iron mine at Lydney Park. This represents evidence for subterranean Roman iron mining but it is not clear how typical this was of the industry as a whole.
[After Wheeler and Wheeler 1932, Society of Antiquaries]

There is also very little evidence for early medieval iron ore mining although goethite, consistent with Forest ore, was used in 8th- to 9th-century smelting at Clearwell Quarry, Stowe (Pine *et al* 2009, 32–3). The Domesday Survey also records 'blooms of iron' paid as rent by tenants at Alvington (Moore 1982), indicating that iron smelting was taking place there at that time. It seems likely that iron smelters in Alvington sourced ore from the Forest, although Alvington may also have had easy trade links (via the River Severn) with iron ore sources in the Bristol region which may also have been mined at that time.

There are many more historical references to iron mines and iron miners in the Forest in the later medieval period. Dean miners were in demand due to their expertise as military engineers to undermine fortifications, or to work in iron mines in other parts of the country (Hart 2002, 19–21) and the customary privileges of the Free Miners (who were licensed by the Crown) were probably officially codified sometime between the mid-13th and early 15th centuries (Hart 2002, 18–19). It is not known whether ores were exploited as surface outcrops, mine pits or subterranean mines, but below-ground mining is assumed to have become more prevalent in the 13th to 15th centuries, perhaps due to increased military demands (Cross 1982), and in 1282 miners were granted access to *coperones* (variously rendered as 'cooper's stuff' or 'lop and top') from the Forest to timber their mines (Maclean 1889–90; Nicholls 1866, 23; Hart 2002, 14). It is not clear, however, whether these applied to coal or iron mines and the timber, assumed to have been used as shoring for underground workings, may equally have been used to construct containers (barrels) for transporting ore or coal, or as fuel for fire setting operations.

Few medieval workings can be precisely located, although an iron mine at Ardlonde recorded in 1270 and 1287 has been identified as St Whites Farm, Cinderford (Jurica 1996d), and in 1282 the Earl of Warwick 'hath a mine in his own wood of Lydeneye', probably in the scowles in Lydney Park (Maclean 1889–90, 369; Nicholls 1866, 23).

Slags from later medieval deposits at Trellech in Monmouthshire and St Briavels in the Forest of Dean have a high uranium content consistent with ores from the western iron ore outcrops and similar slags have been found at the medieval quay at Oldbury, South Gloucestershire, on the eastern side of the Severn (Thomas 2000).

Iron and ochre mining continued in Dean throughout the 17th and 18th centuries mainly in relatively shallow workings above levels which needed pumping to prevent flooding, although some mines were surprisingly deep. Westbury Brook iron mine, for example, was about 140m deep (Ian Standing, pers comm). The industry began to decline from the 18th century as ore bodies above flooding level were worked out and ore was imported from Lancashire and Cumbria to supply the district's numerous ironworks. By 1788 it was reported that there was no regular iron ore mining in Dean with the exception of approximately 20 men collecting ore from old workings, principally in the Parkend area (Hart 1971, 226).

Later miners often encountered evidence of earlier iron mines known as 'Old Men's Workings' (Nicholls 1866, 62–4), and the system of early subterranean mining is doubtless more extensive than records of the discovery of lost mines suggest. These are extremely difficult to date and below-ground mining may have been a feature of the Forest of Dean industry from a much earlier period than is generally thought.

Fig 6.19
Early post-medieval free miner's brass from Newland church. The miner carries a hod on his back and a pick in his hand. In his mouth he holds a candle fixed to a stick with a ball of clay known as a 'nelly'. [© Gloucestershire County Council Archaeology Service. Photo Steve Dorey]

Sometimes artefacts such as ash or oak shovels, ladders, shoe fragments, clay balls (nellies) for attaching a candle to a stick, timbers used as pit props, or the heads of single-pronged picks have been found (Nicholls 1866; Forster Brown 1896–7). Similar items are depicted on late medieval/early post-medieval images of mining, for example the 15th-century font at Abenhall church, the Newland Freeminer's Brass (variously dated from the 15th to the 18th century) or 19th-century engravings of Dean miners (Hart 2002, 22; Jurica 1996d, fig 20), and could date to any of these periods, or earlier.

A wooden pit prop from workings near Clay's Farm, Sling has been dated by dendrochronology to about AD 1650, although the details of where this analysis was undertaken are sketchy (Wildgoose 1993, 141). There was also an interesting 19th-century attempt at objective dating when the rate of decay, mineral replacement and specific gravity of a number of supposedly Roman oak shovels from Westbury Brook iron mine were compared with wooden items of known date which included an oak pile from London Bridge, an Egyptian mummy's coffin and a fragment of the true cross. As a result the shovels were interpreted as relatively recent (and too badly made to be seriously considered Roman) and probably dated to the 17th century (Forster Brown 1896–7, 160).

Iron ore processing

The bloomery smelting process

During the prehistoric, Roman, medieval and early post-medieval periods iron smelting took place in charcoal-fuelled clay furnaces known as bloomeries. Air-flow was controlled by human-powered bellows for much of the bloomery period, although water-powered bellows may have been introduced in the later medieval and early post-medieval periods.

Bloomeries did not reach high enough temperatures to completely separate iron from the ore and a considerable amount of iron-rich slag was a waste product of the bloomery process.

In the early to middle Iron Age (from about 750 to 700 BC) bloomeries were fairly small and slag accumulated at their base, although from the later Iron Age slag tapping bloomeries, which allowed slag to flow from their base, were introduced (Paynter 2011, 3). These were used throughout the Roman period, although slag pit furnaces, where molten slag accumulated

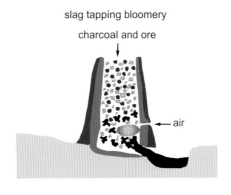

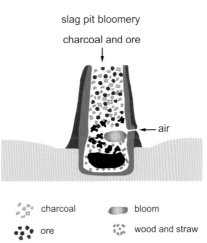

into a pit below the bloomery, were used in the Anglo-Saxon period (Bayley *et al* 2001, 11). Slag tapping bloomeries were reintroduced from about AD 800 (Paynter 2011, 4) and these continued to be used in the Forest of Dean until the introduction of the blast furnace in the later 16th century (Hart 1971, 8).

Although the remains of bloomeries or slag tapping pits can survive as buried archaeological remains, most bloomery smelting sites are identified by dumps of tapped and untapped slag

Fig 6.20 (left)
Slag tapping and slag pit bloomeries. The bloom was a semi-solid spongy mass of metallic iron and slag which formed around the air hole. The hot bloom was removed from the furnace and beaten with hammers to force out slag and consolidate the reasonably uncontaminated iron which could then be taken away for further refining.
[After Paynter 2011. English Heritage]

Fig 6.21 (below)
Typical slag from a slag tapping bloomery furnace. These produced a distinct slag (tap slag), which is the most commonly found evidence for bloomery smelting. It has a clear solidified flow pattern on its upper surface and a rougher lower surface where it flowed over the ground.
[© Gloucestershire County Council Archaeology Service. Photo Paul Nichols]

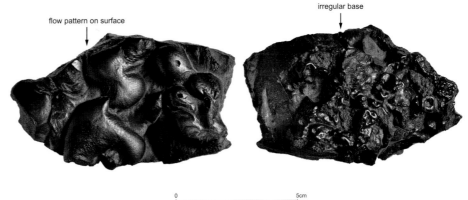

(cinders) and other debris from the smelting process (Cleere and Crossley 1985; Goddard and Juleff 2003). Vast quantities of this material was resmelted following the introduction of the charcoal-fired blast furnace to the Forest in the late 16th century (Bick 1980), and the sale and transportation of this 'unexhaustable quantity' of cinders (Hart 1971, 222) became an industry in its own right. In 1677 it was reported that the digging of iron ore and cinders employed 'an infinite number of men', and cinders were exported to Gloucester, Herefordshire and Monmouthshire and also to Ireland (Hart 1971, 220–3). Exactly how much of this valuable resource for the identification of earlier smelting sites and research into early smelting technologies has now been obliterated is unknown, although it is clearly much diminished and antiquarian accounts record extensive deposits of cinders throughout the Forest of Dean and as far north as Worcester (Wright 1854; Nicholls 1860, 236–7; Herbert 1996a, 291). The precise location of these is generally not specified, although placenames which include the word 'cinder' probably refer to former smelting sites (Hoyle *et al* 2007a, 369–72).

Although a concentration of bloomery slag is a reasonable indication of an early smelting site, the reverse is not necessarily true. There was no surface evidence for the early Roman smelting site in Sallowvallets Wood to the north of Cannop (*see* pp 31–2), although slag charcoal and burnt furnace material were found by excavation (Hoyle 2013a, 31–7), and many early smelting sites may survive in the Forest where no obvious surface indications are visible.

Evidence for bloomery smelting

Pre-Roman and Roman

There are no securely dated pre-Roman smelting sites in the Forest of Dean. Undated non-tapping slag-pit furnaces and slag east of Lydney Road, Yorkley had similarities with known Iron Age examples (Young 2015, 2–3), but could date to the early medieval period (*see* below).

Some early Roman smelting sites may have originated in the late Iron Age and bloomery slag has been found with late Iron Age and early Roman pottery at the Iron Age promontory fort at Symonds Yat (Parry 1994, 67; Walters 1999, 6). Bloomery slag from a 1st-century AD ditch at Reddings Lane, Staunton (Ellis 2013, 12) and from the lower fills of the ditch of the possible early Roman fortlet on Ruardean Hill (Young 2011, 219) may be residues of Late Iron Age smelting. Pre-Roman colluvium in Sallowvallets north of Cannop also contained tiny fragments of iron slag (Hoyle 2013a, 31) although the smelting site was not found.

Unstratified bloomery slag and late Iron Age/early Roman pottery have also been found at Ruardean and Drybrook (Walters 1999, 4), and both Coleford and Blakeney have been identified as 1st-century AD iron-working sites (Walters 1999, figure between pp 57 and 58) although the evidence for this is not clear.

There is much more evidence for Roman smelting although the industry, particularly for the early period, is not well understood. Walters (1992b) suggested that the Forest of Dean was a Roman imperial estate in the 1st and 2nd centuries AD where ore was extracted under direct military control and exported to smelting centres at Ariconium, Monmouth and Whitchurch in Herefordshire, and possibly also Newent and Dymock (Walters 1999, 151). A recent review of the iron industry at Ariconium, however, has questioned the evidence for direct military control of smelting operations at that site (Jackson 2012, 195). Ariconium and Monmouth certainly increased iron production during the early Roman period, presumably in response to increased military needs (Jackson 2012, 194), but the model of a centralised early Roman industry where ore was exported for smelting at large production centres does not really reflect the diverse and complex pattern which is beginning to emerge.

There are a number of sites, both within the Forest of Dean and in its immediate vicinity, where iron slag has been found with 1st-century AD pottery, although few of these have been investigated to any degree (Hoyle *et al* 2007a, 110–11).

A small rural site at Reddings Lane, Staunton was involved in iron smelting during the 1st and 2nd centuries AD (Ellis 2013) and early Severn Valley Ware pottery and charcoal with a radiocarbon date of cal AD 20–140 was excavated along with smelting waste at Sallowvallets, north of Cannop (Hoyle 2013a, 37). The Sallowvallets site was not close to known settlement and smelting appears to have taken place within a small discrete area. A similar scenario has been postulated for some medieval smelting which may have followed the cycle of charcoal production through areas of woodland (Hoyle 2013a, 37).

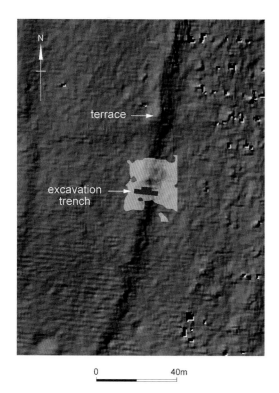

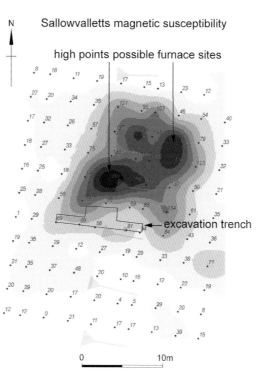

Sallowvalletts magnetic susceptibility

high points possible furnace sites

← excavation trench

0   40m

0   10m

Fig 6.22
Lidar and magnetic susceptibility survey of the early Roman smelting site in Sallowvalletts Wood. This identified high magnetic readings (presumably spreads of magnetic slag) over an area of about 18 × 16m. Particularly high readings in a small area about 3m to the north of the excavation trench, and another about 10m to the north, may be the sites of furnaces.

Villas were essentially at the centre of working estates based on farming (both agricultural and pastoral), although they also operated mixed economies which included industrial activities where resources and need allowed (Branigan 1989, 42). Some Forest villas were certainly involved in iron smelting by the 3rd and 4th centuries AD, although as the production and maintenance of iron items would have been an important aspect of any agricultural estate it cannot be assumed that all evidence for smelting or smithing is necessarily indicative of a commercial enterprise (Branigan 1989, 47).

At the Chesters, Woolaston the foundations of a large timber-framed building contained evidence for a number of iron smelting furnaces, possible ore crushing areas and considerable quantities of tap slag (Fulford and Allen 1992, 205). The total area of industrial activity was estimated at about 7,250m², and this has been interpreted as evidence of 'a highly organised enterprise' dedicated to smelting. It is estimated that between 62 and 180 tonnes of iron were produced at the site and probably traded via the River Severn which was easily accessible from Ley Pill to the west of the villa (Fulford and Allen 1992, 205). The scale of this operation and its level of organisation suggest an organised industrial concern which made a significant contribution to the villa's economy. How impor-

tant this was to the overall economy of the villa is difficult to discern, but at the very least it seems to have been a significant 'side-line' (Hoyle *et al* 2007a, 115–16).

It is not, however, clear how typical this site is of the later Roman iron industry in Dean, as the evidence from other villa sites is much less conclusive.

Park Farm, Aylburton is, like the Chesters, on low ground with relatively easy access to the Severn, and iron slag has been recorded in floor make-up deposits (Fitchett 1986, 27) and as surface finds (Walters 1999, 10). Iron smelting may also have been a significant part of the economy of this villa, perhaps at a scale comparable

Fig 6.23
Early Roman bloomery slag and furnace remains from Sallowvalletts.
[© Gloucestershire County Council Archaeology Service. Photo Paul Nichols]

furnace   bloomery slag

0   5cm

135

to the Chesters, although the evidence for this has not yet been found.

At Boughspring, however, which is on higher ground with no clear access to the Severn, slag has only been recorded as unstratified surface finds (Bridgewater 1973). Iron slag has also been found at Stock Farm, Clearwell on the higher ground in the central part of the Forest, although only in relatively small amounts (Blake 2004, 15; Catchpole 1996, 5; Cook 1995, 2), and evidence for smelting at the Wye-side villas of Huntsham and Hadnock just outside the Forest of Dean is also limited (Taylor 1995, 224; Walters 1992a, 95). While iron smelting may have taken place at these villas, it is difficult to make the case that this was a significant element of their economic basis.

Iron smelting during this period was not confined to villas and there is a growing body of evidence that it was a widespread industry that formed part of the economy of the majority (but not all) of the known Roman sites in the Forest of Dean. Some of these are also associated with evidence for masonry structures and could represent isolated smelting sites, or be part of larger complexes, such as villas or small rural settlements.

Masonry remains and evidence for mid- to late Roman iron smelting were found at Rodmore Farm, St Briavels (Blake 2001, 7; 2002, 15, figs 1 and 2; 2003, 8–11; 2004, fig 3), and at Rossilyn, Alvington (Hood 2013). There was no evidence for domestic occupation at either of these sites, although both could have been associated with larger complexes and possibly a villa. There is also considerable evidence for Roman smelting and masonry buildings dating from the 2nd to 4th centuries AD in the area centred around Blakeney (Barber and Holbrook 2000, 35–9; Johns 2005b; Walters 1990a, 40) and English Bicknor (Milford 2000; Walters 1999) and iron smelting remains associated with 2nd- to 4th-century AD pottery and structural remains have been recorded in the Pope's Hill area to the north of Littledean (Scott-Garrett 1956, 199–202). It is not clear whether the sites in these areas were related to each other, or even operated at the same time, but they may represent evidence for dispersed rural settlements associated with iron smelting, or perhaps out-lying parts of villa estates. Robbed-out foundations of what may have been a rectangular structure with an apsidal addition were also found with bloomery slag and 3rd- and 4th-century AD pottery at High Nash, Coleford. Although this was interpreted as a possible temple (Walters 1987b, 50), these structures may be associated with later Roman iron smelting and/or occupation.

Iron smelting also seems to have been taking place at rural sites which are not clearly associated with villas or larger settlements. There is increasing evidence for 2nd- to 4th-century iron smelting on the gravel terraces to the south-east of Lydney (Barber 2009, 14–15; Brett 2004, 13–14; Wessex Archaeology 2003b, i), at the Mount, Lower Lybrook (Walters 1985a, 24), and probably also at the early Roman enclosure at Ruardean Hill which was occupied in the 3rd century (Hoyle 2013a, 25).

Many other sites are suggested where pottery from the 2nd, 3rd and 4th centuries AD (or which has just been classed as 'Roman') has

Fig 6.24
Evidence for Roman smelting, scowles and villas.

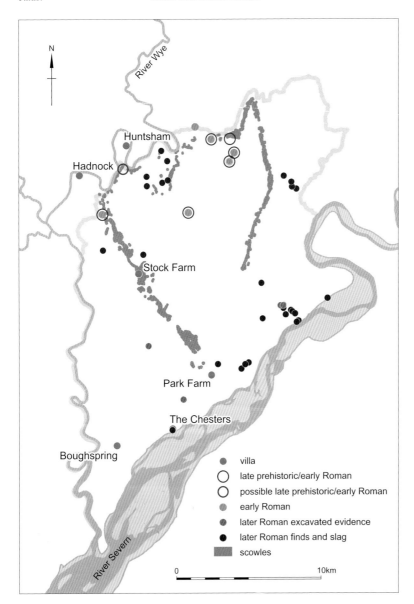

been found (generally as surface scatters or chance finds) along with bloomery slag and other evidence for smelting. Dated 2nd- to 4th-century pottery and bloomery slag have been found at Hangerberry Hill, English Bicknor, and Broom Hill to the south of Soudley, while 'Roman' pottery and bloomery slag is recorded at Holm Farm, Lydney and Pope's Grove, Lydbrook (Hoyle *et al* 2007a, 348–9). Bloomery slag, ore, furnace bases and furnace lining have been found in the same area as 2nd- to 4th-century pottery at Whitescourt, Awre, Horse Pill, Stroat (Walters 1999, 27) and Ley Pill, Woolaston (Allen 2009, 90–1; Allen and Fulford 1987, 275), all of which are close to the Severn and were probably trading along the river. Roman pottery and bloomery slag have been found at Green Bottom, Littledean (Scott-Garrett 1918–58, 14 November 1953), Tidenham (Walters 1999, 20), Hagloe south-east of Blakeney (Johns 2005b) and a complete Roman quern and other quern fragments have been found with bloomery slag at Upper Buttersend, Hartpury (Charlesworth 2007, 7). Iron slag and abraded sherds of Roman pottery (which cannot be precisely dated) have also been recorded on the eastern side of Welshbury Hill associated with an earthwork platform (Jackson *et al* 2016, 22) and iron ore, bloomery slag, and five sherds of Roman pottery have been recovered from molehills within Soudley Camp, Soudley (Hoyle 2014, 6). Slag reported with two 3rd-century AD coins at Cherry Orchard Farm, Newland in 1881 may, however, have been post-medieval and this may not have been a Roman smelting site (Hoyle *et al* 2007a, 350). None of these sites have been investigated further and exactly what these represent is not clear.

Early medieval

There is no firm evidence for smelting in the immediate post-Roman period although evidence for 8th- to 9th-century smelting has been found at Clearwell Quarry, Stowe. The bases of 30 furnaces (probably slag pit type [David Dungworth, pers comm]) were found close to evidence for ore-roasting hearths and charcoal clamps. There were no datable finds but charcoal from three of the furnaces produced radiocarbon dates from between cal AD 763 and cal AD 890. The furnaces were in three discernible clusters which was interpreted as seasonal smelting on the same site, although the time span between smelting operations could not be determined (Pine *et al* 2009, 32–3, table

10). Large non-tapping slag pit furnaces and iron smelting residues have also been recorded to the east of Lydney Road, Yorkley. The furnaces themselves were undated and similar to known Iron Age examples (Young 2015, 2–3), although charcoal from a posthole (over 50m to the west) produced an 8th- to 9th-century AD date (Havard and Guarino 2015, 10, fig 5) and the smelting may date to the early medieval period.

The only other reference to pre-Norman smelting in the Forest is in the Domesday Survey of 1086 which records 'blooms of iron' paid as rent by tenants at Alvington (Moore 1982), although no smelting sites from this period have been identified.

Later medieval

There is considerably more evidence for a major iron industry in the Forest of Dean during the medieval period, although much information is derived from documentary sources and little is known about the scale or organisation of the industry at this time. This is not helped by a lack of precision in the terms used to describe smelting operations, and references to *fabricae*, *forgiae arrantes* or *blissahis* could indicate forges, smithies or bloomeries (Hart 1971, 4). The catch-all term 'forge' (which strictly speaking should indicate a site where iron was processed rather than smelted) is generally used for a smelting site.

Unlike mining, smelting was not governed by customary right, although iron ore was carefully regulated by the Crown and some 13th-century furnaces were under the direct control of the Crown (Hart 1971, 4). Others were held by private individuals under licence from the Crown and some institutions such as Flaxley Abbey were granted smelting rights by the Crown (Watkins 1985, 94). There was, however, considerable abuse of the system (Hart 2002, 146) and there are numerous references to illegal forges whose charcoal needs depleted the Forest's timber supply (Hart 1971, 5–8). The Eyre Roll of 1270 reported that 'there are many itinerant forges and those who hold or have held them have done many evil things both concerning the tall trees as also the underwood, and also by de-branching, so that by reason of these forges a great despoiling has been done to the forest' (Hart 1971).

There were sporadic attempts to regulate smelting and charcoal production and in 1217 the king ordered that all private forges (with six exceptions) should be dismantled. Many of these were returned to their owners within three years, and by the middle of the 13th century between 25 and 30 forges were recorded, a figure which rose to 43 in 1270 and 60 in 1282 (Hart 1971, 6).

The historical evidence for the 12th to 13th centuries records a number of 'itinerant forges' many of them unregulated or operating in a 'grey' semi-official capacity. The precise status of these is not clear and Hart has suggested that 'itinerant' may refer to the operators rather than the furnaces, who were 'itinerant' in their search for charcoal or ore, which they then took to the permanent smelting site (Hart 1971, 4). There appears to have been a close association with charcoal production and smelting in the Royal Demesne, and bloomery slag is often found

Fig 6.25
Evidence for medieval and undated smelting and scowles.

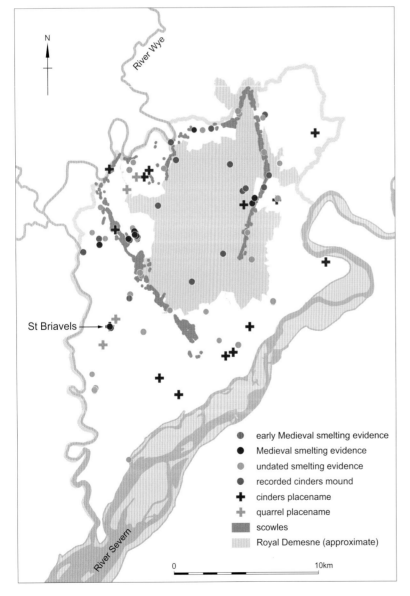

N

River Wye

St Briavels →

- early Medieval smelting evidence
- Medieval smelting evidence
- undated smelting evidence
- recorded cinders mound
- cinders placename
- quarrel placename
- scowles
- Royal Demesne (approximate)

0   10km

River Severn

where there is also evidence for charcoal production (for example Johns 1991; Blake and Briscoe 2002; Monmouth Archaeology 2002; Hoyle 2003a, 2003b) and, in the 13th century, some Forest of Dean charcoal burners also owned forges (Armstrong 1978, 13). 'Itinerant forges' may, therefore, have been relatively temporary bloomery sites which were set up to exploit the charcoal resource in a particular area and then dismantled and moved on as charcoal became depleted. No sites of medieval 'itinerant forges' have been identified with any certainty, although sites at Chestnuts Wood, Littledean and Broom Hill, Soudley where charcoal platforms are associated with bloomery slag, Roman and medieval pottery and flagged stone surfaces and other structural remains (Scott-Garrett 1956; Johns 1991; 2011) have been tentatively suggested as possible sites (Hoyle *et al* 2007a, 119).

There are no references to 'itinerant forges' later in the medieval period and this practice may not have continued much beyond the end of the 14th century. References to 'large' and 'small' furnaces in the reign of Edward III (1327–77) may differentiate between peripatetic 'itinerant forges' (presumably the 'small' furnaces) and more permanent smelting sites attached to settlements.

There is limited excavated evidence, however, for more permanent medieval smelting sites, and nothing is known about how these operated, whether smelting was a seasonal operation, or whether the iron was intended for trade or domestic consumption.

Rock-cut pits (possibly slag tapping pits) and a possible ore roasting hearth (Hart 1971, pl 3) were recorded with bloomery slag, charcoal, fragments of probable furnace base and 13th-century pottery at Warfield Farm, Ruardean (Bridgewater 1966), where surface finds of 'pit slag lumps' and 13th-century pottery have also been found (Hoyle *et al* 2007a, 100).

Slag tapping pits and 12th- to 14th-century pottery have also been excavated close to Rodley Manor, south-east of Lydney, although no furnaces were found (Cooke 2003) and a dump of charcoal and slag with late 12th- to 13th-century pottery excavated at St White's Farm, Cinderford has been interpreted as evidence for iron smelting and primary smithing (Teague 2007, 8). There is also some evidence for early post-medieval bloomery smelting close to the Feathers Hotel, Lydney where smelting residues, an area of burning and a large burnt limestone slab have been found (Townsend 1999; Mack and McDonnell 1999).

Bloomery slag and medieval artefacts have also been found in excavated features at Tidenham House, Tidenham; Tanhouse Farm, Newland; Church Road, Lydney; High Meadow Farm, Newland; and Blakeney Sewage Treatment Works (Hoyle *et al* 2007a, 100, table 45), The Laurels, Ruardean, and Ashfield House, St Briavels, and surface scatters of bloomery slag associated with medieval finds have been found at a number of sites, although apart from the fact that smelting was taking place at these sites little else is known about them.

A third category of iron processing site recorded in the medieval Forest of Dean was the 'great forge of the King' associated with St Briavels Castle (Hart 1971, 4). During the 13th century this site was dedicated to the production of quarrels (crossbow bolt heads) for the Royal Armoury and half a million were produced between 1223 and 1293 (Hart 1966, 272). There was a forge within the castle (Townley 2004, 186, fig 50) which appears to have been a large fabrication centre that imported unforged iron, rather than a smelting site. Other sites in the vicinity may also have been associated with quarrel production as a 'Quarrel field' was recorded in 1608 (Clissold 1982; PRO 1608a) only 1.3km to the south of the castle and another,

less than 0.5km to the north-east, was marked 'Quarrel' on a 17th-century map (GCRO 17th century) and 'Worrals' on the 1608 map and 19th-century tithe map (Clissold 1982; Gwatkin 1993a; PRO 1608a). These may also have been fabrication sites (Webb 2000, 56), although smelting may have been part of this operation as iron slag has been reported from 'Quarrel Field' (Webb 2000, 56) and a large deposit of bloomery slag has been reported at Cinder Hill just over 100m to the west of the castle (Hoyle 2011b).

Quarrels were not the only items manufactured for military use at St Briavels, and horseshoes and nails were made in the early 14th century (Townley 2004, 186), although manufacture appears to have ceased by the later 14th century, perhaps due to a shortage of charcoal from the Forest, and production shifted to the Weald in Kent, partly supplied by Forest of Dean ore (Townley 2004, 186).

Charcoal-fired blast furnaces harnessed water power to achieve greater efficiency through economy of scale, as more ore could be smelted by fewer workers and higher temperatures enabled more iron to be recovered from the ore and also from the waste (cinders) of earlier bloomery smelting. Although blast furnaces were introduced to England in 1496, they were

Fig 6.26
Surface evidence for undated smelting at Hewelsfield showing as a dark spread of slag and charcoal. Numerous bloomery smelting sites survive as spreads of bloomery slag on field surfaces, although many are not associated with datable artefacts and could be evidence for smelting from the late Iron Age through to the early post-medieval period (Hoyle et al 2007a, 102–4).
[© Gloucestershire County Council Archaeology Service]

not adopted in the Forest of Dean region until the late 16th century when furnaces were built at Bishopswood and Whitchurch just over the boundary of the Forest of Dean in Herefordshire, although there was a forge at Lydbrook by the early 1590s (Meredith 2006, 75). There was furnace at Staunton in 1608 (Clissold 1982; PRO 1608a) and by 1612 others had been built at Parkend, Lydbrook (Howbrook furnace) and Cannop, with forges at Parkend, Lydbrook and Cannop (Knight 2011, 41). The introduction of these blast furnaces marked the beginning of the end for bloomery smelting, although the two processes may have coexisted for a period and it is not known for certain when the last bloomery operated in the Forest of Dean.

Fig 6.27
All recorded charcoal platforms.

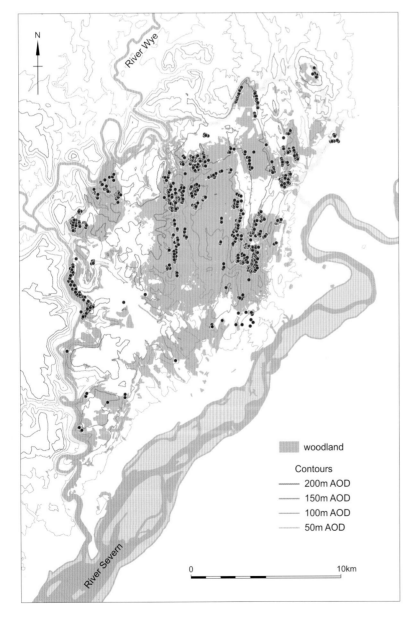

Charcoal production

Charcoal is produced by roasting wood (at around 500 degrees Celsius) in conditions which restrict air supply, preventing the wood from burning and turning to ash but allowing water and other volatile compounds to be released (Armstrong 1978, 8).

Charcoal produces about twice as much heat as wood and was the fuel used for smelting iron, and other industrial processes. Throughout the bloomery period demand for charcoal was high in the Forest of Dean. Estimates of the amount of charcoal required to produce specific quantities of iron are variable and are subject to variations between types of iron ore from different locations, although it has been estimated that Roman iron smelting at Ariconium would have needed 1,000kg of charcoal to smelt 1,000kg of ore to produce 330kg of bloom. A further 1,000kg of charcoal was needed to transform the bloom into 75kg of forgeable iron (Jackson 2012, 193, 196). By this calculation 26.6 tonnes of charcoal were needed to produce 1 tonne of finished iron, which would have used up the produce of 26.6ha of coppiced woodland (Fulford and Allen 1992, 191) or underwood.

Due to its friable nature, charcoal could only be transported about 5–6km without considerable wastage (Cleere and Crossley 1985, 135) and it was more efficient to site bloomeries close to the charcoal source rather than the ore source (Jones 1996, 34). The medieval forges at Parva Dean (Littledean) occasionally used charcoal produced outside the Forest of Dean, and the 13th-century forges at English Bicknor imported charcoal from Wales (Hart 2002, 66), although in both these instances the charcoal may have travelled less than 2–3km. The close relationship between charcoal production and smelting may have been exemplified by medieval 'itinerant forges' (Hart 1971). These may have been relatively temporary operations which smelted in areas where charcoal was available and then relocated to exploit a new source when these were exhausted, perhaps returning when the coppice or underwood had replenished sufficiently for further charcoal production.

Despite the importance of the charcoal resource there has been little research into the practicalities of the industry, how the industry was organised, how the woodland was managed or what production methods were used.

A Roman charcoal store was excavated at the Chesters villa, Woolaston (Fulford and Allen

woodland

Contours
—— 200m AOD
—— 150m AOD
—— 100m AOD
—— 50m AOD

0   10km

1992, 177) and Roman charcoal has been found at a number of sites (*see* below), but no prehistoric or Roman charcoal production sites are known in the Forest and it is not clear how charcoal was made during these periods.

The earliest form of charcoal production may have been in pits with production in above-ground clamps (a stack of timber which was covered in earth and roasted to produce charcoal) being a later innovation. Terminology is inexact and as charcoal clamps are known by a number of names including 'hearths', 'kilns', 'pits' or 'pitsteads' (Armstrong 1978; Rotherham *et al* 2008, 21), medieval records of 'charcoal pits' in the Forest of Dean (Jurica 1996d, 346) probably indicate clamps rather than pits. Evidence for charcoal production in pits is rare in England, although early Bronze Age features in East Anglia and trenches at a Roman smelting site at Wakeley, Northamptonshire may have been used for charcoal production (Tylecote 1986, 225). Recognised examples of charcoal pits tend to be in northern England, Scotland, Ireland and Scandinavia, although few of these have been excavated or dated. Medieval examples are known at Trondheim in Norway and Eyjafjallahreppur in Iceland (Berg 2009, 127; Church *et al* 2007) and early medieval charcoal pits at Russagh, County Offaly in Ireland (Kenny and Dolan nd). A number of charcoal pits in Argyll and Bute, Scotland are either undated or were last used in the post-medieval period (Rennie 1991) and in this part of Scotland charcoal production in above-ground clamps was not introduced until the 16th and 17th centuries in response to increased demand, which needed more efficient production methods (Rennie 1997, 173).

No charcoal pits have been found in the Forest of Dean (or in Gloucestershire) although charcoal platforms, level areas where charcoal was produced in above-ground clamps, are abundant with over 1,200 known sites. Many of these are known from aerial photographs (Small and Stoertz 2006) and field survey (Blake and Briscoe 2002, 9; Monmouth Archaeology 2002; Hoyle 2003a, 2003b; 2008b, 32, 41, 47, 71) although the majority, some 942, were found by lidar. These tend to be in areas with steeper slopes where there are clearly defined platforms, and there are probably many more unrecognised charcoal platforms in the Forest (Hoyle 2008c, 78–9).

Few charcoal platforms in Britain have been excavated or dated, and even when dating evidence is available this need only date the latest burn on a site which may have been periodically reused for generations.

Most dated platforms are either medieval or post-medieval. A platform at Llanelen, Gower dated from the 13th to 14th centuries (Kissock and Wright 2001) and within the Forest of Dean 12th- to 13th-century pottery was found in a charcoal platform at Blakeney Hill (Johns 1991, 10) while post-medieval (16th- to 18th-century) pottery has been found in a charcoal platform in Cadora Woods, south of Lower Redbrook (Monmouth Archaeology 2002). A charcoal platform was also excavated in Welshbury Wood, Blaisdon, where a fragment of charcoal from its base suggested it was in use during the late 18th to early 19th century, probably to supply charcoal for the blast furnaces in the Flaxley Valley (Hoyle 2008b, 28). Undated oval spreads of charcoal

Fig 6.28
Charcoal platforms to the south of Serridge Lodge.

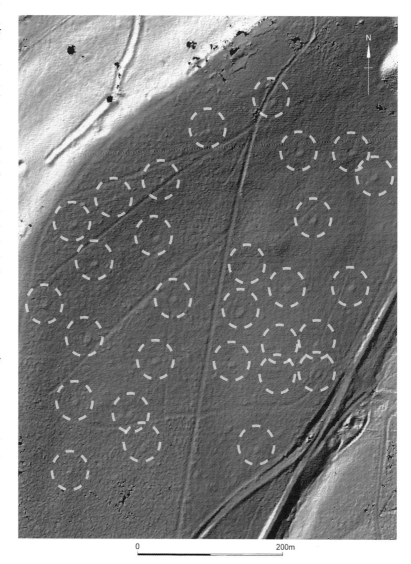

Fig 6.29 (right)
Charcoal production in
a charcoal clamp.
[© Gloucestershire County
Council Archaeology
Service]

Fig 6.30 (below)
Charcoal platform on
Welshbury Hill after
partial removal of loose
overburden.
[© Gloucestershire County
Council Archaeology
Service]

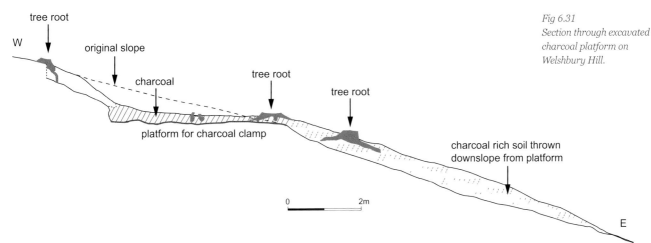

Fig 6.31
Section through excavated
charcoal platform on
Welshbury Hill.

associated with evidence for 7th- to 9th-century smelting at Stowe Quarry, Clearwell may be the bases of charcoal clamps (Pine *et al* 2009, 24–5), and a shallow subcircular scoop (and three similar unexcavated features) east of Lydney Road, Yorkley may also have been charcoal platforms (Havard and Guarino 2015, 8), although the date of smelting at this site is not clear.

Classical writers refer to Roman charcoal production in above ground clamps in the Mediterranean although pits may also have been used (Sim and Ridge 2002, 35) and there is some evidence for Roman charcoal production in clamps in England as a 3m wide area of burning excavated at the 2nd- to 3rd-century iron working settlement at Bardown, Sussex has been interpreted as the base of a charcoal clamp (Cleere and Crossley 1985, 304).The shift from charcoal production in pits to production in above-ground clamps may have been a Roman introduction, perhaps in response to an increased demand for charcoal for the growing iron industry at that time.

Woodland management for charcoal production

Charcoal from excavated sites can provide information on the ways woodland was managed for charcoal production although, in the Forest of Dean, this level of analysis has only been undertaken on Roman sites.

The Romans used charcoal from a range of deciduous trees, and oak heartwood appears to have been most common at early Roman sites such as Sallowvallets Wood, Cannop or Dymock to the north of the Forest (Gale 2007, 213–14; Challinor 2007, 233; Pearson *et al* 2012, 118), although this was less clear at Reddings Lane, Staunton (Ellis 2013, appendix D, table 1). Later

in the Roman period, although oak continued to predominate, charcoals from small deciduous roundwoods (typically hazel, elm, birch or hawthorn) became more common and these were used at the Chesters, Woolaston and Millend, Blakeney during the 3rd and 4th centuries and also for late 2nd-century smelting at Ariconium (Gale 2012, 167). Oak charcoal was still the most common, although this tended to be from small roundwoods, and charcoal from mature heartwood was less common (Figueiral 1992, 191; Gale 2000, 54). The significance of this is not altogether clear, although Cleere and Crossley (1985, 37) have suggested that, in the Weald at least, there is little evidence for deliberate selection of wood for charcoal production and a preference for oak could simply reflect that it was the most common species in the Forest of Dean during the Roman period.

There does appear to have been a preference for oak heartwood during the early Roman period, suggesting that mature trees tended to be used for charcoal production. During the later Roman period there appears to have been greater reliance on charcoal from smaller deciduous roundwoods (including oak) perhaps indicating a decline in the mature oak woodland at this time, perhaps due to over-exploitation. Some of this could also have been the product of the exploitation of natural scrub underwood, although woodland may have been increasingly managed as coppice during this period. Gale (2012, 166) has argued that wide growth rings and a straight rod-like form from charcoal at Ariconium indicated coppiced woodland, while Figueiral (1992, 191) suggested that charcoal from the Chesters, Woolaston was derived from managed coppice as the most recent annual growth rings were very close together. Classical writers indicate that the Romans were aware of the principles of managing woodland as coppice (Columella, *Res rustica* IV, cited in Rackham 1995, 74) and coppicing was used in Britain in the Neolithic Sweet Track in the Somerset Levels (Hey 1996, 505). Bloomery smelting also needed large amounts of charcoal (*see* p 140) and charcoal production for the Roman iron industry would have been a significant industry in its own right (Jackson 2012, 196). Given this demand, the management of large areas of woodland in the Roman period almost certainly involved some form of proactive coppicing to ensure a regular supply, rather than relying on the exploitation of naturally occurring scrub and underwood.

Charcoal from 8th- to 9th-century smelting at Clearwell Quarry, St Briavels was also dominated by mature oak (with a secondary use of hazel, birch, wild cherry or ash) although there was no direct evidence for coppicing (Pine *et al* 2009, 36).

No medieval charcoal assemblages from the Forest have been studied, although medieval charcoal burners in the Royal Demesne were using maple, thorn, hazel and dead wood in 1237 and underwood in 1325. In 1565 'underwood together with the lopping and shredding [branches cut from mature standards]' were sold to the 'ore-smiths' (Hart 1968, 33–4). What is not clear from these records is the extent to which these were the products of coppice or exploitation of naturally occurring underwood and scrub. In 1237 Henry III ordered that underwood should only be cut in the dormant season and in a way which allowed for regrowth so 'that no

damage should befall the coppice [*coepecia*]' and also that areas should be enclosed 'so that no beasts shall enter to browse there' (Hart 1995, 293). This clearly indicates proactive management of the underwood which is difficult not to interpret as coppicing, although how extensive this practice was, to what extent naturally occurring underwood was also exploited and the point at which the two practices can be differentiated in any meaningful way is not clear.

Some of the Forest's woodland was certainly managed as coppice by the late medieval period as eight areas of coppice are recorded on the 'fringes' of the Royal Demesne in the mid-16th century, most notably at Chestnuts Wood, Littledean, Bradley Hill, west of the Soudley Brook, and the Kidnalls, north of Lydney (Herbert 1996j, 362) and by the mid-17th century over 16 coppices were named in legal documents (Hart 1995, 68, 108–11). This may represent an increase in managed coppice, perhaps to ensure a consistent supply for the newly introduced charcoal-fired forges and furnaces (Dave Cranstone, pers comm), although these coppices may have originated at an earlier date.

The limited evidence suggests that some woodland was probably managed as coppice in the Roman and post-medieval periods and possibly also during the Middle Ages. How widespread this was at different times is, however, less clear and mature timber (including removal of smaller branches from standards) and unmanaged underwood and scrub also seems to have been exploited.

7

Management of archaeological sites in the Forest of Dean

One of the aims of the Forest of Dean Archaeological Survey was to improve the management of the archaeological resource in the Forest, and much of the information produced by the survey is now stored in databases that are routinely used for this purpose.

The Historic Environment Record and designated sites

Since the adoption of Planning Policy Guidance 16 (Archaeology and Planning) in 1990, archaeology has been a material consideration in the determination of all planning applications (DoE 1990). This means that whenever a Planning Application is submitted, the archaeological implications of the development are considered and, as a condition of their planning consent, the developer is required to fund appropriate archaeological works. Exactly what these entail would be dependent on the nature of the development and every case is different. Where particularly important remains are anticipated, for example if the development area contains a scheduled monument or listed building, the development could be refused or modified to exclude certain areas. This is rare, however, and it is much more common for the predevelopment works to consist of small-scale excavation to find out exactly what survives below ground, larger excavations to record any archaeological deposits that the development will destroy, or simply maintaining a watching brief of any groundworks in less sensitive areas.

To make the correct decisions about what is an appropriate response, it is vital that the archaeologists who advise the planning authority have the most up-to-date and comprehensive information about what is currently known.

The most important tool for this is the Historic Environment Record (HER), which is an enormous database of known archaeological sites, finds, or even records of investigations which have found nothing, which is managed and updated by the County Archaeology Service based at Shire Hall, Gloucester.

The Gloucestershire Historic Environment Record incorporates all information generated by all stages of the Forest of Dean Archaeological Survey, Rapid Coastal Zone Assessments and National Mapping Programme projects which covered the Forest of Dean. In addition to this, all archaeological contractors who undertake work as part of the planning process are obliged to submit copies of their reports to the HER, and there is also a policy of trawling local and county-wide journals to access information suitable for inclusion in the database. These include the *Transactions of the Bristol and Gloucestershire Archaeological Society*, *Dean Archaeology* (the journal of Dean Archaeology Group), the *Journal of the Gloucestershire Society for Industrial Archaeology* and the *New Regard of the Forest of Dean* (the journal of the Forest of Dean Local History Society). All academic or private researchers who make use of HER information are also requested to submit the results of their research to the HER, although this is not a contractual obligation.

The HER is based around the basic unit of the Area record, each of which can represent an archaeologically important site, structure or artefact, or an archaeological event such as an excavation or watching brief. Individual records vary from chance finds of a single flint or sherd of pottery to complex sites which can contain numerous artefacts or features. The Area record is further subdivided into Monuments which are records of archaeologically significant sites or features, Events which represent records of archaeological work such as excavations or watching briefs, and also Artefacts which represent records of sites where archaeologically significant finds have been recovered (not records of individual finds).

In April 2015, the Gloucestershire County Historic Environment Record contained 6,534 HER Area records for the Forest of Dean, which represented 11,524 separate Monuments, 581 Events and 1,580 Artefact records.

Although the HER cannot contain all information of Archaeological and Historical importance, it is easily the single most comprehensive inventory of archaeological information about the Forest of Dean. Its main purpose is to inform the planning process and as such it is a powerful management tool, but it also has a research function as a 'first port of call' providing basic levels of information about the known archaeological resource and pointing towards sources which can be investigated if further detail is necessary.

Some particularly important sites or buildings are protected through some form of national designation either as Scheduled Monuments or Listed Buildings and no works which affect these, whether they require planning permission or not, can be undertaken without first gaining consent from Historic England.

The Forest of Dean also contains 88 Scheduled Monuments, although 47 of these are different sections of Offa's Dyke (English Heritage 2014). Apart from the sections of Offa's Dyke, these include a diverse range of sites from Iron Age hillforts, Roman villas, medieval moated sites, castles and village crosses, post-medieval industrial sites (such as Dark Hill iron works), a post-medieval bridge across the River Wye and three areas of scowles. Twelve of these (St Briavels Castle, Bigsweir Bridge, Lancaut Church, Lydney Docks, Gunns Mill charcoal-fired blast furnace and seven medieval crosses) are also listed buildings.

Buildings deemed to be of special architectural or historic interest can be protected by designating them as Listed Buildings. The Forest of Dean contains 824 Listed Buildings (English Heritage 2014), which is a diverse group of structures including St Briavels Castle, parish churches and chapels, bridges, domestic, agricultural and industrial structures, village crosses, individual churchyard monuments and milestones. Thirteen of these are listed as Grade I (the highest level of listing reserved for buildings of exceptional interest) including St Briavels Castle, nine parish churches, the remains of Flaxley Abbey and two bridges including the upper Severn Crossing built in 1966.

Other forms of protection also exist and the Forest of Dean contains two gardens (Clearwell Castle and Flaxley Abbey) that are included on Historic England's Register of Parks and Gardens of Special Historic Interest.

This is a lesser protection than listing or scheduling and means that the status of the garden is a material consideration in the event of any works which require planning permission. In such cases the local planning authority would seek advice from Historic England over any proposals, but would not necessarily be bound by their advice.

Management of Forestry Commission woodland

Scheduling and listing are designed to protect sites from development, although there are some works which are permitted on these sites without consent. Emergency works can be

Fig 7.1
All Historic Environment Records, Scheduled Monuments and Listed Buildings in the Forest of Dean.

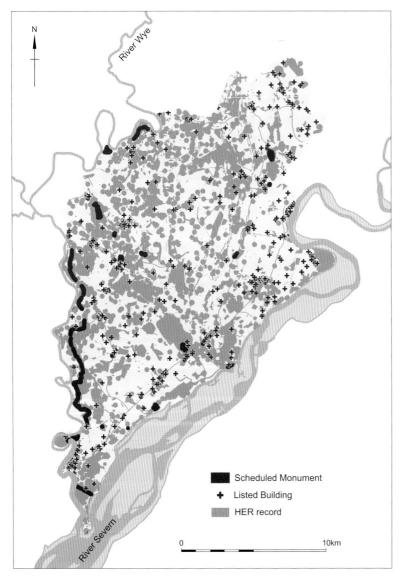

Scheduled Monument
+ Listed Building
HER record

0   10km

undertaken on listed buildings or scheduled monuments without consent and existing agricultural or forestry regimes can be continued on scheduled sites, although it is deemed 'good practice' to notify Historic England of these works and landowners would still be subject to prosecution if they damaged monuments through carelessness during these operations. Registered parks and gardens and undesignated sites are afforded a degree of protection from unsympathetic development which is initiated through the planning process, but there is considerable scope for archaeological sites to be compromised by works which do not require planning consent, and which cannot be monitored.

The most effective way to manage this type of risk is through close liaison with landowners who can be advised on the best way to proceed with operations which may have an impact on surviving archaeology. Clearly it is impracticable for archaeologists to enter into voluntary agreements with all landowners, but a key element of the Forest of Dean Archaeological Survey was to engage directly with the Forestry Commission, the largest single landowner in the Forest of Dean, whose landholdings contain about 30 per cent of the known archaeological sites in the Forest.

The Forestry Commission own most of the woodland in the Forest of Dean. Woodland is arguably less destructive to archaeological deposits than many other land use regimes (for example, agriculture), and earthwork features are often particularly well preserved in areas under long-term woodland. Woodland does, however, have its own management issues. Existing mature trees, particularly on steep slopes, can be at risk from wind-blow and upturned root bowls can cause damage to buried remains. Archaeological deposits are particularly vulnerable to damage from inappropriate machinery which can cause deep rutting, especially where ground is soft, or in wet weather. In the Forest of Dean there is also some risk of damage from wild boar, which are currently feral in the Forest and can grub up large areas in their search for food. Some earthworks, such as Offa's Dyke, are also particularly vulnerable to damage from badgers.

The Forestry Commission manage the archaeology in their land holdings in two ways.

Seven of the Forest of Dean's scheduled monuments (Welshbury and Symond's Yat hillforts, the Dean Road at Blackpool Bridge, Soudley Camp, Darkhill Ironworks and Titanic Steelworks and three areas of scowles in Blakes Wood, Staunton) are on Forestry Commission

land and since 1996 they have commissioned detailed management plans for these.

These plans identify management issues specific to the site and make recommendations to mitigate these. Management issues can range from visitor erosion, natural decay of standing structures, invasive scrub and issues relating to the management of the woodland itself. The plans prioritise management issues and make recommendations to address these. These are tailored to suit the circumstances of the particular site but can include suggesting that mature trees are monitored and felled in advance of tree throw, scrub should be cleared from particular areas, or that sections of eroded earthworks should be repaired. Recommendations can also be made as to what types of machinery can be used and what routes they should take across the site or that

Fig 7.2
All archaeological sites in Forestry Commission land were given a management category (Categories A–D) each of which was assigned general management recommendations.

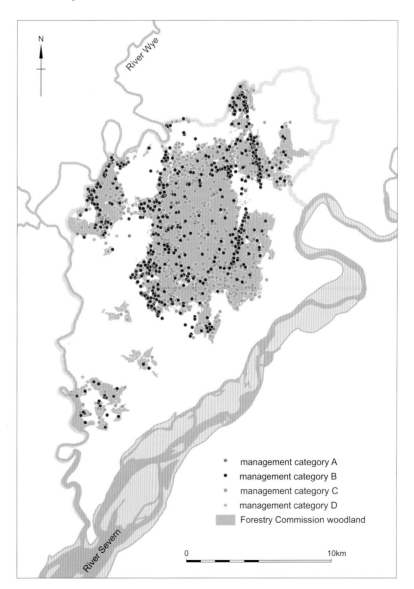

management category A
management category B
management category C
management category D
Forestry Commission woodland

0   10km

Fig 7.3
Forestry management in action. A mechanical harvester, stationed outside the East Wood ring cairn carefully lifts a wind-blown tree from its interior under archaeological supervision. [© Gloucestershire County Council Archaeology Service]

footpaths should be realigned to protect vulnerable earthworks from too much visitor pressure. These management plans are agreed with Historic England before implementation and are reviewed every 10 years.

The seven scheduled monuments represent only 0.1 per cent of the total number of archaeological sites in Forestry Commission land and archaeological sites in woodland are at particular risk from damage during normal forestry operations, particularly where large machinery is involved.

The Forestry Commission are fully aware of this and were involved with the Forest of Dean project from an early stage to discuss ways in which the results could be used to help them to ensure that archaeological sites they managed were protected.

It was agreed that the most important thing was to ensure that the Forestry Commission were aware of all known archaeological sites in their ownership. In the first instance, it was agreed that the project would ensure that the Forestry Commission were provided with basic levels of data from the HER ensuring they had current information about archaeological and historical sites, monuments and structures in a form which could be updated and integrated into their forestry forward planning. The HER is continually changing as new work is undertaken and the information sent to the Forestry Commission is renewed on an annual basis.

Not only were they provided with basic information on the location type, date and extent of known sites, but they were also provided with basic management advice for each site. Clearly the management needs of the known sites in Forestry Commission land are too diverse for all but the most general guidance. All recognised archaeological sites were assigned one of four generalised management categories based on their archaeological significance and perceived sensitivity to the types of operation which are undertaken in normal woodland management.

8

What has the project achieved and what is there still to do?

How has the project added to knowledge of the Forest of Dean?

In 2002, the Historic Environment Record for the Forest contained 4,971 archaeological sites within 2,833 archaeological area records (Hoyle 2008a, 49). In April 2015, this had risen to 12,105 sites within 6,534 area records representing a 130 per cent and 143 per cent increase respectively over 12 years. Although this bald statistic does not in any way accurately reflect what has actually been discovered in the Forest of Dean in those 12 years, it does provide an indication of how far knowledge of that area has advanced in that time.

Clearly not all of this is the result of the work undertaken during the various stages of the Forest of Dean Archaeological Survey and significant finds have been made by other large-scale surveys, such as the National Mapping Programme and the Severn Vale Rapid Coastal Zone Assessment, and also numerous archaeological investigations which have taken place in recent years.

The Forest of Dean Survey has, however, made significant advances in our knowledge of the range and extent of surviving archaeological features in areas of woodland. Not only has the project brought together a vast amount of information from documentary sources, augmenting existing records of the area's post-medieval industrial past, but has demonstrated that lidar is a valuable tool for identifying potential archaeological sites in these areas, and has used this information to identify prehistoric and Roman enclosures and boundary systems which have shed considerable light on earlier land use in areas currently under woodland. The results have also shed light on the early period of Roman occupation of the Dean, the pre-blast furnace-era iron industry and identified extensive areas of surviving earthworks associated with the pre-industrial iron, coal and charcoal industries.

The survey has also shown that the significance of the results of large-scale surveys such as lidar can only begin to be fully understood when they proceed beyond the simple cataloguing, classifying and ground-truthing of identified earthworks to more intensive investigation. Perhaps the most important legacy of the project will not just be what has been found, but the fact that there is now a considerable body of information which has not yet been interpreted but which will act as a focus for future research into the area.

Further research in the Forest of Dean

Although much has been found in recent years there is still a great deal to do to really understand the archaeology of the Forest of Dean. Details of all priorities for further research is beyond the scope of this book although practically any further research has the potential to shed new light on otherwise poorly understood sites or periods, or throw up questions which we have not yet considered. There are, however, a number of general areas where further research would clearly be productive (Hoyle 2017b).

Lidar

Perhaps the most pressing work which needs to be done in the Forest of Dean is further research into many of the features which have been identified by lidar. The recent work by the Forest of Dean Survey has only explored four of the more than 1,500 possible archaeological sites discovered by lidar, and although these sites were carefully selected, and research drew on the expertise of a number of specialists in geophysics, palaeoenvironmental analysis, finds identification, archaeometallurgy and scientific dating, the investigations were very small scale. The results, however, have had a huge impact on the capacity to understand and interpret the significance and complexity of the archaeology within the Forest's woodland. A great deal has been learnt about those earthworks which have been investigated, and a framework within which similar earthworks can be interpreted has been established.

More work needs to be done to determine if these interpretations are correct, and the boundary systems and subrectangular enclosures in woodland need more attention.

Much useful work could also be done in basic ground-truthing of the numerous lidar features, both within and outside woodland, which have not been studied further.

The rapid transcription of lidar data undertaken during Stage 3A of the Forest of Dean survey was limited to recording previously unrecorded archaeological features which had been identified by lidar (Hoyle 2008c, 22). The lidar survey did not just find new sites, but also added significant information to sites which were already known about. The full potential of this has not yet been realised and there is still considerable scope for further enhancement of the HER by integrating the results of the lidar survey with records of sites which were already known about before the lidar survey was undertaken.

Prehistoric

The prehistoric period in the Forest of Dean is still poorly understood, particularly the Palaeolithic.

Work has tended to concentrate on the caves and rock shelters of the Wye Valley (and particularly the Upper Wye Gorge) where new sites undoubtedly await discovery and where high quality *in situ* deposits could be expected. Palaeolithic artefacts have also been recovered in caves in other areas and on the gravel terraces on the northern shore of the Severn and further research in these areas might prove fruitful.

Settlement patterns in the Mesolithic to Iron Age would also warrant further investigation. Since the 1980s a considerable amount of flint has been recovered from the surfaces of ploughed fields in the Forest of Dean. These have produced significant results in terms of a greater understanding of the extent of prehistoric activity, and prior to these findings there was no knowledge of the Mesolithic in the Forest of Dean at all. While this work is to be welcomed, overall it suffers from a lack of consistency in collection methodology and variable levels of analysis and reporting which make it difficult to fully interpret the significance of these finds and also to make comparisons between assemblages recovered at different times or in different places. At the very least existing assemblages should be reassessed as a whole and a strategy should be developed for further fieldwalking exercises in the Forest.

Very little is known about prehistoric ritual activity in the Forest of Dean. There are no known Neolithic long barrows, although a number of undated mounds and other features, particularly in the Tidenham area in the southern part of the Forest, have been tentatively interpreted as Bronze Age ritual sites. Few of these have been investigated and their actual status or date is unknown, and further investigation of some of these sites would certainly be beneficial.

There has been very little exploration of the area's hillforts and questions remain about their date of origin, how they were used, how they related to contemporary non-hillfort settlement, when they fell out of use and whether they were reoccupied in the early post-Roman period.

Roman

Like the prehistoric periods much information about the Roman Forest of Dean takes the form of unstratified finds, often recovered during field walking. These collections would also benefit from some form of review and overview of their significance.

The status of sites which have been interpreted as villas and their relationship with each other, and with contemporary settlement and land use, also needs further research. The economic basis of the Forest's villas should also be reviewed, particularly the extent to which they relied on the iron industry. Although this association is clear at the riverside villa of the Chesters, Woolaston and, to a lesser extent, at Park Farm, Aylburton, how typical was this of other villas in the Forest?

The economic basis of many other Roman settlements is also assumed to have been iron production, although the evidence for this is variable and needs further review.

A number of significant excavations, generally undertaken in the early 20th century, have not been fully published and would warrant review. The Roman villas at Park Farm, Aylburton and Boughspring have only been published in summary form, as have the putative Roman temples at Littledean and High Nash, Coleford, the interpretations of which are controversial. The archives of these excavations should be revisited, and, if appropriate they should be reinterpreted and the results published.

Medieval

The big questions in the pre-Norman Forest of Dean are common to much of England and revolve around issues such as how Romanised was the early post-Roman Forest and how did people live in the 5th and 6th centuries? How and when did the area come under the influence of the Saxons and to what extent did this involve an insurgence of new settlers who founded new communities?

More specifically to the Forest are questions like when did it become part of Mercia and how Mercian was it? Is the earthwork overlooking the Wye Offa's Dyke? If so, how was it used and was it originally built as a single scheme in the 8th century? When did the area which became the Royal Demesne of the Norman Forest become a royal hunting ground and what impact did this have on the local population? Are any of the fortifications which are currently thought to be early Norman, for example the ringworks at Newnham, Stowe and possibly also Soudley, actually late Saxon, perhaps associated with Offa's Dyke?

The impact the arrival of the Normans, and particularly the establishment of the Royal Forest, had on the local population is also an area which needs more research.

The medieval landscape is also poorly understood, particularly the interrelationship between settlement, open fields, more enclosed field patterns and the woodland and waste of the Forest.

Industry

With the Forest's industrial past the big questions are how extensive were these industries at particular times and how did they operate?

These are particularly relevant to the coal and iron ore extraction industries which are known to have existed in the Forest since at least the Iron Age in the case of iron, and the Roman period in the case of coal.

Lidar has identified numerous pre-modern coal extraction sites but the date of very few of these can be determined, and none are known to be earlier than late medieval. Iron ore is presumed to have been extracted from scowles but precisely which scowles were exploited when, how this was organised and whether predominantly surface or underground deposits were extracted at certain periods is unknown.

Scowles come in a number of different forms from shallow hollows to cavernous voids and the question of what different types of scowle represent and precisely how they came by their present form is still a matter of debate.

The bloomery iron industry also has a huge number of unanswered questions. It appears to have been an important industry throughout the Roman and medieval periods, but there are still uncertainties about how extensive it was at given times, how many people were employed and for how much of their time, and how it was organised and what processes were used. Of particular interest is the issue about the extent to which the Roman army was involved in smelting during the early years of occupation and whether this is a question which can be satisfactorily answered by archaeology alone.

Too many questions

Clearly there is still a great deal to learn about the Forest of Dean. When the Forest of Dean Archaeological Survey began much of the Forest, and particularly its large expanse of woodland, was largely an archaeological *terra incognita* about which little was understood and where there was little indication of where to prioritise future research. The Forest is still not fully understood but a framework has been put in place within which future researchers can use their resources to target their investigations in a focused way and begin to understand and interpret the significance and complexity of the archaeology within the Forest of Dean and particularly that which is hidden in its woodland.

Let's hope there are further opportunities to do this.

Appendix 1:
Main archaeological and historic periods

Period	Approximate date range:	
	earliest date	latest date
Lower Palaeolithic	500,000 BC	150,000 BC
Middle Palaeolithic	150,000 BC	40,000 BC
Early Upper Palaeolithic	40,000 BC	25,000 BC
Britain too cold for human occupation between 25,000 BC and 12,000 BC		
Later Upper Palaeolithic	12,000 BC	10,000 BC
Early Mesolithic	10,000 BC	7,000 BC
Late Mesolithic	7,000 BC	4,000 BC
Early Neolithic	4,000 BC	3,000 BC
Middle Neolithic	3,500 BC	2,700 BC
Late Neolithic	3,000 BC	2,200 BC
Early Bronze Age	2,500 BC	1,500 BC
Middle Bronze Age	1,600 BC	1,000 BC
Late Bronze Age	1,000 BC	700 BC
Early Iron Age	800 BC	400 BC
Middle Iron Age	400 BC	100 BC
Late Iron Age	100 BC	AD 43
Roman	AD 43	AD 410
Early medieval	AD 410	1066
Medieval	1066	1540
Post-medieval	1540	1901
Modern	1901	Present

After MIDAS data standard – The Royal Commission on Historic Monuments (England).

Appendix 2:
Phases of the Forest of Dean Archaeological Survey

From the outset, the Forest of Dean survey was envisaged as a staged project that would begin by gathering and checking data over a wide area and gradually home in on more detailed exploration of potentially significant sites or themes. The survey has included desk-based data collection, pilot field survey, lidar survey and analysis, rapid field survey and excavation of selected lidar-detected earthworks (*see* p 8). Two related projects (The Forest of Dean National Mapping Programme, and the Scowles and Associated Iron Industry Survey) took place during the early stages of the project.

Stage 1: Desk-based data collection, 2002 and 2005

The purpose of Stage 1 was to investigate why the Forest of Dean appeared to contain relatively few finds and features predating the post-medieval industrial period. This stage was entirely desk-based and involved working with the Gloucestershire Historic Environment Record (HER), a database of archaeological information maintained by the County Council Archaeology Service.

This involved checking all existing HER records making any necessary amendments, and also systematically trawling through a range of published and unpublished text and map sources.

This added 4,160 new sites to the Gloucestershire HER (representing a 62 per cent increase). Although the majority of these (3,289) were post-medieval or modern sites, and most of these related to the industrial history of the area, this process did identify a further 268 medieval or earlier sites and 581 place names (mostly derived from 19th-century maps) that may indicate the location of prehistoric or Roman sites.

The final part of this stage was to quantify what exactly we knew about the archaeology of the Forest of Dean and whether there were any underlying connections between certain types of archaeological site and other factors such as geology, topography, land use and how the information was collected. This provided an overview of the current state of knowledge, and also showed that woodland was a significant factor in the known distribution of archaeological sites in the Forest.

The Forestry Commission were also provided with up-to-date information about all known archaeological sites in their landholdings, enabling them to manage the archaeological resource in their ownership in an effective manner.

The Scowles and Associated Iron Industry Survey, 2003 and 2004

Between January 2003 and March 2004, the project team undertook the Scowles and Associated Iron Industry Survey, a daughter project of the main survey.

Scowles, landscape features unique to the Forest of Dean, are the main source of iron ore in the Forest, particularly during the prehistoric, Roman and medieval periods. They range from deep irregular quarry-like features to amorphous shallow hollows within the outcrops of Carboniferous Limestones (and particularly the Crease Limestone) around the edge of the central Forest (*see* pp 126–30, Fig 6.12).

This survey included desk-based data collection and field survey concentrated on areas with a solid geology of Carboniferous Limestone. It collected information about scowles and known iron smelting sites that predated the introduction of blast furnaces to the area in the early 17th century.

National Mapping Programme for the Forest of Dean, undertaken by Historic England's Aerial Survey and Investigation team between 2002 and 2004

Historic England is engaged in a long-running national survey (the National Mapping Programme [NMP]) to collect archaeological information from aerial photographs. Between 2002 and 2004 Historic England's Aerial Survey and Investigation team (in partnership with the Forest of Dean Archaeological Survey) studied over 7,000 vertical and oblique aerial photographs covering an area of approximately 625km^2 of the Forest of Dean and adjoining parts of Gloucestershire and the neighbouring county of Herefordshire.

Although cropmarks were not visible in woodland, the NMP team recorded 1,832 new archaeological sites in the Forest of Dean (Small and Stoertz 2006, 1). Just over half of these 55.9 per cent) related to post-medieval industries or communications, while a further 34.9 per cent were agricultural remains (mainly the remains of medieval ridge and furrow) outside the woodland (Small and Stoertz 2006, 142–3). The NMP survey did, however, identify a potentially significant prehistoric enclosure within woodland (Small and Stoertz 2006, 24).

Stage 2: Pilot fieldwork, undertaken in 2005

Stage 2 consisted of a short programme of pilot fieldwork to test a number of archaeological techniques, such as excavation, geophysical survey, palaeoenvironmental sampling and rapid field reconnaissance, at a number of wooded sites across the Forest.

The project team also did some preliminary work to assess the accuracy and value of lidar (*see* p 8) in an area of Flaxley Woods in the north-eastern part of the Forest where a small pilot area of lidar survey had been undertaken in 2004.

The pilot work demonstrated that traditional techniques could produce significant archaeological results in woodland, but could only be effectively applied to known sites, and that the main challenge in woodland was identifying suitable sites to investigate in the first place. It also showed that, while rapid field reconnaissance could identify unrecorded archaeological features in woodland, it was time consuming, physically challenging and had variable results depending on ground cover. It was also difficult to accurately record the location of identified features since visible landmarks were rare in woodland and GPS coverage was extremely variable.

The real value of this work was to highlight the value of lidar as an integral and necessary preliminary to any field survey in woodland. The lidar images accurately depicted the location and form of identified features with a degree of accuracy impossible to achieve without sophisticated surveying equipment, greatly improving the speed and accuracy of field reconnaissance. The lidar provided a landscape-scale overview that showed the full extent of earthworks (particularly linear earthworks) and their relationship with other features in a way that could not be easily discerned at ground level, allowing 'borderline' features to be reassessed and interpreted with greater confidence. It also had the unexpected benefit of aiding navigation though the woods by showing numerous tracks and other landscape features that were not recorded on maps.

Stage 3: Lidar survey and field investigation, 2006 and 2011

Stage 3A: Lidar Survey, 2006 and 2007

As Stage 1 had identified that woodland was the area most in need of further exploration and the Stage 2 pilot work had shown that lidar survey was an essential preliminary to any archaeological exploration of woodland, the first part of Stage 3 was to undertake an extensive lidar survey of approximately 278.3km^2 of the Forest of Dean. This was flown in March 2006 and covered almost all Forestry Commission woodland, and also extensive areas of private woodland. The results were processed to 'remove' the woodland cover and acted as a guide to further investigation.

Archaeology Service staff undertook rapid preliminary analysis of the lidar images to identify previously unrecorded areas of potential archaeological interest that would warrant further, more detailed, analysis or fieldwork. They identified 1,702 potential features, or groups of similar features (none of which had been found by earlier archaeological research) and over 1,000 of which may be archaeologically significant.

Within woodland these included extensive areas of charcoal platforms and the pits and mounds left by early (probably medieval or early post-medieval) mineral workings. The lidar also identified some discrete mounds, a number of subrectangular and subcircular enclosures and some extensive areas of boundaries, many of which seemed to form a coherent pattern as if part of a deliberately laid-out landscape. Outside the woodland, identified features included undated enclosures, boundary systems (many of which may represent the remains of medieval field systems), some areas of ridge and furrow and a number of possible industrial sites.

Stage 3B: Fieldwork

Stage 3B consisted of follow-up fieldwork to ground truth and investigate a relatively small selection of earthworks that had been identified by lidar. This stage of the project was subdivided into two phases.

Phase 1: Rapid field survey of selected earthworks, 2010

This verified, characterised and assessed selected sites identified by lidar, although the first task was to prioritise a selection of the nearly 2,000 previously unrecognised earthworks.

In the first instance, it was decided to focus on the 781 possible sites that had been identified in Forestry Commission woodland, as one of the aims of the project was to assist the Forestry Commission 'to manage archaeological sites on their land' (Hoyle 2001) and better information about these sites was needed.

The next step prioritised types of feature for further research based on which were least understood, rather than an assessment of their relative archaeological value.

Some types were already known in the Forest of Dean (and it had been anticipated that lidar would find more), while others had already been ground-truthed in earlier stages of the project or by local researchers who were already making use of lidar data.

These included post-medieval industrial remains such as tramway cuttings, mineshafts or Crown Forest Enclosure boundaries and also less datable features such as trackways, holloways and stone quarries. It also included the extensive areas of charcoal platforms and surface evidence for shallow, pre-industrial coal extraction, which survived as extensive areas of small pits and mounds. These features are not insignificant, but could be interpreted reasonably confidently from the lidar and accurately mapped, added to the Gloucestershire HER and managed in an appropriate fashion without further field validation at this stage.

The lidar survey had, however, identified a number of undated mounds, boundary systems and enclosures that were unknown before the survey and could not be confidently interpreted without further field survey.

In the winter of 2010, 45 of these (3 subcircular enclosures, 9 subrectangular enclosures, 8 mounds and 25 boundary systems) were selected for rapid field validation. This checked if the lidar images accurately represented what survived on the ground, made a basic record of the height and structure of surviving earthworks and recorded anything else of potential significance, particularly any associated features that had not been identified by lidar.

Phase 2: Field evaluation, 2011

The final stage was more intensive fieldwork (small-scale exploratory excavation, geophysical survey and topographical survey) to investigate a small selection of the earthworks investigated during Phase 1 to explore their significance, date and degree of preservation. This focused on four features (two boundary systems, a subrectangular enclosure and a subcircular enclosure). These were representative of a class of poorly understood features or had the potential to be particularly significant to an understanding of the archaeology of the Forest of Dean and the potential survival of archaeological features.

Appendix 3:
The bloomery smelting process

Before blast furnaces were introduced to the Forest in the later 16th century (Hart 1971, 8), iron smelting took place in charcoal-fuelled furnaces known as bloomeries, which consisted of 'an enclosed combustion chamber' with 'an aperture to enable waste gases to escape' (Cleere and Crossley 1985, 39). Details of these changed over time, although there is some consistency in the way these were built and operated. Bloomeries were basically upright cylindrical clay structures about 1–1.5m high, with either vertical or slightly domed sides. Their internal diameter was generally about 0.3–0.5m (although larger examples are known), and their walls were about 0.2m thick (Bayley *et al* 2001, 10; Dungworth *et al* 2012). They could be freestanding, partly or wholly above ground, or built into the side of a pit or bank, and would have been within a structure of some kind or at least a temporary shelter to protect them from weather damage (Chris Salter, pers comm).

For much of the bloomery period air-flow was controlled by human-powered bellows, and clay cones, called tuyeres, were inserted into air holes to protect the wooden nozzles of the bellows (Tylecote 1986, 141–2). By the later medieval and early post-medieval periods water-powered bellows may have been used, but no evidence for this has been found in the Forest of Dean.

Bloomeries were fuelled by charcoal and a mixture of ore and charcoal was added from the opening at its top. Air was introduced through the blowing hole near its base until the bloomery reached internal temperatures ranging from about 500 degrees Celsius at its top to about 1,300 degrees Celsius around the air hole. Iron does not melt below about 1,538 degrees Celsius, but as the ore approached the higher temperatures around the blowing hole, carbon dioxide produced by burning charcoal reacted with the iron oxide in the ore to reduce it to metallic iron, which began to separate from the slag (a mixture of iron and gangue, the non-ferrous parts of the ore). As the temperature in the bloomery was below the melting point of iron, this separation was not complete and particles of metallic iron and slag merged into a semi-solid, spongy mass, known as the bloom, which formed around the air hole, and which eventually grew large enough to impede air flow. At this point the bloom was removed, generally from the top of the bloomery using large tongs, although it may have been necessary to remove the sides of taller furnaces (Tylecote 1986, 135). The bloom was not pure iron and still included a considerable amount of slag. This needed to be separated from it before reasonably uncontaminated iron,

which could then be taken away for further refining, was produced. This separation process, known as primary smithing, would normally have taken place immediately the bloom was removed from the furnace (while it was still hot) and essentially consisted of beating the hot bloom with hammers to force out slag and consolidate the metallic iron.

Slag has a lower melting point than iron (1,100–1,200 degrees Celsius), and although some coalesced with the bloom, the rest (which would still have included a considerable amount of iron) dropped towards the bottom of the bloomery in a liquid state. In some bloomeries this was simply allowed to collect at the base of the bloomery, or into a pit below the bloomery, although from the later Iron Age bloomeries began to be introduced that had an opening at their base. As slag built up this could be opened to 'tap' the molten slag by allowing it to escape from the base of the furnace and run into a small pit (Dungworth *et al* 2012). The slag produced in this process (tap slag) has a distinct upper surface displaying a clear solidified flow pattern, and a rougher lower surface where it has flowed over the ground surface. This type of slag is the most easily recognised, and most commonly found evidence for bloomery smelting.

In the early to middle Iron Age (from about 750–700 BC) bloomeries were fairly small and had no provision for tapping molten slag from their base. These survive as small pits about 0.3m in diameter, often filled with a cake of slag, which have traditionally been interpreted as 'bowl' furnaces and assumed to have had a domed superstructure with an approximate height/width ratio of 1:1. Experimental work has shown that small domed structures would have been extremely difficult to operate as a bloomery (which would have needed to have been at least 0.5m high below the level at which air was pumped into the furnace) and where these remains have been found they are now generally considered to have been small shaft furnaces with a cylindrical or slightly domed superstructure.

Bloomeries that had the provision for tapping slag were introduced during the later Iron Age (Paynter 2011, 3) and these were used throughout the Roman period, although by the Anglo-Saxon period slag pit furnaces, where molten slag accumulated into a pit below the bloomery, were used (Bayley *et al* 2001, 11). Bloomeries with slag tapping provision were reintroduced from about AD 800 (Paynter 2011, 4) and this type of bloomery continued to be used in the Forest of Dean until the introduction of the blast furnace in the late 16th century.

Appendix 4:
Forestry Commission Management categories

The four Forestry Commission management categories are:

Management category A

This category includes sites of national importance and their settings. Generally, these have statutory protection as scheduled monuments or listed buildings (or wider areas which contain these elements), although this category also includes some other archaeological sites, buildings or structures of significant regional importance that may not have statutory protection. This includes some unscheduled sections of Offa's Dyke, including a number of sites such as the possible Roman fortlets or the Bronze Age ring cairn from East Wood, Tidenham that were identified by lidar.

Management guidance

For sites in this category there is a presumption against any forestry operations such as earth moving, clearfelling or new planting, which may damage archaeological sites, buildings or structures, and the Forestry Commission are advised that any necessary works on sites with statutory protection may require scheduled monument or listed building consent.

Management category B

This category includes sites that are not currently considered to be of national importance, but may be characteristic of the local area and be primary evidence for the archaeology and history of the Forest of Dean. This category includes:

- All structural remains, earthworks or other significant evidence of sites associated with any aspect of the pre-industrial revolution iron or coal industries.
- Structural remains, earthworks or other evidence of sites dating to the prehistoric, Roman or medieval periods, and sites with a strong likelihood of below-ground remains from these periods.
- Surface evidence of pre-20th-century communication routes.
- Structural remains, earthworks or other significant evidence of sites forming part of post-medieval industrial complexes and sites with a strong likelihood of below-ground remains.

- Historic buildings or structures in isolated locations that may meet the criteria for statutory listing, but which have been missed in the review of listed buildings carried out by central government.

Management guidance

There is a presumption that sites in this category should be maintained in a stable condition and protected from potentially damaging operations, although it is recognised that this may not be appropriate in all cases. Gloucestershire County Council Archaeology Service should be consulted where potentially damaging forestry operations cannot be avoided.

Management category C

Sites in this category collectively contribute to the historic landscape of the Forest of Dean. Although they have an intrinsic importance, they are individually less significant and are currently thought unlikely to contain significant archaeological remains. These include:
- Undated or post-medieval stone quarries.
- Undated or post-medieval mineshafts.
- Undated or post-medieval lime kilns.
- Undated or post-medieval wells.
- Undated or post-medieval charcoal burning platforms.
- Other undated or post-medieval features associated with pre-20th-century woodland management (eg 19th-century Crown Enclosure banks, undated sawpits).
- Undated or post-medieval marker stones.
- Undated sites of unknown origin known only from aerial photographic or lidar evidence.
- Probable sites of pre-20th-century communication routes where no surface evidence remains.

Management guidance

Forestry operations affecting sites in this category should as far as is reasonably possible be carried out with regard to retaining these features in their present form. Gloucestershire County Council Archaeology Service should be consulted in advance of any management operations which will have a significant impact on sites in this category.

Management category D

This category consists of sites of undetermined significance, although they have the potential to indicate undiscovered remains of archaeological significance. These include:

- Isolated findspots of archaeological material.
- Areas in which archaeological material has been recovered (generally as surface finds) although the precise location or spread of this material is not known.
- Documented sites of any period that cannot be located precisely.
- Place names that may indicate the site of archaeological features.

Management guidance

No restrictions to forestry operations can be applied to areas containing sites in this category, although Gloucest-ershire County Council Archaeology Service should be notified if structures, deposits or artefacts are encountered in these areas as a result of any forestry management operations.

Areas with no designated management category

It is also recognised that any inventory of archaeo-logical sites can only be an interim statement reflecting the state of knowledge at the time the information is produced.

Areas between known sites should not be regarded as archaeologically sterile, and Gloucestershire County Council Archaeology Service should be notified in the event of any structures, deposits or artefacts being encountered as a result of any forestry management operations.

Bibliography and sources

Adkins, L and Adkins, R A 1982 *The Handbook of British Archaeology*. Newton Abbot: David and Charles

Alcock, L 1972 *By South Cadbury is that Camelot*. London: Thames & Hudson

Allen, D 1944 'The Belgic dynasties and their coins'. *Archaeologia* **90**, 1–46

Allen, D 1961 'A study of Dobunnic coinage' *in* Clifford, E M *Bagendon: A Belgic Oppidum*. Cambridge: W Heffer, 75–147

Allen, J R J 2001 'Sea level, salt marsh and fen: shaping the Severn Estuary levels in the later quaternary (Ipswichian-Holocene)'. *Archaeology in the Severn Estuary* (2000). *Annual Report of the Severn Estuary Levels Research Committee* **11**. Exeter, 13–34

Allen, J R L 2009 'Romano-British iron making on the Severn Estuary Levels; toward a metallurgical landscape'. *Archaeology in the Severn Estuary* (2008). *Annual Report of the Severn Estuary Levels Research Committee* **19**. Exeter, 73–119

Allen, J R L and Fulford, M 1987 'Romano British settlement and industry on the wetlands of the Severn Estuary'. *Antiq J* **62**, 237–89

Allen, J R L and Brown, A (eds) *Archaeology in the Severn Estuary 2005*. *Annual Report of the Severn Estuary Levels Research Committee* **16**. Exeter

Allen, W T 1883–4 'Discovery of interments at St Briavels'. *Trans Bristol Gloucestershire Archaeol Soc* **8 (1)**, 356

Anstis, R 1998 *The Story of Parkend, a Forest of Dean Village*, 2 edn. Lydney: Lightmoor Press

ApSimon, A M and Jacobi, R M 2004 'Getting it right: no Middle Palaeolithic at King Arthur's Cave'. *Proc Univ Bristol Spelaeol Soc* **23 (1)**, 17–26

ApSimon, A M, Smart, P L, MacPhail, R, Scott, K and Taylor, H 1992 'A reassessment of a Middle and Upper Palaeolithic, Mesolithic and Beaker site'. *Proc Univ Bristol Spelaeol Soc* **19 (2)**, 183–239

Armstrong, L 1978 *Woodcolliers and Charcoal Burning*. Coach Publishing House Ltd and the Weald and Downland Open Air Museum, Sussex

Aston, M 1993 *Know the Landscape, Monasteries*. London: Batsford

Atkin, M and Laughlin, W 1992 *Gloucester and the Civil War. A City Under Siege*. Stroud: Alan Sutton Publishing

Atkinson, H D 1986 'Excavations at Stock Farm, Clearwell'. *The New Regard* **2**, 28–35

Atkyns, R 1712 *The Ancient and Present State of Glostershire*. (facsimile edition 1974, EP Publishing, Wakefield 1974)

Bagnall-Oakeley, M E 1881–2 'On Roman coins found in the Forest of Dean'. *Trans Bristol Gloucestershire Archaeol Soc* **6**, 107–22

Bagnall-Oakeley, M E 1890 'Coins found at Caewent and Caerleon', *Numis Chron* **10**, 260–6

Barber, A 2009 'Land east of Lydney, site A (south) Lydney, Gloucestershire'. Cotswold Archaeology unpublished report for Robert Hitchins Ltd. CA Project: 2881, CA Report: 09109, July 2009

Barber, A J and Holbrook, N 2000 'Excavations at Millend, Blakeney'. *Trans Bristol Gloucestershire Archaeol Soc* **118**, 33–60

Barker, P P, Mercer, E J F and Brookes, C F 2000 'A report for Paramount Pictures on a geophysical survey carried out at Lancaut, Gloucestershire'. Unpublished report for Paramount Pictures Ltd

Barnett, C and Savory, H 1961–4 'A Beaker cist at Beachley'. *The Monmouthshire Antiquary* **1**, part 4, 112–16

Bartlett, A D H 1994 'St James's Church Lancaut, Gloucestershire, report on archaeogeophysical survey'. Unpublished Archaeological Investigations Ltd report

Barton, R N E 1993 'An interim report on the survey and excavations in the Wye Valley, 1993'. *Proc Univ Bristol Spelaeol Soc* **19 (3)**, 337–46

Barton, R N E 1994 'Second interim report on the survey and excavations in the Wye Valley, 1994'. *Proc Univ Bristol Spelaeol Soc* **20 (1)**, 63–73

Barton, R N E 1995 'Third interim report on the survey and excavations in the Wye Valley, 1995'. *Proc Univ Bristol Spelaeol Soc* **20 (2)**, 153–9

Barton, R N E 1996 'Fourth interim report on the survey and excavations in the Wye Valley, 1996'. *Proc Univ Bristol Spelaeol Soc* **20 (3)**, 263–73

Barton, R N E 1997 'Fifth interim report on the survey and excavations in the Wye Valley, 1997'. *Proc Univ Bristol Spelaeol Soc* **21 (1)**, 99–108

Bathurst, Revd W H 1879 *Roman Antiquities at Lydney Park, Gloucestershire*. London: Longmans, Green and Co

Bayley, J, Dungworth, D and Paynter, S 2001 *Archaeometallurgy*. Centre for Archaeology Guidelines. English Heritage: Centre for Archaeology Guidelines

Beachus, K 2000 'New sewage pipe, Coleford to Newland, Gloucestershire. Archaeological watching brief'. Unpublished Foundations Archaeology report no 143

Bell, M 2007 *Prehistoric Coastal Communities, The Mesolithic in Western Britain*. York: Counc Brit Archaeol Res Rep **149**

Bellows, J 1877 'Brief notes on Offa's Dyke'. *Proc Cotteswold Nat Fld Club* **6**, 257–60

Berg, R 2009 'Archaeological discoveries of charcoal pits in the close hinterland of medieval Trondheim. Perspectives on charcoal production in central Norway before and after the turn of the 1st Millennium AD'. *Vitark 7, Proceedings of the 58th International Sachsen-symposium*. Trondheim: NTNU Museum of Natural History and Archaeology and Tapir Academic Press, 110–33

Bevan, L 1996 'The flint' *in* Hughes, G (ed) *The Excavation of a Late Prehistoric and Romano-British Settlement at Thornwell Farm, Chepstow, Gwent, 1992*. Oxford: Brit Archaeol Rep Brit Ser **244**

BGS 1974 Geological Survey of Great Britain (England and Wales) Solid and Drift. Sheet 233, Monmouth. Scale 1:50,000

BGS 1981 Geological Survey of Great Britain (England and Wales) Solid and Drift. Sheet 250, Chepstow. Scale 1:50,000

BGS 1992 *British Regional Geology Bristol and Gloucester Region*. 3 edn. London: Her Majesty's Stationery Office

BGS 2014 Digital British Geological Survey data held on Gloucestershire County Council GIS. Accessed 2014

Bick, D 1980 *Old Industries in Dean*. Worcester

Bick, D E 1987 *The Mines of Newent and Ross*. Newent

Bick, D E 1990 'Early iron ore production from the Forest of Dean and District'. *J Hist Metallurg Soc* **24 (1)**, 39–42

Blair, J 1988 'Minster churches in the landscape' *in* Hooke, D (ed) *Anglo-Saxon Settlements*. Oxford: Wiley Blackwell, 35–58

Blake, J 2001 'Rodmore Farm excavations 2000'. *Dean Archaeol* **14**, 6–11

Blake, J 2002 'A geophysical survey at Rodmore Farm'. *Dean Archaeol* **15**, 15–18

Blake, J 2003 'Excavations at Rodmore Farm 2003'. *Dean Archaeol* **16**, 7–13

Blake, J 2004 'Resistivity survey of Stock Farm Villa'. *Dean Archaeol* **17**, 14–15

Blake, J and Briscoe, R 2002 'Broomhill project report'. *Dean Archaeol* **15**, 5–13

Booth, P, Dodd, A, Robinson, M and Smith, A 2007 *The Thames through Time. The Archaeology of the Upper and Middle Thames. The early historical period*. Oxford: Thames Valley Landscapes Monograph **27**

Borthwick, A 1996 'The Beaufort Bridge Project. Concerning Land at Sedbury in the Parish of Tidenham'. Unpublished archaeological desk-top study on behalf of Beaufort Bridge Ltd

Bowden, M 1999 *Unravelling the Landscape: An Inquisitive Approach to Archaeology*. Stroud: Tempus

Bowden, M 2005 *The Malvern Hills, An Ancient Landscape*. Swindon: English Heritage

Bowden, M and McOmish, D 1987 'The required barrie'. *Scottish Archaeol Rev* **4 (2)**, 76–84

Bowen, C R 2003 'Pebble tools from the Forest of Dean'. *Glevensis* **36**, 16

Bradley, R 1998 *The Significance of Monuments. On the Shaping of Human Experience in Neolithic and Bronze Age Europe*. Abingdon: Routledge

Branigan, K 1989 'Specialisation in villa economies' *in* Branigan, K and Miles, D (eds) 1989 *The Economies of Romano-British Villas*. Sheffield: J R Collis Publications, 42–50

Bray, W and Trump, D 1982 *The Penguin Dictionary of Archaeology*. 2 edn. Harmondsworth: Penguin Books

Breeze, D J 1974 'The Roman fortlet at Barburgh Mill, Dumfriesshire'. *Britannia* **5**, 130–62

Breeze, D J 1982 *The Northern Frontiers of Roman Britain*. London: Batsford

Breeze, D J 1994 *Roman Forts in Britain*. Princes Risborough: Shire Archaeology

Brett, M 2004 'Land to the east of Federal Mogul, Lydney, Gloucestershire, Archaeological Evaluation'. Unpublished Cotswold Archaeology report, CA Project: 1750, CA Report: 04157, October 2004

Bridgewater, N 1959 'Ancient Buried Roads in South Herefordshire'. *Trans Woolhope Naturalists Fld Club* **36**, 218–27 and 263–7

Bridgewater, N 1966 'Excavations at Warfield Farm, Ruardean 1966'. *Bull Hist Metallurg Soc* **1 (8)**, 46–7

Bridgewater, N 1968 'The Dean Road'. *Bull Hist Metallurg Group* **2 (1)**, 3

Bridgewater, N P 1973 'Boughspring, Glos'. *Glevensis* **7**, 7–8

Brown, A D 2007 'Mesolithic to Neolithic human activity and impact at the Severn Estuary wetland edge: studies at Llandevenny, Oldbury flats, Hills Flats and Woolaston' *in* Bell, M *Prehistoric Coastal Communities, The Mesolithic in Western Britain*. York: Counc Brit Archaeol Res Rep **149**, 249–62

Brown, A D, Bell, M, Timpany, S and Nayling, N 2006 'Mesolithic to Neolithic and medieval coastal environmental change: intertidal survey at Woolaston, Gloucestershire'. *Archaeology in the Severn Estuary* **16**, 67–83

Bryant, R 2012 *Corpus of Anglo-Saxon Stone Sculpture: Vol. X, The Western Midlands*. Oxford: Oxford University Press/British Academy

Buckman, J 1856 'Proceedings at meetings of the Archaeological Institute, May 2nd 1856'. *Archaeol J* **13**, 281

Burn, A H 1959 'Offa's Dyke–boundary or barrier'. *J Chester North Wales Architect Archaeol Hist Soc* **46**, 25–32

Camden, W 1588 *Britannia, or a Chorographical Description of Great Britain and Ireland together with the Adjacent Islands,* English translation by Edmund Gibson, Web edition published by eBooks@ Adelaide. Derived from https://ebooks.adelaide.edu.au/c/camden/william/britannia-gibson-1722/index.html 6th February 2017

Campbell, J B 1977 *The Upper Palaeolithic of Britain: A Study of Man and Nature in the Ice Age*. Oxford: Clarendon Press

Carew, T 2003 'An assessment of the archaeological excavations, evaluations, test pits, field surveys and watching briefs along the South-east Coastal Strategy pipeline between Chepstow and Magor South Wales'. Unpublished Pre-Construct Archaeology report, February 2003

Casey, D A 1931 'Lydney Castle'. *Antiq J* **11**, 240–61

Casey, P J 1999 *Roman Coinage in Britain*. 3 edn. Princes Risborough: Shire Archaeology

Casey, P J and Hoffmann, B 1999 'Excavations at the Roman temple in Lydney Park, Gloucestershire in 1980 and 1981'. *Antiq J* **79**, 81–143

Catchpole, T C 1993a 'Archaeological recording at Offa's Dyke, Beeches Bungalow, St. Briavels Common'. Unpublished Gloucestershire County Council Archaeology Service report

Catchpole, T C 1993b 'Site visit to Onslow Road, Newent, Gloucestershire'. Unpublished Gloucestershire County Council Archaeology Service

Catchpole, T C 1996 'Clearwell Farm, Newland, Gloucestershire, Archaeological Observations, September 1996'. Unpublished Gloucestershire County Council Archaeology Service report, October 1996

Catchpole, T C, Copeland, T and Maxwell, A 2007 'Roman Dymock: archaeological investigations 1995–2002, introduction'. *Trans Bristol Gloucestershire Archaeol Soc* **125**, 131–6

Challinor, S 2007 'Wood charcoal' *in* Simmonds, A 'Excavations at land adjacent to the Rectory, Dymock, Gloucestershire, 2002'. *Trans Bristol Gloucestershire Archaeol Soc* **125**, 232–4

Chambers, R A 1989 'Drybrook Quarry Extension, Glos, Archaeological Assessment for ARC Southern'. Unpublished Oxford Archaeological Unit report, April 1989

Chamberlain, A T and Williams, J P 2001 'A Gazetteer of English Caves, Fissures and Rock Shelters Containing Human Remains, Revised version June 2001'. *Capra* 1. Derived from http://capra.group.shef.ac.uk/1/caves.html

Chandler, J 1993 *John Leland's Itinerary, Travels in Tudor England*. Stroud: Alan Sutton

Charlesworth, D 2007 'Mapping the landscape: the Iron Age and Roman periods in part of North-West Gloucestershire'. *Glevensis* **40**, 3–12

Child, M 2007 *Discovering Churches and Churchyards*. Princes Risborough: Shire Publications

Church, A J, Dunmore, A J, Mairs, K-A, Millard, A, Cook G T, Sveinbjarnardottir, G, Ascough, P A, Newton A J and Roucoux, K 2007 'Charcoal production during the Norse and early medieval periods in Eyjafjallahreppur, Southern Iceland'. *Radiocarbon* **49 (2)**, 659–72

Clammer, C and Underwood, K 2014 *The Churches and Chapels of the Parish of Tidenham, Their History and Architecture*. Caerphilly: Tidenham Historical Group

Clarke, S 2007 'Buttington Terrace, Sedbury, Chepstow, an archaeological evaluation for Mr D Nightingale'. Unpublished Monmouth Archaeology report, January 2007

Cleere, H and Crossley, D 1985 *The Iron Industry of the Weald*. Leicester: Leicester University Press

Clifford, E M 1933 'The Roman villa, Hucclecote, near Gloucester'. *Trans Bristol Gloucestershire Archaeol Soc* **55**, 323–76

Clifford, E M 1938 'Roman altars in Gloucestershire'. *Trans Bristol Gloucestershire Archaeol Soc* **60**, 297–307

Clifford, E M 1961 'The Hucclecote Roman Villa'. *Trans Bristol Gloucestershire Archaeol Soc* **80**, 42–9

Clissold, G 1982 Rectified copy of 'The West Part of the Plott of the Forest of Deane in The County of Glos. Taken Anno Dni 1608 and Anno Regni Jacobi Sexto' at scale 1:10,560, taken from 2/3 scale copy of original document: Public Record Office MR879. Copy in Standing, I J 1997 'The landscape of the Forest of Dean in the 17th Century, A study based on contemporary maps'. Bristol University Dissertation for an MA in Local History, June 1997

Codrington, T 1905 *Roman Roads in Britain*. 2 edn. London: SPCK

Cole, M 2007 'Human skeletal remains' *in* Catchpole, T C 'Excavations at the Sewage Treatment Works'. *Trans Bristol Gloucestershire Archaeol Soc* **125**, 189–92

Cook, S 1995 'Severn Trent Central Forest Reinforcement main, an archaeological evaluation at Sling Tanks'. Unpublished Gloucestershire County Council Archaeology Service report, October 1995

Cooke, A O 1913 *The Forest of Dean*. London: Constable

Cooke, N 2003 'An archaeological evaluation of land east of Lydney, Gloucestershire'. Unpublished Wessex Archaeology report

Copeland, T 2011 *Roman Gloucestershire*. Stroud

Corney, M and Payne, A 2007 'The regional pattern' *in* Payne, A, Corney, M and Cunliffe, B (eds) *The Wessex Hillforts Project. Extensive Survey of Hillfort Interiors in Central Southern England*. London: English Heritage, 131–50

Court, D and Standing, I 1979 'A ventilation furnace on the Findall Iron Mine, Soudley, Forest of Dean'. *Gloucestershire Soc Indust Archaeol Annual J for 1979*, 9–15

CPAT 2014 Dating Offa's Dyke. Clwyd-Powys Archaeological Trust, May 2014. Accessed from http://www.cpat.org.uk/projects/longer/offachirk/dating_offas_dyke.pdf, 5 April 2017

Craddock-Bennett, L 2015 'English Bicknor Primary School. Archaeological Watching Brief'. Unpublished Headland Archaeology report, HA Job No. EBPG/04, HAS No. 1077, February 2015

Crawford, O G S 1925 *The Long Barrows of the Cotswolds*. Gloucester: John Bellows

Crawley-Boevey, F H 1921 'Some recent discoveries at Flaxley Abbey, Gloucestershire, and their relation to Mr. Middleton's plan made in 1881'. *Trans Bristol Gloucestershire Archaeol Soc* **43**, 57–62

Crew, P 1995 *Currency Bars and Other Forms of Trade Iron*. The Historical Metallurgy Society, Archaeological Data Sheet **8**. Derived from http://hist-met.org/hmsdatasheet08.pdf, 15th April 2015

Crew, P and Crew, S (eds) 1990 *Early Mining in the British Isles. Proceedings of the Early Mining Workshop at Plas Tan y Bwlch: Snowdonia National Park Study Centre, 17–19 November 1989*. Plas Tan y Bwlch, November 1989

Crooks, K 2014 'Archaeological Excavation, Tomack Developments at Western Way, Dymock, Gloucestershire'. Unpublished Border Archaeology report, Report Ref BA1123 LWWD, March 2014

Cross, A G R 1982 *Old Industrial Sites in Wyedean: A Gazetteer*. Wyedean

Crutchley, S and Crow, P 2010 *The Light Fantastic: Using Airborne Laser Scanning in Archaeological Survey*. Swindon: English Heritage

Cunliffe, B 1978 *Iron Age Communities in Britain, an Account of England, Scotland and Wales from the Seventh Century BC until the Roman Conquest*. Rev edn. London: Routledge and Kegan Paul

Cunliffe, B 1984 *Danebury: An Iron Age Hillfort in Hampshire, Volume 1: The Excavations, 1969–1978*. London: Counc Brit Archaeol Res Rep **52**

Cunliffe, B 1995 *English Heritage Book of Iron Age Britain*. London: English Heritage

Cunliffe, B 2003 'Locating the Dobunni' *in* Ecclestone, E, Gardner, K S, Holbrook, N and Smith, A (eds) *The Land of the Dobunni*. Kings Lynn: Heritage Marketing and Publications, 12–16

Cunliffe, B and Poole, C 1991 *Danebury: An Iron Age Hillfort in Hampshire, Volume 4: The Excavations, 1979–1988*. London: Counc Brit Archaeol Res Rep **73**

Current Archaeology 2014 'Offa's Dyke: The work of multiple kings?' *Current Archaeol* **291**

DAG 2000a 'Edge Farm'. *Dean Archaeol* **13**, 26–7

DAG 2000b 'Soudley Camp'. *Dean Archaeol* **13**, 24–5

DAG 2000–2001 'Castle Sites Survey 2000/1. A survey of castle sites, possible and actual in the Forest of Dean and adjoining parishes'. Unpublished Dean Archaeological Group report

Darvill, T 1984 'Neolithic Gloucestershire' *in* Saville, A (ed) *Archaeology in Gloucestershire*. Cheltenham: Cheltenham Art Gallery and Museums, 80–112

Darvill, T 1987 *Prehistoric Gloucestershire*. 1 edn. Gloucester: Alan Sutton

Darvill, T 1988 Monuments Protection Programme, Monument Class Description, Moats, February 1988. Derived from http://www.eng-h.gov.uk/mpp/mcd/mcdtop1.htm, 27th November 2014

Darvill, T 2003 'The Land of the Dobunni' *in* Ecclestone, E, Gardner, K S, Holbrook, N and Smith, A (eds) *The Land of the Dobunni*. Kings Lynn: Heritage Marketing and Publications, 2–11

Darvill, T 2004 *Long Barrows of the Cotswolds and Surroundings Areas*. Stroud: Tempus

Darvill, T 2006 'Early Prehistory' *in* Holbrook, N and Jurica, J (eds) *Twenty-five Years of Archaeology in Gloucestershire: A Review of New Discoveries and New Thinking in Gloucestershire, South Gloucestershire and Bristol 1979–2004*. Cotswold Archaeology Bristol Gloucestershire Archaeol Rep **3**, 5–60

Darvill, T 2011 *Prehistoric Gloucestershire, Forest and Vale and High Blue Hills*. 2 edn. Stroud: Amberley Press

Darvill, T and Fulton, A 1998 *The Monuments at Risk Survey of England 1995, Main Report*. Bournemouth University and English Heritage

Davis, E 2003 'Archaeological Evaluation of land at Spital Meend, Lancaut Lane, Tidenham Gloucestershire. Unpublished Bristol and Regional Archaeological Services report. Report No: 1208/2003, September 2003

Davis, O and Sharples, N 2014 'The Archaeological Evaluation of a Bronze Age Treasure Find at Woolaston, Gloucestershire, 15–16 March 2014'. Unpublished Cardiff University Department of Archaeology report

Dean, R 2012 'An archaeological gradiometer and earth resistance survey, Site so5500/05, East Wood Tidenham, Forest of Dean, Gloucestershire' *in* Hoyle, J P 2013 'The Forest of Dean, Gloucestershire, Forest of Dean Archaeological Survey Stage 3B, Phase 2 Field evaluation of selected lidar-detected earthworks in Forestry Commission woodland, Project Number 5291 SURV'. Unpublished Gloucestershire County Council Archaeology Service report for English Heritage, April 2013, 137–54

Dearne, M J 2000 'Coal' *in* Price, E *Frocester, A Romano-British Settlement, its Antecedents and Successors, Volume* **2**. Stonehouse: Gloucester and District Archaeological Research Group, 259–60

Dinnis, R and Stringer, C 2014 *Britain: One Million Years of the Human Story*. London: Natural History Museum

DoE 1988 List of Buildings of Special Architectural or Historic Interest, District Forest of Dean, (Parishes of Alvington, Aylburton, Hewelsfield, St. Briavels, Tidenham, Woolaston and the town of Lydney). Unpublished document

DoE 1990 Planning Policy Guidance Archaeology and Planning, Her Majesty's Stationery Office, November 1990

Dornier, A 1966 'Bledisloe Excavations, 1964'. *Trans Bristol Gloucestershire Archaeol Soc* **85**, 57–69

Douthwaite, A and Devine, V 1998 'Gloucestershire Historic Towns Survey, Forest of Dean District'. Unpublished Gloucestershire County Council Archaeology Service report

Dreghorn, W 1968 *Geology Explained in the Forest of Dean, and the Wye Valley*. Newton Abbot: David and Charles

Drinkwater, J and Saville, A 1984 'The Bronze Age round barrows of Gloucestershire: a brief review' *in* Saville, A (ed) *Archaeology in Gloucestershire*. Cheltenham: Cheltenham Art Gallery and Museums, 128–39

Duller, G A T 2008 *Luminescence Dating, Guidelines on Using Luminescence Dating in Archaeology*. Swindon: English Heritage

Dungworth, D 2007 'Slag and moulds' *in* Catchpole, T C 'Excavations at the Sewage Treatment Works, Dymock 1995'. *Trans Bristol Gloucestershire Archaeol Soc* **125**, 183–6

Dungworth, D, Crew, P, McDonnell, G 2012 'Iron: bloomery smelting and associated processes'. The Historical Metallurgy Society. Archaeology Datasheet **301**. Derived from http://hist-met.org/images/pdf/HMSdatasheet301.pdf, 20th April 2015

Dyer, J 1992 *Hillforts of England and Wales*. Rev edn. Princes Risborough: Shire Archaeology

Edwards, N and Lane, A (eds) 1992 *The Early Church in Wales and the West. Recent Work in Early Christian Archaeology, History and Place-names*. Oxford: Oxbow monograph **16**

Ekwall, E 1960 *The Concise Oxford Dictionary of English Placenames*. 4 edn. Oxford: Oxford University Press

Ellis, P 1979 'A Watching brief undertaken for the DOE at Birchfield Cottage, St. Briavels, Glos. in December 1978 and January 1979'. Unpublished Committee for Archaeology in Avon, Gloucestershire and Somerset report

Ellis, P 1984 'Earthworks at Bishton Farm, Tidenham. *Trans Bristol Gloucestershire Archaeol Soc* **102**, 204–5

Ellis, C 2013 'Reddings Lane, Staunton, Gloucestershire, Archaeological Evaluation'. Unpublished Cotswold Archaeology report. CA Project: 4393, CA Report: 13433, July 2013

Ellison, A 1977 'A survey of the archaeological implications of forestry in the Forest of Dean'. Unpublished Committee for Rescue Archaeology in Avon, Gloucestershire and Somerset report

Elrington, C R 1972a 'Newnham' *in* Pugh, R B (ed) *The Victoria History of the County of Gloucestershire* **10**, 29–50

Elrington, C R 1972b 'Fretherne and Saul' *in* Pugh, R B (ed) *The Victoria History of the County of Gloucestershire* **10**, 155–69

English Heritage 1988a 'Monuments Protection Programme Single Monument Class Description: Roman Fortlets'. English Heritage

English Heritage 1988b 'Monuments Protection Programme Single Monument Class Description: Romano-British Mansiones'. English Heritage

English Heritage 1989a 'Monuments Protection Programme Single Monument Class Description: Ring Cairns'. English Heritage

English Heritage 1989b 'Monuments Protection Programme Single Monument Class Description: Roads (Romano-British)'. English Heritage

English Heritage 1990 'Monuments Protection Programme Single Monument Class Description: Small Stone Circles'. English Heritage

English Heritage 2011 *Prehistoric Barrows and Burial Monuments*. Introduction to Heritage Assets, English Heritage

Evans, E and Lewis, R 2003 'The Prehistoric Funerary and Ritual Monument Survey of Glamorgan and Gwent: Overviews, Glamorgan and Gwent report for Cadw'. Glamorgan and Gwent Archaeological Trust report no. 2003/068. Pdf copy derived from http://www.ggat.org.uk/cadw/cadw_reports/pdfs/GGAT%2072%20Overviews.pdf

Figueiral, I 1992 'Charcoal' *in* Fulford, M G and Allen, J R L 'Iron-making at the Chesters villa, Woolaston, Gloucestershire, survey and excavation 1987–91'. *Britannia* **23**, 188–91

FISH 2018 The Forum on Information Standards in Heritage, Archaeological Objects Thesaurus. Derived from http://thesaurus.historicengland.org.uk/thesaurus.asp?thes_no=144&thes_name=FISH%20Archaeological%20Objects%20Thesaurus

Fitchett, M 1985 'Littledean Hall'. *The New Regard* **1**, 10–11

Fitchett, M 1986 'Excavations at Park Farm, Lydney'. *The New Regard* **2**, 24–7

Fitchett, M 1987 unpublished correspondence in Gloucestershire County Council Archaeology Service, HER site file 9339, 20th August 1987

Forster Brown, T 1896–7 'Notes on ancient mining tools found in the Forest of Dean'. *Trans Bristol Gloucestershire Archaeol Soc* **20**, 157–60

Fosbroke, T D 1831 'Offa's Dyke, near St Briavels, Gloucester'. *The Gentleman's Magazine,* **101 (2)**, 583

Fosbroke, T D 1832 'Investigation of Offa's Dyke'. *The Gentleman's Magazine* **102 (2)**, 501

Fowler, P J (ed) 1971, 'Excavation, Fieldwork and Finds', *Archaeological Review for 1970, Number 5*. Council for British Archaeology, Department of Extra-Mural Studies, University of Bristol, May 1971

Fowler, P J 1983 *The Farming of Prehistoric Britain,* 2 edn, Cambridge: Cambridge University Press

Fox, Sir C 1931 'Offa's Dyke: A field survey, sixth report: Offa's Dyke in the Wye Valley'. *Archaeologia Cambrensis* **86**, 1–74

Fox, Sir C 1955 *Offa's Dyke*. London: British Academy

Franks, A 1852 'A collection of British antiquities in the British Museum'. *Archaeol J* **9**, 13

Frere, S 1978 *Britannia. A History of Roman Britain*. Rev edn. London: Routledge and Kegan Paul

Fulford, M G 2003 'The canton of the Dobunni' *in* Ecclestone, E, Gardner, K S, Holbrook, N and Smith, A (eds) *The Land of the Dobunni*. Kings Lynn: Heritage Marketing and Publications, 17–23

Fulford, M G and Allen, J R L 1992 'Iron-making at the Chesters Villa, Woolaston, Gloucestershire, survey and excavation 1987–91'. *Britannia* **23**, 159–215

Fulford, M G, Rippon, S, Allen, J R L and Hillam, J 1992 'The medieval quay at Woolaston Grange, Gloucestershire'. *Trans Bristol Gloucestershire Archaeol Soc* **110**, 101–22

GADARG 1982a Card index of sites identified by the Gloucester and District Archaeological Research Group, held as part of Gloucestershire County Council Archaeology Service Historic Environment Record. Card Ruspidge 1

GADARG 1982b Card index of sites identified by the Gloucester and District Archaeological Research Group, held as part of Gloucestershire County Council Archaeology Service Historic Environment Record. Card Newnham 7

Gale, R 2000 'The fuels' *in* Barber, A J and Holbrook, N 'Excavations at Millend, Blakeney'. *Trans Bristol Gloucestershire Archaeol Soc* **118**, 51–57

Gale, R 2007 'Charcoal' *in* Catchpole, T C 'Excavations at the Sewage Treatment Works'. *Trans Bristol Gloucestershire Archaeol Soc* **125**, 212–15

Gale, R 2012 'Charcoal from Bridgewater's 1963 excavation' *in* Jackson, R *Ariconium, Herefordshire, An Iron Age Settlement and Romano-British 'Small Town'*. Oxford: Oxbow, 164–67

Gaunt, P 1987 *The Cromwellian Gazetteer: An Illustrated Guide to Britain in the Civil War and Commonwealth*. Stroud: Alan Sutton

GCRO, 17th century map of parts of Newland, St Briavels, Hewelsfield and Woolaston Parishes, Gloucestershire Archives Document GRO 501

Gelling, M (ed) 1983 *Offa's Dyke Reviewed by Frank Noble*. Oxford: Brit Archaeol Rep Brit Ser **114**, 1–18

Gelling, M 1997 *Signposts to the Past, Place-names and the History of England*. 3 edn. Chichester: Phillimore and Co

Geode Consulting 1998 'The Geological and Conservation Value of 'Scowles' in the Forest of Dean'. Unpublished report for English Nature, January 1998

Gill, M and Newman, P 2015 'An archaeological assessment of coal mining in England' *in* NAMHO 2015 'The Research Framework for the Archaeology of the Extractive Industries in England (Mining and Quarrying)'. Draft documents derived from the National Association of Mining History Organisations (NAMHO) website http://www.namho.org/research.php, 18 March 2015

Glos HER 2015 Unreferenced information derived from the Gloucestershire Historic Environment Record

Goddard, S and Juleff, G 2003 'The excavation season, Sherracombe Ford', *Counc Brit Archaeol Southwest J* **11**

Graham, R 1907 'Flaxley Abbey' *in* Page, W (ed) *The Victoria History of the County of Gloucestershire* **2**, 93–6

Green, S 1989 'Some recent archaeological and faunal discoveries from the Severn Estuary Levels'. *Bull Board Celtic Stud* **36**, 187–99

Green, G W 1992 *British Regional Geology, Bristol and Gloucester Region*. 3 edn. London: HMSO

Grinsell, L V 1968 'City Museum, Bristol. Recent archaeological accessions'. *Bristol Archaeol Res Group Bull* **3 (3)**, 64–5

Grundy, G B 1935–6 'Tidenham'. *Saxon Charters and Fieldnames of Gloucestershire*. **II** Gloucester, 237–53

Grundy, G B 1936 'The ancient woodland of Gloucestershire'. *Trans Bristol Gloucestershire Archaeol Soc* **58**, 65–155

GSGB 1957–9 *Geological Survey of Great Britain (England and Wales). Reconstituted Geological Sheets, at scale 6" to 1 mile*. Sheets SO50NE, SO51SE, SO61NW, SO61NE, SO61SE

Gutierrez, A and Roe, F 1998 'Stone objects' *in* Timby, J *Excavations in Kingscote and Wycomb, Glos. A Roman Estate Centre and Small Town in the Cotswolds with Notes on Related Settlements*. Cirencester: Cotswold Archaeology, 176–9

Gwatkin, G 1992a Rectified copy of Mitcheldean Tithe Map (1840), Abinghall Tithe Map (1838) and Longhope Tithe Map (1841) at scale 1:10,560 (Map No 11)

Gwatkin, G 1992b Rectified copy of Littledean and Newnham Tithe Map (1839) at scale 1:10,560 (Map no: 8)

Gwatkin, G 1993a Rectified copy of St Briavels (1842) and Hewelsfield (1841) Tithe Map including Brockweir at scale 1:10,560 (Map no: 22)

Gwatkin, G 1993b Rectified copy of Alvington Enclosure Map (1813) and Woolaston Tithe Map (1841) at scale 1:10,560 (Map no: 25)

Gwatkin, G 1993c Rectified copy of English Bicknor Tithe Map (1838) and Staunton (1845) at scale 1:10,560 (Map no: 20)

Gwatkin, G 1994a Rectified copy of Newland Tithe Map including Coleford (1840) at scale 1:10,560 (Map no: 47)

Gwatkin, G 1994b Rectified copy of Aylburton and Bream Tithe Map (1840) at scale 1:10,560 (Map no: 49)

Gwatkin, G 1995a Rectified copy of Tidenham Tithe Map (1845) including Lancaut (1839) at scale 1:10,560 (Map no: 82)

Gwatkin, G 1995b Rectified copy of Awre Tithe Map (1840) at scale 1:10,560 (Map no: 54)

Gwatkin, G 1996 Rectified map of West Dean (North) including Lydbrook (1836) at scale 1:10,560 (Map no: 104)

Gwatkin, G 1997a Rectified map of East Dean including Ruardean and Drybrook (1836) at scale 1:10, 560 (Map no: 106)

Gwatkin, G 1997b Rectified map of East Dean: Cinderford (1836) at scale 1:10,560 (Map 107)

Gwatkin, G 1997c Rectified map of East Dean including Cinderford, Ruspidge, Soudley and Shakemantle (1836) at scale 1:10,560 (Map no: 108)

Gwatkin, G 1997d Rectified map of West Dean (South): Parkend (1834–35/1840) at scale 1:10,560 (Map no 116)

Hannaford, H R 1999 'Archaeological Investigation of Wat's Dyke at Maes-y-Clawdd, Oswestry'. Shropshire County Council Archaeology Service

Harding, A F and Lee, G E 1987 *Henge Monuments and Related Sites of Great Britain. Air Photographic Evidence and Catalogue*. Oxford: Brit Archaeol Rep Brit Ser **175**, Oxford

Hare, M and Heighway, C 2012 'Historical introduction' *in* Bryant, R *Corpus of Anglo-Saxon Stone Sculpture: Vol. X, The Western Midlands*. Oxford: Oxford University Press/British Academy, 5–18

Harley, J B 1970b Cartographical notes prepared on facsimiles of late 19th century editions of the 1st Edition 1" to 1 mile scale Ordnance Survey maps published by David and Charles, Second Impression 1980. Sheet 68, Bristol

Harley, J B 1970b Cartographical notes prepared by J B Harley reproduced on facsimiles of late 19th century editions of the 1st Edition 1" to 1 mile scale Ordnance Survey maps published by David and Charles. Sheet 68, Bristol

Harris, F H 1936 'A hand hammer and jug, Lydney'. *Trans Bristol Gloucestershire Archaeol Soc* **58**, 283–4

Harris, F H 1937 'Roman pottery, Lydney'. *Trans Bristol Gloucestershire Archaeol Soc* **59**, 327

Harris, F H 1938 'Strainer and pottery, Lydney'. *Trans Bristol Gloucestershire Archaeol Soc* **60**, 346–7

Hart, C E 1945 'Metes and bounds of the Forest of Dean'. *Trans Bristol Gloucestershire Archaeol Soc* **66**, 166–207

Hart, C E 1966 *Royal Forest, A History of Dean's Woods as Producers of Timber*, Oxford: Clarendon Press

Hart, C E 1967 *Archaeology in Dean*. Gloucester: John Bellows

Hart, C E 1968 'Charcoal burning in the Royal Forest of Dean'. *Bull Hist Metall Soc* **1**, 33–39

Hart, C E 1971 *The Industrial History of Dean*. Newton Abbot: David and Charles

Hart, C E 1995 *The Forest of Dean: New History 1550–1818*. Stroud: Sutton Publishing

Hart, C E 2002 *The Free Miners of the Royal Forest of Dean and the Hundred of St Briavels*. 2 edn. Lydney: Lightmoor Press

Hart, C E with Clissold, G 2000 'Ancient Locations in the Forest of Dean'. *The New Regard* **15**, 17–29

Havard, T and Guarino, P 2015 Land east of Lydney Road, Yorkley, Gloucestershire, Archaeological Evaluation, Cotswold Archaeology unpublished report, CA Project 5627, CA Report: 15796, November 2015

Hayes, T and Mallim, T 2008 'The date and nature of Wat's Dyke'. *Anglo-Saxon Studies in Archaeology and History* **15**, 147–79

Hedges, R E M and Salter, C 1979 'Source determination of currency bars through analysis of the slag inclusions'. *Archaeometry* **21**, 161–75

Heighway, C 1987 *Anglo-Saxon Gloucestershire*. Gloucester: Sutton Publishing

Henig, M 1984 *Religion in Roman Britain*. London: Batsford

Herbert, N M 1972a 'Tidenham' in Pugh, R B (ed) *The Victoria History of the County of Gloucestershire* **10**, 50–79

Herbert, N M 1972b 'Westbury-on-Severn' in Pugh, R B (ed) *The Victoria History of the County of Gloucestershire* **10**, 79–102

Herbert, N M 1996a 'The Forest of Dean' in Herbert, N M (ed) *The Victoria History of the County of Gloucestershire* **5**, 285–94

Herbert, N M 1996b 'Flaxley' in Herbert, N M (ed) *The Victoria History of the County of Gloucestershire* **5**, 138–50

Herbert, N M 1996c 'Hewelsfield and Brockweir' in Herbert, N M (ed) *The Victoria History of the County of Gloucestershire* **5**, 150–9

Herbert, N M 1996d 'Staunton' in Herbert, N M (ed) *The Victoria History of the County of Gloucestershire* **5**, 272–84

Herbert, N M 1996e 'Lydney' in Herbert, N M (ed) *The Victoria History of the County of Gloucestershire* **5**, 46–85

Herbert, N M 1996f 'St Briavels' in Herbert, N M (ed) *The Victoria History of the County of Gloucestershire* **5**, 247–72

Herbert, N M 1996g 'Newland' in Herbert, N M (ed) *The Victoria History of the County of Gloucestershire* **5**, 195–231

Herbert, N M 1996h 'Awre' in Herbert, N M (ed) *The Victoria History of the County of Gloucestershire* **5**, 1446

Herbert, N M 1996i 'Ruardean' in Herbert, N M (ed) *The Victoria History of the County of Gloucestershire* **5**, 231–47

Herbert, N M 1996j 'Forest Administration' in Herbert, N M (ed) *The Victoria History of the County of Gloucestershire* **5**, 354–75

Herbert, N M 1996k 'Bounds of the Forest' in Herbert, N M (ed) *The Victoria History of the County of Gloucestershire* **5**, 295–300

Herbert, N M 1996l 'St Briavels Hundred' in Herbert, N M (ed) *The Victoria History of the County of Gloucestershire* **5**, 85–92

Hey, D (ed) 1996 *The Oxford Companion to Local and Family History*. Oxford: Oxford University Press

Hickling, S 2007 'An Archaeological Desk-based Assessment and Level 2 Building Recording at The Malt House, Brockweir'. Unpublished Gloucestershire County Council Archaeology Service report

Hill, D 1977 'Notes on Offa's and Wat's Dykes' in Webster, L E and Cherry, J (eds) 'Medieval Britain in 1976'. *Medieval Archaeol* **21**, 219–22

Hill, D 1981 'Notes on work on Offa's Dyke' in Youngs, S M and Clark, J (eds) 'Medieval Britain in 1980'. *Medieval Archaeol* **25**, 184–5

Hill, D 1985 'The construction of Offa's Dyke'. *Antiq J* **65**, 140–2

Hill, D 1986 'The Offa's and Wat's Dyke Project' in Youngs, S M, Clark, J and Barry, T (eds) 'Medieval Britain and Ireland in 1985'. *Medieval Archaeol* **30**, 150–3

Hill, D 1996a 'Gloucestershire, Sedbury, Allotment', Manchester Centre for Anglo Saxon Studies (Offa's Dyke Project)' unpublished note in Gloucestershire HER Site File 16340

Hill, J D 1996b 'Hill-forts and the Iron Age of Wessex' in Champion, T C and Collis, J R (eds) *The Iron Age in Britain and Ireland: Recent Trends*. Sheffield: University of Sheffield, 95–116

Hill, D and Worthington, M 2003, *Offa's Dyke: History and Guide*. Stroud: Tempus Publishing

Hirst, R P 1998 *Old Stone Crosses in Gloucestershire*. Lydney: Lightmoor Press

Hirst, R P 1999 'More local crosses of west Gloucestershire'. *The New Regard* **14**, 61

Historic England 2019 The National Heritage List for England. Listed Buildings: Information. Derived from the Historic England website https://historicengland.org.uk/listing/the-list/advanced-search?searchType=nhleadvancedsearch

Holbrook, N 1994 'Corinium Dobunnorum: Roman Civitas Capital and Provincial Capital' in Darvill, T C and Gerrard, C *Cirencester: Town and Landscape, an urban archaeological assessment*. Cirencester: Cotswold Archaeology, 57–86

Hood, A 2013 'Evidence for Roman iron working at Church Lane, Alvington, Forest of Dean'. *Trans Bristol Gloucestershire Archaeol Soc* **131**, 103–22

Hooke, D 2009 *The Anglo-Saxon Landscape, The Kingdom of the Hwicce*. Manchester: Manchester University Press

Hosfield, R, Straker, V and Gardner, P 2008 'Palaeolithic and Mesolithic', in Webster, C J (ed) 2008 *The Archaeology of South West England, South West Archaeological Research Framework, Resource Assessment and Research Agenda*. Taunton: Somerset County Council, 23–59

Hoyle, J P 1992 Western Stowfield Quarry, Staunton, Gloucestershire, A preliminary archaeological assessment. Unpublished Gloucestershire County Council Archaeology Service report, HER Source Work Reference 679

Hoyle, J P 1996a 'Offa's Dyke Management Survey 1995–6'. *Glevensis* **29**, 29–31

Hoyle, J P 1996b 'Archaeological Watching Brief at Mercian Way, Sedbury, Gloucestershire'. Unpublished Gloucestershire County Council Archaeology Service report, August 1996

Hoyle, J P 2001 'The Forest of Dean, Gloucestershire: Archaeological Survey Project design for Stage 1 and 2 and outline proposal for Stages 3–4'. Unpublished project design for English Heritage, August 2001

Hoyle, J P 2003a 'Welshbury Woods, Blaisdon Gloucestershire, A report on a rapid walk-over field survey'. Unpublished Gloucestershire County Council Archaeology Service report for the Forestry Commission, May 2003

Hoyle, J P 2003b 'Chestnuts Wood, Littledean, Gloucestershire, A report on archaeological desk-based data collection and field survey'. Unpublished Gloucestershire County Council Archaeology Service report, May 2003

Hoyle, J P 2004 'Report on a site visit to May Hill, Longhope, 18/04/04'. Unpublished Gloucestershire County Council Archaeology Service site visit report date 19/04/04

Hoyle, J P 2006 'Historic Landscape Characterisation, Gloucestershire, The Cotswolds Area of Outstanding Natural Beauty, The Wye Valley Area of Outstanding Natural Beauty'. Unpublished Gloucestershire County Council Archaeology Service report, September 2006, and digital HLC data held by Gloucestershire County Council Archaeology service as part of the HER

Hoyle, J P 2008a 'The Forest of Dean, Gloucestershire, Stage 1: Desk-based data collection, Project Number 2727'. Unpublished Gloucestershire County Council Archaeology Service report for English Heritage, November 2008

Hoyle, J P 2008b 'The Forest of Dean, Gloucestershire, Stage 2: Pilot Field Survey, Project Number 2727'. Unpublished Gloucestershire County Council Archaeology Service report for English Heritage, November 2008

Hoyle, J P 2008c 'The Forest of Dean, Gloucestershire, Lidar survey of selected areas of woodland and the Aggregates Resource Area: Forest of Dean Archaeological Survey Stage 3A, English Heritage Project Number 4798 MAIN'. Unpublished Gloucestershire County Council Archaeology Service report for English Heritage, March 2007

Hoyle, J P 2009a 'The Forest of Dean, Gloucestershire, Forest of Dean Archaeological Survey Stage 3B: Survey for management of lidar-detected earthworks in Forestry Commission woodland, Project Design, Project Number 5291 PD'. Unpublished Gloucestershire County Council Archaeology Service project design for English Heritage, March 2009

Hoyle, J P 2009b 'Cinderford Northern Quarter, Heritage and Archaeological Assessment'. Unpublished Gloucestershire County Council Archaeology Service report for the Forest of Dean District Council, September 2009

Hoyle, J P 2011a 'The Forest of Dean, Gloucestershire, Forest of Dean Archaeological Survey Stage 3B, Phase 1 Rapid field validation and scoping analysis for characterisation of archaeology in woodland, Project Number 5291 SURV'. Unpublished Gloucestershire County Council Archaeology Service report for English Heritage, January 2011

Hoyle, J P 2011b 'Observations at Church Farm St Briavels 15/02/2011'. Unpublished Gloucestershire County Council Archaeology Service report

Hoyle, J P 2013a 'The Forest of Dean, Gloucestershire, Forest of Dean Archaeological Survey Stage 3B, Phase 2 Field evaluation of selected lidar-detected earthworks in Forestry Commission woodland, Project Number 5291 SURV'. Unpublished Gloucestershire County Council Archaeology Service report for English Heritage, April 2013

Hoyle, J P 2013b 'Report on a rapid archaeological evaluation of land at Keynsham Lane, Woolaston, Gloucestershire, 15th November 2013'. Unpublished Gloucestershire County Council Archaeology Service report, 17th December 2014

Hoyle, J P 2014 'Soudley Camp, Soudley, Gloucestershire: Management Plan'. Unpublished Gloucestershire County Council Archaeology Service management plan for Forest Enterprise, January 2014

Hoyle, J P 2017a 'Report on site visit to the Dean Road between Soilwell and Oldcroft 09/10/2016'. Unpublished Gloucestershire County Council Archaeology Service site visit report, January 2017

Hoyle, J P 2017b Forest of Dean Archaeological Survey Stage 4: Module 3, Research Framework for Forest of Dean District, Project Number 5291 ANL, Unpublished Gloucestershire County Council Archaeology Service report for Historic England, March 2017

Hoyle, J P, Butler, L, Tait, G and Wootton, D 2007a 'The Forest of Dean Gloucestershire, The Scowles and Associated Iron Industry Survey: Project Number 3342'. Unpublished Gloucestershire County Council Archaeology Service report for English Heritage, March 2007

Hoyle, J P, Owen, D, Rowlatt, S and Studholme, C 2007b 'Scowles in the Forest of Dean, Gloucestershire: Their geological, archaeological and ecological significance'. *Proc Cotteswold Nat Fd Club* **44 (1)**, 40–62

Hoyle, J P and Vallender, J 1997 'Offa's Dyke in Gloucestershire. Management Survey'. Unpublished Gloucestershire County Council Archaeology Service report for English Heritage

Hoyle, J P and Armstrong, A 2011 Cupstone at Beeches Farm, Glos HER 22305, NGR 354530200425. Unpublished Gloucestershire County Council Archaeology Service site visit report, October 2011

Hurst, H R 1985 *Kingsholm*. Gloucester: Gloucester Archaeol Rep **1**

Iles, R 2017 Lancaut Village Earthworks. Unpublished topographical survey report for the Forest of Dean Buildings Preservation Trust, February 2017

Jackson, R 2012 *Ariconium, Herefordshire, An Iron Age Settlement and Romano-British 'Small Town'*. Oxford: Oxbow

Jacobi, R M and Higham, T F G 2011 'The later Upper Palaeolithic recolonisation of Britain: new results from AMS radiocarbon dating' *in* Ashton, N M, Lewis, S G and Stringer, C B (eds) *The Ancient Human Occupation of Britain*. Amsterdam: Elsevier, 223–47

Jackson, R, Walsh, A and Wheeler, J 2016 Foresters' Forest: Unearthing our Heritage, Development Stage, Forest of Dean Gloucestershire, Worcestershire Archive and Archaeology Service report for the Forestry Commission, 30 August 2016, Version 2 (final), Report reference 2369

James, T and Walters, B 1988 'Some recent prehistoric finds in Dean'. *Dean Archaeol* **1**, 39–44

Jarman, R 2015 Welshbury Hillfort, Gloucestershire, unpublished preliminary report of survey prepared for discussion meeting on 19 November 2015

Johns, B 1990 'Cup stones and arrow stones'. *The New Regard of the Forest of Dean* **6**, 19–25

Johns, B 1991 'Attempts to date a hearth site, charcoal hearth survey, Blakeney Hill Woodland'. *The New Regard of the Forest of Dean* **7**, 8–10

Johns, B 1995 'Dowsing – a track line investigated'. *The New Regard* **10**, 40–8

Johns, B 2005a 'Roman altar. An attempt at deciphering the inscriptions on its sides'. *The New Regard* **20**, 38–40

Johns, B 2005b Unpublished list of sites identified by B Johns to the south of Blakeney, Gloucestershire County Council Archaeology Service HER site file 27852-27856 and 27858-27869. March 2005

Johns, B 2011 'Attempts to date a hearth site, an update of research in Blakeney Hill, woodland as outlined in previous reports in the New Regards 5, 6 and 7'. *The New Regard* **25**, 66–71

Jones, B and Maude, K 1987 'Excavations at Dean Hall, Littledean, 1985'. *Manchester Archaeol Bull* **1**, 38–41

Jones, M J 1975 *Roman Fort Defences to AD 117*. Oxford: Brit Archaeol Rep Brit Ser **21**

Jones, W 1996 *Dictionary of Industrial Archaeology*. Stroud: Sutton Publishing

Jones, E M 2006 'Monuments and memories set in stone; a Cornish Bronze Age ceremonial complex in its landscape (on Stanton Down)'. *Proc Prehist Soc* **72**, 341–65

Jurica, A R J 1996a 'Ruardean' *in* Herbert, N M (ed) *The Victoria County History of Gloucestershire* **5**, 231–47

Jurica, A R J 1996b 'Littledean' *in* Herbert, N M (ed) *The Victoria County History of Gloucestershire* **5**, 159–73

Jurica, A R J 1996c 'English Bicknor' *in* Herbert, N M (ed) *The Victoria County History of Gloucestershire* **5**, 101–17

Jurica, A R J 1996d 'Industry' *in* Herbert, N M (ed) *The Victoria County History of Gloucestershire* **5**, 326–54

Jurica, A R J 1996e 'Mitcheldean' *in* Herbert, N M (ed) *The Victoria County History of Gloucestershire* **5**, 173–95

Jurica, A R J 1996f 'Coleford' *in* Herbert, N M (ed) *The Victoria County History of Gloucestershire* **5**, 117–38

Jurica, A R J 1996g 'Flaxley' *in* Herbert, N M (ed) *The Victoria County History of Gloucestershire* **5**, 138–50

Jurica, A R J 2010 'Longhope' *in* Jurica, A R J (ed) *The Victoria County History of Gloucestershire* **12**, 223–54

Kenny, N and Dolan, B nd Traditional Charcoal Making, Experimental Archaeology, Undated web page derived from http://charcoal. seandalaiocht.com/uploads/3/5/0/8/3508898/leaflet_on_trad_charcoal_making_for_experiment.pdf, 20 February 2015

Keynes, S 2005 'The kingdom of the Mercians in the eighth century' *in* Hill, D and Worthington, M (eds) *Aethelbald and Offa, Two Eighth-Century Kings of Mercia*. Oxford: Brit Archaeol Rep Brit Ser **383**, 1–26

Kissock, J and Wright, N 2001 'The excavation of a charcoal-burning platform at Llanelen, Gower'. *Studia Celtica* **25**, 143–59

Knight, A 2011 'The King's Ironworks in the Forest of Dean 1612–1674'. *The New Regard* **25**, 40–52

Leach, P 1988a Monuments Protection Programme, Monument Class Description, 'Ringworks'. English Heritage

Leach, P 1988b Monuments Protection Programme, Monument Class Description, 'Motte and Bailey Castles'. English Heritage

Leach, P 1988c Monuments Protection Programme, Monument Class Description 'Shell Keeps'. English Heritage

Leach, P 1989 Monuments Protection Programme, Monument Class Description 'Tower Keep Castles'. English Heritage

Leech, R 1981 *Historic Towns in Gloucestershire*. Gloucester: The Committee for Rescue Archaeology in Avon Gloucestershire and Somerset, Survey **3**

Lelong, O and Pollard, T 1998 'Excavation of a Bronze Age ring cairn at Cloburn Quarry, Cairngryffe, Lanarkshire'. *Proc Soc Antiq Scotland* **128**, 105–42

Lewis, J M 1963 'A section of Offa's Dyke at Buttington Tump, Tidenham'. *Trans Bristol Gloucestershire Archaeol Soc* **82**, 202–4

Lewis, G R and Vellacott, C H 1907 'Mining' *in* Page, W (ed) *The Victoria History of the County of Gloucestershire* **2**, 215–38

Ling, T 1968 *A History of Religion East and West*. 1974 edition. London

Lovell, J, Wakeman, G, Timby, J and Allen, M J 2007 'Excavation at Bishop's Cleeve, 1998 and 2004'. *Trans Bristol Gloucestershire Archaeol Soc* **125**, 95–129

Lowe, D J 1989 'Limestones and caves in the Forest of Dean' *in* Ford, T D (ed) *Limestones and Caves of Wales*. Cambridge: Cambridge University Press, 106–16

Lowe, D J 1993 'The Forest of Dean caves and karst: inception horizons and iron ore deposits'. *Cave Science* **20 (2)**, 31–43

L U A U 1998 'M.P.P. Iron and Steel Industries Step 3. Introduction to site assessments'. Unpublished Lancaster University Archaeological Unit report for the English Heritage Monuments Protection Programme. October 1998

Lynch, F 1979a 'Ring cairns of Britain and Ireland: their design and purpose'. *Ulster J Archaeol* **42**, 1–19

Lynch, F 1979b 'Ring cairns and related monuments in Wales'. *Scottish Archaeol Forum* **4**, 61–80

Manning, W H 1981 *Report on the Excavations at Usk 1965–76: The Fortress Excavations 1968–71*. Cardiff: University of Wales Press for Board of Celtic Studies

Macer-Wright, D M and Fitchett, M 1984 'Littledean Hall Roman temple, Gloucestershire, 1st Interim Report, 1984'. Unpublished report held in Gloucestershire County Council Historic Environment Record file 9782

Macinnes, L 1986 'The protection and management of Offa's and Wat's Dykes: A Welsh perspective' *in* Hughs, M and Rowley, L (eds) *The Management and Presentation of Field Monuments*. Oxford: Oxford University Department of External Studies, 87–93

Maclean, Sir J 1879–80 'Notice of earthworks in the parish of English Bicknor'. *Trans Bristol Gloucestershire Archaeol Soc* **4**, 301–12

Maclean, Sir J 1882–3 'History of the manor and advowson of Staunton, in the Forest of Dean'. *Trans Bristol Gloucestershire Archaeol Soc* **7**, 227–66

Maclean, Sir J 1889–90 'A perambulation of the Forest of Dean, in the county of Gloucestershire, 10th Ed I (1281–2)'. *Trans Bristol Gloucestershire Archaeol Soc* **14**, 356–69

Maclean, Sir J 1893–4 'The course of Offa's Dyke in Gloucestershire'. *Trans Bristol Gloucestershire Archaeol Soc* **18**, 3–31

Mack, I and McDonnell, G 1999 'Preliminary report on the slags and residues from Lydney'. Unpublished Avon Archaeological Unit report

Margary, I D 1957 *Roman Roads in Britain, 2, North of the Foss Way – Bristol Channel*. London

Mason, C and Egging Dinwiddy, K 2014 'Land at Lower Lane, Berry Hill, Coleford, Gloucestershire'. Unpublished Wessex Archaeology report, Ref: 106080.02, October 2014

McGrath, P and Cannon, J (eds) 1976 *Essays in Bristol and Gloucestershire History*. Bristol: Bristol and Gloucestershire Archaeological Society

McOmish, D S and Smith, N A 1996 'Welshbury Hillfort: A new survey by the Royal Commission on the Historical Monuments of England'. *Trans Bristol Gloucestershire Archaeol Soc* **114**, 55–64

McWhirr, A D 1981 *Roman Gloucestershire*. Gloucester: Sutton Publishing

McWhirr, A D 1986 'Beeches Road excavations 1970–73' *in* McWhirr, A D (ed) *Houses in Roman Cirencester*. Cirencester: Cirencester Excavations III, 19–176

Mellars, P A 1974 'The Palaeolithic and Mesolithic' *in* Renfrew, C (ed) *British Prehistory: A New Outline*. London: Duckworth, 41–99

Meredith, J 2006 *The Iron Industry of the Forest of Dean*. Stroud: The History Press

Middleton, J H 1881–2 'Flaxley Abbey – the existing remains'. *Trans Bristol Gloucestershire Archaeol Soc* **6**, 280–3

Milford, B P 2000 'Whitehouse Farm, English Bicknor – SO 57901485'. Unpublished note in Gloucestershire County Council Archaeology Service HER file 9060, January 2000

Millett, M 1990 *The Romanization of Britain. An Essay in Archaeological Interpretation*. Cambridge: Cambridge University Press

M'Kenny Hughes, T 1892 'On Offa's Dyke'. *Archaeologia* **53 (2)**, 2 Ser **3 (2)**, 465–84

Monmouth Archaeology, 2002 'Woodland Trust, Cadora Wood Project, A Programme of Archaeological Recording for Woodland Trust'. Unpublished Monmouth Archaeology report, November 2002

Moore, J S 1982 *Domesday Book: 15 – Gloucestershire*. History from the Sources, J Morris (ed). Chichester: Phillimore

Moore, J S 1987 'The Gloucestershire section of Domesday Book: geographical problems of the text, part 1'. *Trans Bristol Gloucestershire Archaeol Soc* **105**, 109–32

Moore, T 2006a *Iron Age Societies in the Severn-Cotswolds. Developing Narratives of Social and Landscape Change*. Oxford: Brit Archaeol Rep Brit Ser, **421**

Moore, T 2006b 'The Iron Age', in Holbrook, N and Jurica, J (eds) *Twenty-five years of Archaeology in Gloucestershire. A Review of New Discoveries and New Thinking in Gloucestershire, South Gloucestershire and Bristol, 1979–2004*. Cotswold Archaeology, Bristol and Gloucestershire Archaeological Report No. **3**, 61–96

Moore, T 2012 'Interim report on geophysical survey at Hailey Wood Camp, Sapperton, Gloucestershire'. Unpublished Durham University, Department of Archaeology report

Moore, T and Reece, R 2001 'The Dobunni'. *Glevensis* **34**, 17–26

Morris, R 1990 'Monuments Protection Programme: Single Monument Class Description, Parish Churches'. English Heritage

Muckelroy, K W 1976 'Ambulatories in Romano-Celtic temples in Britain'. *Britannia* **7**, 173–91

Mullin, D 1988 'Some millstone quarry locations in the Forest of Dean'. *The New Regard* **4**, 53

Mullin, D 1990 'Some millstone quarry locations in the Forest of Dean – Part II'. *The New Regard* **6**, 30–7

Mullin, D, Brunning, R and Chadwick, A 2009 'Coastal change on the English side of the Severn Estuary from the Palaeolithic to the present day' *in* Mullin *et al* 'Severn Estuary Rapid Coastal Zone Assessment Survey, Phase 1 report, HEEP project No. 3885'. Unpublished Gloucestershire County Council and Somerset County Council report for English Heritage, Version 3 Final, December 2009

Murphy, K 1983 'Excavations at Penycoed, Llangynog, Dyfed'. *The Carmarthenshire Antiquary* **21**, 75–112

Neal, D S and Walker, B 1988 'A mosaic from Boughspring Roman Villa, Tidenham, Gloucestershire'. *Britannia* **19**, 191–7

Newman, R 1988 'The development of the rural landscape of West Gloucestershire circa 1550–1800'. Unpublished PhD thesis, University College, Cardiff

Nicholls, H G 1858 *The Forest of Dean: An Historical and Descriptive Account*. London: John Murray

Nicholls, H G 1860 'The ancient iron trade of the Forest of Dean, Gloucestershire'. *Archaeol J* **17**, 227–39

Nicholls, H G 1866 *Iron Making in Olden Times*. (facsim edn Coleford 1981)

Oldham, T 2002 *The Mines of the Forest of Dean and Surrounding Areas*. Cardigan

O'Neil, H E 1946–7–8 'The Rev. C F Stopford'. *Trans Cotteswold Nat Fld Club* **67**, 420–1

O'Neil, H and Grinsell, L V 1960 'Gloucestershire barrows'. *Trans Bristol Gloucestershire Archaeol Soc* **79 (I)**, 5–138

Ormerod, G 1841 'An account of some Ancient remains existing in the District adjacent to the confluence of the Wye and the Severn, in the counties of Gloucestershire and Monmouth'. *Archaeologia* **29**, 5–31

Ormerod, G 1861 *Strigulensia, Archaeological memoirs relating to the district adjacent to the confluence of the Severn and the Wye*. Privately published limited edition. London

OS 1881 Ordnance Survey 1st Edition County Series 25" scale (1:25,000) map, Sheet 46:12

OS 1880–1 Ordnance Survey 1st Edition County Series 25" scale (1:25,000) map, Sheet 47:6

OS 1881–6 Ordnance Survey 1st Edition County Series 25" scale (1:25,000) map, Sheet 54:7

OS 1878–91 Ordnance Survey 1st Edition County Series 25" scale (1:25,000) map, Sheet 31:2

OS 1884 Ordnance Survey 1st Edition County Series 25" scale (1:25,000) map, Sheet 32:9

OS 1902a Ordnance Survey 2nd Edition County Series 25" scale 1:25,000) map, Sheet 46:11

OS 1902b Ordnance Survey 2nd Edition County Series 25" scale (1:25,000) map, Sheet 54:7

OS 1902–3 Ordnance Survey 2nd Edition County Series 25" scale (1:25,000) map, Sheet 47:6

OS 1921a Ordnance Survey 3rd Edition County Series 25" scale (1:25,000) map, Sheet 47:6

OS 1921b Ordnance Survey 3rd Edition County Series 25" scale (1:25,000) map, Sheet 54:7

OS 1967 Ordnance Survey 1:25,000 Sheet SO6102

OS 1974 Ordnance Survey 1:25,000 Sheet SO5496

Overy, C G D (ed) 1989 'Monuments Protection Programme: Single Monument Class Description, Standing Stones'. English Heritage

Owen, E 1897 'Circular churchyards' *in* Andrews, W (ed) *Antiquities and Curiosities of the Church*. London: W Andrews and Co, 229–36

Parker Pearson, M 1993 *English Heritage Book of Bronze Age Britain*. 1996 edition. London: English Heritage

Parry, C J 1990 'A survey of St. James's church, Lancaut, Gloucestershire'. *Trans Bristol Gloucestershire Archaeol Soc* **108**, 53–103

Parry, C J 1994 'Symonds Yat Promontory Fort'. *Trans Bristol Gloucestershire Archaeol Soc* **112**, 59–72

Parry, C J 1998 'Excavation near Birdlip'. *Trans Bristol Gloucestershire Archaeol Soc* **116**, 25–92

Paynter, S 2006 'Provenancing iron – is slag the key?' *Research News. Newsletter of the English Heritage Research Department* **3**, 32–33

Paynter, S 2011 *Pre-industrial Ironworks*. Introduction to Heritage Assets, English Heritage, May 2011

PCNFC 1914 'Excursions–Forest of Dean', *Proc Cotteswold Nat Fd Club* **38**, 201–2

Pearson, E, Daffern, N and Wilkinson, D 2012 'Palaeoenvironmental assessment of Cannop Brook, Forest of Dean' *in* Hoyle, J P 2013a 'The Forest of Dean, Gloucestershire, Forest of Dean Archaeological Survey Stage 3B, Phase 2 Field evaluation of selected lidar-detected earthworks in Forestry Commission woodland, Project Number 5291 SURV'. Unpublished Gloucestershire County Council Archaeology Service report for English Heritage, April 2013, Appendix A, 95–136

Phillips, C W 1931 'Final report on the excavations at Merlin's Cave, Symonds Yat'. *Proc Univ Bristol Speleol Soc* **4**, 11–33

Philpott, R 1991 *Burial Practices in Roman Britain. A Survey of Grave Treatment and Furnishings AD 43–410*. Oxford: Brit Archaeol Rep Brit Ser **219**

Pine, J, Allen, J R L and Challinor, D 2009 'Saxon iron smelting at Clearwell Quarry St. Briavels, Lydney, Gloucestershire'. *Archaeology of the Severn Estuary 2009. Annual Report of the Severn Estuary Levels Research Committee* **20**, 9–40

Playne, G F 1876 'On the recent destruction of a Gloucestershire menhire'. *Trans Bristol Gloucestershire Archaeol Soc* **1**, 105–6

Playne, G F 1877 'On the Ancient Camps of Gloucestershire'. *Proc Cotteswold Nat Fd Club* **6**, 202–46

Pollard, J and Healy, F 2008 'Neolithic and Early Bronze Age' *in* Webster, C J (ed) The *Archaeology of South West England. South West Archaeological Research Framework: Resource Assessment and Research Agenda*. Taunton: Somerset County Council, 75–102

Price, A 1991 'A smithing hearth from East Dean'. *The New Regard* **7**, 51–3

Price, E 2000a *Frocester. A Romano-British Settlement, its Antecedents and Successors, Volume 1. The Sites*. Stonehouse: Gloucester and District Archaeological Research Group

Price, E 2000b *Frocester. A Romano-British Settlement, its Antecedents and Successors, Volume 2. The Finds*. Stonehouse: Gloucester and District Archaeological Research Group

Price, W 2001 'A flint adze from the Wye at English Bicknor'. *Glevensis* **37**, 72–3

PRO 1608a The West Part of the Plott of the Forest of Deane in the County of Glos. Taken Anno Dni 1608 and Anno Regni Jacobi Sexto. Bromide copy of Public Record Office Document formerly held at The Wilderness Field Studies Centre, Mitcheldean, Public Record Office document F17/1 MR 879

PRO 1608b The Plott of Rewardine Baylywick parte of the forrest of Deane in the countye of Gloucester taken in Anno 1608. Accessed as 1:10,560 rectified copy of Public Record Office document SP 14/40 MR 129 produced by Gordon Clissold and reproduced in Standing 1997

PRO 1618 The survai of the Mannoar of Rudle within the Countie of Glostar. Being parte of the possessions of the Right Noble Henry Poole of Cirencester. Taken in August One thousand six Hundred and eighteen by me Elias Allen. Accessed as 1:10,560 rectified copy of Public Record Office document SP 14/40 MR 129 researched by Ian Standing and drawn by Gordon Clissold (October 1987) and reproduced in Standing 1997

PRO *c* 1700 A Description of the Forest of Deane as it lyes in sev.l parcels w.th the Inclosures. Bromide copy of Public Record Office Document formerly held at The Wilderness Field Studies Centre, Mitcheldean, Public Record Office document F17/7 M BP297

PRO 1782 The Forest of Dean 1782 Bromide copy of Public Record Office Document formerly held at The Wilderness Field Studies Centre, Mitcheldean, Public Record Office document F17 4 BP150

Pullinger, J 1990 'Excavation report – the Roman villa at Boughspring'. *Dean Archaeol* **3**, 12–25

Putley, J 1999 *Riverine Dean. The Maritime and Waterfront Archaeology of the Forest of Dean*. Lydney: Dean Archaeological Group Occasional Publication **5**

Rackham, O 1995 *The History of the Countryside*. 3 edn. London: Weidenfeld Nicolson

Rawes, B 1981 'The Romano-British site at Brockworth, Glos'. *Britannia* **12**, 45–77

Rawes, B 1984 'The Romano-British site on the Portway, near Gloucester'. *Trans Bristol Gloucestershire Archaeol Soc* **102**, 23–72

Rawes, B 1986 'The Romano-British settlement at Haymes, Cleeve hill, near Cheltenham'. *Trans Bristol Gloucestershire Archaeol Soc* **104**, 61–93

Rawes, B 1987 'Archaeological review for 1986'. *Trans Bristol Gloucestershire Archaeol Soc* **105**, 243–50

Rawes, B 1991'Archaeological review for 1990'. *Trans Bristol Gloucestershire Archaeol Soc* **109**, 223–38

Ray, K and Bapty, I 2016 *Offa's Dyke, Landscape Hegemony in Eighth-Century Britain*. Oxford: Oxbow

Raymond, F 2013 'The Bronze Age pottery' *in* Hoyle, J P 'Report on a rapid archaeological evaluation of land at Keynsham Lane, Woolaston, Gloucestershire, 15th November 2013'. Unpublished Gloucestershire County Council Archaeology Service report, 17th December 2014, Appendix C, 14

RCAHMW 2015 'Little Hadnock Roman Site'. Royal Commission on the Ancient and Historical Monuments of Wales, Site 400333. Derived from http://map.coflein.gov.uk/index.php?action=do_panel&cache_name=cG5wcm4sNDAwMzMzX3NlYXJjaHR5cGUsYWR2YW5jZWRfb3Jh, 9 June 2015

RCHME 1984 'Measured survey at scale 1:500 of earthwork on Cern Hill, Aylesford, Awre (SO 6650 0890)'. Unpublished Royal Commission on the Historical Monuments of England survey. Historic England archive reference 839520

Reece, R 1987 *Coinage in Roman Britain*. London: Seaby

Rennie, E B 1991 'Records of charcoal pits at Kilail Burn, Dunloskin, Sunfield, Archyline, Tom A Choraghasich and Fearnoch in Argyll'. *Discovery and Excavation Scotland 1990*, 45–62

Rennie, E B 1997 *The Recessed Platforms of Argyll, Bute and Inverness*. Oxford: Brit Archaeol Rep Brit Ser **253**

Reynolds, P J 1974 'Experimental Iron Age storage pits: an interim report'. *Proc Prehist Soc* **40**, 118–31

Reynolds, S 1977 *An Introduction to the History of English Medieval Towns*. Oxford: Oxford University Press

Rhodes, J 1965 'Offa's Dyke in Lippets Grove, Tidenham'. Unpublished Gloucester City Museum report

Rhodes, J 1974 'The Oldcroft Hoard'. *Glevensis* **8**, 15

Rhodes, J and Wild, J P 1974 'The Oldcroft (1971–2) hoard of bronze coins and silver objects'. *Numis Chron* **14**, 65–70

Riches, P 2009 'Lidar survey of the Forest of Dean'. *Dean Archaeol* **21**, 20–3

Riches, P (ed) 2011–12 'Pottery finds'. *Dean Archaeol* **23**, 32–5

Riley, R 2010 '6 Buttington Terrace, Beachley, Tidenham, Gloucestershire, Archaeological watching brief'. Unpublished Cotswold Archaeology report, September 2010

Robinson, D (ed) 1998 *The Cistercian Abbeys of Britain*. London: Cistercian Studies Inc

Roe, F nd 'Gloucester, Magistrates Court Site, Ladybellegate Street GLOS 15454 32/95, Assessment of worked stone'. Unpublished assessment report in Gloucestershire County Council Archaeology Service excavation archive, Historic Environment Record Number 15454, Accession Number GMAG 1995.32

Roe, F 1993 'Worked stone' *in* Woodward, A and Leech, P *The Uley Shrine. Excavation of a Ritual Complex on West Hill, Uley, Gloucestershire: 1977–9*. London: English Heritage Archaeological Report **17**, 197–201

Roe, F 2000 'Worked stone' *in* Barber, A J and Holbrook, N 'Excavations at Millend, Blakeney'. *Trans Bristol Gloucestershire Archaeol Soc* **118**, 48–51

Roe, F 2003 'Worked Stone' *in* Thomas, A, Holbrook, N and Bateman, C *Later Prehistoric and Romano-British Burial and Settlement at Hucclecote, Gloucestershire: Excavations in advance of the Gloucester Business Park Link Road, 1998*. Cirencester: Cotswold Archaeology Report **2**, 50–1

Rooke, Major H 1777 'Correspondence'. *Archaeologia* **207**

Roseveare, M J 2018a 'Lancaut Promontory Fort, Gloucestershire, Geophysical Survey Report'. Unpublished TigerGeo report for Dean Historic Buildings Group and Wye Valley AONB, Project code SMG171, Version 1.0, 10th January 2018

Roseveare, M J 2018b 'Lancaut Church, Gloucestershire, Geophysical Survey Report'. Unpublished TigerGeo report for Dean Historic Buildings Group and Wye Valley AONB, Project code SMG171, Version 1.0, 8th January 2018

Rotherham, D, Jones, M, Smith, L and Handley, C (eds) 2008 *The Woodland Heritage Manual*. Sheffield: Wildtrack Publishing

Rudge, T 1803 *The History of the County of Gloucestershire, compressed and brought down to the year 1808. Volume 2*. Gloucester

Russell, B 2010 *Sarcophagi in Roman Britain*. Bollettino di Archeologia on line I 2010/ Volume speciale E / E10 / 2. Derived from www.archeologia.beniculturali.it/pages/pubblicazioni.html

Salter, M 1998 *A Guide to St Briavels Castle in the Royal Forest of Dean*. Worcester: Folly Publications

Salway, P 1993 *The Oxford Illustrated History of Roman Britain*. QPD edition, Oxford University Press.

Saville, A 1984a 'Palaeolithic and Mesolithic evidence from Gloucestershire' *in* Saville, A (ed) *Archaeology in Gloucestershire*. Cheltenham: Cheltenham Art Gallery and Museums, 59–79

Saville, A 1984b 'The Iron Age in Gloucestershire. a review of the evidence' *in* Saville, A (ed) *Archaeology in Gloucestershire*. Cheltenham: Cheltenham Art Gallery and Museums, 140–178

Saville, A 1986 'Mesolithic finds from west Gloucestershire'. *Trans Bristol Gloucestershire Archaeol Soc* **104**, 228–30

Savory, H N 1976 'Welsh hillforts: A reappraisal of recent research' *in* Harding, D W (ed) *Hillforts: Later Prehistoric Earthworks in Britain and Ireland*. London: Academic Press, 237–91

Scarth, The Revd Canon 1880–1 'Remarks on the ancient baptismal font in Staunton church, Gloucestershire'. *Trans Bristol Gloucestershire Archaeol Soc* **5**, 67–9

Scott-Garrett, C 1918–58 'Ramblings of a Dean Archaeologist'. Unpublished notebooks of Scott-Garrett. Gloucestershire Archives, GRO D3921/II/41

Scott-Garrett, C 1954 'Gazebo or folly on Tidenham Chase'. *Trans Bristol Gloucestershire Archaeol Soc* **73**, 237–41

Scott-Garrett, C 1955 'Tidenham Chase Barrow'. *Trans Bristol Gloucestershire Archaeol Soc* **74**, 15–34

Scott-Garrett, C 1956 'Romano-British sites at Chestnuts Hill and Popes Hill, Forest of Dean'. *Trans Bristol Gloucestershire Archaeol Soc* **75**, 199–202

Scott-Garrett, C 1958 'Littledean Camp'. *Trans Bristol Gloucestershire Archaeol Soc* **77**, 48–60

Scott-Garrett, C 1959 'Roman iron mine in Lydney Camp'. *Trans Bristol Gloucestershire Archaeol Soc* **78**, 86–91

Scott-Garrett, C 1960 'Stamped tiles found in Gloucestershire'. *Trans Bristol Gloucestershire Archaeol Soc* **79 (2)**, 302

Scott-Garrett, C and Grinsell, L V 1957 'Two socketed bronze axes from Gloucestershire'. *Trans Bristol Gloucestershire Archaeol Soc* **76**, 146–9

Scott-Garrett, C and Harris, F H 1932 'Field Observations between Severn and Wye'. Unpublished notes. Gloucestershire Archives AR21

Scott-Garrett, C and Harris, F 1938 'Chesters Roman Villa, Woolaston, Glos'. *Archaeologia Cambrensis* **93**, 93–125

Seymour, W A (ed) 1980 *A History of the Ordnance Survey,* Folkestone: Dawson Publishing

Shaffrey, R 2012 'Stone tile' *in* Catchpole, T and Chadwick, A M 'Archaeological investigations undertaken in connection with the construction of the A417 Brockworth Bypass, Gloucestershire, 1990–1994 Gloucester'. Unpublished Gloucestershire County Council Archaeology Service report, 50–3 Library of Unpublished Fieldwork Reports [data set], York: Archaeology Data Service [distributor] (doi:10.5284/1027558)

Sheldon, S, McSloy, E R and Watts, M 2010 'Excavations at Kingsmead School/All Saints Academy, Cheltenham –interim report'. *Glevensis* **43**, 1–6

Sim, D and Ridge, I 2002 *Iron for the Eagles. The Iron Industry of Roman Britain.* Stroud: Tempus Publishing

Sindrey, G 1990 *Roman Dean, The Forest of Dean in the Roman Period.* Dean Archaeological Group Occasional Publication **1**

Small, F and Stoertz, C (eds) 2006 'Gloucestershire, Forest of Dean, National Mapping Programme Report'. English Heritage Research Department Report Series no. 28/2006

Smith, A H 1964a *The Place-names of Gloucestershire. Part III.* English Place-name Society **40**, Cambridge: Cambridge University Press

Smith, A H 1964b *The Place-names of Gloucestershire. Part IV.* English Place-name Society **40**, Cambridge: Cambridge University Press

Smith, B 1972a 'The Hundred of Westbury' *in* Pugh, R B (ed) *The Victoria History of the County of Gloucestershire* **10**, 1–5

Smith, B S 1972b 'Woolaston' *in* Pugh, R B (ed) *The Victoria History of the County of Gloucestershire* **10**, 102–18

Smith, J T 1985 'Building at Littledean Hall, Littledean, Gloucestershire'. Unpublished correspondence in Gloucestershire County Council Archaeology Service Historic Environment Record site file 9738

Smith, N 1999 'The earthwork remains of enclosure in the New Forest'. *Proc Hampshire Fld Club Archaeol Soc* **54**, 1–56

Solari, R A and Lowe, D J 1974 Various short articles in *Cave Projects Group, Newsletter Five,* June 1974

Sopwith, T 1835 Plan of the coal and iron districts in the Forest of Dean surveyed by order of HM Commissioners of Woods, Forests and Revenues, Gloucestershire Archives document D232

Standing, I J 1986 'Review of Archaeology in the Forest of Dean, 1985–86'. *Glevensis* **20**, 33–35

Standing, I J 1987 'The industrial heritage of Bixhead and Bixslade in the Forest of Dean'. *Gloucestershire Society for Industrial Archaeology Annual Journal for 1987*, 17–32

Standing, I J 1988 'Dating the Dean Road'. *The New Regard* **4**, 35–43

Standing, I J 1997 'The landscape of the Forest of Dean in the 17th Century, A study based on contemporary maps'. Unpublished Bristol University MA

Standing, I J 2000 'Iron working residues' *in* Price, E *Frocester. A Romano-British Settlement, its Antecedents and Successors, Volume 2. The Finds.* Stonehouse: Gloucester and District Archaeological Research Group, 92–4

Standing, I J and Coates, S 1979 'Historical sites of industrial importance on Forestry Commission land in Dean'. *Gloucestershire Society for Industrial Archaeology Annual Journal for 1979*, 16–20

Standing, I J and Tylecote, R F 1977 'The Drummer Boy Stone, Forest of Dean'. *J Hist Metall Soc* **11 (2)**, 84–5

Standing, I J and Wills, J 1988 'Earthwork at Lydney' *in* Standing, I J (ed) '1988 archaeological notes'. *The New Regard* **4**, 62

Stenton, F 1998 *Anglo-Saxon England.* 3 edn. Oxford: Oxford University Press

Stoertz, C 2004 'The Marches Uplands Mapping Project; a report for the National Mapping Programme'. English Heritage Aerial Survey Report Series AER/1/2004

Strassburger, E nd 'Early Ochre-Mining in the Forest of Dean, Gloucestershire'. Unpublished document for Clearwell Caves Mining Museum. Copy in Gloucestershire County Council Archaeology Service HER site file 20827

Stratoscan 2013 'Sedbury Park, Geophysical Survey Report' *in* Garland, N 'Archaeological Desk-based Assessment: Land east of Sedbury Park, Forest of Dean, Gloucestershire'. Unpublished Heritage Collective report, August 2013, Appendix A

Substrata 2005a 'Gradiometer survey at Welshbury Hillfort, Gloucestershire' *in* Hoyle, J P 2013 'The Forest of Dean, Gloucestershire, Forest of Dean Archaeological Survey Stage 3B, Phase 2 Field evaluation of selected lidar-detected earthworks in Forestry Commission woodland, Project Number 5291 SURV'. Unpublished Gloucestershire County Council Archaeology Service report for English Heritage, April 2013, Appendix ii

Substrata 2005b 'Gradiometer survey at Fairplay Enclosure, Gloucestershire' *in* Hoyle, J P 2013 'The Forest of Dean, Gloucestershire, Forest of Dean Archaeological Survey Stage 3B, Phase 2 Field evaluation of selected lidar-detected earthworks in Forestry Commission woodland, Project Number 5291 SURV'. Unpublished Gloucestershire County Council Archaeology Service report for English Heritage, April 2013, Appendix i

Sullivan, D P 1991 *The Old Stones of Gloucestershire. A survey of Megaliths and Mark Stones Past and Present.* Cheltenham: Reardon and Son

Swan, V G 1988 *Pottery in Roman Britain.* 4 edn. Princes Risborough: Shire Archaeology

Symonds, Revd W S 1871 'On the contents of a hyena's den on the Great Doward, Whitchurch, Ross'. *The Geological Magazine* **88**, 433–8

Taylor, E 1995 'Report on the excavation of Huntsham Romano British villa and Iron Age enclosure 1959–1970'. *Trans Woolhope Nat Fld Club* **48 (II)**, 224–81

Taylor, I 1777 'Isaac Taylor's 1" to 1 mile map of Gloucestershire' *in A Gloucestershire and Bristol Atlas.* (facsim edn Bristol and Gloucestershire Archaeological Society 1961)

Taylor, B and Bagnall, A 1990 'Finds' *in* Wilson, D 1990 *Excavations of a Romano-British Villa at Wortley, Gloucestershire. 6th Interim Report.* Keele, 12–26

TBGAS 1881–2 'Transactions at a special meeting for the West Gloucestershire Division held on 23rd May, 1882'. *Trans Bristol Gloucestershire Archaeol Soc* **6**, 357–66

Teague, S 2007 'St White's Farm, Cinderford, Gloucestershire, Archaeological Evaluation Report'. Unpublished Oxford Archaeology report, OA Job Number 3671, August 2007

Thomas, D 2000 'Cadora Woods, Wye Valley. An Archaeological and Historic Assessment'. Unpublished report

Timberlake, S 1990 'Excavations at Parys Mountain and Nantyreira' *in* Crew, P and Crew, S (eds) *Early Mining in the British Isles.* Proceedings of the Early Mining Workshop at Plas Tan y Bwlch: Snowdonia National Park Study, Centre, 17–19 November 1989, 15–21, Plas Tan y Bwlch 1990

Timberlake, S 2001 Unpublished correspondence between Simon Timberlake of the Copa Hill Bronze Age mine research project and Jonathan Wright of the Clearwell Caves mining museum. Gloucestershire County Council Archaeology Service HER Site File No. 20829

Timby, J 2012 'Pottery from Ruardean Woodside' *in* Hoyle, J P 2013 'The Forest of Dean, Gloucestershire, Forest of Dean Archaeological Survey Stage 3B, Phase 2 Field evaluation of selected lidar-detected earthworks in Forestry Commission woodland, Project Number 5291 SURV'. Unpublished Gloucestershire County Council Archaeology Service report for English Heritage, April 2013, 213–15

Toms, P, Cook, G, Bronk Ramsey, C and Bayliss, A 2012 *Forest of Dean Archaeology Survey, Scientific dating of earthworks systems so6013/04 and so6013/26*. Research Report Series 53–2012, English Heritage. (Reproduced in Hoyle, J P 2013, Appendix D)

Townley, E L 2004 'The medieval landscape and economy of the Forest of Dean'. Unpublished PhD thesis. University of Bristol

Townsend, A J P 1999 'Site of the Feathers Hotel, High Street, Lydney, Gloucestershire: Archaeological Documentary Research and Field Evaluation'. Unpublished Avon Archaeological Unit report, August 1999

Travis, J R 2008 *Coal in Roman Britain*. Oxford: Brit Archaeol Rep Brit Ser **468**

Trotter, A W 1936 *The Dean Road*. Gloucester

Trotter, F M 1942 *Geology of the Forest of Dean Coal and Iron-Ore Field*. London: HMSO, Reprinted 1964

Turner-Flynn, B, Garner, D J, Sproat, D and Walker, W S 1995 Ffrith Farm, Ffrith, near Wrexham: An Archaeological Evaluation. Unpublished Earthworks Archaeology Report E140

Tylecote, R F 1986 *The Prehistory of Metallurgy in the British Isles*. Kings Lynn

Vallender, J 2002 An Archaeological and Historical Assessment: Condition Survey and Management Proposals of Ruardean Castle, Gloucestershire. Unpublished Gloucestershire County Council Archaeology Service report, December 2002

Verey, D 1970 *The Buildings of England, Gloucestershire: The Vale and the Forest of Dean*. 1979 edn. Harmondsworth: Penguin Books.

Verey, D 1981 *The Diary of a Cotswolds Parson*. Trowbridge and Esher: Alan Sutton

Verey, D and Brooks, A 2002 *The Buildings of England, Gloucestershire: The Vale and the Forest of Dean*. 3 edn. New Haven and London: Yale University Press

Wainwright, G J 1971 'The excavation of a fortified settlement at Walesland Rath, Pembrokeshire'. *Britannia* **2**, 48–108

Walker, E A 2004 'The Mesolithic: The final hunter-gatherer-fisher societies of south-eastern Wales' in Aldhouse-Green, M and Howell, R (eds) *The Gwent County History Volume I: Gwent in Prehistory and Early History*. Cardiff: University of Wales Press, 29–55

Walker, E A 2015 'Scratching the surface: new late glacial lithic artefacts from south-east Wales' in Ashton, N and Harris, C (eds) *No Stone Unturned: papers in honour of Roger Jacobi*. London: Lithic Studies Society, 113–25

Walters, R C S 1928 *Ancient Wells, Springs and Holy Wells of Gloucestershire*. Bristol: The St Stephen's Press

Walters, B (ed) 1985a 'Archaeological notes'. *The New Regard* **1**, 21–38

Walters, B 1985b 'Dean Road excavation near Soudley'. *The New Regard* **1**, 5–9

Walters, B (ed) 1986 'Forest of Dean: site reports'. *Glevensis* **20**, 36

Walters, B (ed) 1987a 'Archaeological notes'. *The New Regard* **3**, 59–86

Walters, B 1987b 'Archaeology in Dean'. *Glevensis* **21**, 50

Walters, B 1988 'The distribution of prehistoric flint artefacts in Dean'. *Dean Archaeol* **1**, 36–8

Walters, B 1989 'A survey of prehistory in Dean circa 12,000BC to AD43'. *Dean Archaeol* **2**, 9–22

Walters, M 1990a 'Rescue excavations on the Roman occupation site at Legg House, Blakeney Forest of Dean, Glos'. *Dean Archaeol* **3**, 40–4

Walters, B 1990b 'The Forest of Dean – A Roman imperial estate?' *Dean Archaeol* **3**, 45–6

Walters, B (ed) 1991a 'Summary observations and additions to the archaeological record'. *Dean Archaeol* **4**, 38–47

Walters, M 1991b 'A new Roman coin hoard from the Forest of Dean: Oldcroft 2'. *Dean Archaeol* **4**, 4–15

Walters, B 1992a *The Archaeology and History of Ancient Dean and the Wye Valley*. Cheltenham: Thornhill Press

Walters, M 1992b 'Excavations of the Roman occupation site at Legg House, Blakeney Forest of Dean, Gloucestershire (second interim report 1991/92)'. *Dean Archaeol* **5**, 5–11

Walters, M 1996 'Flints from Bream Cross'. *Dean Archaeol* **9**, 11

Walters, B 1999 *The Forest of Dean Iron Industry*. Dean Archaeological Group Occasional Publication **4**

Walters, B and Walters, M 1987 'Excavation of Romano-British iron smelting shaft furnace at Barnfield, Eastbach Court, SO 59395 15161, Easter 1987'. *The New Regard* **3**, 50–3

Watkin, W 1878 'On the Roman stations 'Burrium', 'Gobannium' and 'Blestium' of the Twelfth and Thirteenth Iters of Antoninus' *Archaeol J,* **35**, 19–43

Watkins, B 1985 *The Story of Flaxley Abbey and the Cistercian Monks in the Forest of Dean*. Gloucester

Waygood, G 2003 'The Dean Forest lodges, part I'. *The New Regard* **18**, 5–17

Waygood, G 2004 'The Dean Forest lodges, part II'. *The New Regard* **19**, 5–26

Webb, A 1992 'St. Briavels Castle – The king's great arsenal'. *Dean Archaeol* **5**, 19–24

Webb, A 1997a 'Metallic finds: axe and spearhead'. *Dean Archaeol* **10**, 15

Webb, A 1997b 'St Briavels, Brook Farm, Mork' in Rawes, J and Wills J (eds) 'Archaeological Review No. 21, 1996', *Trans Bristol Gloucestershire Archaeol Soc* **115**, 291

Webb, A 1998 'Ceramic finds: glass beads, pottery'. *Dean Archaeol* **11**, 6–7

Webb, A 2000 *Early Medieval Dean, the Forest of Dean and West Gloucestershire, 409 to 1272 AD*. Dean Archaeological Group Occasional Publication **6**

Webb, A 2005 'Lithic finds'. *Dean Archaeol* **18**, 23–31

Webster, G 1989 'Part of a late Celtic sword-belt found at Coleford, Gloucestershire in 1987'. *Dean Archaeol* **2**, 30–1

Webster, G 1990 'A late Celtic sword-belt with a ring and button found at Coleford, Gloucestershire'. *Britannia* **21**, 294–5

Webster, P 2015 'Oxford Ware Analysis' in Jarman, R 2015 Welshbury Hillfort, Gloucestershire. Unpublished preliminary report of survey prepared for discussion meeting on 19th November 2015, Appendix 2, 25/04/2015

Wessex Archaeology 2003a 'Land east of Lydney, Gloucestershire'. Unpublished Wessex Archaeology report. Ref: 53846.01, November 2003

Wessex Archaeology 2003b 'Land at Hurst Farm Lydney, Gloucestershire'. Unpublished, Wessex Archaeology report. Ref: 53846.02, November 2003

Wheeler, R E M and Wheeler, T V 1932 *Report on the Excavation of the Prehistoric, Roman, and post-Roman Site in Lydney Park, Gloucestershire*. Reports of the Research Committee of the Society of Antiquities in London **9**. Oxford

Wheeler, J and Walsh, A 2019 'Mining the Forest's secrets: recent archaeological excavations at Yorkley and Soudley' *The New Regard* **33**, 6–9

Whitten, D G A and Brooks, J R V 1972 *The Penguin Dictionary of Geology*. 1987 edn. Harmondsworth: Penguin Books

Wildgoose, P 1993 'The Forest of Dean as a major centre of the iron industry from Roman to medieval times'. Unpublished MLitt thesis, University of Bristol

Wilkin, N 2014 'Report on possible treasure for H M Coroner for Gloucestershire 2013 T805; A hoard of probable Middle Bronze Age ornaments from Woolaston, Gloucestershire'. Unpublished British Museum report, 9th April 2014

Wilkinson, K and Straker, V 2008 'Neolithic and Early Bronze Age environmental background' *in* Webster, C J (ed) *The Archaeology of South West England, South West Archaeological Research Framework, Resource Assessment and Research Agenda*. Taunton: Somerset County Council, 63–73

Williams, V 1988 'Analysis of 'Roman' coal from Monmouth, Glendower Street School excavations'. *Dean Archaeol* **1**, 10–11

Williams, B 2011 'An interim report on an archaeological excavation on land at Tewkesbury Road, Uckington (Uckington fire station), Gloucestershire 2011'. Unpublished Gloucestershire County Council Archaeology Service report, May 2011

Wills, J 1986 'A report on a watching brief at Devil's Pulpit, Offa's Dyke'. Unpublished Gloucestershire County Council Archaeology Service report in Gloucestershire County Council Archaeology Service Historic Environment Record site file 502

Witts, G B 1880 *Archaeological Handbook to Gloucestershire*. Cheltenham

Wood, J G 1900–1 to April 1902 'Notes on the portions of Offa's Dyke called the Stone Row and Rowe Ditch'. *Trans Woolhope Nat Fld Club* 1900–April 1902, 148–51

Wood, M 1981 *In Search of the Dark Ages*, London: BBC

Woodward, A 1995 'Pottery Report' *in* James, T 'Excavations at Rodmore Farm 1994'. *Dean Archaeol* **8**, 15–20

Wright, R 1980 *Secret Forest*. Cinderford: Douglas McLean

Wright, T 1854 *Wanderings of an Antiquary*. London: J B Nichols

Wyrall, G 1878 '"Observations on the iron cinders found in the Forest of Dean and its neighbourhood", Communicated by Sir John Maclean, 27th January 1780'. *Trans Bristol Gloucestershire Archaeol Soc* **2**, 216–34

Youles, T 2004 'Delving in Dean: The Delves. An area of unrecorded early coal mining (part two)'. *Gloucestershire Soc Industrial Archaeol, Annual Journal for 2004*, 3–11

Youles, T, Fernando, P, Burton, T, and Colls, F 2008 'Delving in Dean: The Delves. An area of unrecorded early coal mining (part three)'. *Gloucestershire Soc Industrial Archaeol, Annual Journal for 2008*, 37–52

Young, T P 2011 'Evaluation of archaeometallurgical residues from the Forest of Dean Archaeological Survey, Stage 3B phase 2 (37920/37921/37923/37924, GeoArch Report 2011/32: Residues from Cannop' *in* Hoyle, J P 'The Forest of Dean, Gloucestershire, Forest of Dean Archaeological Survey Stage 3B, Phase 2 Field evaluation of selected lidar-detected earthworks in Forestry Commission woodland, Project Number 5291 SURV'. Unpublished Gloucestershire County Council Archaeology Service report for English Heritage, April 2013, 218–31

Young, T 2012 'Petrographic and chemical analysis' *in* Jackson, R 2012 *Ariconium, Herefordshire, An Iron Age Settlement and Romano-British 'Small Town'*. Oxford: Oxbow, 163–4

Young, T P 2013 'Analysis of archaeometallurgical residues, Cannop, Glos (Glos HER 37920), GeoArch Report 2014/05: Residues from Cannop' *in* Hoyle, J P 'The Forest of Dean, Gloucestershire, Forest of Dean Archaeological Survey Stage 3B, Phase 2 Field evaluation of selected lidar-detected earthworks in Forestry Commission woodland, Project Number 5291 SURV'. Unpublished Gloucestershire County Council Archaeology Service report for English Heritage, April 2013, 238–42

Young, T P 2015 'Assessment of archaeometallurgical residues from Yorkley, Gloucestershire, GeoArch Report 2015/24', *in* Harvard, T and Guarino, P 'Land east of Lydney Road, Yorkley, Gloucestershire, Archaeological Evaluation'. Cotswold Archaeology unpublished report, CA Project 5627, CA Report: 15796, November 2015, Appendix B

Young, T P and Macdonald, P 1998 'Lydney Park Geophysical Survey, March/April 1998, Interim Report'. Unpublished Cardiff Geoarchaeology report 98/01

Index

172